Peter Rollberg, Marlene Laruelle (eds.)

MASS MEDIA IN THE POST-SOVIET WORLD

Market Forces, State Actors, and Political Manipulation in the Informational Environment after Communism

ibidem-Verlag
Stuttgart

Bibliographic information published by the Deutsche Nationalbibliothek
Die Deutsche Nationalbibliothek lists this publication in the Deutsche Nationalbibliografie;
detailed bibliographic data are available in the Internet at http://dnb.d-nb.de.

Bibliografische Information der Deutschen Nationalbibliothek
Die Deutsche Nationalbibliothek verzeichnet diese Publikation in der Deutschen
Nationalbibliografie; detaillierte bibliografische Daten sind im Internet über http://dnb.d-nb.de
abrufbar.

Cover picture: narin chauhan/Shutterstock

ISSN: 1614-3515
ISBN-13: 978-3-8382-1116-9
© *ibidem*-Verlag / *ibidem* Press
Stuttgart, Germany 2018

Alle Rechte vorbehalten

Das Werk einschließlich aller seiner Teile ist urheberrechtlich geschützt. Jede Verwertung außerhalb der engen Grenzen des Urheberrechtsgesetzes ist ohne Zustimmung des Verlages unzulässig und strafbar. Dies gilt insbesondere für Vervielfältigungen, Übersetzungen, Mikroverfilmungen und elektronische Speicherformen sowie die Einspeicherung und Verarbeitung in elektronischen Systemen.

All rights reserved

No part of this publication may be reproduced,
stored in or introduced into a retrieval system, or transmitted, in any form,
or by any means (electronical, mechanical, photocopying, recording or otherwise)
without the prior written permission of the publisher.
Any person who does any unauthorized act in relation to this publication may be liable to
criminal prosecution and civil claims for damages.

Printed in the United States of America

Table of Contents

Introduction: Mass Media in the Post-Soviet World 7
Peter Rollberg and Marlene Laruelle

I. National Trends 15

Politics of International Media Rankings 15
Tudor Vlad, Lee B. Becker, and Jack Snyder

Russia's Nongovernmental Media under Assault 41
Maria Lipman

Russia and the New Authoritarians 57
Jonathan Becker

Ukraine's Media in the Context
of Global Cultural Convergence 79
Marta Dyczok

Media in Post-Soviet Belarus: Between
Democratization and Reinforcing Authoritarianism 111
Oleg Manaev

Mass Media Consumption in Post-Soviet
Kyrgyzstan and Kazakhstan: The View from Below 139
Barbara Junisbai, Azamat Junisbai, and Nicola Ying Fry

Networked Apathy:
Georgian Party Politics and the Role of Social Media 169
Kornely Kakachia, Tamara Pataraia, and Michael Cecire

II. Television 197

Coercion or Conformism? Censorship and Self-
Censorship among Russian Media Personalities
and Reporters in the 2010s 197
Elisabeth Schimpfossl and Ilya Yablokov

The "Russian Idea" on the Small Screen:
Staging National Identity on Russia's TV 219
Marlene Laruelle

Peter the Great, Statism, and Axiological
Continuity in Contemporary Russian Television 247
Peter Rollberg

In Search of Kazakhness: The Televisual Landscape
and Screening of Nation in Kazakhstan 275
Marlene Laruelle

Small Screen Nation-Building: *Astana – My Love* 301
Peter Rollberg

III. Social Media 325

Glasnost 2.0 325
Sarah Oates

The Persistence of Media Control under
Consolidated Authoritarianism:
Containing Kazakhstan's Digital Media 347
Luca Anceschi

Friends, Foes, and Facebook:
Blocking the Internet in Tajikistan 371
Abdulfattoh Shafiev and Marintha Miles

Youth Media Consumption and Perceptions
of Electoral Integrity in Kazakhstan and Kyrgyzstan 399
Olena Nikolayenko

Social Media and Online Public Debate
in Central Asia: A Journalist's Perspective 425
Navbahor Imamova

Introduction: Mass Media in the Post-Soviet World

Peter Rollberg and Marlene Laruelle, The George Washington University

For the past two decades, global mass media have been in the middle of a radical transformative process. To a certain degree, this transformation is spontaneous, a side effect of revolutionary technical innovation. However, it is also guided by specific power structures and interest groups. While social media have led to an unprecedented communicative empowerment of the individual, the concentration of traditional media in fewer and fewer hands caused global information monopolization that presents a severe threat to democracy everywhere. The media environments in formerly Communist societies, which a mere three decades ago were integral elements of totalitarian systems, are no exception: innovations in electronic media spread in Russia or Ukraine almost as fast as in the West, while the commercialization and monopolization of traditional media have reached an unprecedented, dangerous level, as has the collusion between private and state interests. The issue of insufficient media freedom is particularly precarious in Central Asia, although it is problematic in all post-Soviet nations. The present volume aims at highlighting major trends in the media environment of the post-Communist world, with special focus on Russia and the post-Soviet space. The term "media environment" is applied in a rather broad manner, implying not just traditional print and electronic media, but new media as well, and ranges from the political to the entertainment and artistic spheres.

Scholarly research on post-Communist and specifically post-Soviet media was in high demand in the late 1990s and in the first years of the new millennium. The large number of media-focused academic publications indicates that this field was seen as one with a strong potential for the future. However, in recent years, a noticeable disillusionment in the emancipative potential of mass media has taken place—the expected progress has rarely materialized. Media in post-Soviet societies in particular present a moving target, influenced by complex geopolitical and cultural factors. That makes it hard, if not impossible, to arrive at a lasting analytical consensus about the post-Soviet media sphere, whether in regards to Russia, which keeps dominating its "near abroad" through media, or Ukraine and Belarus—one in turmoil, the other frozen, in the Republic of Georgia, or in the five Central Asian states. And yet, the complicated and often contradictory process of democratization in Russia and the post-Soviet space is both dependent on and reflected by the transformation of these countries' mass media. As print and electronic media are essential factors in a functioning civil society, they often represent embattled territory. The violent deaths of over 30 journalists in the past decade—the cases of Georgy Gongadze in Ukraine in 2000 and of Anna Politkovskaya in Russia in 2006 made worldwide headlines—drastically demonstrate the significance attributed to media in post-Soviet societies.

Despite the absence of universally acknowledged concepts of media democratization, there is broad consensus that post-Soviet media—particularly the dominant medium, television—have "helped to re-consolidate elite power rather than empower citizens."[1] What is subject to debate is the question of which societal elements facilitate and constrain the independence and freedom of media, especially television. What role do market forces play in the process of media democratization, and how do state structures regulate, suppress, or use capitalism toward their own gain? What degree of informational pluralism has been achieved in the newly independent republics? What are the prospects for transparency and the participation of civil society in Russian and Eurasian media? And to what degree to trends in post-Communist media reflect global trends? In other words, is there a worldwide convergence both in regards to media formats and political messaging?

---

1   Sarah Oates, "The Neo-Soviet Model of the Media," *Europe-Asia Studies* 59:8 (2007): 1280.

Using the classical four fundamental models proposed by Siebert et al.,[2] it can be assumed that the majority of post-Soviet media underwent an evolution from a *Social Responsibility* model that had emerged in the last years of perestroika and glasnost and matured in the first post-communist phase, to an *Authoritarian* model that was forcefully implemented in the early 2000s. However, the classification requires some fine-tuning: even in the most liberal years of glasnost, the Soviet media environment retained essential features of what Siebert called "the Soviet model," and even in the most intrusive years of the Putin presidency (2002–2003, after 2012), the Authoritarian model contains prominent libertarian and consumer-driven features. Moreover, it is obvious that the post-Soviet republics, while sharing certain features, do not form a homogenous space—far from it. Take, for example, Central Asia: the media in Kyrgyzstan, with all their imperfections, are closer to the *Social Responsibility* model, whereas those in Turkmenistan are the closest to the *Authoritarian* model of which Kazakhstan, Tajikistan, and Uzbekistan represent variations. Of course, even the most authoritarian systems strive to present themselves as socially responsible, protecting civil society and discouraging anti-social behavior while facilitating a sense of common values and strengthening nationhood.

However, the real ownership and decision-making structures—often carefully hidden from society—demonstrate that the majority of post-Soviet media are, above all, geared toward reinforcing the authoritarian status quo. Economic and political power structures are so closely intertwined that serious media challenges to the ruling establishments are the exception. For this reason, both journalists and artists working in the post-Soviet media systems look at media as patron-guided political players in themselves, promoting the values of the owners, not the common good, and audiences have come to accept this reality, using digital media as an individual corrective. Indeed, at the dawn of the Internet, many observers assumed that the rise of the Internet and, subsequently, of

---

[2] Fred S. Siebert, Theodore Peterson, and Wilbur Schramm, *Four Theories of the Press* (Urbana-Champaign, Ill.: University of Illinois Press, 1963).

social media would progressively reduce the stranglehold of the state authorities. However, the Internet/social media revolution should not be exaggerated. Authoritarian post-Soviet regimes have learned that their stability and legitimacy can be challenged by "connected" movements, but these regimes have other tools to influence public opinion in their countries. More and more efficiently, the local elites manage to limit and control the socio-cultural influence of Western media, non-governmental organizations, and individual activists. Audiences are thirsty for news, but even more for entertainment, a combination that the two main media, television and the Internet, offer in parallel. The demand for screen content has contributed to the marginalization of newspapers and radio, which provide news but less entertainment.

The familiar low rankings of media freedom in most-post-Soviet nations issued by Western agencies capture only a small part of these countries' media environments. Such rankings focus mostly on legal issues and limitations orchestrated by authoritarian regimes, as well as journalists' rights, but do not take into consideration the other side of the coin, that of the audiences. The rankings, therefore, are only able to capture a partial picture of the more involved set of roles played by the media in post-Soviet societies. Moreover, these indexes come with some conceptual limitations, including the assumption that freer media automatically create new support for democratization—in reality, freer media can also give rise to illiberal ideologies and to more vocal nationalisms.

Determining the ratio between different elements in a certain media environment presents serious challenges and demands consistent monitoring and ongoing analysis. Even when a common terminology is applied, it requires adjustment depending on each case within a certain time frame—thus, the exact meaning of notions such as "censorship" or "self-censorship" can no longer be taken for granted since the terms originated from totalitarian society models. Equally problematic is the undifferentiated usage of the notion of "transition" from authoritarianism toward democracy, which has dominated the academic discourse on media for many years. As Tina Burrett has observed, the

> continued application of the transition paradigm creates a false dichotomy. (…) The frustration that analysts express over the democratic deficit in the Russian media system must be replaced with realistic, empirically grounded expectations about the trajectory of political development in contemporary Russia.[3]

Still, to completely avoid normative statements regarding the realization of democratic values in mass media would be just as unproductive. Without denying national specifics for individual media systems, it seems fair to juxtapose the predominant western media models to the authoritarian/corporate media of post-Soviet nations. John Dunn aptly noted that

> a modern western-type democracy is polycentric, with competing centers of power and influence, all of which have clearly defined functions and clearly delineated boundaries established by laws, constitutions or, failing that, long-established custom and practice; the corporate state does not allow for competing or alternative centers of power and influence, but instead the sole function of all structures is to serve the overall aims and priorities of the corporate centre.[4]

A sore point for all post-Soviet media environments is the role of the Russian media. A large number of people in formerly Soviet republics are still bilingual; the older generation was brought up with the constant presence of Russian television, a factor which certainly yielded lasting effects on the following generations as well. Russian has maintained its position as the lingua franca in many places, regardless of efforts to promote the respective native languages as the official means of communication. This, together with the high production value of Russian television, with which no other post-Soviet nation can compete, has secured the Russian elites an enormous advantage over the hearts and minds of people in the majority of post-Soviet republics, in addition to their dependence on the remissions sent by millions of migrant workers from the powerful

---

3   Tina Burrett, "The end of independent television? Elite conflict and the reconstruction of the Russian television landscape," in Birgit Beumers, Stephen Hutchings, and Natalia Ryulova, eds., *The Post-Soviet Russian Media: Conflicting Signals* (London and New York: Routledge, 2009), 72–73.

4   John Dunn, "Where did it all go wrong? Russian television in the Putin era," in Beumers, Hutchings, and Rulyova, eds., *The Post-Soviet Russian Media*, 50.

neighbor. Thus, the symbiotic relationship between the Russian and non-Russian media environments, who not only share a common past but also close economic ties in the present, will likely remain a factor that must be taken into consideration when analyzing mass media in the post-Soviet world. And indeed, what would be the alternative? Conspicuously, the authoritarian values masked as democratic that form the ideological foundation of contemporary Russian media are in many ways similar to those of the other post-Soviet elites who often prefer a variation of "mild authoritarianism" to full-fledged emulation of western-style democracies. The safest consensus everywhere is the commercial one—in all post-Soviet countries, profit-making is considered a fundamental value, whether admitted or not. Indeed, what post-Soviet media environments share with the West is their high degree of commercialization. However, its impact on political opinion-formation is much more direct and visible than in parliamentary, free market-based democracies.

Western observers usually pay the keenest attention to the role of media in Russia and Eurasia during national elections. While this is certainly a valid focus, the present volume aims at understanding the deeper overall media philosophies that characterize post-Soviet media systems and environments, and the type of identity formation that they are promoting. This includes information outlets and entertainment on all levels, from news programs to talk shows and serious artistic production.

As several chapters in the present volume demonstrate, growing segments of the population in the post-Soviet world, and the young generation in particular, make increasing use of digital media that are harder to control than television and print media. The heightened attention to the national media environment is in part a reaction to experiences of the 1990s, including experiments with Western media models. Under these conditions, the "import model" which is based on the expectation that Western values can be introduced through the formation of western-educated media elites whose work will successively promote liberal values, has largely failed because the ruling elites in post-Soviet societies are unwilling to passively permit such processes to unfold since they will eventually undermine their position. Still, despite authoritarian regulations and multifaceted repression, the electronic, print, and social media in the post-Soviet world are both forum and battlefield of political agendas, economic interests, activist idealism, and pragmatic cynicism. Through their respective mass media, the ruling establishments engage with their civil societies in a wide variety of communicative processes, ranging from genuine dialogue to unabashed censorship and from subtle manipulation to brutal pressure. The ongoing minor and major scuffles over access to digital media demonstrate the significance attributed to media in these societies beyond doubt. It seems safe to say that, the more illiberal a society, the more the control of its media is viewed as a condition for maintaining the power status quo overall.

What, then, are the real prospects for freedom and transparency in post-Soviet media? The interest of Western engagement is no longer as strong and idealistic as it was in the 1990s, while the local elites have learned to limit and control the socio-cultural influence of Western media representative, NGOs, and individual activists. Social media are harder to manage, as the cat-and-mouse games that government officials and young activists engage amply demonstrate. On the one hand, the developments in post-Soviet mass media environments will to a large extent be determined by geopolitical developments, depending on the degree of success that China, Russia, the United States, and Europe can achieve in pursuing their agendas. On the other hand, each individual will likely have more and more choices in selecting his sources of information, and the higher the number of sources, the greater the individual's relative independence from each source will be. Thus, much as post-Soviet establishments may try, and much as large segments of the population may be willing to accept it, the state control over media can never fully eliminate the emancipatory potential of the growing and diversifying global media.[5]

---

5   In the interest of consistency, the Chicago Manual of Style (16th edition) was used for Russian transliteration throughout the volume.

****

We would like to express our deep gratitude to a number of people who helped us make this project happen. First and foremost, our thanks go to the anonymous donor of two SOAR grants at GW's Elliott School of International Affairs, which allowed us to organize two workshops on post-Communist media in 2013 and 2014. We would also like to thank Robert Orttung, editor of *Demokratizatsiya: The Journal of Post-Soviet Democratization*, for granting us permission to reprint articles from two special media issues. Bryan Rosenthal, Evan Alterman, and Marya Rozanova were extremely helpful with preparing the manuscript. Our thanks go to Andreas Umland for accepting this volume as part of the 'Soviet and Post-Soviet Politics and Society' series.

I. National Trends

Politics of International Media Rankings

Tudor Vlad, University of Georgia; Lee B. Becker, University of Georgia; and Jack Snyder, Columbia University

Governmental and nongovernmental organizations have heavily invested in media assistance projects in developing countries each year, with the assumption that, ultimately, these programs will contribute to fostering democracy and stability. Spending has been distributed around the world, with eastern and central Europe, the former Soviet space, and African countries having been major recipients since the early 1990s. The U.S. and other western assistance programs have been created on the theory that development of free media performed by well-trained journalists leads to the development of democratic regimes. The evidence to support that assumption, however, is not robust. Relatively little work has been done to empirically evaluate the media assistance programs.

More than 100 organizations throughout the world have been engaged in some form of local, national or regional media system and press freedom assessment. Three of them (Freedom House, Reporters Without Borders, and International Research & Exchanges Board) have a global approach and have developed specific measures of media freedom or media sustainability. Their methodologies have evolved across the time to capture the changes in the media and in communication technologies and the new challenges brought to the press in post-totalitarian regimes. These indices and reports have been often used by governments and NGOs. They also have been repeatedly questioned and contested. As an example, the Freedom House ranking has been criticized that it reflected U.S. perspectives on political and economic pressures on the media in different countries and on their judicial regulations related to the press. Some argue that the Reporters Without Borders index has been created as an alternative tool to the FH ranking.

The Freedom House and Reporters Without Borders methodologies are different, while IREX assesses the sustainability of media systems (not press freedom). The conclusions of all three annual reports, however, on the state of the media in most of the countries that belong to the former Soviet space have many common points.

Analyzing the year-by-year rankings, ratings and reports after 1989, there is evidence that a short period of diversification in terms of media content and ownership occurred after the fall of communism in the region. This trend was encouraged and supported by U.S. and Western investments in media independence and professionalization through a variety of assistance programs.

This era was followed by a consolidation of ownership or a partial re-monopolization in the media landscape, the effect of which has been a decline of press independence. In some cases, this increased control has been imposed directly by authoritarian regimes in the region. In other cases, media groups were created or purchased by business or political groups or by oligarchs (many of them with ties to the government), who wanted and were allowed to use the media as attack dogs.

The economic crisis, which brought a significant decline in the advertising budgets in the former Soviet space, accelerated this process and aggravated its consequences on media freedom.

Another important characteristic in this region is the existence of Russian-speaking minorities in every country and the penetration of programs and publications in Russian, either produced in Russia or locally. Kremlin-friendly media have become more and more sophisticated in manipulating the news content and flow in Central Asian and the Baltic States, Ukraine and the Republic of Moldova.

The assessment of media freedom is a complex endeavor: variation exists from one type of media to another and from national to local outlets. The Internet and the new media it has generated are not always captured in these measurements.

What the reports of Freedom House, Reporters Without Borders and IREX suggest is that currently, with the notable exception of the Baltic countries, in most of the former Soviet states media are under political, economic or judicial pressure, and many journalists face major risks when they are trying to do their job. As a consequence, these countries' rankings in the press freedom indexes are low, with Turkmenistan, Uzbekistan, Belarus and — more recently, Crimea — being constantly listed in the group of states or regions where media are oppressed.

The Freedom House indicators are more consistent across time for countries in the regionn, in part because the scale (0 to 100) has been unchanged. The higher variability in the Reporters Without Borders ratings can be explained in part by the weight that attacks on journalists has in their assessment and by the fact that the organization has used scales varying between 0 to 85 and 0 to 140. IREX measures different characteristics of media systems to evaluate sustainability, on a scale from 0 to 4, where 4 indicates fully sustainable media.

This chapter begins with a survey of how media freedom has been measured, discusses the reliability of those measures, and examines their validity in the narrow sense of media freedom as an end in itself. We close with a discussion — relevant to challenges that media and journalists are facing in the former soviet space — of what would be needed to examine the causal relationship between media freedom and democracy, including mechanisms that would be relevant to democracy promotion efforts.

Researchers began creating measures of press freedom and linking those measures to both antecedents and consequences of that freedom in the early 1960s. Freedom House, a media advocacy group, began its rankings of press freedom in 1980, and today, competing rankings are being produced by other organizations with similar goals. These public ratings have become the dominant indicators of media freedom used by academics and non-academics alike.

The existing rankings have both methodological and conceptual limitations, exacerbated by the dramatic changes taking place in the media landscape around the world. We find that existing rating systems perform reasonably well by the criterion of reliability. That is, the measures used by media rating organizations are generally applied in internally consistent ways across countries and over time, and different rating organizations tend to agree on variations in press freedom across countries and over time. To the extent that ratings diverge somewhat across rating systems, this can largely be explained by conceptual differences in the weight assigned to different criteria, such as physical attacks on journalists, government control over media, and public availability of information, which may vary somewhat independently even though all are valid considerations in an overall assessment of media freedom.

More problematic is the validity of these measures as a guide to improving media freedom and stabilizing democracy in transitional countries. Media freedom is an end in itself, a right enshrined in Article 19 of the Universal Declaration of Human Rights, which propounds the freedom "to receive and impart information and ideas through any media." Existing measures for the most part reflect fairly casual conceptualizations of this right. At the same time, media freedom is also thought to be causally or functionally related to the success of democratic governance. Efforts to promote media freedom are normally justified in part as contributing to the larger agenda of democracy promotion. It is not accidental that Freedom House is a leader in rating both democracy and media freedom.

Despite the presumed link of media freedom to democratic governance, very little attention so far has been paid to demonstrating empirically whether or how improvements in media freedom lead to improvements in democracy. At the grossest level over the long run, it is not disputed that greater media freedom tends to be associated with more democracy. At a more fine-grained level, however, measures of media freedom are not chosen with a view toward assessing specific mechanisms by which improvements in the media environment might lead to better democratic outcomes. Very little hypothesis testing of this kind has been attempted. To the extent that it has, it turns out that increased media openness sometimes leads to worse outcomes for democracy and human rights, for example, because newly freed media may be hijacked by populist demagogues and scapegoaters.

1. Measurement of Media Freedom

The indicators of three different organizations are most prominent in the discussion of media freedom. The best-known and most widely used measure of the press freedom is that of Freedom House. A non-governmental organization based in Washington, D.C., Freedom House was founded in 1941 to promote democracy globally. In 1980, it began conducting its media freedom survey — "Freedom of the Press: A Global Survey of Media Independence" — which in 2015 covered 199 countries and territories.[1]

To measure the press freedom concept, Freedom House attempts to assess the political, legal, and economic environments of each country and evaluate whether the countries promote and do not restrict the free flow of information. The ratings are reviewed individually and on a comparative basis in a series of six regional meeting with the analysts, ratings advisers with expertise in each region, other invited participants and Freedom House staff. Freedom House then compares the ratings with the previous year's findings. These reviews are followed by cross-regional assessments in which efforts are made to ensure comparability and consistency in the findings. Freedom House asks the raters to use questions divided into three broad categories covering the legal environment, the political environment and the economic environment.

In 2011, Freedom House added a new instrument, "Freedom on the Net," to assess a broad range of elements that comprise digital media freedom, and 65 countries were included in the survey.[2]

Freedom House has its main office in Washington, and the organization's operation there is often associated with conservative elements of U.S. foreign policy. Freedom House conducts the research for its Freedom in the World and Press Freedom indices out of its office in New York, and it states that these surveys are funded

---

1 "Freedom of the Press 2016," Freedom House, https://freedomhouse.org/report/freedom-press/freedom-press-2016?gclid=CJSg_oC56tlCFVUvgQod_2IJww.
2 "Freedom on the Net 2016," Freedom House, https://freedomhouse.org/report/freedom-net/freedom-net-2016.

separately from other Freedom House activities and not funded by the United States Government.

Reporters Without Borders (RWB) has released annually since 2002 a Worldwide Press Freedom report and ranking of individual nations. Based in Paris, RWB defends journalists and media outlets by condemning attacks on press freedom worldwide, by publishing a variety of annual and special reports on media freedom, and by appealing to governments and international organizations on behalf of journalists and media organizations. The RWB index has been seen as a French and European counterpoint to the Freedom House measures.[3]

RWB bases the score for each of the 180 countries on responses of its selected panelists to a questionnaire that was revised in 2013 to reflect changes in the media challenges and challenges faced by the media. The questionnaire includes questions about the number of journalists, media assistants and netizens who were jailed or killed in the connection with their activities, the number of journalists abducted, the number that fled into exile, the number of physical attacks and arrests, and the number of media censored. In addition, the questionnaire focuses on issues that are hard to quantify such as the degree to which news providers censor themselves, government interference in editorial content, or the transparency of government decision-making. Legislation is the subject of some questions. Questions have been added or expanded, to address issues such as concentration of media ownership, allocation of subsidies or state advertising, discrimination in access to journalism and journalism training.[4] The questionnaire is sent to freedom of expression groups, to a network of correspondents around the world, and to journalists, researchers, jurists and human rights activists.

---

[3] Christina Holtz-Bacha, "Freedom of the Press: Is a Worldwide Comparison Possible and what Is it Good for?" in Monroe Price and Susan Abbot, eds., *Measures of Press Freedom and Media Contributions to Development* (New York: Peter Lang, 2011).

[4] "World Press Freedom Index," Reporters Without Borders, https://rsf.org/en/ranking.

Funding for Reporters Without Borders has come from organizations such as the European Instrument for Democracy and Human Rights of the European Commission, the French Development Agency, the Organization for Security and Co-operation in Europe, UNESCO, the Organisation internationale de la francophonie, and the National Endowment for Democracy, a branch of the U.S. State Department.

A third organization, International Research & Exchanges Board (IREX), also conducts evaluations of media systems. IREX is a nonprofit organization based in Washington, D.C., that was founded in 1968 by U.S. universities to promote exchanges with the Soviet Union and Eastern Europe. IREX focuses on higher education, independent media, Internet development, and civil society in the United States and internationally. In 2001, IREX, in cooperation with USAID, prepared its first Media Sustainability Index (MSI) to evaluate the global development of independent media. IREX began with the idea of doing something more than and different from what Freedom House was doing. IREX said its MSI measures five criteria of a successful, independent media system. First, IREX measures the extent to which legal and social norms protect and promote free speech and access to public information. Second, IREX measures whether the journalism in the media system meets professional standards of quality. Third, the MSI determines whether the system has multiple news sources that provide citizens with reliable and objective news. The fourth criterion is whether the media are well-managed businesses, allowing editorial independence. Finally, MSI examines the supporting institutions in society to determine if they function in the professional interests of independent media.[5]

Media systems are scored in two steps. First, IREX assembles a panel of experts in each country, drawn from representatives of local media, NGOs, professional associations and media-development implementers. The panelists' scores are reviewed by IREX, in-country staff and/or Washington, DC, media staff, which then

---

5   "Media Sustainability Index — Europe & Eurasia," IREX, http://www.irex.org/project/media-sustainability-index-msi-europe-eurasia.

score the countries independently of the MSI panel. IREX says that the final scores are a combination of these two scores.

2. Reliability and Validity of Measures

In their early work on media freedom assessment, researchers at the University of Georgia focused on the internal and across-time reliability of the Freedom House, Reporters Without Borders and IREX measures, on the internal consistency of the measured dimensions of the Freedom House and IREX measures, on the relationships among those three measures, and on the ability of the Freedom House measures to identify dramatic changes across time.[6] They found that the measures were reliable across time, that they were internally consistent, that they largely measured the same concept or at least highly correlated concepts, and that the Freedom House measures reflected the major changes in the media environment associated with the collapse of communism in eastern and central Europe in the last decade of the last century.

Those analyses were later extended to data collected and reported to the end of 2008.[7] They focused again on reliability across time and on the interrelationships among the Freedom House, Reporters Without Borders and IREX measures. The Freedom House measures of Press Freedom to that point stretched across 28 years. The average correlation year-to-year for the Freedom House measures was .96 (Pearson r). By tracking the ratings across time, however, it is possible to see that the Freedom House measures are not static. The correlation, for example, between the measure of Press Freedom in 1980, when the scores were first used, with 1981, was .92. The correlation between the 1981 measure and the 2008 measure, however, was .57. This is true across time.

---

6   Lee Becker, Tudor Vlad, and Nancy Nusser, "An Evaluation of Press Freedom Indicators," *The International Communication Gazette* 61 (2007): 5–28.

7   Lee Becker and Tudor Vlad, "Validating Country-level Measures of Media Freedom with Survey Data" (paper presented at the Midwest Association for Public Opinion Research meeting, Chicago, 20–21 November 2009).

The Reporters Without Borders measures of Press Freedom also were found to be consistent year-to-year. The average correlation was .94. The Reporters Without Borders measures were available only across seven years, but they, too, show evidence of decreasing correlations across time. The 2002 measure of press freedom correlated .94 with the 2003 measure but only .83 with the 2008 measure.

It was possible to examine the correlations between the Freedom House and MSI index across seven years. The actual countries measured changed significantly across time, making comparisons a little difficult to evaluate. The correlations did vary, but overall they were high. The average across the seven years was 0.87. Across the five years in which the countries evaluated were roughly the same, that correlation was 0.90.

3. Conceptualization

Both the Freedom House and the Reporters Without Borders measures of press freedom come from the world of media advocacy. Freedom House was founded to promote democracy globally. Reporters Without Borders defends journalists and media outlets by condemning attacks on press freedom worldwide, by publishing a variety of annual and special reports on media freedom, and by appealing to governments and international organizations on behalf of journalists and media organizations.

Neither organization provides much by way of a conceptualization of the concept of press freedom. Freedom House says the concept is linked to Article 19 of the Universal Declaration of Human Rights. Article 19 holds that everyone has the right to freedom of opinion and expression, including freedom to hold opinions and to seek, receive, and impart information and ideas through any media. Freedom House says it seeks to provide a picture of the entire "enabling environment" in which the media in each country operate and to assess the degree of news and information diversity available to the public in any given country, from either local or transnational sources. Reporters Without Borders says its measure reflects the degree of freedom that journalists and news organizations enjoy in each country and the efforts made by the authorities to respect and ensure respect for this freedom.

IREX says its Sustainability Index assesses the development of independent media systems, that is, the hoped-for outcome of media assistance. Sustainability is defined as the extent to which political, legal, social, and economic circumstances and institutions, as well as professional standards within independent media, promote and/or permit independent media to survive over time.

When Freedom House began its work on press freedom, the concept already was in use in the political science and mass communication literature. Freedoms of association, information, and communication were listed as essential components of democracy.[8] Mass media were called the "connective tissue of democracy."[9]

In the literature of mass communication, Siebert, Peterson, and Schramm[10] were particularly influential. They identified four models or theoretical types of media. The first, historically, was the authoritarian type, where the government controlled the press through prior censorship and through punishment after publication. They labeled a more current variant of the authoritarian model the Soviet Communist type. The libertarian model was seen as the counterpoint to the authoritarian model. The primary feature is the absence of government control. The fourth model, social responsibility, holds that the media have obligations to society that accompany their freedom. The work of Siebert, Peterson, and Schramm is normative, though it did make reference to historical change. Hallin and Mancini provided a rare empirical test of these models and found them wanting.[11] They focused exclusively on 18 nations in Europe and North America and found that they best clustered into three models, based on their media systems. One was called the

---

8 Juan Linz, "Totalitarian and Authoritarian Regimes," in Fred I. Greenstein and Nelson W. Polsby, eds., *Handbook of political science*, Vol. 3 (Reading, Mass.: Addison-Wesley, 1975).

9 Richard Gunther and Anthony Mughan, eds., *Democracy and the Media: A Comparative Perspective* (Cambridge: Cambridge University Press, 2000).

10 Fred Siebert, Theodore Peterson, and Wilbur Schramm, *Four Theories of the Press* (Urbana-Champaign, Ill.: University of Illinois Press, 1963).

11 Daniel Hallin and Paolo Mancini, *Comparing Media Systems: Three Models of Media and Politics* (Cambridge: Cambridge University Press, 2004).

Mediterranean or "Polarized Pluralist" model. The second was called the North/Central European or "Democratic Corporatist" Model. The third was the North Atlantic or "Liberal Model." Subsequently, they edited a volume that included contributions from scholars examining a wider range of countries.[12]

Perhaps because of this early formulation by Siebert, Peterson, and Schramm, definitions of press freedom in the mass communication literature focus primarily on freedom from government control. Weaver distinguished three components of press freedom: the relative absence of government restraints on the media, the relative absence of nongovernmental restraints, and the existence of conditions to insure the dissemination of diverse ideas and opinions to large audiences.[13] Others distinguished between negative press freedom (the absence of legal controls, such as censorship) and positive press freedom (the ability of individuals to use the media).[14]

Some have argued that definitions of media freedom should include other concepts, such as the role of media in nation building, economic development, overcoming illiteracy and poverty, and building political consciousness.[15]

In another view, press freedom was called one type of freedom of communication.[16] Others have distinguished between the classic liberal perspective on media freedom and the radical democratic perspective.[17] The classic liberal perspective focuses on the freedom

---

12 Daniel Hallin and Paolo Mancini, "Conclusion," in Hallin and Mancini, eds., *Comparing Media Systems Beyond the Western World*.
13 David Weaver, "The Press and Government Restriction: A Cross-National Study over Time," *The International Communication Gazette* 23 (1997): 152-70.
14 Robert Picard, *The Press and the Decline of Democracy: The Democratic Socialist Response in Public Policy* (Westport, Conn.: Greenwood Publishing Group, 1985).
15 Ingunn Hagen, "Democratic communication: Media and social participation," in Janet Wasko and Vincent Mosco, eds., *Democratic communications in the information age* (Toronto: Garamond Press, 1992).
16 Christian Breunig, *Kommunikationsfreiheiten: Ein internationaler Vergleich* (Konstanz: Universitaetsverlag, 1994).
17 James Curran, "Media and Democracy: The Third Route," in Michael Bruun Andersen, ed., *Media and Democracy: Papers from an International Seminar* (Oslo: University of Oslo, 1996).

of the media to publish or broadcast. The radical democratic perspective focuses on how mass communications can equitably mediate conflict and competition between social groups in society. According to McQuail, the concept of media freedom should include both the degree of freedom enjoyed by the media and the degree of freedom and access of citizens to media content.[18] One view is that for a media system to be free there must be a diffusion of control and access supported by a nation's legal, institutional, economic and social-cultural systems. Thus, free and independent media "exist within a structure which is effectively demonopolized of the control of any concentrated social groups or forces and in which access is both equally and effectively guaranteed."[19] While there is not consensus in the academic literature on the proper conceptualization of media freedom, there does seem to be agreement that it should not be restricted to government constraints, or even to constraints from the marketplace. And media freedom should include some notion of the needs of citizens. McQuail's position that media freedom should include freedom of the media and freedom and rights for the citizen captures this sentiment. In this regard, the measures of press freedom of Freedom House and Reporters Without Borders are too limited, focusing most heavily on government constraints and attacks on the media, mostly from official channels. The Media Sustainability Index also has a bias toward media needs and rights, rather than towards those of the citizens.

4. Elite vs. Citizen Measures of Press Freedom

The Freedom House, Reporters Without Borders, IREX (and African Media Barometer) measures are all based on evaluations of media systems by elite evaluators. We also now have examined the relationship between the measures of media systems prepared by

---

[18] Dennis McQuail, *McQuail's Mass Communication Theory*, 5th ed. (London: Sage Publications, 2005).

[19] Beate Rozumilowicz, "Democratic Change: A Theoretical Approach," in Monroe Price, Beate Rozumilowicz, and G. Verhulst, eds., *Media Reform: Democratizing the Media, Democratizing the State* (London: Routledge, 2002).

these three organizations and the measures reflected in public opinion surveys of the BBC World Service Poll, the Gallup World Poll, and WorldPublicOpinion.Org also have been examined.[20] In 2007, The BBC World Service Poll included a question that asked respondents in 14 countries to use a 5-point scale to indicate how free they thought the media in their country were to report the news accurately, truthfully and without bias. In 2008, WorldPublicOpinion.Org, based at the University of Maryland, asked respondents to surveys conducted in 20 countries how much freedom the media in their country have.

The relationship between the measure of public perceptions of press freedom and the Freedom House measure of press freedom for the 14 countries included in the 2007 BBC World Service Poll was only .23 (Spearman rho). The correlation between the BBC World Service Poll measures and the Reporters Without Borders was .25 (Spearman). The relationship between the WorldPublicOpinion.Org measure of press freedom from the point of view of the citizens and the Freedom House measure was a much stronger .76, while the relationship between the WPO measure and the Reporters Without Borders measure was .71. The discrepancy between the findings from the two surveys was surprising. The surveys did use two different measures, and the BBC World Service Poll item was more complex and reverse scored. The more straightforward WorldPublicOpinion.org measure did produce the stronger relationship.

Additional analyses of the relationship between public opinion measures and the elite evaluations of media systems were undertaken using Gallup data. The Gallup World Poll included a measure of confidence in the media in its core battery of items from 2005 to 2010. Respondents were asked if they had confidence in the quality and integrity of the media. The Gallup measure of confidence was unrelated to Press Freedom as measured by Freedom House and by Reporters Without Borders. The correlations for the

---

20   Lee B. Becker and Tudor Vlad, "Linking Elite Measures of Media Freedom and Public Opinion Data: A Validation Exercise" (paper presented at the World Journalism Education Conference, Grahamstown, South Africa, 2010).

IREX measures were slightly positive. The IREX measure of Media Sustainability contains as one of its five components a measure of Journalistic Performance. The correlations increased slightly when this measure was used alone, suggesting that there is at least some slight link between Press Performance as measured by IREX and confidence in the press as measured by Gallup. The media systems with more professionally solid performance garner more confidence from their citizens.

Another analysis of confidence in the media as measured by the Gallup core item and press freedom as measured by Freedom House was conducted later with a much richer data set, namely data gathered as part of the World Poll in years 2005, 2006, 2007, 2008 and 2009.[21] In the last three of these years, we had more than 100 countries surveyed. The data showed that the relationship between the confidence measures and the elite evaluations was masked. In those countries in which repression of freedom of expression was low, free media was associated with low levels of confidence in the media relative to confidence in other institutions in society. When repression of freedom of expression was high, however, press freedom was associated with high levels of confidence in the media. In free societies, it seems, the media suffer from their critical stance relative to other institutions in society. In restricted societies, the media benefit from a more independent and critical stance. That finding replicated across the three years for which data were available for this analysis, namely 2007, 2008 and 2009.

Subsequently we analyzed the relationship between the Gallup measure of press freedom and the Gallup measure of confidence in the media was analyzed.[22] Across the sample of countries, the belief that the media have a lot of freedom was correlated only

---

21 Lee B. Becker, Tudor Vlad, and Cynthia English, "Examining the Linkage between Journalistic Performance and Citizen Assessments of Media" (paper presented at the Journalism Research and Education Section of the International Association for Media and Communication Research, Braga, Portugal, 2010).

22 Lee B. Becker, Cynthia English, and Tudor Vlad, "Understanding the Link between Public Confidence in the Media and Media Freedom" (paper presented at the World Association for Public Opinion Research meeting, Amsterdam, The Netherlands, 2011).

mildly with confidence in the media. The correlation coefficient was .21. The belief that the media are free is correlated slightly more strongly with confidence in other institutions, but in no case is the correlation strong. The belief that the media are free is unrelated to a measure of approval of the national leadership. Confidence in the media, in contrast, is more strongly correlated with confidence in the national government, financial institutions and religious organizations. As in the past, the elite evaluations of media freedom were only slightly correlated with confidence in the media in 2010. The relationship was negative rather than positive. The correlation between confidence in the media and the Freedom House measure of press freedom was -.18, while the correlation between confidence in the media and the Reporters Without Borders measure of press freedom was -0.17.

5. What Now We Know About Measures of Media Freedom

The questions are simple: Could these indicators be used as a way of monitoring changes in the media systems of countries? Is there a way to test the impact of media assistance efforts?

In recent years, Freedom House, Reporters Without Borders and IREX have become more transparent in their methodologies. They also have become more rigorous. They are competing for media attention and for support, and the competition has been a stimulant to innovation and improvement. The indicators are consistent across time, but not so consistent as to miss change. We know that Freedom House and IREX, which use subindices, produce internally consistent measures, but the subindices do report meaningful variability. All three organizations produce quite similar results, indicating that variability due to the particular rater's political orientation or advocacy goals is minimal.

The differences that do exist can be understood in terms of meaningful differences in the raters' approach. The Reporters Without Borders and Freedom House measures purport to measure the same concept. On closer examination, however it is clear that the former places much more emphasis on attacks on journalists than does the later. Some analyses of discrepancies in the two measures confirm this difference.[23] So the concept of press freedom is narrower from the RWB perspective. Media Sustainability, as measured by IREX, is highly correlated with Press Freedom, as measured both by Reporters Without Borders and Freedom House. But it does not appear to be the same thing. The finding that the IREX measure is more highly correlated with the Freedom House measure than with the Reporters Without Borders measure again suggests the narrower focus of the latter.

A somewhat related question is whether the high correlations between the Freedom House and Reporters Without Borders measures are the result of extreme cases. To put it another way, the question is whether the extreme cases mask higher variability in the middle range of measures. There is no evidence that variability is greater in the middle range than on the extremes. In sum, the two measures by and large produce similar results, the similarity is the same whether the countries are low, moderate or high in terms of press freedom, and the variability seems to be explained by differences in the conceptual bases of the measures rather than anything else.

The indices largely satisfy the criterion of reliability. The evidence is that random error is not a serious problem. We also feel that the three measures have some distinctiveness, with the Freedom House being the broader measure of press freedom than Reporters Without Borders measure. And we feel that media sustainability is a related but separate concept.

The question of validity is more complex. Freedom House, Reporters Without Borders and IREX are not conceptually well developed, as we have noted. The measures and procedures used certainly are consistent in a very general sense with the term press or media freedom. It is hard to argue, however, that the measures on

---

[23] Lee B. Becker, Laura Schneider, and Tudor Vlad, "A Systematic Analysis of the Discrepancies between Press Freedom as Measured by Reporters Without Borders and Freedom House" (paper presented at the International Conference Media and the Public Sphere, Lyon, France, 2012).

their face reflect the full range of the concept. The most obvious limitation is that all of the measures focus most heavily on constraints to press freedom that result from government action. They are less sensitive to limitations from the market or from other factors, such as journalistic or organizational incompetence. None of the measures reflects the concern of McQuail and others that a robust media freedom measure must incorporate audience needs and the rights of audience members to a free and complete flow of information. In this sense, the existing measures cover only half of the meaning of media freedom, namely the half represented by the freedoms of the media operatives.

All three measures are limited in other important ways. The first results from technological change in the media environment and its impact on media structure and journalistic behavior. All of the indices reflect some of these concerns. Freedom House has even gone so far as to create a separate index of Net Freedom. The challenge to the indices on this front is great, however, and it is likely to require modification of procedures in the future. The very definition of journalism and of journalists is changing rapidly. What affects the traditional media and what affects citizens acting as journalists may be quite different. Media freedom or some broader concept of journalistic freedom must incorporate both in today's world.

A broader issue is how to incorporate into the measure of media freedom in a single country the activities of media outside that country. Nation-state borders have come to mean less in the age of satellite broadcasting. And while countries have demonstrated some success in controlling what comes in through the Internet, the techniques are not perfect, and many work hard to overcome them. This is a fundamental challenge to the idea that the nation-state is the proper unit of analysis for the study of media freedom.

Another challenge is that the degree of media freedom within a nation-state may vary from one regional media market to another. The market in the capital, for example, might be more or less free than the markets outside the governmental center. Yet the existing measures ignore these differences by creating a single measure that attempts to incorporate the internal variability. The existing measures also do not differentiate between freedoms enjoyed by one form of the media but not by others. In many countries, the printed media differ from the visual and oral media in terms of the freedoms they enjoy. The existing measures are not explicit in how they handle these disparities.

The indicators also give less attention to the matter of content than would seem to be ideal. The IREX index does contain a subindex of press performance, and all of the indicators give some attention to this matter. But the quality of media content is not their primary concern.

The analyses have shown that the public largely agrees with the elite evaluators in their assessments of media freedom. We found that the public has the broader perspective of media freedom as measured by Freedom House, rather than the narrower perspective of Reporters Without Borders with its focus on attacks on the media and on journalists. The public's notion of confidence in the media is more highly correlated with the IREX measure of Sustainability than with the Freedom House and Reporters Without Borders measures of press freedom. This is consistent with the idea that sustainability is a related but distinguishable concept from press freedom.

These analyses raise the question as to whether a more robust measure of media freedom would include both elite evaluations and those of individual citizens. Should the elite evaluators and the public have to agree that the media are free for the country to score highly on a media freedom index? What weight might be given to public assessments of media freedom in such an index? Consistent with this view, some have Bajomi-Lazar (2008) has argued that the consolidation of media freedom in a society occurs only when there is institutional support for that freedom, the media behave in a free fashion, and the public is supportive of media freedom.[24]

An alternative strategy is to view the elite evaluations and the public evaluations as separate concepts. Such a strategy suggests

---

24 Peter Bajomi-Lazar, "The Consolidation of Media Freedom in Post-Communist Countries," in Karol Jakubowicz and Miklos Sukosd, eds., *Finding the Right Place on the Map: Central and Eastern European Media Change in a Global Perspective* (Bristol, UK: Intellect Books, 2008).

that media freedom might have different effects in conditions in which the public was less convinced that the media were, in fact, free than when the public agreed with elite assessments. While no empirical work has examined this question, related work is consistent with it.

The existing indices, in sum, suffer from their limited conceptualization. And the conceptual weakness is a reflection of the limited theoretical development on the role of the media in the functioning of a society. The presumption here is that we should not only be concerned with media freedom as something of importance on its own, but rather we should be concerned with media freedom because we believe such freedom determines important society outcomes, such as creation of a functioning democracy and economy. The basic question, in the end, is what kinds of content are needed for democratic and economic development.

6. Mechanisms by which Media Freedom Affects Democracy

The starting point of this discussion of media freedom has been that freedom of news and of communications media is one of the central pillars of political life in stable democracies. Without media freedom, citizens would lack the information to evaluate public issues, organize political groups, choose prudently among candidates for office, and hold officials accountable. Consequently, democrats typically take it for granted that increases in media freedom in countries that lack it will contribute to democratization, the enhancement of rights, the rule of law, and social stability.

On average, and over the long run, they are certainly correct. In the short run, however, the impact of increased media freedom on these desirable outcomes is much more complex and varied. Media openings in dictatorships or culturally divided countries sometimes exacerbate power struggles between regimes and their subjects, or between ethnic and religious groups.[25] Media freedom may

---

25   Jack Snyder and Karen Ballentine, "Nationalism and the Marketplace of Ideas," *International Security* 21 (Autumn 1996): 5–40.

stir up opposition to abuses, which is countered by repression, or it may open channels for hate speech by opportunists who play the ethnic card.[26] Satellite TV and new communications media have contributed to a dramatic increase in the opportunities for political expression in the Middle East, but the consequences for democracy, rights, law, and stability are mixed in the short run and indeterminate in the longer run.

Divisive voices may hijack debate in a newly freed marketplace of ideas, because opportunists can exploit "market imperfections" in a situation where media resources are unequally distributed, audiences are divided by language and culture, journalists lack professionalism, and corruption and intimidation are rampant. In such settings, no invisible hand guarantees that the free contestation of ideas will cause the truth to triumph. In this setting, more speech can sometimes ironically lead to a detour away from the institutionalization of media and information freedom.

Although financial support for media freedom projects has been growing and diversifying, the knowledge base needed to design such programs has major gaps. Precisely because media freedom is so crucial to the progress of democracy, rights, law, and social peace, efforts to enhance media freedom should be based on a finer-grained understanding of the mechanisms by which media openness affects political outcomes, and how different circumstances affect the working of these mechanisms.

In liberal theory, media freedom is thought to affect political processes and outcomes through two general routes: by increasing the freedom of political contestation, and by providing improved information. Both contestation and information are needed to make democracy work. One without the other sets up potentially perilous contradictions. If media contributes to contestation without improving information, coercive struggle rather than stable democracy may result. Conversely, if increased media openness improves public information without simultaneously institutionalizing mass

---

26 Jenifer Whitten-Woodring, "Watchdog or Lapdog? Media Freedom, Regime Type, and Government Respect for Human Rights," *International Studies Quarterly* 53 (September 2009): 595–625.

political contestation, a volatile social science experiment is set in motion. The post-Jazeera Arab World, China in the Internet era, and Singapore are running that experiment now, just as Britain did in 1704 when it ended press censorship, and as South Africa did under apartheid.

Although the world has been running such experiments for some time now, social scientists have just begun to study their results. The barrier has not been the lack of systematic, global measures of media freedom, which have been available for a couple of decades. Rather, the lag has been in examining the impact of changes in media freedom on the specific causal mechanisms that are believed to affect the quality of democracy, rights, law, and social peace.

Liberal theory expects that greater media freedom will lead to these good results through five mechanisms: increased media freedom is expected to improve media quality, lead to a better informed public that can choose wisely and hold leaders accountable, create a common political discourse within the nation, make political discourse more reasonable, and have a moderating effect on political attitudes. Do these five mechanisms operate as expected in transitional societies?

a)   How does an increase in media freedom affect media quality?
Starting with John Milton and continuing through John Stuart Mill's *On Liberty*, it has been axiomatic for liberals that a more open media will contain better ideas and information than a closed one. They acknowledge that false or destructive ideas may be voiced in open media, just as they may be when media are controlled, but bad ideas in a free marketplace can be scrutinized, confronted in debate, and discredited.

Are free media, especially newly free media, in fact better in the quality of the ideas and information that they convey? Do quality media flourish under free competition, or does intense market competition lead to pandering to mass tastes and prejudices? Are poorly professionalized, partially free media in transitional societies especially susceptible to manipulation that undercuts the expected benefits of increased media freedom?

Answering these questions requires first that we be able to measure media quality. A good, but limited attempt to do this is IREX's rating of media quality, first in 20 post-communist states, then in the Middle East and North Africa, and now also in Sub-Saharan Africa. IREX asked expert panels to rate objectivity, fairness, and sourcing of reporting; ethical standards of journalists; self-censorship; corruption and adequacy of pay; ratio of news to entertainment content; quality of technical equipment; and existence of investigative and other specialized reporting. A cross-national statistical comparison using this data has shown that quality was low when competition was absent, better when competition was moderate, but also low when commercial pressure to compete induced a race to the lowest common denominator of media content. This is just a start at answering a hard question.

b)   *How does an increase in media freedom affect political knowledge?*
Some experts argue that the public needs only a little political knowledge to pick up on the cues it needs to effectively play its role in monitoring its elected representatives.[27] If so, free media need only vet opinions and monitor gross outcomes. Normally, however, proponents of a free press insist on a higher standard: quality media must help attentive elites and publics evaluate opinions against facts.

Scholars are just beginning to study whether media freedom actually does improve political knowledge. A study showed that the public gains more political knowledge in the less competitive, more elite-controlled Finnish media setting than in the more mass-competitive US media environment, and that the mixed British system produces intermediate knowledge results.[28] An analysis tried to assess the impact on political knowledge in Spain of reading higher quality print media, compared to consuming lower quality news sources—and to tease apart these effects from the influence of

---

27 John Zaller, *The Nature and Origins of Mass Opinion* (Cambridge: Cambridge University Press, 1992).
28 Toril Aalberg, Peter van Aelst, and James Curran, "Media Systems and the Political Information Environment: A Cross-National Comparison," *International Journal of Press/Politics* 15 (2010): 255–71.

other factors, such as education and motivation.[29] Though a good start, these studies highlight the need to find factual questions that are relevant to real political issues, allow comparison across countries or over time, and take into account confounding factors other than media freedom and quality that may affect political knowledge. None of them examines the impact of change over time in media freedom on political knowledge, nor do they extend beyond the global North.

c) *Does an increase in media freedom lead to more integrated or more segmented media markets?*

The advent of print capitalism created a sense of an "imagined community" among those who shared a common reading experience in their vernacular language, and thus established a prerequisite for national self-determination.[30] However, increases in media freedom may Balkanize political discourse if each ethnolinguistic group, religious sect, or partisan faction gains its own media voice. This literally happened in the Balkans when the federal decentralization of Yugoslavia allowed ethnic demagogues to hijack television broadcasting to captive audiences.

It is a largely unstudied empirical question whether, and under what conditions, increases in media freedom tend to strengthen the market share of integrative national media or lead to the regional dispersal of media markets. Likewise, there have not been systematic studies of how political content and topics differ between national and regional media markets during media openings. Nor do we know whether free media increases or decreases the likelihood that different views get debated in settings moderated by professional journalists rather than presented as unanswered monologues aimed at the speaker's core support group.

---

29 Marta Fraile, "Widening or Reducing the Knowledge Gap? Testing the Media Effects on Political Knowledge in Spain (2004–2006)," *The International Journal of Press/Politics* 16 (2011): 163–82.

30 Benedict Anderson, *Imagined Communities* (London: Verso, 1983).

d) *How does an increase in media freedom affect the provocativeness or radicalism of media content?*

Those of us brought up in the democratic media environment presided over by Walter Cronkite and the McNeil-Lehrer Newshour might assume that free media automatically tend to moderate discourse, since rebuttal in open debate reported by professional journalists will quickly expose and humiliate baseless provocateurs. But even in the professionalized, well-institutionalized U.S. media setting, McCarthyism and "swiftboating" have made their impact. In the very early days of free media (in the U.S. and elsewhere), slander and mythmaking are even more pervasive. Thomas Jefferson himself complained that nothing can now be believed which is seen in a newspaper. Truth itself becomes suspicious by being put into that polluted vehicle. Notwithstanding plenty of such anecdotes, there is no systematic study of the impact of increased media freedom on the provocativeness and immoderation of discourse.

e) *Does an increase in media freedom increase social consensus, or does it polarize opinions?*

We know that civil war and ethnic conflict are less common in established democracies, and we know that media freedom is greater in established democracies, so it seems intuitive that increased press freedom might somehow contribute to the moderation of political opinion, which underpins this social peace. Perhaps disagreements are settled by open, fair argument or by compromise-based political bargaining among factions whose disagreements have become moderated by the exchange of well-vetted information. The deliberation school of democratic theory makes arguments of this kind.[31]

Apart from anecdotal knowledge, we are unaware of any effort to study whether, or under what conditions, increased press freedom moderates or polarizes political attitudes. Of course, this topic would be difficult to study in cases of a sudden transition

---

31 Jon Elster, ed., *Deliberative Democracy* (Cambridge: Cambridge University Press, 1998).

from a totally closed society, where public opinion surveys are impossible or unreliable. However, the effects on attitudes of improvements in media freedom in mixed regimes could be studied in this way. For example, attitude surveys on topics like religious and ethnic intolerance have been carried out in Turkey over a time period in which media freedom has both improved and worsened.[32] Likewise, opinion barometers in various countries ask repeat questions about contentious issues, so opinion polarization can be compared over time as media freedom changes.

Finally, scholars and activists are also interested in learning whether increases in media freedom correlate with ultimate goals such as democracy, human rights, rule of law, and social peace. However, problems of causal inference are particularly difficult to disentangle at this macro level, since many independent factors in addition to the media environment can affect such outcomes. Unless we can show that the causal mechanisms posited by liberal free media theory are at work, it could be that any such correlation might not be causal, but rather an effect of some third variable, such as improved education, per capita income, or the influence of U.S. geopolitical hegemony.

Media assistance programs are facing an increasingly complex environment in which social movements with diverse and often illiberal ideologies deploy a range of new and old media technologies in wildly different contexts of rapid political change. The old verities of free media doctrine were never well tested against systematic empirical evidence. Now, changing circumstances redouble the need to take a fresh look at the effectiveness and relevance of existing strategies for measuring and promoting free media.[33]

---

32 Hennie Kotzé and Pierre du Toit, "Civic Tolerance and Religiosity: Elites and Publics Compared," in Ursula J. van Beek, ed., *Democracy Under Scrutiny: Elites, Citizens, Cultures* (Opladen and Farmington Hills, MI: Barbara Budrich Publishers, 2010).

33 Anne Nelson, "Continental Shift: New Trends in Private U.S. Funding for Media Development," http://www.cima.ned.org/resource/continental-shift-new-trends-in-private-u-s-funding-for-media-development/.

Russia's Nongovernmental Media under Assault

Maria Lipman, journal Counterpoint *chief editor*

In developed democracies, the news media are an inseparable element of a network of checks and balances that help society to ensure the accountability of powerful actors (first and foremost, the government). At least, such is the understanding, even if in real life the news media do not always live up to these expectations and the goal of public accountability is not easily achieved.

In Vladimir Putin's Russia—long before his return to the Kremlin in 2012 and the shift toward a harder authoritarian model—political power was heavily monopolized, and democratic checks and balances existed only nominally. While the collapse of the Soviet communist system created a promise of democracy—the 1993 constitution defined a multiparty system with the separation of powers and mechanisms of public participation—the new institutions did not take root, and as soon as Putin came to power in 2000, they were steadily and radically eviscerated. The system of governance that Putin built virtually eliminated public accountability.

Despite some obvious similarities, Putin's system was not a return to the Soviet model. In the media realm Putin's Kremlin did not seek to reintroduce preliminary censorship across the board, the key element of the Soviet media scene. Far from it: though the national TV networks with the largest audience were taken under control within just a few years after Putin became president, elsewhere opportunities for self-expression remained. A range of media continued to pursue reasonably independent editorial lines; some were even openly anti-government.

These nongovernment media[1] occasionally exposed government abuse of authority and reported other politically meaningful

---

1 The term "nongovernmental media" is used here to designate those media outlets whose editorial policy is not guided by the desire to demonstrate their

information, yet actors who could follow up on these reports and use them in politically relevant ways were missing. In the absence of an independent parliament or genuine political opposition, media reports remained mere political texts that were not converted into political events. In other words, in the early 2000s press freedom as a democratic institution that could hold the government to account ceased to exist.[2]

The establishment of the Kremlin's political monopoly, as well as the elimination of press freedom, were facilitated by a weak public demand for political rights and civil liberties, media freedom being no exception. Put more broadly, the long decades of Soviet oppression precluded the emergence in Russia of a sense of "we, the people," or a belief that the people can hold the government to account.

By the end of the 2000s, however, a minority that did not share the habitual sense of acquiescence toward government authority began to emerge. It was this constituency that in December 2011 took to the streets chanting "Russia without Putin." The protests continued through 2012, and in May that year the government responded with a crackdown and a conservative shift that the protesters were too weak to oppose. The freedom of expression remaining at that time did not make much difference. Moreover, in 2012-2013 the nongovernment media came under increasing pressure. The crisis in Ukraine followed by Russia's annexation of Crimea exacerbated the oppressive trend: the TV networks have been turned into raw propaganda machines,[3] and dissenting voices were

---

loyalty to the powers that be. Their degree of independence may vary. The form of ownership is of less importance, since in Russia the borderline between state and private property is blurred. The media that are technically private commonly shape their editorial policy strictly in the interests of the government.

[2] On the media in Putin's Russia, see, for instance, Maria Lipman, "Freedom of Expression Without Freedom of the Press," *Journal of International Affairs* 63:2 (Spring/Summer 2010): 153-69.

[3] "1984 in 2014," *The Economist*, http://www.economist.com/news/europe/21599829-new-propaganda-war-underpins-kremlins-clash-west-1984-2014.

condemned as natsional predateli ("traitors of the people").[4] In late 2013–early 2014, the regime dealt several critical blows to what was left of the nongovernment media realm, leaving in doubt the viability of those nongovernment media outlets that have not been destroyed or submitted.

1. Putin's Kremlin and the Media Realm in 2000–2008

Putin's political monopoly sought to neutralize the political challenges faced by his predecessor and anointer, Russia's first president Boris Yeltsin. By the end of Putin's first term both chambers of the Russian parliament, the Duma and the Federation Council, regional governors, political parties, big business — all previously independent (and not infrequently unruly) political actors — were taken under control. National TV networks — Russia's largest-audience media — were among the first targets.

It should be pointed out, however, that from the start the Kremlin refrained from harassing or persecuting those independent media figures who had enjoyed broad public popularity. Instead, the Kremlin opted for less straightforward tactics — that of a redistribution of media property. Putin's Kremlin promptly got rid of the two biggest media tycoons — Vladimir Gusinsky and Boris Berezovsky — who sought to preserve their status of political players gained in the 1990s. Both fled abroad, their major media assets either redistributed in favor of the state itself or entrusted with politically reliable owners.

In the framework of this property redistribution, the national gas monopoly Gazprom (Gazprom-media holding) took over Russia's largest privately-owned media holding, *Media MOST*, which had been created by Vladimir Gusinsky. NTV, a national TV network that Gusinsky had built from scratch, was the crown jewel of his media empire. In the spring of 2001 there were two protest ral-

---

4   Joshua Yaffa, "Putin's New War on 'Traitors'," *The New Yorker*, http://www.newyorker.com/online/blogs/newsdesk/2014/03/putin-new-hunt-for-internal-enemies.html.

lies, with the first bringing 15,000 people to the street and the second mobilizing 10,000 in Moscow to denounce the "capture of *NTV*." People strongly sympathized with their beloved journalists who had run afoul of the government, but since the journalists remained safe and at large, the protests promptly faded away. A national survey conducted in 2001 showed that a mere four percent of Russians regarded the squelching of *NTV* as an encroachment on media freedom; likewise, an overwhelming majority did not see it as an infringement on their own civil liberties.

The government promptly turned the three major national TV networks into its own political resource, a one-way communication tube that it has since used effectively to shape public opinion. Since the crisis in Ukraine began to unfold in late 2013 the national TV networks have shifted to disseminating raw propaganda.

The Kremlin did not completely squash the freedom of expression: a number of smaller-audience nongovernment outlets continued to operate, but the bulk of the Russian audience remained with TV. After the national TV networks had been turned into government mouthpieces, the viewing audience did not rush to read or listen to alternative, nongovernment media.[5] The latter remained "niche" outlets for a critically minded and politically concerned minority.

The Kremlin policy vis-à-vis the Russian media thus included: Constraints on media freedom through the redistribution of media assets, not through the repression of journalists; and allowing a reasonable degree of freedom of expression in smaller-audience media, yet turning it politically irrelevant through tight controls on the political realm.

The change of ownership did not necessarily entail an immediate change in the editorial line. For example, both *NTV* and *Ekho Moskvy* (formerly parts of Gusinsky's *Media MOST* group) were owned by Gazprom-media, but, as far as the political coverage was concerned, their editorial lines differed quite substantially: *NTV*,

---

[5] Still today, and even in modernized Moscow, national TV networks remain by far the most popular source of information for the Russian people, the sharp rise of the number of Internet users notwithstanding.

like other national TV broadcasters with news programming, was tightly controlled so nothing unexpected or unpleasant for the Kremlin would ever appear on air. Meanwhile, *Ekho Moskvy*, Russia's most popular political talk radio, continued to offer the listener a diversity of voices, many of them fairly critical of the government. But the ownership factor ensured that those media that pursued a relatively independent editorial line remained at the government's discretion.

The limited freedom of expression that the Kremlin permitted served regime interests by working as a means to let off steam among those who did not support the status quo. Yet, this freedom remained politically innocuous since the authorities maintained secure control over both the political and business realms and benefitted from broad public acquiescence to their continued rule, ensured by a combination of growing living standards, carefully orchestrated TV coverage and a low demand for nongovernment sources of information.

The nongovernment media of the mid-2000s and their audiences were often described as "ghettos" or "islands." And they were, for the most part, preaching to the converted. The "converted"—roughly speaking, the liberal constituency—may have enjoyed listening to the critical voices, but, just like the rest of their compatriots, they acquiesced to controlled politics and to being denied political participation. That is the way the system worked through the end of Putin's second term in 2008.

2. Tandem Rule: Societal Shifts and Media Developments

The period of Dmitry Medvedev's presidency, better known as the "tandem rule" (Putin, who had moved to the position of the prime minister, remained Russia's most powerful man) was marked by a societal modernization which also affected the realm of public communication. The following factors contributed to this process:

- The high and rising price of oil had produced extensive new wealth and stimulated the emergence of a post-industrial economy, especially in Moscow. This gave rise to a new, "non-Soviet" constituency that no longer shared the habitual Soviet paternalism and developed an interest in charitable activities and civic activism. Journalists were an important element of this constituency
- President Medvedev's liberal rhetoric, such as his famous line "freedom is better than nonfreedom," generated a new sense of liberty among younger constituencies as well as broader civil society circles, journalists included.
- Rapid penetration of the Internet in Russian society and the spread of social networks facilitated the exchange of information and opinions.

During Medvedev's presidency, Russian citizens began to use freedom of expression more avidly, the media environment grew more vibrant, and a modicum of political liberty emerged even on TV. For example, the *NTV* network launched a few late-night shows that took liberties with sensitive political subjects. A number of new niche outlets, such as *Dozhd'* (*Rain*) and *Kommersant FM* radio station began broadcasting in 2010 and targeted younger, liberal audiences. Some of the glossy journals and the so-called "hipster press," such as *Afisha* or *Bolshoy Gorod*, grew politicized.[6] In short, the "ghetto" life grew more intense.

Meanwhile, the redistribution of media assets continued. Putin's government took pride in ridding Russia of "oligarchic media," but during the years of Putin's leadership the concentration of media properties significantly exceeded that of Gusinsky's or Berezovsky's holdings in the 1990s. The difference between the "media oligarchs" of the 1990s and the media magnates of Putin's Russia is

---

6   Russian *Esquire* magazine was the first among the glossies to turn to political themes. For instance, in its October 2008 issue it published an interview with the jailed tycoon Mikhail Khodorkovsky by a highly popular author, Boris Akunin (three years later Akunin was among the most prominent figures of the Moscow protests). In the interview-by-correspondence, Khodorkovsky admitted that Akunin was his first "understanding and interested" interviewer.

that the latter are fully loyal to Putin. Among the magnates who vastly expanded their media holdings under Putin, the most prominent is Yury Kovalchuk. Numerous press reports indicate that he and Putin have long-term personal ties. Kovalchuk's Natsionalnaya Media Gruppa (National Media Group) included two national television networks and a range of print and Internet resources. In 2010 his affiliated business interests became 100 percent owners of Video International, a major company that sells advertising on TV, and, in particular, on Russia's largest TV network *Pervyy kanal* (*Channel 1*)[7] In early 2011 Kovalchuk further increased his holdings by purchasing a 25 percent share in *Pervyy kanal*, Russia's largest-audience national network. Other major owners included Gazprom-media (see also footnote 12) and Alisher Usmanov, a metal tycoon and Russia's richest man. And, of course, the state itself.

While Dmitry Medvedev's presidency brought a whiff of liberty, the general political pattern, that of unchallenged centralized power, remained unchanged. Politics was still tightly controlled, business companies and entrepreneurs depended on the benevolence of the powers that be, and public participation existed only on paper.

In September 2011 Medvedev announced that he would "vacate" the presidency for Putin. The switcheroo — Putin promptly announced that he would appoint Medvedev his prime minister — is a graphic illustration of the Kremlin's political pattern in which decisions are made secretly by a close circle of people at the very top. Both Medvedev and Putin made it clear[8] that they had agreed a few years earlier on who would run for president in 2012. To many in Russia such statements, which read like "we decided who would be

---

[7] Konstantin Gaaze, "Otdel'no vzyatyy telekanal," *Forbes.ru*, 9 February 2011, www.forbes.ru/ekonomika-opinion/vlast/63087-otdelno-vzyatyi-telekanal; Aleksandr Polivanov, "Pervyy plyus Pyatyy," *Lenta.ru*, 11 February 2011, www.lenta.ru/articles/2011/02/10first/; Ksenia Boletskaya, "Who owns Video International," *Vedomosti*, 29 June 2010.

[8] "Medvedev i Putin reshili pomenyat'sya mestami," *Reuters*, 24 September 2011, http://ru.reuters.com/article/topNews/idRURXE78N00320110924; and "Tretiy srok Putina," *Rambler.ru*, 24 September 2011, http://news.rambler.ru/11196015/.

president beyond 2012," sounded like utter contempt for the people.

The outrage over the "job swap" was further exacerbated by the egregiously rigged parliamentary election in December 2011. These events triggered a series of mass protests that lasted in Moscow through the first half of 2012. The most common slogan was "Russia without Putin." For the first time since he came to power over a decade earlier, Putin faced large-scale public defiance.

3. Putin's Response to the Protests and the Contraction of the Mass Communications Realm

As soon as Putin returned to the Kremlin, the Medvedev-era flirtations with liberty vanished. The timid signs of political liberty promptly disappeared from *NTV*. In 2012, the Kremlin shifted to repressive policies that included the prosecution and harassment of activists and protesters. In May, a protest rally for the first time ended with clashes with the police. Subsequently, about three dozen participants were arrested and charged with "mass unrest," leading to trials known as the *Bolotnoe delo* (the Bolotnoe Affair). [9] New pieces of legislation encroaching on the rights and freedoms passed through the parliament in quick succession with barely any debate or amendment (this law-making frenzy earned the Duma a nickname "a printer gone wild").

---

9   The *Bolotnaya* affair is named after Bolotnaya Square where the rally was staged. The court hearings in the case were a demonstration of the lawlessness and egregious anti-defendant bias common to all politically motivated trials in Russia. Of the almost 30 defendants who had been charged in the Bolotnaya case, two opted for a plea bargain and were sentenced to long terms in jail nonetheless. One person was locked up in a psychiatric asylum. A few were amnestied in December 2013. In February 2014, seven protesters were sentenced to 2.5 to 4 years of prison camp and one to house arrest (members of this group had spent 16 to 21 months in pretrial detention). See "Figurantam "Bolotnogo dela" dali do 4 let kolonii," *Lenta.ru*, 24 Febraury 2014, http://lenta.ru/news/2014/02/24/sentence/. Up to one thousand people came to the courthouse on the day when the verdict was announced; several hundred were detained, many of them roughed up by the police. The most common punishment was a fine; in a few cases the detainees had to spend a few days in jail. As of this writing four more participants of the May 6 rally are in pretrial detention awaiting trial.

Nongovernment organizations that received foreign funding came under pressure. Other elements of the crackdown included a harsh campaign of anti-Western and anti-liberal propaganda and a shift toward social conservatism. The government's rhetoric increasingly focused on issues such as faith, sex, school curriculum, art and culture and condemned "nontraditional" practices. The goal of the new policy was to consolidate the conservative majority and pit it against the modernized minorities. What began as a tactical move aimed at discrediting and neutralizing the excessively modernized trouble-makers has gradually evolved as a new "ideological choice": Russian traditions and morality vs. the decadent and immoral West and its "fifth column" within Russia that included liberals, gays, activists, and protesters. Any criticism of conservative laws and policies came to be seen as unpatriotic and undermining Russia's traditional values.

The nongovernment media thoroughly covered the surge of civic activism and the protests, and many journalists took an active part in the protest activities. Yet, unlike the nongovernmental organizations, media outlets did not become a direct target of harassment. There are no journalists among those prosecuted for "mass unrest" in Bolotnaya Square. But the nongovernment media have come under pressure in a different way.

Just as during the early stages of Putin's presidency, control through ownership proved to be an effective tool to impose constraints on media. The new round of pressure can be traced back to late 2011 when staffers of gazeta.ru quit as a sign of protest against the owner's interference with the coverage of the parliamentary campaign.[10] The *gazeta.ru* staff has since been thoroughly reshuffled and its top editors replaced twice. Beginning in early 2012, numerous journalists and editors lost their jobs (dismissed or forced to quit) and a few media outlets that pursued independent editorial lines have been closed. In all these cases the immediate "offender" was not the Kremlin or a biased judge: it was the owner, and the

---

10   Nataliya Rostova, "Roman Badanin: "V Rossii v rassledovateli perekvalifitsiruyutsya zhurnal pro uspekh i gazeta pro trendy," *Slon.ru*, 2 December 2013, http://slon.ru/russia/roman_badanin-1027489.xhtml.

dismissals and closures were explained by purely economic reasons, if they were explained at all.

Media outlets are additionally vulnerable because business in general, just as any nongovernment actors, is at the discretion of the Kremlin. Profitable media outlets can be easily stripped of advertising revenues—no firm would want to displease the Kremlin by placing its ads in a publication deemed unwelcome by the powers that be. *The New Times* weekly magazine, arguably the most uncompromising and daring publication, has lost all its advertisers. It struggles to survive and lives off private donations and subscription fees.

The nature of control differs for big and small businesses. Magnates like Usmanov, who owns the Kommersant media holding, are especially keen to avoid political risks because of their large-scale and diverse business interests. Anxious to maintain good relations with the Kremlin, such major owners often preempt political "instructions" or "requests" and make sure their media do not show disloyalty. But small-scale owners or media managers who are still ready to take some risk and let their media practice a degree of editorial freedom are aware that sooner or later they will face the Kremlin's displeasure. Nikolay Uskov, the editor-in-chief of the media project *Snob*, said in late November 2013: "Any media outlet that seeks to be objective can fall under the government's steamroller or lose the advertising revenues drawn from state corporations."[11]

The "owner factor" gained additional potency after the stepped-up concentration of media assets and coincided with Putin's return to the Kremlin. In late 2013 Gazprom-media purchased the TV and radio holdings of ProfMedia. "The Kovalchuks'

---

11 "'Vernulis' vremena lishnikh lyudey': Interv'yu s glavnym redaktorom proekta 'Snov' Nikolaem Uskovym," *Lenta.ru*, 27 November 2013, http://lenta.ru/articles/2013/11/26/uskov/?utm_source=rubrics&utm_medium=clicks&utm_campaign=ClickFromRubrics.

empire" now controls 11 of Russia's 17 largest TV networks, according to *The New Times* weekly.[12]

There is little doubt that the closures of outlets and programs and dismissals of journalists, whether explained by economic factors or not explained at all, reflected growing political constraints. *Kommersant*, once Russia's best mainstream newspaper, lost about a dozen journalists. The first in the line of dismissals in the *Kommersant* media holding was Maksim Kovalsky, the editor-in-chief of the weekly magazine *Kommersant-Vlast'*. Shortly after Putin's election in March 2013, Kovalsky ran a photo of a ballot on which a voter had scribbled a profanity referring to Putin.

The top editor of *Kommersant FM*, a radio station that had been launched in the freer atmosphere of Medvedev's presidency, was replaced twice. The current editor's background is in regional government administration.[13] A new high-quality magazine, *CITIZEN K* (another publication of the *Kommersant* media holding), was closed soon after its launch. Those who remain employed by Kommersant publications complained—in private—about the growing interference of the owner in the editorial line. In another example,

---

12 Dmitriy Kamyshev, Ol'ga Beshley, and Zhanna Ul'yanova, "Kooperativ 'Ozero': efir vzyat!," *The New Times*, 2 December 2013, http://www.newtimes.ru/articles/detail/74981?sphrase_id=237051. Gazprom-media which was originally launched as the media company of Gazprom, in recent years has gradually come under the control of Kovalchuk's business structures. According to a report published in *The New Times* weekly magazine, "structures controlled by Yuri Kovalchuk" through various property schemes own "at least a blocking package" in all major media holdings except for VGTRK (All-Russian State Television and Radio company). *The New Times* magazine quotes Russia's leading media expert Anna Kachkaeva: "The new giant media holding (of Yuri Kovalchuk) reaches out to maximum-sized audiences as applies to age, social groups as well as the segments of politically active and apolitical citizens." The purchase of ProfMedia marks yet another radical expansion of the Kovalchuk's media empire to include a few of Russia's best entertainment TV channels. The total daily audience share of the TV channels connected to the Kovalchuk brothers is close to 60 percent; their share of Russian TV advertising revenues is about 80 percent.

13 "Kommersant FM vozglavila eks-zammera Saratova po ideologii," *Forbes*, 5 July 2013, http://www.forbes.ru/news/241727-kommersant-fm-vozglavila-eks-zammera-saratova-po-ideologii.

Bolshoi Gorod, a Moscow youth magazine whose coverage grew politicized during the period of mass protests, lost its top editor, and its editorial policy was subsequently reformatted in order to avoid risky, political subjects.

In the summer of 2013 Gleb Pavlovsky, once a Kremlin insider and currently an insightful and critical commentator, said:

> The reorganization of the media (that employ) disloyal journalists is done by a transfer of property from one owner to another. It is done quietly ... The journalists assume that they have a professional and reputational weight and can quietly move to another outlet. They fail to see that the space... is shrinking. And they begin to ... censor themselves... They may write about the same [topics], but they try not to cross an invisible line.[14]

There are other ways to "tame" excessively independent journalists and editors. For instance, in early 2012 Gazprom-media initiated an urgent reshuffling of the board of directors of *Ekho Moskvy*. In February 2014 the new board that is now dominated by the government loyalists fired the station's executive director Yury Fedutinov. For many years Fedutinov worked in close cooperation with *Ekho*'s legendary top editor Aleksey Venediktov. He has been replaced by a woman whose background is in government media. Her appointment to the position of executive director means that Venediktov's authority in editorial decision-making will be significantly constrained.

Several other major blows were dealt to journalistic freedom in late 2013 and early 2014. In December the government announced that it was abolishing its major news agency, *RIA Novosti*, and replacing it with the international information agency *Rossiya segodnia* (Russia Today).[15] The announcement came as a complete surprise to everyone in the media community. Many in the liberal journalistic circles were shocked by the liquidation itself: *RIA*

---

14   "'Molchanie organizovano obshchestvom, a ne vlast'yu:' Interv'yu s Glebom Pavlovskim," *Lenta.ru*, 18 June 2013, http://lenta.ru/articles/2013/06/18/newsmi/.

15   "Ukaz o merakh po povysheniyu effektivnosti deyatel'nosti gosudarstvennykh SMI," Office of the President of Russia, http://www.kremlin.ru/acts/19805.

Novosti was Russia's best and most modern news agency whose operation, despite its government status, was guided by high professional standards. But an even deeper shock came with the appointment of Dmitry Kiselev as the top manager of the newly created information agency. *RIA Novosti* had been run for many years by Svetlana Mironyuk and she enjoyed considerable respect in nongovernment media circles. Kiselev, one of the aggressive loyalists who gained prominence and promotions since Putin's return to the Kremlin, is notorious for his raving anti-Ukrainian and anti-gay statements (in March 2014 Kiselev became a target of European Union sanctions following Russia's annexation of Crimea). Besides, he has little, if any, managerial experience.[16]

The next victim of the assault against press freedom was *Dozhd'* (Rain), a private TV channel launched in 2010, at first as an Internet TV outlet, and later included in cable packages. *Dozhd'*'s target audience was mostly younger, urban, well-educated professionals—the same social group as the participants of the Moscow mass protests of 2011–2012. The editorial independence and defiant reportage of *Dozhd'* undoubtedly irritated the Kremlin. Besides, the channel made powerful enemies because it exposed the abuse of authority by high-ranking officials. In January 2014, *Dozhd'* came under an orchestrated public attack after an online vote question it had posted on its website was deemed "unpatriotic."[17] Almost instantly nearly every cable provider terminated its contract with *Dozhd'*. In

---

16   Two opinions on the liquidation of RIA Novosti and the appointment of Dmitry Kiselev cited by a pro-Kremlin website Nakanune.ru are interesting in the way they reflect the current political atmosphere. Both come from journalists who, like Kiselev, can be referred to as aggressive loyalists. "Svetlana (Mironyuk) is a good professional and not a bad person, but she was ideologically inappropriate. She was loyal, she accomplished corporate tasks, but ideologically she was unfit".... "The state wants to have more influence on the media realm as it prepares for difficult media wars that will be unleashed by the liberal media..." Sergey Tabarintsev-Romanov, "Peredel rossiyskogo mediaprostranstva prokhodit pod znakom usileniya 'suverennogo kryla'," *Nakanune.ru*, 12 December 2013, http://www.nakanune.ru/articles/18417.

17   Masha Lipman, "Asking the Wrong Question on Russian TV," *The New Yorker*, 5 February 2014, http://www.newyorker.com/online/blogs/comment/2014/02/asking-the-wrong-question-on-russian-tv.html.

March the station's owner and top manager announced that the broadcaster would not survive more than a few months.[18]

The next major event in this line was the firing of Galina Timchenko, the top editor of *lenta.ru*, Russia's most popular online news and analysis website.[19] Obviously, this dismissal will not be the last attack on the Russian media.

4. The Internet as a Public Realm

Internet outlets are no less vulnerable to the government crackdown than are traditional media. Today Russian social networks still remain a realm of free expression, but in early 2014 the most popular among them, VKontakte, with its 60 million daily users, came under the control of businessmen allied with the Kremlin.[20] Over the past years the Russian government has developed a variety of tools to facilitate restrictions for online communication. This tool set includes a number of new legal norms, such as the "Internet black lists" or the "anti-piracy law" that can be used to impose constraints on the Web. A much more radical piece of legislation that grants the government the authority to block websites without a court ruling[21] was passed in February 2014. In March, three non-government websites were blocked, as well as Aleksey Navalny's

---

18   "Gendirektor 'Dozhdya' otvela kanalu odin mesyats raboty," *Lenta.ru*, 4 March 2014, http://lenta.ru/news/2014/03/04/months/. In March, TV *Dozhd'* launched a crowdfunding campaign and was able to collect enough funds to last about 30 or 40 days. "Telekanal 'Dozhd' za pyat' dney marafona sobral sredstva na 35 dney veshchaniya," *Kommersant.ru*, 28 March 2014, http://www.kommersant.ru/doc/2440645.

19   "Eurasia Outlook," Carnegie Russia, http://carnegie.ru/eurasiaoutlook/?fa=54951; "Glavnyy redaktor Lenta.ru Galina Timchenko uvolena. Ee smenit eks-glava 'Vzglyad.ru'," *NewsRu*, 12 March 2014, http://www.newsru.com/russia/12mar2014/lentaruu.html. Most lenta.ru staffers quit as a sign of solidarity with their top editor.

20   Nickolay Kononov, "The Kremlin's Social Media Takeover," *The New York Times*, 10 March 2014, http://www.nytimes.com/2014/03/11/opinion/the-kremlins-social-media-takeover.html?_r=0.

21   "Zakon o dosudebnoy blokirovke saytov vstupil v silu," *Voice of America*, 1 February 2014, http://www.golos-ameriki.ru/content/internet-block/1842488.html.

page on LiveJournal.[22] According to Internet experts, the relevant government agencies have made significant progress in establishing censorship of the Web. Specialists in this field point to Russia's highly effective filtration of websites as well as total surveillance of communications organized during the 2014 Winter Olympics Games in Sochi[23] and forecast that the Russian authorities will eventually force global platforms such as Google, Gmail or Facebook operating in Russia to register as Russian legal entities.[24]

Given today's level of communications, it is hardly possible to entirely block information exchange as in the Soviet Union, but the nongovernment media, both the traditional outlets and Internet communications alike, are unable to defend themselves from the current assault on media freedom. The liberal constituency is too small and weak, and the pubic at large appears to be in favor of the government's censorship.[25] After the military intervention and the annexation of Crimea there is every reason to expect further constraints on press freedom as well as other civil liberties.

---

22 "ZhZh Naval'nogo, Kasparov.ru, Grani.ru i EZh zapreshcheny," *BBC*, 13 March 2014, http://www.bbc.co.uk/russian/russia/2014/03/140313_russia_oppo_sites_blocked.shtml.

23 Andrei Soldatov, "Why We Should Care About Russia's Stance on the Internet," http://www.cyberdialogue.ca/2014/03/why-we-should-care-about-russias-stance-on-the-internet-by-andrei-soldatov/.

24 "Do chego mozhet doyti Kreml', reguliruya internet," Agentura.ru, http://agentura.ru/projects/identification/Internetregulating.

25 In a national poll conducted in March 2014, 62 percent said they have more trust in government media and only 16 percent prefer nongovernment outlets. Over 70 percent do not mind if, in some cases, information is withheld in pursuit of the government's interests, and over 50 percent see nothing wrong if, in order to meet the government's goals, information is intentionally distorted. "O sredstvakh massovoy informatsii," Fom.ru, http://fom.ru/SMI-i-internet/11427.

Russia and the New Authoritarians

Jonathan Becker, Bard College

More than twenty years after the collapse of the Soviet Union, and twenty-five years after Soviet Communist General Secretary Mikhail Gorbachev unleashed the heretofore moribund Soviet press with the policy of *glasnost*, the landscape of media in the post-Soviet space has changed. And for the worse. After the liberalization of the late 1980s and relative freedom amidst the chaos of the 1990s, the press has taken a big step backwards in the Putin era, and not just in Russia. In the 2013 Freedom House rankings, nine of the fifteen post-Soviet countries were rated "not free," with Georgia, Moldova, and Ukraine listed as "partly free," and only the three Baltic states, now European Union and NATO members, free.[1] Russia has ignominiously made the Committee to Protect Journalists' Impunity Index's top ten list for countries "where journalists are slain and the killers go free."[2] Reporters without Borders expresses a similar view, with their map of the former Soviet space (with the exception of the Baltics and Kyrgyz Republic) swathed in red and black, their lowest categories of press freedom. They also name Russia's Vladimir Putin and Belarus' Alexandr Lukashenka as leading "enemies of press freedom."[3]

That things have not gone well for the media in most of the former Soviet states is undeniable. But it does not necessarily follow that the current challenges are the same as those during the Soviet period. The primary purpose of this paper is to answer the following question: Is there something uniquely post-"Soviet" in media systems in Russia and many of the countries which emerged from

---

1 "Freedom of the Press 2013: Global Press Freedom Rankings," Freedom House, http://www.freedomhouse.org/sites/default/files/Global%20and%20regional%20tables.pdf.
2 "Getting Away with Murder: 2013 Impunity Index," Committee to Protect Journalists, http://www.cpj.org/reports/2013/05/impunity-index-getting-away-with-murder.php.
3 "Press Freedom Index 2013," Reporters without Borders, http://en.rsf.org/press-freedom-index-2013,1054.html.

the collapse of the Soviet Union? In other words, in using the word "Soviet," whether the modifier is "neo" or "post," are we speaking of a geographic space or specific and unique legacies of the Soviet era that continue to shape and impact the media in those countries?

I will argue that the media landscape, particularly in the critical sphere of government control, has more in common with other authoritarian countries than it does with the immediate Soviet past. In this context, the media systems are better described as "neo-authoritarian" than "post-" or "neo-" "Soviet."[4] This distinction is important for two reasons. From a politics perspective, it helps to clarify analytically that what is taking place in the post-Soviet space is very different from Soviet times: authoritarianism may be on the rise after the failure of the democratic hopes of the 1990s and the colored revolutions of the 2000s, but we are by no means witnessing the rebirth of the Soviet Union. Second, from a media studies perspective, it moves forward the analysis of differences between various forms of non-democratic media systems, a subject which media scholars often lament as understudied.[5]

In order to answer the primary question, a number of related questions will be addressed: What is a neo-authoritarian press and how does it differ from the post-totalitarian press that typified the Soviet Union? How is the current Russian press similar to and different form the Soviet press? How is it similar to and different from media in authoritarian counties outside of the former Soviet space and what does that mean about the relationship between the current press and Soviet legacies? Finally, what are the implications of similarities and differences of current media vis-à-vis Soviet times and other authoritarian media (historically and not) and what do these mean for countries' future? The paper will first and foremost

---

[4] See Sarah Oates, "The Neo-Soviet Model of the Media," *Europe-Asia Studies* 39:8 (December 2007) or Clifford May, "Vladimir Putin, the Neo Soviet Man," *National Review*, 19 September 2013. http://www.nationalreview.com/article/358894/vladimir-putin-neo-soviet-man-clifford-d-may.

[5] Kaarle Nordenstreng, "Normative Theories of the Media: Lessons from Russia," in Yassen N. Zassoursky and Elena Vartanova, eds., *Media, Communications and the Open Society* (Moscow: IKAR, 1999), 150. See also Oates, "The Neo-Soviet Model."

concentrate on Russia because of its size and influence on its Eurasian neighbors, but other post-Soviet states will be brought into the discussion to illustrate some of the key points.

1. Soviet (Post-Totalitarian) vs. Neo-Authoritarian Media Systems

In order to understand where the media in Russia and many of the states of the former Soviet Union stand today, we need to step back to look at the conceptual distinctions between the Soviet (or what I have previously termed "post-totalitarian") press system[6] and neo-authoritarian media systems. Differences emerge in terms of the perceived role of the press, access, the relative autonomy of the press vs. the center of power, and the interaction between censorship and ideology.

The role of the press in the Soviet Union was utilitarian: it was a form of ideological education, the party's main tool to shape public opinion. Indeed, the Soviet approach to the press emerged in part because of the modern belief in the indoctrinating and transformative power of mass communications. Access to the entire press in the Soviet Union was controlled by the Communist Party. The party/state owned all print and broadcast facilities and exerted both positive and negative control through an elaborate system of management that included guiding the education of journalists, power over the appointment of media personnel, and the imposition of a complex system of pre-and post-publication censorship.[7] The press enjoyed no relative autonomy vis-à-vis the party/state.[8] Journalists operated as extensions of the party apparatus, behaving no differently than others who worked in the sphere of ideological education. In this context the nature of the ideology was critically important: because the Soviet ideology, Marxism-Leninism, was

---

6   Jonathan Becker, *Soviet and Russian Press Coverage of the United States: Press, Politics and Identity in Transition* (London: Palgrave, 2002).
7   For a complete discussion of totalitarian media systems, see Becker, *Soviet and Russian Press*, 1–45.
8   Robert A. Dahl, *Dilemmas of Pluralist Democracy: Autonomy vs. Control* (New Haven, Conn.: Yale University Press, 1982), 26.

supposedly based on scientifically determined truths that explain history and the nature of human order, the Soviet press was the object of ideological censorship that meant that journalists were not only restricted in what they could say, but in the language they could use. Journalists were bound by a special discourse that suffused all public communication and words became so loaded with evaluative connotations that it was difficult for them to express ideas beyond the accepted, official beliefs.[9] As Young put it, "for every politically significant word, one meaning; for every historical event, one interpretation; for every social problem, one solution..."[10] The citizen, in the words of one Soviet journalist paraphrasing Lenin, was treated as "an imbecile who doesn't know what is good for him and therefore has to be agitated, propagandized and collectively organized."[11]

It should be noted that there were always small amounts of manufactured diversity, small differences in press coverage encouraged by the party/state in order to appeal to audiences of different regions, educational levels and occupations.[12] With the decline of ideological fervor in the late (pre-*glasnost*) Soviet period, there was even sanctioned diversity or what has been called "permitted dissent,"[13] which suggests the appearance of non-uniform press content that, although not explicitly endorsed by the leadership, is tolerated by it. However, in the Soviet case the relaxation of controls was both narrow and selective. Sanctioned diversity was most likely to be found in publications with extremely limited, elite

---

9   Jeffery C. Gordfarb, *Beyond Glasnost: The Post-Totalitarian Mind* (Chicago: University of Chicago Press, 1991), 55.

10   John Wesley Young, *Totalitarian Language* (Charlottesville, Va.: University Press of Virginia, 1991), 31.

11   Alexander Pumpyansky, "Are We Really So Tired of the Truth?," *New Times* 14 (1990): 8–14.

12   Juan Linz, "Totalitarian and Authoritarian Regimes," in Fred I. Greenstein and Nelson W. Polsby, eds., *Macropolitical Theory* (Reading, Mass.: Addison Wesley Publishing, 1975), 191.

13   Diane R. Spechler, *Permitted Dissent in the USSR* (New York: Praeger, 1982).

audiences, such as cultural and literary journals, or in specialty academic journals.[14] The press remained identified with and subordinated to the Party, which retained and regularly exercised strict positive and negative control over the entire press. Finally, even as the ideology lost its vibrancy, strict ideological control continued, binding society in a common language and in so doing limiting any potential opposition to the regime.

Neo-authoritarian media systems, on the other hand, are an essential element of the tactical choice that many modern authoritarian leaders make: to allow some elements of openness and contestation in exchange for greater legitimacy both domestically and internationally. As Krastev argues, these leaders recognize the "status of democracy and elections as the only acceptable sources of legitimacy in the modern world," and "the increasing costs of violence as an instrument for preserving political power."[15] They therefore choose to allow simulated forms of democratic governance, including elections, but ensure that in doing so they create "conditions of radical unfairness" in the competition for political power.[16] For these new autocrats who seek "to reap the fruits of electoral legitimacy without running the risks of democratic uncertainty,"[17] the mass media is perhaps the most important tool in limiting meaningful pluralism and undermining the capacity of citizens to make informed choices.[18]

---

14 Goldfarb, *Beyond Glasnost*, 57; Becker, *Soviet and Russian Press*, 25.
15 According to Krastev, "Democracy's doubles can best be understood as an attempt to construct political regimes that mimic democratic institutions but work outside the logic of political representation and seek to repress any trace of genuine political pluralism." See Ivan Krastev, "Democracy's 'Doubles'," *Journal of Democracy* 17:2 (April 2006): 54.
16 Andreas Schedler, "The Menu of Manipulation," *Journal of Democracy* 13:2 (April 2002): 43. See also Steven Levitsky and Lucan Way, "The Rise of Competitive Authoritarianism," *Journal of Democracy* 13:2 (April 2002): 53.
17 Schedler, "Menu of Manipulation," 36.
18 From this perspective, neo-authoritarian systems differ from more traditional ones because in the current environment the control over television and other forms of mass communication is not the product of technological necessity, as it was in the early days of the airwaves, but of a conscious political choice.

Neo-authoritarian leaders recognize that in today's world of relatively low-cost international travel, cell phones, instant messaging, the Internet, and satellite television, they cannot, without great cost, seal their citizens off from alternative messages, as did totalitarian and authoritarian leaders of old. With an increasing emphasis on participation in the world economy, and the technological openness that that entails, and an emerging, sophisticated and mobile middle-class, the hermetic seal of the past has too many negative social and economic consequences. They therefore assert a rhetorical commitment to a free press, eschewing totalitarian and post-totalitarian claims that the role of the press is to support state- or party-determined ideological priorities. While such claims of press freedom are grossly overstated, the breadth and depth of control are both different and less robust than in the Soviet system described above.

The mechanisms for controlling media, like other important institutions, are often more subtle than in Soviet or traditional authoritarian systems. The center of power asserts control over the most popular forms of communication, usually television, while allowing relative autonomy in media that have a more limited reach and impact. The state asserts control in a variety of ways. It institutes rules on government ownership and erodes barriers that are meant to ensure the autonomy of public broadcast outlets. It co-opts private media through mutually beneficial relations with owners, who often have a symbiotic relationship with the political leadership. The political center may direct subsidies and advertising revenue to sympathetic media organs.[19] If owners of opposition media resist the blandishments of the center of political power they are likely to face various forms of intimidation. They might find themselves the subjects of quasi-legal processes involving issues like registration and license requirements. They may also find themselves the focus of the selective enforcement of tax codes. Imprisonment and exile are not unheard of. The stage is set for dis-

---

19   Jonathan Becker, "Lessons from Russia: A Neo-Authoritarian System," *European Journal of Communication* 19:2 (June 2004): 139–63.

loyal owners to surrender control over high impact media to private entities with close links to the state. It is also often the case that in countries with neo-authoritarian systems, foreign ownership, which might be more insulated from pressures, is limited and discouraged. Alternative forms of communication, including satellite television and the Internet, often face hurdles—financial, technological, linguistic, or legal—that limit their impact and allow the media controlled by the new autocrats to continue to dominate.

Message shaping in neo-authoritarian systems is neither as extensive nor intensive as in post-totalitarian systems, because there is no all-encompassing ideology. The media landscape as a whole is influenced by market forces, and thus focused often on least common denominator popular programming rather than ideological education. While tight reins may be placed on current events topics, and on television in particular, they are not as ubiquitous, and there may exist windows of pluralism, and even privately owned stations, which, although often with limited reach, may offer criticism of leaders and their policies. There might exist vibrant print media, or at least publications, that are independently owned (by individuals, parties, or foreign corporations), relatively autonomous, accessible to the population, and highly critical of the regime, in spite of periodic harassment, violence and closures. The same is the case for radio.

As far as content is concerned, the closer any issue may rest to the heart of the political leadership, the greater the assertion of control. For example, during elections, large audience media are regularly mobilized to improve the position of the center of political power and its selected candidates. The party of power gets the vast majority of (usually adulatory) coverage, while the opposition faces some combination of "information blockade" and merciless attacks, often from prominent journalists who in the former Soviet space have earned the sobriquet "information killers," for their brutal attacks on opposition politicians.[20] Similarly aggressive message control may extend over such

---

20 Marta Dyczok, "Breaking Through the Information Blockade: Election and Revolution in Ukraine 2004," *Canadian Slavonic Papers* 47 (September–December 2005): 242.

critical issues as internal unrest, corruption, and governmental responses to manmade and natural disasters. The mass media may still contain sharp criticism on such issues. However, critical voices would normally appear in media with limited effective public reach and/or drowned out in a sea of regime-sympathetic messages.

Journalists in neo-authoritarian systems also face a litany of hurdles that limit their capacity to criticize the center of power. They are often told in formal and informal ways by politicians and activist owners where the limits are, and they may be dismissed if they cross the line of acceptable dissent. They are often confronted with an array of laws related to professional licensing, access to information, and state secrets that impede their freedom of action. They are also increasingly the victims of civil and criminal defamation and libel laws, including laws barring insults to state leaders, which effectively preclude criticism of political decisions.[21] Foreign journalists, who often pave the way for satellite and/or Internet coverage, often face challenging visa regimes. Finally, they are the objects of physical attacks, imprisonment, and even murder. Journalists are always cognizant that there may be an exorbitant cost for criticism, either personal or financial, thus promoting self-censorship, the most ubiquitous limit on freedom of expression worldwide.

The neo-authoritarian approach has found resonance across the globe. Whether it is in Yemen,[22] Ethiopia,[23] Singapore,[24] or Venezuela,[25] leaders pay homage to the importance of freedom of expression and attempt to bask in the glow of democratic legitimacy while at

---

21   Marina Ottaway, *Democracy Challenged* (Washington: Carnegie Endowment for International Peace, 2003), 52–155; "Defining Defamation," Article 19, http://www.article19.org/pdfs/standards/definingdefamation.pdf.
22   Joel Campagna, "Attacks, censorship, and dirty tricks: In Yemen, the press climate is deteriorating," Committee to Protect Journalists, http://www.cpj.org/reports/2006/03/yemen-press.php.
23   Mohamed Ademo, "Media Restrictions Tighten in Ethiopia," Committee to Protect Journalists, http://www.cjr.org/behind_the_news/ethiopia_news_crackdown.php?page=all.
24   Garry Rodan, "Embracing electron media but suppressing civil society: authoritarian consolidation in Singapore," *The Pacific Review* 16:4 (2003): 503–24.
25   Boris Munoz, "The Media and the Citizen in Venezuela," *New Yorker*, August 30, 2013, http://www.newyorker.com/online/blogs/currency/2013/08/venezuela-the-media-and-the-citizen.html.

the same time supporting an environment that fundamentally undermines political competition. Today's Russian press fits in well with the neo-authoritarian approach. Indeed, as Leon Willems and Arch Puddington have argued, "Under Vladimir Putin, Russia has emerged as a laboratory for the development of methods to suppress media freedom in the post-totalitarian era."[26]

2. Russian vs. Soviet Media

The Russian press has experienced tremendous backsliding since the halcyon days of *glasnost* and the early days of the 1990s. Typical of neo-authoritarian leaders, Putin professes support for a free press, calling media freedom "one of the cornerstones of democracy" and asserting that "if we don't have a free mass media, we shall very soon slide back into the past."[27] However, his actions are not consistent with these priorities. There are some important similarities to the Soviet era. The Russian government continues to dominate the media landscape. It owns or controls through sympathetic parties the vast majority of news media, including the most important form of communication, television. The media is viewed in instrumental terms: control is used to achieve the ends of the party of power, both in terms of promoting government leaders and policies and assailing enemies. There is limited pluralism and diversity: television is President-centric, especially when it is Vladimir Putin's turn to be president, and opposition voices are severely constrained. Due to the political and economic environment, self-censorship remains a critical and ubiquitous problem whether the media is publicly or privately owned. As Masha Gessen said,

---

[26] Leon Willems and Arch Puddington, "Russian Model Gains as Press Freedom Declines," Freedom House, http://www.freedomhouse.org/blog/russian-model-gains-press-freedom-declines.

[27] "Communication Law in Transition: A Newsletter," University of Oxford, November 1999, http://pcmlp.socleg.ox.ac.uk/transition/.

> Where the Soviet regime used direct censorship, with a specially assigned person at every media outlet clearing every story before publication, the instrument of control today is fear. Reporters, editors and media owners are constantly looking over their shoulder.[28]

In spite of the bleak picture in Russia, it is still the case that things are substantially different from the Soviet period in terms of the breadth and depth of control of the media as well as methods of control, differences that reflect the neo-authoritarian approaches discussed above and witnessed increasingly across the globe. They occur in key areas such as diversity of content, the role of ideology, access to media, and the scope and methods of control.

The Russian media are undoubtedly more diverse than throughout the vast majority of the Soviet period, particularly when they are not covering sensitive domestic concerns like Chechnya, or important international topics like Georgia or Syria. In terms of print media, while the major national daily newspapers and most major weeklies toe the president's line, on the streets, at least in big cities, one can purchase newspapers covering a wide array of views. There are several hundred titles available, more than in Soviet times, although it should be noted that several of the most popular publications are tabloid in style and substance, and not well trusted.[29] Alternative views are also heard over the radio waves via *Ekho Moskvy*, which has maintained its approach of presenting divergent and even critical voices, in spite of the fact that it is owned by the state energy giant Gazprom. However, its reach (and that of other alternative radio voices) remains limited, ranking as only the tenth most popular station in the country.[30] Per the neo-authoritarian playbook, television remains largely controlled by the Kremlin: the top five television stations by audience reach (*Pervyy kanal, Rossiya 1, NTV, TNT* and *Pyatyy kanal*) are all controlled by

---

28 Masha Gessen, "As Russian Journalists, our lives are dark comedy and tragedy," *Globe and Mail*, 3 May 2013, http://www.theglobeandmail.com/globe-debate/as-russian-journalists-our-lives-are-black-comedy-and-dark-traged y/article11687214/.
29 Oates, "Neo-Soviet Model," 1286.
30 Olga Khostumova, "A Complete Guide to Who Controls the Russian News Media," Index on Censorship, http://www.indexoncensorship.org/2013/1 2/brief-history-russian-media/#sdfootnote2sym.

the state or state enterprises.[31] The leadership's focus on television still appears to have merit: around 90 percent of the population prefers to get news from television and around 50 percent cite it as the most trusted form of communication.[32] It should be noted that even on the president-centric television, news and current events programs occasionally have alternative voices, debates and disagreements, and the opposition can even make the occasional appearance. The cable and Internet TV station *Dozhd'* offered robust coverage of the post-2011 election protests and regularly presents opposition figures. As *Dozhd's* editor-in-chief Mikhail Zyagar said, "We're not an opposition TV channel, we're just a normal TV channel giving the floor to representatives of different movements and people with different points of view."[33] In this context, it is also important to note that the Internet has grown rapidly in Russia in recent years, reaching between 50–60 percent of the population, up from around 10 percent a decade earlier, with the vast majority of that group, particularly those in large cities, being regular users. Broadband usage is also growing greatly.[34] The Internet has more diverse ownership and more voices, and social media is thriving. While there have been rumblings of efforts at greater control over Internet service providers, the state has yet to show the inclination

---

31 Khostumova, "Who Controls Russian Media."

32 "88% of Russians Prefer to Get News from TV," *The Moscow Times*, 8 July 2013, http://www.themoscowtimes.com/print/article/88-of-russians-prefer-to-get-news-from-tv/482864.html. See also Khostumova, "Who Controls Russian Media."

33 Courtney Weaver, "Dozhd' TV: A Breath of Fresh Air," *Financial Times*, 27 February 2012, http://blogs.ft.com/beyond-brics/2012/02/27/dozhd-tv-agust-of-fresh-air/#axzz2mgiM5pC4.

34 "According to Public Opinion Fund data for autumn 2012, Russia has a monthly internet audience of 61.2 million people over 18 years of age — which is more than 52% of the adult population. For the majority of users, the internet has become a regular part of everyday life. Three-quarters of users (almost 47 million people) are online daily. According to TNS data, in cities with a population of more than 100,000 people, practically all users (94%) have internet access at home and the majority have broadband." See "Development of Media in Russia's Regions," Yandex, http://download.yandex.ru/company/ya_russian_regions_report_2013.pdf.

or the capacity to take a Chinese-style approach of control. The Internet certainly played an important role in the protests that followed the parliamentary elections of 2011.

One key issue that distinguishes the Russian from the Soviet press is that there is no highly developed ideology. Indeed, if anything, with new market pressures, the press has shifted from being highly politicized in Soviet times to largely de-politicized, with the media welcoming the same entertainment and tabloid dross that dominates entertainment systems around the world.[35] To the extent that it is politicized, the Russian media is more sultanistic (in which, according to Linz and Stepan, there is "almost never political pluralism, because political power is so directly related to the ruler's person")[36] than totalitarian: while there may be a cult of leader, there is no guiding ideology, no claims to truths that are scientifically determined and which can transform human history.[37] As a consequence of this, particularly combined with the diverse forms of ownership, there is nothing like the highly developed system of ideological control that existed during the Soviet period. There is no all-encompassing system of ideological education from cradle to grave, a less distinct "party line," and no GLAVLIT censors conducting pre-publication censorship at all media outlets. As Owen Mathews explained,

---

35 Oates, "Neo-Soviet Model," 1286.
36 On sultanism, Linz and Stepan declare: "In sultanism, there is a high fusion by the ruler of the private and the public. The sultanistic polity becomes the personal domain of the sultan. In this domain there is no rule of law and there is low institutionalization… [There] is almost never political pluralism, because political power is so directly related to the ruler's person." See Juan Linz and Alfred Stepan, *Problems of Democratic Transition and Consolidation* (Baltimore: Johns Hopkins Press, 1996), 52.
37 As Peter Pomerantsev said in relation to Russian television, particularly RT, "Russia's view on the world" turns out to be less about proposing one's own ideology as the USSR did than undermining western narratives." See Pomerantsev, "The Kremlin's attempt at soft power is back-to-front," *Financial Times*, 6 December 2013, 11.

> The Kremlin's approach to media control was and is essentially pragmatic rather than ideological—the rule of thumb is that newspapers such as *Novaya Gazeta* or radio stations like Radio Ekho Moskvy are allowed to be critical, as long as they are not too widely listened to or circulated. [38]

The neo-authoritarian approach is also manifested in methods of control. With the absence of ideology to justify subordination of the entire legal press to the party/state, more subtle and creative methods are used to ensure that the most important parts of the media system are subordinated to the party of power.

One of the key trends in Russian media ownership since the 2000s has been a transformation of media ownership from commercial capital to state and mixed (state and private, non-media) capital.[39] Ownership of key media organs has been secured by stripping some-time hostile owners of control through steps ranging from licensing, to fire, safety, and sanitary regulations, to customs and tax rules that target both publications and their owners.[40] The latter came to the fore early in the Putin era when some of the most important opposition owners came under attack, including Vladimir Gusinsky and Boris Berezovsky, whose holdings included the all-important television stations. The crippling of Gusinsky's *Media-Most* empire, including the transfer of *NTV*, the leading source of non-state broadcast news and the only station with a national reach that was not state-owned and controlled, was the most devastating. Through the selective application of tax and criminal law, including the arrest, and subsequent exiling, of Gusinsky, the invasion of *Media-Most* premises by hooded and heavily armed tax police, the direct pressure of the Ministry of Press, Radio and Television, and boardroom intrigue, *Media-Most* collapsed.[41] This is not to say that Gusinsky or Berezovsky were paragons of press freedom—they were activist owners interested in promoting their own agendas—but the impact of the assault on them, and the message it sent, were

---

38 Owen Mathews, "The Real Reasons Newsweek Russia Folded," *Newsweek*, 20 October 2010, http://www.newsweek.com/real-reasons-newsweek-russia-folded-73747.
39 See Khostumova, "Who Controls Russian Media."
40 Khostumova, "Who Controls Russian Media."
41 Becker, "Lessons from Russia."

devastating, with the state reaping the benefits and sympathetic owners swept in to claim the orphaned assets and instill more sympathetic, if not sycophantic, editorial lines.

The state has not simply acted from on high: it has used a number of other political, economic, and legal tools to pressure journalists. It has controlled journalists by selectively providing and limiting access to information, official events and press conferences. Criminal and civil defamation lawsuits have been unleashed to intimidate and silence journalists.[42] In the case of Gregory Pasko, known for his reporting on environmental and nuclear safety issues related to Russia's Pacific fleet, charges related to revealing official secrets resulted in a lengthy imprisonment. After the 2011–12 protests, the Russian leadership reinvigorated what it has called in the past the "dictatorship of law" to assure compliance. A law was passed in July 2013 to reintroduce criminal defamation, including fines of up to five million rubles (US$153,000) and criminal penalties of up to 12 weeks of forced correctional labor for violations.[43] Blogger and opposition organizer Aleksei Navalny, who published several allegations about official corruption among government officials, was charged with criminal fraud and, in addition to being arrested, was thoroughly smeared in the official media.

Others face attacks whose origins are more murky. *Newsweek Russia* (since closed) editor Mikhail Fishman was outed as an oversexed, drug-using degenerate, when a heavily edited video of him with a scantily clad woman named Moomoo and a white powder, allegedly cocaine, popped up on YouTube.[44] Far more insidious has been the well-documented list of crusading Russian journalists who have been murdered in crimes that largely remain unsolved. The most notable was Anna Politkovskaya, who wrote extensively on the war in Chechnya and was a strong critic of President Putin, including in her book *Putin's Russia*. In response to the assassination,

---

42 Khostumova, "Who Controls Russian Media."
43 "Freedom of the Press 2013, Russia," Freedom House, http://www.freedomhouse.org/report/freedom-press/2013/russia.
44 Michael Idov, "Russia's Amazing Drugs and Hookers Scandal," The Daily Beast, 23 March 2010, http://www.thedailybeast.com/articles/2010/03/23/russias-amazing-drugs-and-hookers-scandal.html.

Putin demonstrated the pathos of an unchallenged and undaunted authoritarian, dismissing her as "insignificant" and "well-known only in the West."

The picture painted here gets to the heart of the neo-authoritarian approach. It is not that journalists cannot speak out against the state or political leadership in some media: unlike in communist times, they can. The problem is that it takes great bravery to do so, and the uncertainty of the situation creates significant disincentives for journalists to challenge the state or press the limits of what it (or anxious owners) will tolerate.[45] This institutionalized uncertainty and the pressures of market forces breed doubt and self-censorship. This is not the ubiquitous system of heavy-handed ideological control, which was described by Gorbachev's immediate predecessor Konstantin Chernenko as a "well-tempered orchestra, where every instrument has its voice and plays its part, and harmony is achieved by skillful conducting."[46] Present-day Russia has a less elaborate, but more varied and chaotic structure in which the center of political power has employed a wider array of techniques to gradually reclaim control when and where it sees fit.

3. Implications of Neo-Authoritarianism and Conclusions

What are the implications of neo-authoritarianism for our understanding of media systems and for the future of Russia and the post-Soviet space? From a media studies perspective, it is important to draw analytical distinctions between different types of authoritarian media systems: it is clear that the current system in Russia is different from the Soviet past in terms of breadth, depth, and mechanisms of control, as well as the role of ideology.

---

45 In describing what he calls "hybrid regimes," Diamond sees the situation as follows: There may be an "arena of contestation," but it is sufficiently distorted so that "while an opposition victory is not impossible... it requires a level of oppositional mobilization, unity and skill and heroism far beyond what would normally be required for victory in democracy." See Larry Diamond, "Thinking about Hybrid Regimes" *Journal of Democracy* 13:2 (April 2002): 24.

46 Konstantin Chernenko, *Pravda*, 12 December 1984, 1.

It should be noted that some students of comparative media, who primarily focus on evils of the market in so-called "democratic" or "free" media systems, find Russia unremarkable, the state in their eyes being just a different, but equally malevolent, center of power compared with the corporate concentration that dominates the West.[47] But as I have argued previously, this analysis ignores the fact that both historically and in the present era the state poses the greatest threat to freedom of expression.[48] There may be a variety of sources of power, but the state retains the greatest potential to encroach upon media autonomy, limit pluralism, unleash violence, and turn the media into a tool of political manipulation.[49] It is likely that most journalists in Russia, or Uzbekistan, or Somalia would gladly trade their "enabling environment for freedom of expression" with those of colleagues who work in the United States, United Kingdom, or France.[50] The same can be said of the citizens: whatever the limits of commercially-oriented media, and whatever convergence might be occurring in terms of concentration of media power, it is difficult to conclude that citizens in Russia are not in a

---

47 See John Downing, *Internationalizing Media Theory* (London: Sage, 1996) and Colin Sparks, "Media Theory after the Fall of Communism," in James Curran and Myung-Jin Park, eds., *De-Westernizing Media Studies* (New York: Routledge, 2000), 35–49.

48 Becker, "Lessons from Russia," 20. See also Jonathan Becker, "Keeping Track of Press Freedom," *European Journal of Communication* 18:1 (2003): 107–12.

49 It is difficult to argue with Lee's conclusion that "if a liberal state is considered both an enemy and friend of democracy... the authoritarian state is... nothing but an enemy of democracy... because it dominates, if not monopolizes, the political and economic resources upon which the media depend." See Chin-Chuan Lee, "Rethinking Political Economy: Implications for Media and Democracy in Greater China," *The Public* 8 (2001): 86. See also a World Bank study of 97 countries which found that "countries with more prevalent state ownership of the media have less free press, fewer political rights for citizens, inferior governance, less developed markets and strikingly inferior outcomes in the areas of education and health." (Simeon Djankov, Caralee McLiesh, Tatiana Nenova, and Andrei Schleifer, "Who Owns the Media?," The World Bank, http://econ.worldbank.org/wdr/subpage.php?sp=2391.

50 See "Camden Principles on Freedom of Expression," Article 19, http://www.article19.org/resources.php/resource/1214/en/camden-principles-on-freedom-of-expression-and-equality.

disadvantageous position in terms of their capacity to make political decisions "on the basis of informed choice," vis-à-vis citizens in much of Europe and North America and countries around the world in which the state's control over the media is reasonably circumscribed.[51]

A politics lens provides further clarity as to the distinctions between neo-authoritarian and (post) totalitarian systems, and also provides a silver lining. The relative weakness of the neo-authoritarian system compared with the Soviet/post-totalitarian systems leaves open opportunities at strategic times for potential challenges to the leadership. In the past, in more traditional authoritarian regimes, such as in Iberia and Latin America,, the existence of private ownership, the regular presence of minority discordant voices in the media, and the absence of a highly developed ideology became pivotally important when transformative moments for change emerged, such as after the death of a leader or following a military defeat or economic shock.[52] Masha Gessen is correct when she points out that private owners in Russia are subjected to tremendous pressures from the state. However, as the experience in more traditional authoritarian countries has demonstrated, this does not mean that the interests of all private owners are the same: in periods of crisis or change this can become significant. At such times, when the press already enjoys significant pockets of freedom, journalists can take advantage of leadership fissures to make a quick transition to more open forms of communication that challenge leaders and orthodoxies.

---

51 Richard Gunther and Anthony Mughan, "The Media in Democratic and Nondemocratic Regimes: A Multilevel Perspective," in Richard Gunther and Anthony Mughan, eds., *Democracy and the Media* (Cambridge: Cambridge University Press, 2000), 3–5.

52 International Press Institute, "The Press in Authoritarian Countries," IPI Survey 5 (Berne: International Press Institute, 1958), 139–55; Stanley G. Payne, *The Franco Regime* (Madison: University of Wisconsin Press, 1987), 420; Jean Seaton and Ben Pimlott, "The Role of the Media in the Portuguese Revolution," in Anthony Smith, ed., *Newspapers and Democracy* (Cambridge, Mass.: MIT Press, 1980), 177; Eugenio Tironi and Guillermo Sunkel, "The Modernization of Communications: The Media in the Transition to Democracy in Chile," in Gunther and Mughan, eds., *Democracy and the Media*, 171.

This is precisely what happened in Georgia during the 2003 Rose Revolution and Ukraine in the 2004 Orange Revolution. In both countries, the media were dominated by the party of power, but both, unlike in Soviet times, had pockets of openness, including on television. In the case of Georgia, the private television station *Rustavi-2* showed significant autonomy in the run-up to the fraudulent parliamentary elections, and then reported extensively on the electoral fraud, becoming in the words of David Anable, "the voice and vision" of the revolution.[53] Central control was even tighter in Ukraine on the eve of the Orange Revolution, but the regime's media monopoly was pierced by *Pyatyy kanal* (*Channel 5*), which played a pivotal role in informing the public about fraud allegations and the protests, in spite of the fact that it reached only 37 percent of the population. Together with opposition newspapers and websites, it not only covered the rigged elections and subsequent protests, but in so doing placed pressure on journalists from other print and broadcast venues to acknowledge what was taking place and emboldening others to act.[54]

The Ukrainian and Georgian cases are indicative of the dilemmas faced by authoritarian leaders who aspire to some form of democratic legitimacy: They seek to control the press without too obviously appearing to do so, but this dynamic is imperfect, and in allowing some freedoms openings can emerge that can become critical at pivotal moments, presenting transformative opportunities.

The challenge faced in the former Soviet space is that having witnessed what took place in Georgia and Ukraine (and Serbia before it), many leaders, led by Vladimir Putin, have redoubled their efforts to assert control of the press, particularly over television. As Ivan Krastev has said: "The response of people in power to the rise of 'people power' has been the politics of total manipulation."[55] In Russia, as stated above, there is an increasing attention to all facets

---

[53] David Anable, "The Role of Georgia's Media—And Western Aid—in the Rose Revolution," *Press/Politics* 11:3 (2006): 18–20.

[54] Lucan Way, "Kuchma's Failed Authoritarianism," *Journal of Democracy* 16:2 (2005): 137; Dyczok, "Breaking the Blockade," 243–62; Anable, "Georgia's Media," 18–20.

[55] Krastev, "Democracy's 'Doubles'," 61.

of information dissemination at home and abroad. The recent closing of the state-run *RIA Novosti* news agency and its folding into the new *Russia Today* under a staunch Kremlin ally demonstrates how concern over central control extends even to state-run media organs. As *RIA Novosti*'s report on its own demise said, the changes "appear to point toward a tightening of state control in the already heavily regulated media sector."[56] As the Sochi Olympics come to a close and echoes of revolution again emerge in Ukraine, this trend appears to be confirmed. Gazprom media has replaced the long serving business manager of *Ekho Moskvy*, Yuri Fedutinov, in what he described as a "totally political decision" aimed at changing editorial policy.[57] *Dozhd' TV* saw its audience cut by 80 percent when cable and satellite providers dropped it supposedly in response to an insensitive poll concerning the Second World War.[58] There is no doubt that a bad situation is worsening.

The result is that while the current Russian press fits the broad description of neo-authoritarianism, the leadership, having recognized the threat of even small windows of pluralism, increasingly sees the benefits of severely constricting alternative voices in mass audience media as outweighing the damage that such actions have on democratic legitimacy. In political science terms one might say that they have made the transition from a competitive neo-authoritarian to a hegemonic neo-authoritarian system, in which, to paraphrase Diamond, the institutionalized ruling party increasingly monopolizes the political arena, using media control, as well as coercion, patronage, and electoral fraud to deny formally legal opposition parties any real chance of competing for power.[59]

---

56 Amar Toor, "Putin's controversial news Agency Merger Tightens Grip on Media," *The Verge*, 11 December 2013, http://www.theverge.com/2013/12/11/5199516/putin-tightens-his-grip-over-russia-media-dissolves-ria-novosti.
57 "Russian Ekho Moskvy Radio director Fedutinov dismissed," *BBC*, 18 February 2014, http://www.bbc.co.uk/news/world-europe-26239715.
58 Courtney Weaver, "Russian TV Dozhd loses distributors after crossing 'red line'," *Financial Times*, 4 February 2014, http://www.ft.com/cms/s/0/ef0398b0-8dba-11e3-bbe7-00144feab7de.html#axzz2uFzcJaib.
59 Diamond, "Hybrid Regimes," 21–35.

Significantly, Russia is not alone. Although it is difficult to track causality, the growth of neo-authoritarian tendencies in the wake of the "colored" revolutions and Arab Spring suggest that much authoritarian learning is occurring and spreading in a wave across the globe, particularly within the former Soviet states, Asia, the Middle East and Africa. As Freedom House points out in its 2013 report, "the percentage of people worldwide who enjoy a free media environment fell to its lowest point in more than a decade."[60] It should also be noted that this learning also appears to incorporate the worst practices of governments in countries more traditionally associated with press freedom, including national security responses that emerged as a part of the "war on terror." As one Russian journalist lamented, "Here in Russia the authorities are always eager to borrow from the worst elements of western experience."[61]

The Russian experience demonstrates that transitions are not a unilinear process and that change can occur in multiple directions. The Russian press today is radically different from during the Soviet period, and yet it leaves free press advocates feeling cold and getting colder. When the Soviet regime was collapsing, and Russia was emerging, the press enjoyed the best of all worlds with a highly engaged citizenry, massive state support, and relatively little state/party control. The current situation is the most challenging since the Soviet period, with a corrosive market, meddling owners, and an intrusive state that both imposes tremendous punitive actions on journalists and owners, and actively seeks to depoliticize media and the citizenry. But this still leaves present day Russia

---

60 See "Freedom of the Press 2013," Freedom House, http://www.freedomhouse.org/report/freedom-press/freedom-press-2013. Reporters without Borders, in its World Press Index 2014, writes, "Alarmed by the Arab Spring turmoil, authoritarian regimes in the Arabian Peninsula and Central Asia have stepped up media censorship and surveillance to head off any "attempt at destabilization." See "World Press Index 2014," Reporters without Borders, http://rsf.org/index2014/en-index2014.php#. Nuamnjoh describes the "clawback measures" which are taking place "across the (African) continent." Francis B. Nyamnjoh, *Africa's Media: Democracy and the Politics of Belonging* (London: Zed Books, 2005), 134.

61 Ann Cooper. Quoted in Richard McGill Murphy, ed., *Attacks on the Press in 2001: A Worldwide Survey by the Committee to Protect Journalists* (New York: Committee to Protect Journalists, 2001).

more akin to traditional authoritarian regimes like Franco's Spain, Salazar's Portugal, or the military dictatorships of Latin America, than to the Soviet past, with its all-encompassing ideological straight-jacket.

The pockets of freedom that currently exist, in contradistinction to the Soviet period, may prove important at some point in the future. For now, however, the Russian state is not only unremittingly tightening its control over the media, but its approach sets an example for new authoritarians everywhere.

Ukraine's Media in the Context of Global Cultural Convergence

Marta Dyczok, University of Western Ontario

Ukraine became independent when modern globalization went into high gear.[1] Thus the new country with an ancient history has been re-defining its identity and relations with the world in the larger context of global cultural convergence.[2] Mass media are at the center of this process, both reflecting and influencing it. In Ukraine, the state has not systematically imposed a single vision of identity from above, and no consensus has emerged from below on what it means to be Ukrainian today. At the same time, the media system changed radically. Thus the media can be seen as a site where the struggle for representation power, or identity, is visible. In many ways Ukraine is following larger global trends.[3]

A quick look at media consumption patterns and trends shows that Ukrainians now have many comparable tastes and habits to other Europeans and North Americans. In 2012 the most watched TV shows in Ukraine were strikingly similar to those in the US and UK: sports, reality shows, sitcoms, and drama.[4] Over 30

---

1 Tehri Rantanen, *The Global and the National. Media and Communications in Post-Communist Russia* (Lanham, Md: Rowman & Littlefield, 2002).
2 Tim Dwyer, *Media Convergence* (New York, McGraw Hill, 2010); Isabelle Rigoni and Eugenie Saiita, eds., *Mediating Cultural Diversity in a Globalised Public Space* (Houndmills and New York, Palgrave: 2013).
3 I am grateful to the Social Sciences and Humanities Research Council of Canada, the Woodrow Wilson International Center for Scholars, and Western Ontario University for funding this research. My thanks also go to members of the Harvard University's Post-Communist Politics and Economics Workshop, Columbia University's Ukrainian Program, the University of Toronto's Ukraine Research Group, and anonymous reviewers for their comments on earlier drafts. This paper was written in the summer of 2013.
4 For Ukraine, see "Top naireytingovyshikh transliatsiy 2012 roku na kanalakh 'velykoy shistky'," *Telekritika*, 1 January 2013, http://www.telekritika.ua/news/2013-01-09/78047. For the US, see Lisa de Moraes, "What were the Top 10 most-watched shows this season?," *Washington Post*, 23 May 2012, http://www.washingtonpost.com/blogs/tv-column/post/what-were-the-top-10-most-watched-shows-this-season/2012/05/23/gJQANudXlU_blog

million social network accounts were registered in Ukraine in 2012[5], approximately 66 percent of the total population, which puts it on par with the US[6] and UK.[7] The current state of affairs is dramatically different from the situation in 1991 when Ukrainians were watching Soviet-sanctioned programming on the three state-owned TV channels and the Internet, still in its infancy, was not yet available in Ukraine.

In today's globalized world, media is one factor causing identity to be fluid, and this is certainly visible in Ukraine. After twenty years of independence, no consensus has emerged on what it means to be Ukrainian, and media representations show that a number of competing visions coexist. One is a cosmopolitan, pro-Western Ukrainian identity which embraces the forces of globalization. Another is a residual Soviet Ukrainian identity that is open to some change but has a strong cultural affinity to Russia. A third is a new/old Ukrainian identity that draws on deep-rooted local (national) values, which often coincide with more universal ones such as democracy, but with a contemporary flavor and without a Russian dimension. These three are simultaneously distinct yet overlapping.[8]

.html; and "Nielsen Tops of 2012: Television," Nielsen, http://blog.nielsen.com/nielsenwire/consumer/nielsen-tops-of-2012-television/. For the UK, see Alex Fletcher, "Most-watched TV shows of 2012 so far—In pictures," *Digital Spy*, 13 November 2012, http://www.digitalspy.ca/british-tv/news/a437899/most-watched-tv-shows-of-2012-so-far-in-pictures.html.

5   "Expert: More than 30 million Ukrainians Subscribed to Social Media," *Ukraine Business Online*, 12 September 2012, http://www.ukrainebusiness.com.ua/news/7110.html.

6   According to Pew, as of August 2012, 69 percent of US online adults used social networking sites: "Social Media Fact Sheet," Pew Research Center, Internet and Technology, http://pewinternet.org/Commentary/2012/March/Pew-Internet-Social-Networking-full-detail.aspx.

7   The Office of National Statistics (ONS) reported that in 2011 57 percent of Britons used social media, up from 43 percent in 2010. See Matt Scott, "Office of National Statistics internet survey shows UK surge in social network use," Computer Weekly, http://www.computerweekly.com/news/2240105511/Office-of-National-Statistics-internet-survey-shows-UK-surge-in-social-network-use.

8   Mykola Riabchuk suggested two Ukrainian identities in Mykola Riabchuk, "Two Ukraines?," *East European Reporter* 5:4 (July–August 1992): 18–22; Mykola Riabchuk, *Dvi Ukraïny: real 'ni mezhi, virtual 'ni viiny* (Kyiv: Krytyka,

Ukrainians' evolving identities have profound implications for democracy. While Ukraine's media watchers have focused on censorship,[9] other political scientists and media scholars have been noticing that mass media are transforming politics and identities globally. A new style of politics has emerged in established democracies, where media are changing symbolic frameworks and transforming citizens into audiences.[10] This approach has also become the norm in Ukraine, where politicians reach out to society directly through media and use cultural icons and symbols to construct their public images.

This chapter presents an overview of how Ukraine's media changed from the Soviet era through the first twenty years of independence, both in terms of the structure of the system and media content. It argues that Ukraine's media and society are in many ways following global patterns of changing media preferences and values.

1. Ukraine, Identity, Mass Media, Globalization, Cultural Convergence, and New Politics

When the USSR collapsed, a Soviet identity category disappeared, and discussions re-emerged about what it meant to be Ukrainian. People needed to re-define who they are, how they want to be governed, what kind of society they want to live in, and how they want to interact with the world. French theorist Pierre Bourdieu has suggested that when elements of collective identities are being re-

---

2003), 6. Iaroslav Hrytsak suggested 22 in Iaroslav Hrytsak, *Strasti za natsionalizm: Istorychni ese* (Kyiv: Krytyka, 2011), 216–28; Andriy Kulykov suggested three in Andriy Kulykov, "Novi' rus'ki': Trudnoshchi perekladu," *UkraiNext*, 3 October 2009, http://issuu.com/ukrainext/docs/ukrainext?e=1368478/2974728.

9 Marta Dyczok, "Was Kuchma's Censorship Effective? Mass media in Ukraine before 2004," *Europe-Asia Studies* 58:2 (March 2006): 215–38.

10 Lance W. Bennett and Robert Entman, eds., *Mediated Politics: Communication in the Future of Democracy* (Cambridge: Cambridge University Press, 2001); Ronald Inglehart, *The Silent Revolution: Changing Values and Political Styles Among Western Publics* (Princeton: Princeton University Press, 1977); Robert Putnam, "Bowling Alone: America's Declining Social Capital," *Journal of Democracy* 6:1 (January 1995): 65–78.

sorted, as is the case in Ukraine, the process involves a combination of changes in institutional structure, social interaction, and subjective meaning.[11]

Most discussions about Ukrainian identity overlook these issues and focus on regional divisions, historical legacies, language issues related to the post-communist transformation, Ukrainian-Russian relations, and whether Ukraine will make a pro-Russian or pro-Western choice.[12] Although important, such analyses all miss the point that for over 20 years Ukraine has been part of the global community, and through mass media, engaged in transnational cultural flows. Ukrainian society, identity, and, consequently, its politics, are profoundly changing as a result of becoming part of McLuhan's global village. Todd Gitlin aptly noted the worldwide trend where Habermas's public sphere has splintered into public sphericules and media have become a public arena where different ideological positions confront each other.[13] This is precisely what is happening in Ukraine.

Communications scholars study how international communications systems shape cultural change and influence national cultures, and the discussions are polarized. Some argue that globalization and the shift towards convergent digital media weakens state influence over media institutions and content, and erodes national

---

11   Pierre Bourdieu, *Distinction: A Social Critique of the Judgment of Taste*, trans. Richard Nice (Cambridge, Mass.: Harvard University Press, 1984); Pierre Bourdieu, *The field of cultural production* (New York: Columbia University Press, 1993).

12   Yitzhak Brudny and Evgeny Finkel, "Why Ukraine Is Not Russia: Hegemonic National Identity and Democracy in Russia and Ukraine," *East European Politics & Societies* 25:4 (November 2011): 813–33; John-Paul Himka, "The Basic Historical Identity Formations in Ukraine: A Typology," *Harvard Ukrainian Studies* 28:1–4 (2006): 483–500; Volodymyr Kulyk, "Language identity, linguistic diversity and political cleavages: evidence from Ukraine," *Nations and Nationalism* 17:3 (July 2011): 627–48; Mykola Riabchyk, "Ukraine's 'muddling through': National identity and postcommunist transition," *Communist and Post-Communist Studies* 45:3–4 (September 2012): 439–46.

13   Todd Gitlin, "Public sphere or public sphericules?," in Tamar Liebes and James Curran, eds., *Media, Ritual, and Identity* (London and New York: Routledge, 1998), 168–75.

cultures.[14] Others contend that national governments remain the key players in regulating, thus shaping, media.[15] Globalization optimists view the integration of media systems as a positive development that leads to global norms, practices and thus global stability and prosperity,[16] while critical theorists raise concerns about cultural imperialism because the production, dissemination and marketing of media and cultural products are dominated by a handful of countries led by the U.S. [17] They also note that the U.S. media model is driven by market forces rather than the liberal, normative "watchdog of the state" principle, and this model, aimed at delivering audiences to advertisers, is being exported globally.[18]

A recent study by Harvard's Pippa Norris and Ronald Inglehart shows that the impact of global cultural convergence appears to be mixed.[19] While some countries are adopting the global model and others reject foreign ideas,[20] many appear to amalgamate aspects of the imported culture into their own and produce a hybrid.[21]

---

14 Paula Chakravatty and Yuezhi Zhao, eds., *Global communications: toward a transcultural political economy* (Lanham, Md.: Rowman & Littlefield Publishers, 2008); Robert Hackett and Yuezhi Zhao, *Democratizing global media: One world, many struggles* (Lanham, Md.: Rowman & Littlefield Publishers, 2005).

15 Tim Dwyer, *Media convergence* (Maidenhead, UK and New York: McGraw Hill, 2010).

16 David Held, *Globalization Theory: Approaches and Controversies* (London: Polity Press, 2007).

17 Andrew Calabrese and Colin Sparks, *Toward a political economy of culture: Capitalism and communication in the twenty-first century* (Lanham, Md.: Rowman & Littlefield Publishers, 2004); Edward S. Herman and Robert W. McChesney, *The global media: The missionaries of global capitalism* (London and Washington: Cassell, 1997); Herbert I. Schiller, *Communication and Cultural Domination* (White Plains, NY: M. E. Sharpe, 1976).

18 Robert W. McChesney, *The Political Economy of Media* (New York: Monthly Review Press, 2008); Daya Kishan Thussu, ed., *Electronic Empires: Global Media and Local Resistance* (London and New York: Arnold, 1998).

19 Pippa Norris and Ronald Inglehart, *Cosmopolitan Communications: Cultural Diversity in a Globalized World* (Cambridge: Cambridge University Press, 2009).

20 Benjamin R. Barber, *Jihad vs McWorld* (New York: Ballantine Books, 2001); Meic Pearse, *Why the Rest Hates the West: Understanding the Roots of Global Rage* (Downer Grove, Ill.: InterVarsity Press, 2004); Daya Kishan Thussu, ed., *Electronic Empires*.

21 Marwan M. Kraidy, *Hybridity, or the cultural logic of globalization* (Philadelphia, Temple University Press, 2005).

Thus, it is difficult to establish direct causality between media use and social values. In Ukraine trans-cultural flows are more complex than the usual global-national dynamic because in addition to globalization, the new/old country continues to be affected by the legacy of Russian/Soviet cultural domination and continued Russian influence.[22] The result is a complex triangular pattern of internal and external forces engaged in a cultural competition, which in turn is influencing politics. Media, and particularly television, are at the center of this process. As Italian media scholar Mancini noted, "Television with its messages, values and view of the world, interferes continuously with politics and determines and shapes its values."[23] He, as well as others, argues that the new 21st century "Lifestyle Politics" are now the norm in established democracies.[24] Traditional institutions like political parties, unions, and civic organizations have weakened and mass media became the key agent of socialization. In Ukraine, as elsewhere, politicians use television to reach their electorate,[25] citizens are treated increasingly as audiences, and political messages are mixed in with entertainment and consumption.[26]

By looking at media developments, especially television, this chapter explores the relationship between media and identity in Ukraine in the context of a globalized world. Moving away from a normative approach that asks how free or independent the media

---

22 Russia is also influenced by globalization. See Natalia Rulyova, "Domesticating the Western Format in Russian TV: Subversive Glocalisation in the Game Show *Pole Chudes* (Field of Miracles)," *Europe-Asia Studies* 59 (December 2007): 1367–86.
23 Paolo Mancini, *Between Commodification and Lifestyle Politics: Does Silvio Berlusconi Provide a New Model of Politics for the Twenty-First Century?* (Oxford: RISJ, 2011), 8.
24 Peter Dahlgren, *Media and political engagement: citizens, communication, and democracy* (Cambridge: Cambridge University Press, 2009); Putnam, "Bowling Alone."
25 Peter Dalhgren, "Media, Citizenship and Civic Culture," in James Curran and Michael Gurevitch, eds., *Mass Media and Society* (London: Hodder Arnold, 2005); Yves Meny and Yves Surel, eds., *Democracies and the Populist Challenge* (New York: Palgrave, 2002).
26 Bernard Manin, *The Principles of Representative Government* (Cambridge and New York: Cambridge University Press, 1997).

are,[27] it instead follows Carothers and tries to show what is really going on.[28] It argues that the power struggle over identity is ongoing, visible in media representations, and Western-led global forces are just as important as the Russia factor.

2. The Imperfect Soviet Hegemon

Ukraine's current struggle over identity is shaped by both present realities and the past. In 1991 Ukrainians rejected the USSR, but legacies from the Soviet era are still an important reference point for habits, beliefs, and values for many Ukrainians today, albeit in different ways.

For seventy years Soviet authorities used the media in a hegemonic way to try and construct a Soviet identity, the "*homo sovieticus.*"[29] Yet Soviet identity was neither static nor monolithic, and although strongly dominated by Russian cultural imperialism,[30] it also contained international and multi-national dimensions.[31]

---

27   Diana Dutsyk, "Media Ownership Structure in Ukraine: Political Aspects," in Olexiy Khabyuk and Manfred Kops, eds., "Public Service Broadcasting: A German-Ukrainian Exchange of Opinions," *Working Paper* No. 277, Institute of Broadcasting Economics University of Cologne, December 2010; Marta Dyczok, "The Politics of Media in Ukraine: Election 2002," in Nicolas Hayoz and Andrej N. Lushnycky, eds., *Ukraine at a Crossroads* (New York, Oxford and Vienna: Peter Lang Publishers, 2005), 63–99; Volodymyr Kulyk, *Dyskurs ukraïnskykh medii: Identychnosti, ideolohiï, vladni stosunky* (Kyiv: Krytyka, 2010); Andrei Richter, "The Partial Transition: Ukraine's Post-Communist Media," in Monroe Price, Beata Rozumilowicz and Stefaan G. Verhulst, eds., *Media Reform: Democratizing the Media, Democratizing the State* (New York: Routledge, 2002); Natalya Ryabinska, "The Media Market and Media Ownership in Post Communist Ukraine: Impact on Media Independence and Pluralism," *Problems of Post Communism* 58:6 (November–December 2011): 3–20.

28   Thomas Carothers, "The End of the Transition Paradigm," *Journal of Democracy* 13:1 (January 2002): 5–21.

29   A. N. Burmistenko, ed. and trans., *Lenin about the press* (Prague: International Organization of Journalists, 1972). See also RadNarKom RSFSR Decree on the Press, October 1918.

30   Ivan Dziuba, *Internationalism or Russification. A Study in the Soviet Nationalities Problem*, 2nd ed. (London: Weidenfeld and Nicholson, 1970).

31   Terry Martin, *The Affirmative Action Empire: Nations and Nationalism in the Soviet Union, 1923–1939* (Ithaca, NY: Cornell University Press, 2001).

The complex, multi-layered Soviet identity was visible in the media system. Constructed like a series of concentric circles, a Russian language central media covered the entire territory of the USSR; within it, on the level of Soviet national republics, media subsystems existed that used regional and local languages. Central media were better funded and of higher quality than those in the Soviet republics, yet the republican systems produced their own content. Thus a Soviet Ukrainian identity existed as part of the larger *homo sovieticus*, and alternative ideas circulated through the *samizdat* (*samvydav*) underground media.

During Gorbachev's *glasnost*, the representational struggle widened. It is well known that media liberalization was intended to gain support for reforms but led to a broader public discourse about ideology and identity.[32] Media content became more diverse during this time. Both conservative and reform messages appeared in central and republican media, pro-democracy messages grew from emerging alternative media, and exposure to the outside world increased. Things in Ukraine changed more slowly than in Moscow: as late as 1990 the Communist Party of Ukraine (CPU) was instructing newspaper editors how to cover elections.[33] That said, already in 1989 the official Writer's Union paper, *Literaturna Ukraina,* published RUKH's draft program, republican state TV aired debates between the Communist Party and RUKH, and the youth TV program *HART* began reporting previously taboo subjects, such as the crackdown on protesters in Lithuania in January 1991. Informal newspapers appeared all over the country from L'viv to Dnipropetrovs'k and Simferopol, containing a variety of visions of what kind of Ukraine people wanted to live in, but all critical of the status quo and advocating change.[34]

---

32   Joseph Gibbs, *Gorbachev's Glasnost: The Soviet Media in The First Phase Of Perestroika* (College Station: Texas A & M University Press, 1999).

33   Svitlana Oleksandrivna Kostyleva, *Drukovani Zasoby masovoii kommunitaktsii Ukrainy (1986–2000 rr). Istoriya stanovlenniya, tendentsii i rozvytku* (Kyiv: Ministerstvo Osvity Ukrainy, 2001), 39.

34   Kostyleva, *Drukovani Zasoby*, 249; Bekir Memutov, journalist. Interviewed by Marta Dyczok, Simferopol, 16 September 2004; Oleksander Kryvenko, journalist. Interviewed by Marta Dyczok, Kyiv, 22 December 2001; Vadym

International media played an important role during this time as well. Foreign journalists started working in Kyiv, so news about Ukraine was no longer reported by Moscow-based correspondents like *The Guardian's* Jonathan Steele who found it difficult to believe that Ukrainians were openly advocating independence as late as 1991.[35] Western journalists also provided contacts for Ukrainian journalists, ideas, and employment opportunities at western media outlets.

Thus, although the Soviet state had a monopoly on the media, it perhaps should be thought of as an imperfect hegemon, since a degree of struggle over representation issues and identity was always present.

3. Early Independence: What Kind of Ukraine? and Opening Up to the World

After Ukrainians voted overwhelmingly for independence in December 1991, the media became an important site for discussing what kind of Ukraine to build. As already mentioned, the state did not take it upon itself to exercise a hegemonic role through media representations. In a 2011 interview, first President Leonid Kravchuk could not answer the question, "what kind of media system did you envision?"[36] Some Ukrainian scholars viewed it as a failing that "in the early years of independence, the new state failed to fill the ideological vacuum, did not create an integrated set of values, new ideology."[37]

Institutional changes were made to the media system in the early years, including changes to legislation and upgrading infrastructure. Ukraine began integrating into transnational networks

---

Ryzhkov, journalist. Interviewed by Marta Dyczok, Dnipropetrovs'k, 18 October 2004.

[35] The author heard this repeatedly while working as *The Guardian's* correspondent in Kyiv between May 1991 and June 1992.

[36] Leonid Kravchuk, First President of Ukraine. Interviewed by Marta Dyczok, Kyiv, 22 August 2011.

[37] Valeriy Bebyk and Oleksander M. Sydorenko, *Zasoby masovoï informatsiï postkomunistychnoï Ukraïny* (Kyiv: Mizhrehional'na akademiya upravlinniya personalom, 1996), 54.

like the European Broadcasting Union, but its media system remained part of the old Soviet communications network. Russian Ostankino remained the most watched TV channel because it continued to broadcast on the most powerful TV frequency.[38] Thus the Soviet Ukrainian identity remained quite strong. Private media ownership was legal since 1990, and small private media outlets began to appear "like mushrooms after the rain,"[39] but due to the economic crisis most of the media system remained state owned.

Perhaps most importantly media content began to change quite significantly, beginning the process of global cultural convergence. In the early 1990s, Western media content increased, and Ukrainian media outlets began experimenting with new ideas and formats. Programs ranging from Latin American soap operas,[40] U.S. sitcoms, Hollywood films, and *BBC* and *CNN* news gained large audiences. In December 1991 American Story First Communications created a private TV station, *ICTV*.[41] They were only able to gain broadcast licenses on regional state-owned channels, but within a year became the fourth most popular channel by showing Western entertainment programs. This appetite for Western formats revealed that part of Ukrainian society was open to the world, saw itself in cosmopolitan terms, as part of a larger global community. In these early years small advertising companies also began appearing, starting new patterns of consumerism in Ukraine.

Ukrainians also began creating new media products that reflected both their own ideas and influences from the West. Oleksandr Tkachenko revolutionized Ukrainian television with his weekly news program, *PislaMova,* introducing innovations like live

---

[38] Ukrainian Media Monitor, September 1994 (Prepared by Socis-Gallup International).

[39] Svitlana Eremenko, journalist. Interviewed by Marta Dyczok, Donetsk, 11 October 2004.

[40] *Los Ricos También Lloran*, telenovela produced in Mexico in 1979, broadcast on *UT2* in 1993.

[41] Ivan Mashchenko, *Telebachennia Ukrainy: De facto. Tom Pershyi* (Kyiv: Tetra, 1998), 338.

interviews, talking heads, expert commentary, original camera angles, and seating the host in the center of the screen rather than at the side next to a phone, the Soviet model.[42]

Global, or rather Western, influences also appeared in the form of funding and training. U.S. based NGO InterMedia allocated a US$7 million USAID grant to Ukraine in the early 1990s, to develop independent media. The funds were used to create an independent news agency, UNIAN, and produce new radio and television programming with the assistance of Western journalists. By 1994 six new shows were broadcast on state TV channel *UT2* that reached wide audiences, including news and commentary — *Vikna Novyny* (Yuri Horban, producer), *Vikna Plus* (Heorhii Gongadze, producer), *Vikna v Svit* (Oleksander Myroniuk, producer), sports, economics and culture.[43]

Simultaneously, Ukrainian journalists began exploring their old/new Ukrainian identity, perhaps best illustrated by a series of historical films called *Nevidoma Ukraina* (The Unknown Ukraine), which were produced by Adrian Shmotolokha and Danylo Yanevs'kyi and aired on the state broadcaster. These films showed Ukrainians aspects of their history that had previously been silenced, or framed from the Soviet perspective.[44]

Thus the early years of independent media developments show two simultaneous trends: Ukrainians began exploring their identity in the context of a nation-state that was called Ukraine rather than the USSR, and exploring the world, largely through mass media. During this period the pro-Western cosmopolitan and new/old Ukrainian identities are most visible.

---

42 Oleksander Tkachenko, journalist (for *UT1*, *Studio 1+1*) and media manager (CEO of *Novyy kanal* (*New Channel*), *Studio 1+1*). Interviewed by Marta Dyczok, Kyiv, 25 July 2005.

43 Andriy Kulykov, journalist and general producer of InterMedia funded programs in Ukraine, 1995. Interviewed by Marta Dyczok, by phone from Kyiv, 15 June 2010.

44 Danylo Yanevs'kyi, journalist (*Studio 1+1*). Interviewed by Marta Dyczok, Kyiv, 6 July 2011. See http://ukr-film.ucoz.ua/publ/serial_quot_nevidoma_ukrajina_quot/12.

4. Competing Visions of Ukrainian Identity Become Clearly Visible

By the mid-1990s deepening economic crisis led to different views on how to proceed, which in turn reflected the increasingly divergent views on identity. Some believed the best way to move ahead was to embrace Westernization and push ahead with rapid market reforms. Others felt that is was safer to retain close relations with Russia and reform more gradually. A third view was that Ukraine needed to find its own path, draw on its own ideas and traditions, although there was no clear vision on what that was. Media representations clearly show these competing visions of identity.

When Leonid Kuchma became president in 1994 he pursued an aggressive privatization program, secured Ukraine's international position vis-à-vis Russia and the U.S., and reformed the media system. Although his legacy will always be linked to the disappearance of opposition journalist Heorhii Gongadze and the gradual restriction on the freedom of speech, he did not try and use the media to construct a Ukrainian identity.[45]

Kuchma's goal was to make the media system work more efficiently and protect Ukraine from continuing uncontrolled Russian influences. In January 1995 he was quoted as saying, "My position is that rather than occasional, shall we say, fireman-like measures,[46] it is desirable to move to a clear government policy in the information sphere."[47] Freedom of speech was codified in the 1996 Constitution, and a Press and Information Ministry and National Council on Television and Radio Broadcasting were created.[48] The Russian TV channel *Ostankino* was removed from the country's most

---

45   Serhiy Vasiliev, Head of the Presidential Administration of Ukraine (2002–2004). Interviewed by Marta Dyczok, Kyiv, 19 June 2003.
46   Kuchma's words were "pozhezhni zakhody."
47   Leonid Kuchma, quoted in *Uriadovyi Kurier*, 14 January 1995.
48   I. H. Boyko, Head of Ministry of Press and Information, *Radianska Zhytomyrshchyna*, 12 January 1995, http://www.nrada.gov.ua/en/1283520327.html

powerful broadcast frequency through a 1995 Presidential decree; thus, Ukraine gained control over broadcasting on its territory.[49]

Perhaps the most important change Kuchma introduced was the privatization of major state media outlets. The non-transparent way this was done produced a rather corrupt system where media suffers from both state and corporate pressures. Kuchma viewed media largely as an asset, and television was privatized much the same way as everything else: certain actors were given privileged access, while foreign capital was allowed in, but limited.[50] According to insiders involved in the process, early business groups would come to Kuchma and say, "Papa, here is a state TV enterprise that is failing, let us have it, we'll make it work, and make it profitable."[51] Thus media owners became dependent on good relations with the president, a pattern which continues to the present.

Kuchma did not privatize the entire broadcast sector. The most powerful national TV channel, *UT1*,[52] remained in state hands. It positioned itself as representing the state and its identity, and broadcast exclusively in Ukrainian. But innovations from the early 1990s disappeared and *UT1* returned to its Soviet-era flavor because senior management did not change, and innovators moved to the new private channels. *UT1* continued to produce important programming on culture, for children, and public service information like explaining legislation about privatization, but it lacked vision. There was no guidance from state policy and *UT1* became known as "the channel with no image." Once a private sector emerged, it steadily lost audience share.

---

49 Presidential Decree No. 296/95, 11 April 1995, followed by Ministry of Information Nakaz (Directive) No. 72, "Pro tymchasovyi rozpodil zasobiv rozpovsiudzhennia derzhavnyk prohram telebachennia," 18 August 1995.
50 For the media sector, this was 30 percent.
51 Olexiy Mustafin, journalist and news director of *INTER TV* and *STB TV*. Interviewed by Marta Dyczok, Kyiv, 26 September 2006. Similar narratives were recounted by Mykyta Poturaev, Journalist, Kyiv, 27 September 2006; Oleksander Tkachenko, Kyiv, 22 June 2003 and 26 September 2006; and Oleksander Martynenko, director, *InterFax Ukraine*, Kyiv, 20 June 2003 (all interviewed by Marta Dyczok).
52 At the time *UT1* had the greatest technical broadcast reach.

Two new private channels appeared in the mid-1990s and presented very different representations of what it was to be Ukrainian, although neither articulated the identity issue in national terms. Both were *de facto* transferred into private hands, commercially oriented, and allowed to develop with little state interference in terms of content.[53] Both attracted large audiences yet each had very different ideas about how to do this.

Studio 1+1[54] began broadcasting in October of 1995 and projected a cosmopolitan Ukrainian identity. From the beginning it used only the Ukrainian language, and projected a hip, youthful image from the screen. Initially it aired mainly Western films and entertainment shows, but within a year created the top newsroom in the country by bringing together talented journalists from all over Ukraine, providing them with resources and a free hand. The first news director, Oleksandr Tkachenko, later recalled those days, "this sort of thing happens once in a lifetime. We had a dream team and were not restricted in what we did."[55]

The channel was created by three key individuals: Oleksandr Rodnyanskiy, a Kyiv-born filmmaker who had spent the late 1980s working in Germany; Vadym Rabinovych, a somewhat controversial early Ukrainian businessman; and U.S. billionaire Ronald Lauder. Their vision was very much Western and European-oriented. "It [the channel] was supposed to be substantively Ukrainian, and as such was meant to play a role in social change in the country," recounts Ol'ha Herasymiuk, one of the station's early employees who went on to become a big TV star.[56] The cosmopolitan ideas of the founders came from different motivations. Rodnianskyi had the creative vision that contemporary Ukraine was part of a European cultural landscape. Rabinovych seemingly intuitively understood the importance of advertising, and that profits would initially come from abroad, while Lauder's ambition was to create

---

53   The state retained ownership of the infrastructure of both *UT2* and *UT3* but granted broadcast licenses to the two new private companies.
54   "Home Page," *1+1*, http://www.1plus1.ua/.
55   Tkachenko interview, Kyiv, 26 September 2006.
56   Olha Herasymiuk, journalist. Interviewed by Marta Dyczok, Kyiv, 27 September 2006.

an East European media corporation that could then enter the global arena.[57] Each of them viewed Ukraine as part of the larger global community whose future lay with the West. The channel gained popularity immediately and remained one of the top two audience favorites until it came under attack by political censorship.

The second private TV company, *INTER*,[58] first aired in April 1996 and began by projecting the residual Soviet Ukrainian identity. Russian was the primary language, the main evening news was Vremya, produced by Russia's *ORT TV*,[59] and initially much of the entertainment programming was either Soviet era classics or new Russian media products.

The main force behind creating *INTER* was Kyiv businessman Ievhen Pluzhnikov, who was a key member of the then powerful Kyiv clan and the SDPU(o) party. His business partners were the Ukrainian State Property Fund and the Russian TV company *ORT*. From the beginning it seemed that this was conceived as both a business project and political instrument, and was oriented on the Russian-speaking part of Ukrainian society.

The creators of this channel viewed Ukrainian identity through a Russian lens, drawing on the shared cultural heritage and orientation along familiar patterns. This channel, too, attracted large audiences, showing that some Ukrainians continued to prefer the old, well-known media content and style, and, although prepared to change somewhat, were more comfortable moving along with Russia rather than directly embracing global values.

This all suggests how Ukrainians were viewing themselves in rather different ways. The popularity of both *Studio 1+1* and *INTER* shows that the cosmopolitan identity resonated among large sectors of society, while simultaneously the residual Soviet Ukrainian

---

57   Lauder created Central European Media Enterprises in 1994. See "Home Page," Central European Media Enterprises, http://www.cetv-net.com/en/index.shtml.
58   "Home Page," *Inter.ua,* http://inter.ua/uk/.
59   This was the successor of Soviet era *VREMYA*, and the pattern continued until 2001. Ukrainian news was also produced, but was broadcast during non-prime time slots.

identity resurfaced as an enduring alternative. Both were forward looking but in different directions—Russia vs. the West. The new/old identity seemed somewhat directionless at this stage, or perhaps lacking in well placed advocates.

5. Unusual Convergence and Contradictions: The Worst of Both Worlds?

By the late 1990s and the beginning of the new millennium, an unusual cultural convergence became visible in Ukraine and its media, which one analyst called "combining the worst of all worlds."[60] Many positive values from the Soviet era, such as social justice, had all but disappeared from public discourse, while negative behavior patterns like corruption had increased. Excesses of consumer capitalism and unfettered individualism grew in a society that was not enjoying the benefits of democracy and the rule of law. The larger context is significant here—Ukraine's economy had begun to stabilize and grow, while simultaneously democracy was seriously backsliding. To a large degree these changes were driven by structural, economic, and political factors that led to the gradual change in value systems.

This period coincides with Kuchma's second term in office, which was overshadowed by the Gongadze case. On September 16, 2000, Internet journalist Heorhii Gongadze disappeared, soon afterwards a headless corpse was found, and the president was implicated in the case. This led to domestic protests, international isolation, and increasing authoritarianism that included intensified censorship.[61] However, as already noted, Kuchma was largely uninterested in issues of identity, and the censorship was directed at whitewashing his regime. Information needed for the economy was al-

---

60   Yevhen Fedchenko, Dean, School of Journalism, NaUKMA. Interviewed by Marta Dyczok, Kyiv, 1 June 2005.
61   Dyczok, "Was Kuchma's Censorship Effective?"

lowed to circulate freely, as were various representations of identity.[62] In part because news became distorted, audiences tended to prefer entertainment programming.

However, apart from the intensified censorship, during these years Ukraine's media system continued to follow many global patterns, including growing concentration of ownership and media content shifting towards infotainment. Most foreign investors were bought out by Ukrainian businessmen who began creating large media corporations (called holdings in Ukraine). Victor Pinchuk, Kuchma's son-in-law, purchased *ICTV* from Story First Communications, *Novyy kanal* (*New Channel*) from Russia's Alpha Bank,[63] and *STB*[64] from Russia's Lukoil.[65] When in 2000 Ukraine's economy went into growth for the first time since independence, media finally became profitable because advertising revenues grew, even though real profits were often hidden.[66]

That meant that media companies had more resources to spend on content, and entertainment programming continued to gain popularity. New products continued to appear some domestically produced, others purchased from abroad.[67] At the turn of the millennium, quiz shows were all the rage internationally. In 2001, *Studio 1+1* purchased the "Who Wants to be a Millionaire" format and broadcast a Ukrainian version to great popular success. A year

---

62   Iryna Pohorelova, journalist. Interviewed by Marta Dyczok, Kyiv, 20 June 2003.

63   MIGnews.com.ua reported this on 11 February 2003.

64   *STB* was created with *INTERNEWS* funds to be an independent TV station. In 1996, it was privatized, and although the owners remained in the shadows, it was widely reported that Lukoil had purchased a significant portion of the shares.

65   In the next phase, this media corporation would grow further to include entertainment TV channels, newspapers, radio, and Internet sites, and become known as the StarLightMedia Group.

66   *Studio 1+1* profits reportedly reached US$10,543,000.00 in the first half of 2001, compared with a loss of US$334,000.00 the year before. *Ukrainian Media Bulletin*, No. 7, August 2001, distributed by European Institute for the Media (EIM). However, State broadcast regulator, Borys Kholod, announced that half of advertising revenues were "in the shadows" (*Interfax Ukraine*, 15 December 2003).

67   See Natalia Dankova, "Vid 'Pershoho miliona' do 'X-faktora'," *Telekritika Magazine* 11–12:76 (November 2010), 60.

later it repeated this feat, purchasing the British format "Brainiest,"[68] and producing it as "Nairozumnishyi." *INTER* also followed this trend, but when they adapted "Blind Date" into the Ukrainian "Kokhannia z Pershoho Pohliadu," they opted for both Russian and Ukrainian speaking co-hosts. There were also examples where Ukrainian and Russian companies jointly purchased formats and produced a single show.[69]

In these years all TV channels began broadcasting content that reflected the three visions of identity, with the aim of attracting audiences. Thus, Ukrainians continued to be exposed to an ever-widening range of media formats, images, messages, and value systems, and private channels began diversifying their content.

State media were underfunded by the Kuchma administration, given no direction or incentive to produce programming which would foster a common identity, and as a result considered uninteresting at best, and "media with no character" at worst. Their main function was, as one journalist put it, "to create obedient citizens who would be loyal to the state regardless of what the state did."[70] Clearly, this did not succeed, since a massive protest erupted in 2004, known as the Orange Revolution.

---

68 Created and owned by Celador.
69 For example, *Studio 1+1* co-produced *Harem*, purchased from Styx, with Russia's *STS*.
70 Kulykov interview, 27 March 2010.

Figure 1. Audience Share Dynamic, 1998–2004

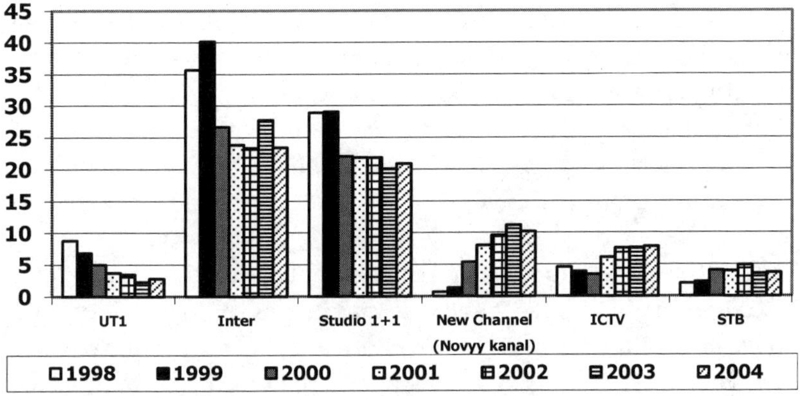

Source: Oleksander Tkachenko, CEO, *Studio 1+1* TV Channel

6. 2004: Collision, Explosion, Reframing

The 2004 Orange Revolution reframed media representations once again. An estimated one in five Ukrainians took to the streets to protest when Victor Yanukovych allegedly stole the presidential election from Victor Yushchenko. The media played a key role in these events, although a more complex one than usually portrayed.[71] The journalists' revolution showed a submerged desire for democracy, transparency and accountability quickly coming to the surface, seemingly re-framing the representational struggle into one over political values as the key component of identity, a combination of new/old values and cosmopolitan ones.

However, despite the excitement of the revolutionary events, there was still no consensus on values. Ukrainians had been receiving a distorted picture of political events for years, yet a handful of journalists in alternative media outlets had been actively opposing

---

71 For a discussion, see, Marta Dyczok, "Breaking Through the Information Blockade: Election and Revolution in Ukraine 2004," *Canadian Slavonic Papers/Revue canadienne des slavistes*, XLVII:3–4 (September–December 2005): 241–66.

censorship and used their technologically savvy international contacts to draw attention to the issue as best they could.[72] During the revolutionary events many others joined them, suggesting that while they had exercised self-censorship under neo-authoritarian conditions, they did hold democratic values. The best example is that the entire *Studio 1+1* news team went on strike on the second day of protests, and later made a live public apology for having lied in the past. Others continued to present news in a rather dubious way. Once widely respected journalist Volodymyr Ruban denounced the revolution as an American plot aimed at destabilizing Ukraine. *TRK Ukraine*[73] reported mainly anti-revolutionary meetings, including the infamous hysterical speech by Yanukovych's wife where she accused protesters of distributing oranges laced with American hallucinogenic drugs.

An interesting dimension of the revolution and media representations is that despite the apparent clash between cosmopolitan and residual Soviet views of identity, both sides used cultural symbols, references and formats that seemed incongruent with that identification. Yushchenko supporters, the orange side, regularly played *Orangevoie Nebo*, a Soviet era classic sung by Georgian singer Irma Sokhadze,[74] and used Soviet era Cat Leopold cartoons to ridicule Yanukovych,[75] while the blue side that supported Yanukovych held Western-style rallies with music, lighting, and DJs as recommended by U.S. PR experts.

7. Aftermath: Change and Continuity

After Yushchenko became president in the wake of the revolution, Ukraine's media continued to evolve. Heavy-handed state censorship ended but the media system continued to be profoundly influenced by the forces of globalization and the Russia factor.

---

72 *Ukrainska pravda, Telekritika, Kanal 5*, Independent Journalists' Union.
73 *TRK Ukraine* is owned by Rinat Akhmetov, who was financing Yanukovych.
74 "Irma Sokhadze—Orange Song," YouTube, http://www.youtube.com/watch?v=wqwJvPSiL_I.
75 "Leopold the Cat," Wikipedia, http://en.wikipedia.org/wiki/Leopold_the_Cat.

Yushchenko made efforts to improve relations between journalists, the state, and society. He created a National Commission for Consolidation of Freedom of Speech and Development of the Information Sphere,[76] changed the management of the state broadcaster and state media regulatory agencies,[77] talked about introducing public broadcasting,[78] had regular televised "fireside chats" and tried to limit negative Russian influences into Ukraine's media space.[79] He also viewed media as a vehicle to promote a united Ukrainian identity that would draw on the historical past as well as cosmopolitan (Western, European) values. News reporting became more objective and complete. However, checkbook journalism, known as "jeans" in Ukraine increased, showing that market forces were also a threat to free speech, a trend that media scholars have long noted in established democracies.[80]

In terms of political economy, the pattern of media ownership did not radically change, but a number of important media assets changed hands, political actors became media owners, and media corporations grew in size.[81] For example, the once powerful Kyiv clan lost control over the lucrative *INTER TV*. It was purchased initially by the Russian corporation EVRAZ, later it came under the ownership of Valery Khoroshkovs'kyi, then Deputy Secretary of

---

76   See Presidential Decree No. 493/2006, http://zakon4.rada.gov.ua/laws/show/493/2006.
77   See "Stets'kiv ide na UT1 iak na front, shchob rozchystyty avhievi staini," *Ukrainska Pravda*, 24 February 2005, http://www.pravda.com.ua/news/2005/02/24/3007404/; "Obrano kerivnyi sklad Hatsrady a pytan' teleradiomovlennia," *Telekritika*, 13 April 2005, http://www.telekritika.ua/news/2005-04-13/23636.
78   See "Hromads'ke movlennia maie buty profesiinishym za kometrsiine," *Telekritika*, 13 April 2005, http://www.telekritika.ua/news/2005-04-13/23632.
79   "RNBO povidomliaie pro zavershnnia roboty had rishenniam Rady ta proiektom Ukrazu prezydenta za naslidkamy rozhliadu pytannia pro informatsiinu bezpeku Ukrainy," Press Division, RNBOU, 25 March 2008, http://www.rainbow.gov.ua/news/665.html?PrintVersion.
80   For a fuller argument, see Marta Dyczok, "Threats to Free Speech in Ukraine: The Bigger Picture," in Giovanna Brogi, Marta Dyczok, and Oxana Pachlovska, eds., *Ukraine Twenty Years After Independence: Assessments, Perspectives, Challenges* (Bern: Peter Lang, 2014).
81   For an overview of media ownership, see Dutsyk, "Media Ownership Structure in Ukraine."

the National Security Council. A year after taking control of INTER TV, Khoroshkovs'kyi formed a new media giant, UA INTER Media Group Ltd, made up of 70 media companies.[82]

The global process of media convergence intensified in Ukraine during this period. As everywhere, technological advancement began altering media usage by society, particularly as Internet penetration increased. The infotainment model, which had come to dominate in established democracies, also became the norm in Ukraine. *Studio 1+1's* PR director proudly announced, "The channel's news programs are mastering a new genre known as infotainment. *TSN*, the main news program on *Studio 1+1*, has been operating in this new format for several months now and their ratings are steadily on the rise. This proves that viewers like the new format."[83] That said, in the spirit of the new freedom of speech, live political talk shows became popular. The format first appeared on *ICTV* in 2005 with the "Svoboda slova" show hosted by Savik Shuster, who brought the format to Ukraine after being closed down on Russia's *NTV* in 2004.

Western programs and films continued to be broadcast on all TV channels; there was an increase in Ukrainian and Russian adaptations of Western formats. Celebrity talent shows became particularly fashionable. Six national TV networks led the market in terms of ratings, commonly known as 'the big Six,' and to a large degree are considered to be the most influential media in the country. They are: *INTER, Studio 1+1, STB, Novyy kanal, ICTV,* and *TRK Ukraina.*

---

[82] "Khoroshkovsky Creates New Media Giant in Ukraine," *Kommersant*, 27 June 2007, http://www.kommersant.com/p778375/r_500/%D0%9A1_%D0%9A2_Megasport_Inter/.

[83] Olesya Ostafiyeva, "Unbearable lightness of TV: Changes in Ukraine's entertainment," *Kyiv Weekly*, 24 December 2008, http://www.kyivweekly.com/?art=1230123744.

Figure 2. Changes in Audience Share of the Channels, 2000–2010

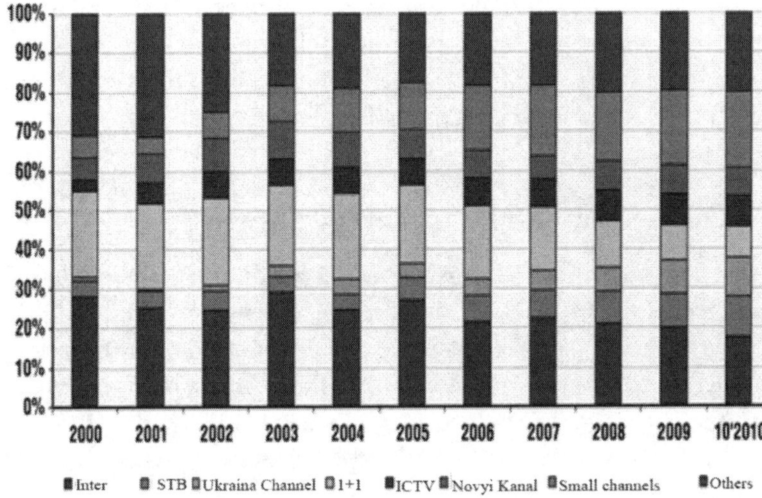

■ Inter ■ STB ■ Ukraina Channel ■ 1+1 ■ ICTV ■ Novyi Kanal ■ Small channels ■ Others

Source: Telekritika Magazine 11–12:76 (November 2010), 72

Yushchenko was the first Ukrainian president to make the issue of identity a subject of public discourse, thus it would seem that the old/new vision of Ukrainian identity would have become strong in this period. Yet when one looks at media representations, audience preferences, and images presented by political actors, what is evident is that cultural and identity reference points became increasingly blurred, while the trend towards lifestyle politics grew. Yushchenko did promote the old/new Ukrainian identity, but it tended to merge with the cosmopolitan one. The fireside chat format was directly borrowed from the U.S. His pro-European, pro-Western values are well documented in public statements, and when he travelled abroad he looked indistinguishable from other Western leaders. At home in Ukraine, however, he would often sport a traditional embroidered shirt, usually paired with designer trousers or suits.

Then PM Yulia Tymoshenko, on the other hand, retreated from the cosmopolitan image, and increasingly wore folk-inspired clothing and/or Ukrainian fashion designers. Then opposition leader Victor Yanukovych is the most difficult to categorize during this phase. He began to use mainly the Ukrainian language in his media appearances, but also adopted a Berlusconi-like stance, selling a lifestyle of power and glamour.[84] At a 2007 Regions Party Conference he was photographed smiling broadly as "Dancing with the Stars" celebrity Nataliya Mohylevs'ka spun him around on the dance floor.[85]

8. 2010: New Challenges, Old Threats[86]

When in 2010 Yanukovych was elected president, there were fears that he would roll back Yushchenko's reforms and steer Ukraine closer to Russia. These fears were not unfounded. Within months of the election, state pressures on mass media had increased. Ukraine's top media analyst, Nataliya Ligachova, noted that censorship had increased to the highest levels ever, worse than the darkest days of the Kuchma regime.[87] These pressures took on a devastating form combining coercion, co-option, and control through ownership. A new journalists' movement, Stop Censorship, sprung up, but the state largely ignored its efforts.[88] Yanukovych abolished the Media Advisory Council set up by Yushchenko,[89] Parliament reduced the quota for Ukrainian language in broadcast media to 25 percent,[90] Russian speaking Yegor Benkendorf was appointed Director of the State TV channel, and for the

---

84 Yanukovych had hired the U.S. PR firm Paul Manafort, which helped him transform his image.
85 See "Yanukovych stav partnerom Mohylavs'koii," *Ukrainska Pravda*, 8 July 2007, http://tabloid.pravda.com.ua/photos/471dff9fde3bd/.
86 Title of Andriy Kulykov's Keynote Address, "Breaking News: Censorship, Media, and Ukraine" (delivered at Columbia University, 21 February 2013).
87 Nataliya Ligachova, Founder and Editor, *Telekritika*. Interviewed by Marta Dyczok, Kyiv, 31 August 2011.
88 Stop Tsenzuri was formed on 22 May 2010. See *Telekritika*, http://www.telekritika.ua/news/2010-05-22/53128.
89 Presidential Decree No. 493/2010, 2 April 2010, http://zakon4.rada.gov.ua/laws/show/493/2010.
90 Law No. 6342 proposed 26 April 2010, adopted 1 February 2011, http://w1.c1.rada.gov.ua/pls/zweb_n/webproc4_2?id=&pf3516=6342&skl=7.

first time since independence, Russian appeared on the state broadcaster.[91]

There were few changes in ownership structures with one notable exception—in April 2010 the last significant foreign owner, CME, sold its shares in *Studio 1+1* and left Ukraine, leaving the main assets in Ukraine's media market in Ukrainian hands. The remaining changes were intra-elite competition, illustrating the larger political power struggles which were occurring behind the scenes.[92] For example, when Khoroshkovs'kyi, many times minister under various presidents and prime ministers, sold his controlling interest in *INTER* to then head of the Presidential Administration, Serhiy Lyovochkin, it was clear that he had fallen out of favor.[93] A few analysts noted that media are not the primary source of income for media owners and are often used for political purposes.[94]

Yet if one looks at media content and audience preferences, the cultural competition remains clearly visible. Despite the seeming establishment move towards a pro-Russian (residual Soviet) stance after 2010, the impact of globalization (or Westernization) continues strongly, as does the search for a new/old Ukrainian identity, while society drifts more and more towards audience democracy and lifestyle politics.

Live political talk shows continued to attract surprisingly large audiences through the end of 2012. In 2010 Shuster Live regularly drew 13 percent ratings; Svoboda slova with Andriy Kulykov on *ICTV* averaged 12–15 percent, and Velyka polityka with Evgeni Kiselyev on *INTER* attracted 14–17 percent ratings.[95]

---

91 "Zhyrnalisty ta hromadsist' vymahaiut' vid Benkendorfa ukrainomovnoii Olimpiady," *Telekritika*, 6 August 2012, http://www.telekritika.ua/news/20 12-08-06/73919.

92 For more on media as a site where political power is contested, see Dyczok, 2009.

93 "Firtash kupyv hrupu 'INTER.' Top-menedzhment bude zmineno?," *Telekritika*, 1 February 2013, http://www.telekritika.ua/news/2013-02-01/78704.

94 Dutsyk, "Media Ownership Structure in Ukraine"; Ryabinska, "The Media Market and Media Ownership."

95 *Telekritika* posts ratings compiled by market research firms GfK, Neilsen. See, for example, "Proiekt Kiselova znov vyperedyv Shustera," http://www.telekritika.ua/news/2011-02-07/59938.

But, as elsewhere, entertainment programming remains much more popular in Ukraine than news and information shows, suggesting that global cultural influences are strengthening the cosmopolitan vision of identity. In 2010, adaptations of Western format talent shows topped the ratings: the Ukrainian version of *Ukraine Has Talent* (*STB*, 30–35 percent), *X-Factor* (*STB*, 25–30), and *So You Think You Can Dance* (16–20 percent). When *ICTV* purchased the *Survivor* format and broadcast it as *Ostannyy Heroy* in 2011, it got the highest ratings ever in Ukrainian television.[96]

The residual-Soviet identity continues to resonate with many Ukrainians, as witnessed by the fact that the second most popular entertainment programming on Ukrainian television is Russian TV shows. In 2010, *Svaty* on *INTER* topped the ratings with 22–29 percent, followed by *Bratany* on *ICTV* (11–13 percent) and *Interny* on *Studio 1+1* (7–10 percent).[97]

The new/old Ukrainian identity remains the weakest of the three, yet continues to hold its own. To celebrate twenty years of independence, all TV channels produced special programming about the event, without directives from above. *INTER*, traditionally oriented towards the Russian-speaking audiences, aired a series of Ukrainian language shows, *Nashi Dvadtsiats'*, and *Legendary Castles of Ukraine*. Benkendorf, who introduced Russian onto the state broadcaster, raised funds among his corporate friends to produce *20 Steps towards a Dream*, a series of 20 short historical films which adopt Hrushevs'kiy's historiographic scheme and handle controversial topics with sensitivity and respect for various perspectives.[98] His second project, "Faces of Ukrainian History," includes figures ranging from Kniahynia Ol'ha and Pylyp Orlyk, through Stepan Bandera and Mykola Amosov.[99]

96　Natalia Dankova, "Iak dyvylysia top-6 kanaliv u pershomu pivrichich 2013-oho," *Telekritika*, 12 July 2013, http://www.telekritika.ua/rinok/2013-07-12/83234.

97　Nataliya Dan'kova, "Vid Pershoho miliona do X-faktora. Istoriia adaptatsii mizhnarodnykh teleformativ na Ukrains'komu telebachenni," *Zhurnal Telekrytyka* 11–12/76 (November-December 2010): 60–66.

98　"20 Krokiv do Mrii," *1tv*, http://1tv.com.ua/uk/programs/20_krokiv.

99　"Oblichchia ukrains'koi istorii," *1tv*, http://1tv.com.ua/uk/programs/faces_history.

Two other important developments during these years are the intensification of media convergence, and the explosion of new and social media. Internet usage grew steadily, and although Ukraine has not yet reached European or North American penetration levels, it has the highest rate of growth in Europe.[100] Here, too, the competing influences of globalization and the Russia factor are clearly visible, perhaps best illustrated by which websites Ukrainians visit most often. In 2011, one sees that similar to Canada or the U.S., Google, YouTube, Wikipedia, and Facebook are popular, as well as the Russian VKontakte, Mail.ru, and Yandex (both the .ru and .ua versions), and a few Ukrainian sites (Google.com.ua, Ukr.net). Television is increasingly viewed on-line, such as TVi, and this is providing both commercial opportunities and the ability to get around government pressures on alternative media.[101]

Table 1. Most Visited Websites in Ukraine, 2011

	According to Alexa.com		According to InMind
1.	Google.com.ua	1.	Google
2.	VKontakte.ru	2.	Mail.ru
3.	Google.com	3.	VKontakte.ru
4.	Mail.ru	4.	Yandex
5.	YouTube.com	5.	YouTube
6.	Yandex.ua	6.	Wikipedia.org
7.	Yandex.ru	7.	Facebook.com
8.	Facebook.com	8.	Marketgrid.com
9.	Wikipedia.com	9.	Ukr.net
10.	LiveJournal.com	10.	Odnoklassniki

Source: http://www.alexa.com/topsites/countries/UA; http://ain.ua/2011/01/19/40868

This evidence shows that symbolic values continue to shift, and competition for cultural capital is ongoing. What does this mean for

---

100 Olha Minchenko, "V Ukraini 19.3 mil korystuvachiv internet u vitsi 15+," *Watcher*, 25 February 2013, http://watcher.com.ua/2013/02/25/v-ukrayini-19-3-mln-korystuvachiv-internetu-u-vitsi-15/.

101 Mykola Kniazhyts'kyi, then Director, TVi. Interviewed by Marta Dyczok, Kyiv, 5 July 2012.

democracy? Here global trends of media, especially TV, are clearly visible. Politicians continue to use TV as the primary vehicle for communicating with society, thus undermining the importance of traditional institutions, such as political parties. With the ever-deepening corruption and disregard for the rule of law, manipulation and abuse of media professionals and the simultaneous projection of a certain lifestyle, two trends are visible in society. On the one hand, there is a disengagement from the political process, as witnessed by low voter turnout in the 2012 parliamentary election, particularly the youth vote. Simultaneously there is an increase in activism on the local level, on issues such as preserving historical monuments.[102] Both of these parallel developments in established democracies.

9. Conclusion

Ukraine is often viewed in isolation (what is happening in Ukraine, Ukraine's politics, Ukraine's media) or compared to normative standards that do not really exist anywhere (how close or far is Ukraine to a consolidated democracy, how free and independent are Ukraine's media). This misses the point that for over 20 years Ukraine has been part of the global community, through mass media engaged in transnational cultural flows. In many ways Ukraine's media system and content have become very similar to those in other parts of Europe and North America.

Television and the Internet have been bringing the world into Ukrainian living rooms for over twenty years, and this is changing values, from growing consumerism to a shift in political views on individualism vs. collectivism. Ukrainians have embraced technology and lifestyle changes, [103] and these innovations are not coming from Russia, but rather from the West.

---

102 See Marta Dyczok, "Fighting the developers in Kyiv," *OpenDemocracy*, 20 February 2013, http://www.opendemocracy.net/od-russia/marta-dyczok/fighting-developers-in-kyiv.

103 In 2013, four Ukrainian IT companies were listed among the top 100 in the Global Outsourcing 100 ranking (Intetics, Luxoft, EPAM Systems and Miratech). See "Chotiri ukrains'ki IT-kompanii yviishli do sotni naikrashchikx b cviti," *TSN*, 3 March 2013, http://tsn.ua/ukrayina/chotiri-ukrayinski-it-

Ukraine is still struggling to define its identity and global media trends are having a powerful impact on this process. While much attention has rightly focused on the political censorship that Ukraine has experienced during various phases of its independence, what has been overlooked is that media owners are more interested in profits than politics. They accommodate political elites to gain influence and protect their other business interests, but in terms of media content, they are equally accommodating market forces and provide audiences with the same media product that global media corporations are selling and Ukrainians are consuming.

Ukrainian audiences display a wide range of preferences, but in many ways are similar to global audiences in that they prefer entertainment over information, are open to new ideas, and Western (global) media formats have steadily gained popularity. Whereas in the mid-1990s, *INTER TV* succeeded by broadcasting mainly Russian/Soviet media content, 15 years later it had adopted many Western formats in the competition for ratings.[104] Russian programming remains popular, but it, too, has increasingly adopted Western formats. Thus, in some ways globalization is coming to Ukraine through a Russian lens. Ukrainian media products also continue to attract audiences.

Media representations show that there are a variety of competing visions on Ukrainian identity. Certain parts of Ukrainian society have consistently demonstrated an interest in and desire to define themselves as part of a larger, cosmopolitan, global community, others feel more comfortable in a Russian cultural space, while others still are looking for a unique Ukrainian identity.

There are different ways to interpret this. One is that Ukraine has not developed a strong national idea around which society has

---

kompaniyi-uviyshli-do-sotni-naykraschih-v-sviti-284506.html?fb_action_ids=136932006483382&fb_action_types=og.recommends&fb_source=timeline_og&action_object_map={%22136932006483382%22%3A534074393282504}&action_type_map={%22136932006483382%22%3A%22og.recommends%22}&action_ref_map.

104 Ekaterina Shapoval, "INTER: Vtoroe prishestvie," *Forbes Ukraine*, 7 August 2013, http://forbes.ua/magazine/forbes/1355859-inter-vtoroe-prishestvie.

united. This view continues to be voiced in Ukraine, as it has been since the early 1990s.[105] Another is that Ukrainian society is diverse, that the state has not behaved in a hegemonic manner and imposed a vision from above, and media representations demonstrate a high degree of tolerance toward alternative views. A third is that Ukraine is in keeping with global trends, where identities are changing as a result of cultural and media convergence.

10. Epilogue

This chapter was completed in the summer of 2013, before the events shook Ukraine in the subsequent autumn, winter, and spring. Much of what happened from November 2013 through April 2014 was about identity and media.

By sheer coincidence, a few months before protests erupted, a number of new independent, Internet-based media outlets had appeared, created by journalists who were tired of state and corporate pressures in the existing media.[106] They served as a counter-hegemonic force that challenged censorship and provided alternative, largely objective news on the protests, and later invasion by Russia. As events unfolded, the impact of media convergence became even more evident. Live streamed TV and social media became important information sources which were picked up and disseminated by mainstream and global media outlets. After President Victor Yanukovych fled the country on February 21, 2014, state censorship largely ended and the once compliant media corporations began to show a relatively clear picture of the news and call for national reconciliation and unity. All the main TV stations added the same logo onto their screens: the Ukrainian flag and the words United Ukraine in both Russian and Ukrainian languages.

At the time of this writing, April 2014, it is too early to tell what the long term impact of these events will be. However, it seems

---

105   Heorhii Pocheptsov, "Informatsiiniy prostir iak kliuchevyi dlia rozvytku krainy," *MediaSapiens*, 3 March 2013, http://osvita.mediasapiens.ua/material/15890.
106   These outlets include *Hromadske Radio* (http://hromadskeradio.org/) and *Hromadske TV* (http://hromadske.tv/).

ironic that Russian President Putin went to so much trouble to destabilize and divide Ukraine from within, yet the result of his actions, particularly the military invasion of Crimea, served to unite Ukrainians. The three strands of identity outlined in this chapter seem to be congealing into a single multi-dimensional Ukrainian identity, where cosmopolitan views blended with old/new visions of identity as well as the cultural affinity with Russia. From available polls and media reports, language, ethnicity, and even foreign policy orientation no longer seem to be dividing Ukrainians. Whichever direction they're looking, towards the European Union or Russia, few want to live in a corrupt state or be invaded by Russia.

Media in Post-Soviet Belarus: Between Democratization and Reinforcing Authoritarianism

Oleg Manaev, European Humanities University

The Republic of Belarus is a shining example of a "hybrid regime" or "competitive autocracy" in the post-Soviet space.[1] As William Dobson stressed, "Although these regimes are much more tactically subtle and adaptive than the old-school communist regimes and military juntas of the past, at their core these systems are still about maintaining power through coercion. The regimes are smart enough to know that they cannot squelch all dissent and should not even try. Instead, they focus on what counts."[2] Thus, after the collapse of the USSR in December 1991, Belarus became an independent state and declared democracy and rule of law as its constitutional principles. But after Alexander Lukashenka's victory in the relatively free and fair presidential election in 1994, he employed a simple strategy for ruling the country: He rebuilt the Soviet-style command economy and isolated Belarus from the economic chaos that encompassed the rest of the USSR in the mid-1990s. By reducing the unemployment level to below 1 percent and providing moderate, but stable, economic growth, he satisfied public expectations. During the first years of his rule, he also marginalized or eliminated any political alternatives. The concentration of economic and political power allowed him to exert direct personal control over the state. In turn, the state put most of society under its control.

---

1 Kimitaka Matsuzato, "A Populist Island in an Ocean of Clan Politics: The Lukashenka Regime as an Exception among CIS Counties," *Europe-Asia Studies* 56:2 (2004); Javier Corrales, "Hugo Boss," *Foreign Policy* (January–February 2006); Dmitriy Furman, "Problema 2008: Obshchee i osobennoe v protsessakh perekhoda postsovetskikh gosudarstv," *Polit.ru*, http://polit.ru/article/2007/10/19/furman/; Ivan Krastev, "Paradoxes of the New Authoritarianism," *Journal of Democracy* 22:2 (April 2012).

2 William J. Dobson, *The Dictator's Learning Curve: Inside the Global Battle for Democracy* (New York: Doubleday, 2012).

The state-run media became one of the key-stones of this control system.

Despite this extensive state control, around 30 percent of the country's economy is private; there are 15 officially registered political parties, and over 2,000 non-governmental organizations, independent business associations, human rights groups, think tanks and other organizations that comprise Belarusian civil society. Despite constant pressures from the state, unequal resources, and adversarial political, economic, legal, and technological conditions, independent media continue to exist and make significant contribution to the development of civil society and elements of democracy.

The present chapter examines how this "dual system" works, explores its peculiarities and commonalities with other post-Soviet countries, and predicts its prospects. For this purpose, I will locate the Belarus media system in the world media freedom landscape, analyze its unique characteristics with a special emphasis on the media's elections coverage, the social grounds of media system duality, and media's role in generating trust as a "lubricant for cooperation" in both social and media systems. Moreover, I will define what Belarus can tell us about media in non-democratic regimes and social science theory more generally. The main contribution here is the "Islands in the Stream" model.

1. Belarus in the World Media Freedom Landscape

Perceived media freedom varies widely across countries, with as many as 97 percent in Finland and as few as 26 percent in Belarus saying their media are free. Expert evaluations of media freedom fall in line with these assessments by the public. Ten out of the 13 countries with the lowest percentage of adults saying their media are free are rated "not free," according to Freedom House's 2013 evaluations of press freedom (see Table 1).[3]

---

3 "Freedom of the Press 2013," Freedom House, http://www.freedomhouse.org/report-types/freedom-press.

Residents in many of these countries with the lowest percentage of adults saying their media are free have consistently expressed skepticism about the presence of media freedom. As one can see from the Freedom House "Nations in Transit" statistics, Belarus had low levels of media independence over the last decade (see Table 2).[4]

Table 1.   Lowest Perceived Media Freedom Worldwide, Percent

	Yes	No	Don't Know/ Refused	Freedom House Press Freedom Status
Belarus	26	47	27	Not free
Gabon	32	62	6	Not free
Chad	32	65	2	Not free
Zimbabwe	32	54	13	Not free
Palestinian Territories	33	56	10	Not free
Armenia	35	49	15	Not free
Sudan	37	57	5	Not free
Congo (Brazzvillle)	37	59	4	Partly free
Russia	38	41	21	Not free
Congo (Kinshasa)	38	48	14	Not free
Mauritania	38	57	5	Partly free
Macedonia	39	45	16	Partly free
Yemen	40	27	33	Not free

Source: Gallup. Data collected in 133 countries in 2012

---

4   "Nations in Transit 2013: Belarus," Freedom House, http://www.freedomhouse.org/report/nations-transit/2012/belarus.

Table 2.   Belarus Nations in Transit Ratings and Average Scores

Features	'03	'04	'05	'06	'07	'08	'09	'10	'11	'12
National Democratic Governance	N/A	N/A	6.75	7.00	7.00	7.00	6.75	6.75	6.75	6.75
Electoral Process	6.75	6.75	7.00	7.00	7.00	7.00	6.75	6.75	7.00	7.00
Civil Society	6.50	6.75	6.75	6.75	6.50	6.50	6.25	6.00	6.00	6.25
Independent Media	6.75	6.75	6.75	6.75	6.75	6.75	6.50	6.75	6.75	6.75
Local Democratic Governance	N/A	N/A	6.50	6.50	6.50	6.75	6.75	6.75	6.75	6.75
Judicial Framework and Independence	6.75	6.75	6.75	6.75	6.75	6.75	6.75	6.75	6.75	7.00
Corruption	5.50	5.75	6.00	6.25	6.25	6.25	6.00	6.00	6.00	6.25
Democracy Score	6.46	5.54	6.64	6.71	6.68	6.71	6.57	6.50	6.57	6.68

Source: Freedom House

2. Peculiarities of the Belarusian Media

According to the State Media Register, as of January 1, 2014, Belarus had registered 1,556 periodicals (including 410 state-run and 1,146 private), 262 radio and TV stations (178 state and 84 non-state), and 9 information agencies (2 state and 7 non-state).[5] The Belarusian Association of Journalists (a professional organization uniting approxiately 1,500 journalists primarily from non-state media) noted that less than 30 of the registered non-state periodicals are focused on covering public or socio-political issues, the rest are focused on business, entertainment, sports, cultural affairs, and ads. Almost

---

5   "Belarus Media Data 2014," Republic of Belarus Ministry of Information, http://www.mininform.gov.by/smi/.

half of them were expelled from the state—owned distribution networks before the previous presidential election in 2005.[6] In terms of periodicity, circulation and air-time, the state—run media dominate the media landscape—the ratio between them and independent media is approximately 9 to 1.[7]

Broadcasting in Belarus remains under strict government control. Most importantly, national television networks are state—owned. According to the Freedom House "Freedom of the Press 2012" report, "the state maintains a virtual monopoly on domestic broadcast media, which consistently glorify Lukashenka and vilify the opposition. Only state media broadcast nationwide, and the content of smaller television and radio stations is tightly restricted."[8]

The state-owned media are in a beneficial position compared to the independent media: they enjoy subsidized rent, salaries, distribution, printing, tax exemptions and direct funding from the government, as the International Fact-Finding Mission to the Republic of Belarus report "For Free and Fair Media in Belarus" indicates.[9] In 2010, the Council of Ministers approved special resolution No. 855, which includes a list of print media whose editorial boards were entitled to subsidies from the state budget that year. The list of state subsidized media outlets includes twenty four publications. Not surprisingly, *Sovetskaya Belorussiya*, the Belarusian newspaper with the largest circulation (2.5 million copies weekly) founded by the Presidential Administration, is among them. Support for the

---

[6] "Mass Media in Belarus 2012," Belarusian Association of Journalists, http://baj.by/sites/default/files/monitoring_pdf/mediamonitoring2012en.pdf.

[7] Oleg Manaev, Natalie Manayeva, and Dmitry Yuran, "Islands in the Stream: Reflections on Media Development in Belarus," in Peter Gross and Karol Jakubowicz, eds., *Media Transformations in the Post—Communist World: Eastern Europe's Tortured Path to Change* (New York: Lexington Books, 2012), 195–215.

[8] "Freedom of the Press 2011," Freedom House, http://www.freedomhouse.org/uploads/pfs/371.pdf.

[9] http://www.i-m-s.dk/files/publications/1528%20Belarus.web%20final.pdf.

state-run media outlets is rapidly growing: from 2002 to 2009, financial support for the state media from the state budget grew almost fourfold, from US$24 million to over US$90 million.[10]

As a result of the economic, political, and legal preferences for the state-run media and discrimination against the non-state media, the number of non-state media has decreased twofold during the last decade, and the Ministry of Information refuses to register new independent media outlets. The editors of state-run media are appointed by the president or local authorities. Such control over personnel gives the state enormous influence in shaping editorial policy and presents a fertile environment for editorial bias.

The Internet remains the most liberalized sector in Belarus's information space. The number of Web-users exceeds 5 million people (over 60 percent of the adult population, and the same number of people use social networks): this audience increased by more than 10 times since the late 1990s. Authorities have reacted to the growing influence of the Internet on Belarusians by attempting to take control of the Web. Thus, Presidential Order No. 60 of February 1, 2010, "On Measures to Improve the Use of the National Segment of the Internet" came into effect on July 1, 2010, and introduced various restrictions. But an even more important factor that limits the Internet role as a counterbalance to state-run media dominance is the way that people use it. Thus, according to an Independent Institute for Social, Economic, and Political Studies (IISEPS) March 2013 poll, only 21.8 percent of all Internet users go on-line to obtain political information; the rest use if for communication and entertainment.

Belarus adopted a new media law in 2008 and it took effect in 2009. The law set up a number of obstacles for independent journalists and media outlets, shortening the list of journalistic rights. Some of these control measures include: having journalists go through a three-step accreditation process after which they can be denied accreditation without any explanation; increasing the au-

---

10   "Media in Belarus 2008," Belarusian Association of Journalists, http://baj.by/sites/default/files/monitoring_pdf/mediamonitoring2012en.pdf.

thority to penalize journalists and mass media outlets for vague reasons, such as "dissemination of inaccurate information that might cause harm to state and public interests" for which journalists could be fined and operations of media outlets could be suspended or terminated; requiring all print and broadcast media outlets to re-register with the Ministry of Information (at least half a dozen independent media outlets were denied registration); sanctions when media materials are found to violate requirements for "compliance with reality"; and foreign ownership of media being restricted to 30 percent. Other laws detrimental to freedom of speech and the press include "The Law on Public Service," "The Law on Counteracting Extremism," and "The Criminal Code."[11]

3. Peculiarities of Media Elections Coverage

These characteristics of the Belarusian media determine what they can say and do. This state control naturally has a huge impact on the way that the Belarusian media cover elections. "By focusing their attention on one candidate, i.e. the incumbent, and giving him positive coverage while negatively assessing his opponents, the state-owned media violated the principle of equal opportunities and equal access to the media," according to a Belarus Association of Journalists (BAJ) Analytic Report on "Coverage of the 2010 Presidential Election in the Belarusian Media" which summed up the findings of presidential election coverage from October 11 to December 25, 2010, in 18 media, including the national state-owned TV and radio networks, Internet resources, regional TV and radio stations and both the state-owned and independent press.

State media provided biased coverage of the opposition candidates and did not offer them a chance to rebut. By citing only negative opinions about them and negative assessments of their agendas, the state-owned media in fact censored public opinion, depriving the opposition candidates' supporters of their voice. Thus, during the election, the state-owned media did not reflect the interests

---

11 Natalie Manayeva, Anna Aniskevich, and Anton Dinerstein, "Mass Media under the Eye of Big Brother: Governmental Control Over Mass Media in Belarus," *Otázky žurnalistiky* 3–4 (2011): 3–19.

of all social groups. In fact, they actively demonstrated their loyalty to the incumbent by acting as an instrument of power and an ideological tool.

Just like in the previous elections, by adopting a low-key approach to the election and marginalizing the opponents of the current regime, the state-owned media contributed to undermining political competition and the contest of ideas. In this way, they actually excluded, or at least diverted, voters from political competition. State-run media do not adhere to professional standards or the ethical principles of journalism.

Although the independent print press offered a varied picture of the election, their limited circulation prevented them from becoming a competitive information source. For the same reason, they could not efficiently oppose the practice of ignoring government opponents or their negative representation in the state-owned media."[12]

Figures 3–6 prove the conclusion about different media subsystems in Belarus producing different discourses—one reflecting an authoritarian "picture of the world," and the other a democratic one. The state-owned media focused heavily on Lukashenka in its election coverage (Figures 1 and 3). However, television spent little time on the elections, preferring to distract popular attention away from this topic by focusing on other topics (Figure 2). The opposition did not have access to state television, but gained much more coverage in the independent press (Figure 4).

---

12   "Coverage of the 2010 Presidential Election in the Belarusian Media (Final Report)," Belarusian Association of Journalists Media Monitoring, http://baj.by/sites/default/files/monitoring_pdf/Coverageofthe2010PresidentialElectionintheBelarusianMedia-final-2010.pdf.

Figure 1. Coverage of the 2010 Presidential Elections by State TV (Actors), Percent

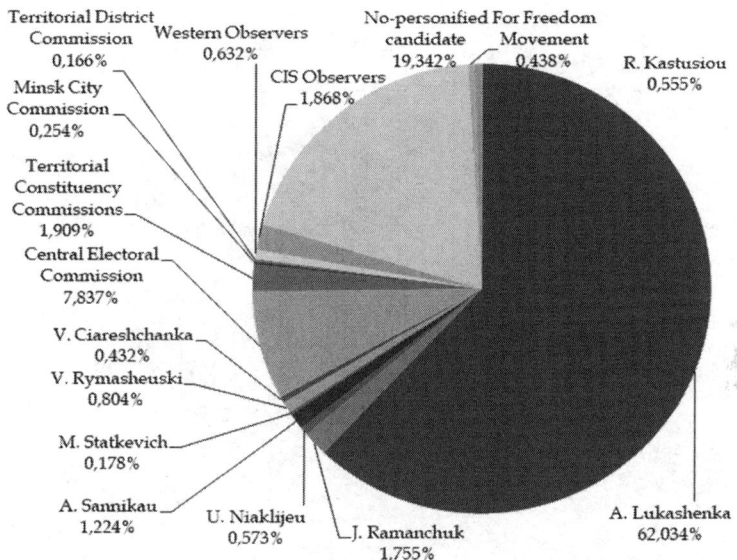

Source: Author's own calculation

Figure 2. Coverage of the 2010 Presidential Elections by State TV (by Subject), Percent

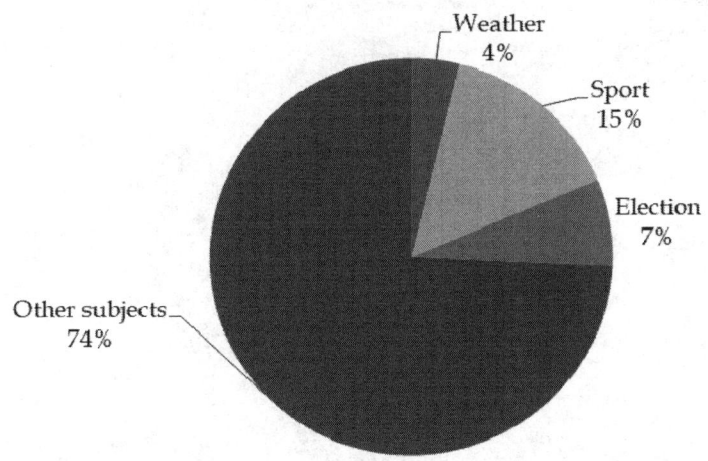

Source: Author's own calculation

Figure 3. Coverage of of the 2010 Presidential Elections by the State-run Newspaper *Sovetskaya Belorussiya*, Percent

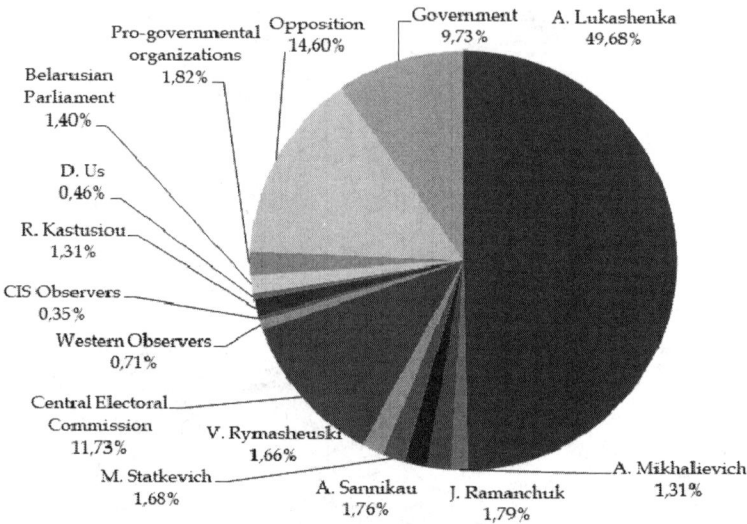

Source: Author's own calculation

Figure 4. Coverage of of the 2010 Presidential Elections by the Independent Newspaper *Nasha Niva*, Percent

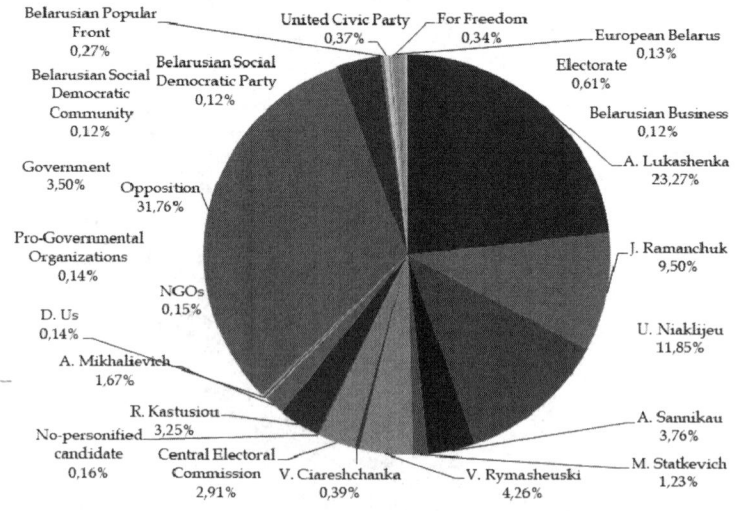

Source: Author's own calculation

Thus, according to Siebert, Peterson, and Schramm's classification,[13] the Belarusian media model could be identified as authoritarian: the function of the state-run media is to support the policies of the authorities; state-run media fosters support for the president, as well as social and national unity; and the state has the right to control mass media by enforcing a repressive media law and other means. According to Jakubowicz's classification,[14] Belarus falls into the category of non-competitive regimes and its media system is very different from media systems in Western Europe, or even from those of the Baltic States, Ukraine, or Poland, Belarus's closest neighbors.

The dominant "media philosophy" was clearly formulated by Belarus President Lukashenka in various public statements:

- "Journalism is probably a state profession, and journalists are the state's men" (1999).
- "Freedom of the press does not constitute total permissibility, but is an 'inside editor.' And we should not intend to avoid such an editor, let him serve society" (1999).
- (About Western media projects for Belarus) "Our country falls into a disinformation circle" (2005).
- "Mass media today is a weapon of mass destruction. The most powerful one. This is a war that never ends" (2006, two months before the presidential election of 2006).
- "On the eve of the presidential election, Belarus was exposed to massive information pressure from the outside, which is still growing" (2006, two months after the presidential election of 2006).

---

13   Fred Siebert, Theodore Peterson, and Wilbur Schramm, *Four theories of the press: The authoritarian, libertarian, social responsibility and Soviet communist concepts of what the press should be and do* (Urbana-Champaign, Ill.: University of Illinois Press, 1963).

14   Karol Jakubowicz, *Rude awakening: Social and media change in Central and Eastern Europe* (New York: Hampton Press, 2007).

- (Addressing journalists) "You are the most powerful weapon of the president for the purpose of state governing" (2008).[15]

Under Lukashenka the Belarusian political system, however, has not collapsed over the course of two decades and the Belarusian authorities do not face massive public protests. Several attempts to introduce "colored revolutions" during the last decade failed, not only due to brutal repression but mostly because of the lack of massive public support. According to an IISEPS public opinion poll conducted in June 2011, 53.3 percent of respondents think that the mass media in the country are dependent (31.2 percent answered "some media are independent, and some not," 10.3 percent said "media are independent"). And most of them have no doubts on whom the media depend: three quarters named the president and other authorities, while only 13.2 percent named the audience, 7.1 percent — political parties and NGOs, and only 1.7 percent — private business. However, responding to the question if they have enough access to information about current life in Belarus, 52.9 percent of respondent said "no," while 46.7 percent said "yes," and to the question "to what extent does information that you get from official sources correspond to your real life?" 48.3 percent said that it "does not correspond completely/to some extent," while 51.2 percent said that it "corresponds completely/to some extent."[16] These numbers mean that many people who consider the media to be dependent on the state see nothing wrong with this state of affairs.

The image of Belarusian mass media is surrounded by myths. And these views are common in Belarus and in the West, among journalists and politicians. These myths are deeply rooted in society. According to one myth, the state-run media are bad while independent media are good. According to another myth, if all Belarusians use only independent media, Belarus will evolve into a

---

15 Vladimir Podgol, ed., *Tsitaty Lukashenko iz kollektsii Podgola* (Minsk: Peredvizhnoe izdatel'stvo im. Skoriny, 2007).
16 Results of National Opinion Poll conducted in June 2011, IISEPS, http://iiseps.org/dannye/8/lang/en.

democratic country. Sometimes journalists publish excellent articles but they do not gain public interest and support. Occasionally ordinary publications raise important issues. Why does the system work like this? Answers must be sought in society and not in the media.

4. Peculiarities of Belarusian Society

In response to the above data and statements, one could ask: Why do so many Belarusians who consider the media to be dependent on the state see nothing wrong with this? Similarly, one can ask a related question: Why does the regime allow independent print media to exist at all and why does it not block access to websites it does not like following the Chinese example? To answer these questions, it is necessary to invoke the peculiarities of Belarusian society.

Most of the peculiarities are deeply rooted in Belarus's history, culture and geography which can explain Belarusian authoritarianism and its vitality: (1) the gradual separation from the USSR and its heritage, (2) the growing breakdown of political and social values in society, (3) the redrawing of its social landscape, (4) the Belarusians' unformed national identity, and (5) their consequent ambivalence about the country's geopolitical orientation.[17]

Hallin and Mancini, who developed one of the most comprehensive comparative analyses of media systems and politics in the post-Communist countries, stressed, "The free media that evolved in Eastern Europe in the 1990s were not born out of nothing" and speak about "the legacy of the Communist system."[18] This is true, of course, but "Belarusian peculiarities" cannot be reduced simply and

---

17 Oleg Manaev, Natelie Manayeva, and Dzmitri Yuran, "More state than nation: Lukashenka's Belarus," *Journal of International Affairs* 65:1 (2011).
18 Daniel Hallin and Paolo Mancini, *Comparing Media Systems: Three Models of Media and Politics* (Cambridge: Cambridge University Press, 2004); Daniel Hallin and Paolo Mancini, eds., *Comparing Media Systems Beyond the Western World* (Cambridge: Cambridge University Press, 2011); Daniel Hallin and Paolo Mancini, "Comparing media systems between Eastern and Western Europe," in Peter Gross and Karol Jakubowicz, eds., *Media Transformations in the Post – Communist World: Eastern Europe's Tortured Path to Change* (New York, Lexington Books, 2012), 18–35.

solely to this legacy. The Soviet heritage is gradually but steadily being overcome by Belarusians: the number of respondents in favor of restoring the USSR fell to half the previous level over 18 years, while opposition to its restoration increased 2.7 times. The number of respondents uncertain about such a restoration also dropped. This is evidence that the nature of Belarusian authoritarianism differs from that of its Soviet past.

Another important feature of Belarusian authoritarianism is the significant split in society. The observation that "winners get everything and losers nothing" fits this country: it means not just the replacement of one ruling elite by another, but the replacement of one value system with another. The new values of national independence, political democracy, the rule of law, a market economy, and "the return to the European family" inspired Belarusian democrats of the "perestroika wave" and led to the emergence of independence and democracy in the early 1990s, but were replaced by patriarchic values of the rule of "the father of the people," "a fair distribution of prosperity," and the "restoration of the historic and cultural union/friendship with Russia." Moreover, the latter values of the "common majority" were consolidated while the democratic ones of the "advanced minority" were marginalized via various political, legal, economic, informational, educational, and other means. Instead of a system of checks and balances, Belarus ended up with a system based on one group's absolute domination.

Analysis proves that the split has not only been of a social-demographic nature, but also of a value nature in a way pre-determined by the legacy of the Soviet and Russian Empire, including a lack of initiative, responsibility, and trust on the one hand, and a tendency to rely on the authorities, on the other. Thus, Lukashenka convinced supporters to come out against privatizing state property; they do not see infringement of human rights or problems with the political climate and state of democracy; and a majority of them supported Lukashenka's candidates in the parliamentary and local elections that they consider free and fair. In contrast, his convinced opponents speak out for privatization and are seriously concerned over human rights infringements, the political climate and the state of democracy. They mostly supported alternative and independent candidates in the parliamentary and local elections which they considered neither free nor fair. The correlation between those who believe the best form of government is democracy and those who chose "a strong hand" is 48 percent vs. 43 percent among those trusted to Lukashenka, while 82 percent vs. 10 percent among those who do not trust him.[19]

Strengthening the societal split with a "stick and carrot" policy had much more fundamental consequences for the country than simply a promotion of one set of values and the marginalization of others. Lukashenka's policy affects the very social structure of society. During the first decade of Lukashenka's rule, the social position of several socio-professional groups has been downgraded, while the status and position of other groups has increased. Unlike the Bolshevik revolution of 1917, this change occurred without mass violence. However, this "quiet revolution" has already had serious consequences for Belarusian society and the state because it marks a significant redistribution of power, re-allocation of property, and access to social resources, such as healthcare, education, and a culture that stands behind the redistribution of social statuses.

One additional important feature of Belarusian society is its incomplete national identity. I define national identity as a system of institutional and cultural features that clearly sets the Belarusian nation, state and society apart from others. After a three centuries break in its nation and state building, Belarusians faced a serious challenge of self-identification: Who are we? To what culture, or, broadly speaking, civilization, do we belong? These questions might sound strange for almost all of our neighbors—Poles, Baltic peoples, Russians, Ukrainians, but not for many Belarusians. The weakness of the national identity makes Belarusian society unstable and creates a need for some "unifying basis." Lukashenka used this situation effectively, introducing himself as the essence of the "unifying" base.[20]

---

19   Manaev, Manayeva, and Yuran, "More state than nation."
20   David Marples, *Belarus: A Denationalized Nation* (Newark: Harwood Academic, 1999); Grigory Ioffe, *Understanding Belarus and How Western Foreign*

According to Samuel Huntington's theory, Belarusian history, as well as the histories of Ukraine and Moldova, can be viewed as examples of "torn" or "cleft states" on a "civilization fault line" between the Western European Catholic/Protestant and the Eurasian Orthodox civilizations.[21] Under these circumstances, Belarus's incomplete national identity turned into the ambivalence of its geopolitical choice: while the more "advanced minority" looks up to Europe, the "common majority" looks up to Russia. Throughout his career, Lukashenka masterfully used these internal and external contradictions. On the one hand, for twenty years he demonstrated a strong pro-Russian political orientation domestically, thus getting support from the majority. On the other hand, he played a game with both Russia and the West, and managed to get support from both sides (mostly from Russia but sometimes from the West as well).

5. Trust as a "Lubricant for Cooperation"

Thus, the coexistence of state and non-state media that became a key feature of the post-Communist Belarusian media system is deeply rooted in the country's history and culture, both at the structural and cultural levels. The state-run "media sub-system" follows political, legal, economic, cultural, and professional standards supported by the "common majority" and the state, while the independent media follow the "advanced minority" and to some extent the West.

At first glance, the Belarusian media system looks as if it were at the intermediate stage of transformation in Central and East European post-Communist countries, where non-state media gradually replace the state-run media. But this similarity is deceptive. In Belarus both media sub-systems came into being at the beginning

---

Policy Misses the Mark (New York: Rowman & Littlefield Publishers, 2008); Ryszard Radzik, *Bialorusini Miedzy Wschodem a Zachodem* (Lublin: UMCS, 2012).

21 Samuel Huntington, *The Clash of Civilizations and the Remaking of World Order* (New York: Simon and Schuster, 1997).

of the 1990s and during the two following decades continued to reproduce themselves with some minor deviations. The state-run segment of the Belarusian media became more visible and prominent, while the independent media appear less visible. This discrepancy leads to a problem in assessing their real role in society. Which "media sub-system" is more influential and effective?

To answer this question, I use one important "cumulative" indicator that has broad theoretical and other implications: public trust in the media. One of the basic reasons why trust is essential for society is its complex relationship with cooperation. On the one hand, trust is a necessary precondition for cooperation; on the other hand, trust is a product of successful cooperation. According to Putnam, "trust is an essential component of social capital... it lubricates cooperation."[22] At the same time, Gambetta stressed that distrust destroys cooperation: "If distrust is complete, cooperation will fail among free agents."[23]

The Polish sociologist Peter Sztompka asserted that after the collapse of the Soviet system many post-communist societies experienced "a cultural trauma," which includes crises for trust and confidence in institutions.[24] The result is an "atomized society" in which trust is confined to small local pockets of inter-personal interaction. With the erosion of confidence in social institutions, people prefer to solve problems using personal connections.

According to the December 2010 IISEPS public opinion polls displayed in Table 3, those Belarusians who trust the state media and those who put their faith in the independent media differ significantly in their attitudes towards basic social institutions in the country. For example, those who trust state media have much more trust in the president than those who rely on independent media.

---

22   Robert Putnam, *Making democracy work: civic traditions in modern Italy* (Princeton: Princeton University Press, 1993).
23   Diego Gambetta, ed., *Trust: making and breaking cooperative relations* (Oxford: Basil Blackwell, 1988).
24   Peter Sztompka, *Trust: A Sociological Theory* (Cambridge: Cambridge University Press, 1999).

The data[25] here support our conclusion that in Belarus different media sub-systems are based on different social-political sub-systems.

Table 3.   Trust for Mass Media and Confidence in Selected Social Institutions

Of Those Who Trust Independent Media	Of Those Who Trust State Media
The President	*The President*
48.8 percent have confidence in the President and 42.2 percent do not.	89.3 percent have confidence in the President and 7.1 percent do not.
The Military	*The Military*
50.4 percent have confidence in Belarusian Military and 36.9 percent do not.	76 percent have confidence in Belarusian Military and 15.5 percent do not.
Opposition Political Parties	*Opposition Political Parties*
22.9 percent have confidence in opposition political parties and 59.4 percent do not.	15 percent have confidence in opposition political parties and 72 percent do not.
Independent Labor Unions	*Independent Labor Unions*
47.3 percent have confidence in the independent labor unions and 32.6 percent do not.	42.3 percent have confidence in the independent labor unions and 35.4 percent do not.

Table 4 examines the evolution of public trust for different media sub-systems. Based on these public opinion polls, we conclude that in the past 17 years:

- The total average level of trust (i.e. ratio between trust and distrust) for the state media is higher than for the non-state media;
- The total average level of distrust (i.e. ratio between distrust and trust) for both state and non-state media has significantly grown;

---

25   Dzmitri Yuran, "Public confidence in social institutions and media coverage: A case of Belarus" (master's thesis), http://trace.utk.edu/cgi/viewcontent.cgi?article=2000&context=utk_gradthes.

- Distrust for the state media has grown more rapidly than for the non-state media.

Table 4. Dynamics of Public Trust in Different Media Sub-Systems, Percent

Years	State Media		Non-State Media	
	Trust	Distrust	Trust	Distrust
06'2013	33.6	53.0	31.1	51.6
06'2012	32.4	58.4	35.5	48.1
09'2011	25.7	62.2	32.8	52.2
09'2010	35.9	48.7	30.4	49.4
09'2009	44.7	42.1	45.3	35.5
06'2008	47.7	46.9	49.6	48.5
05'2007	51.0	39.7	50.6	35.5
06'2006	57.0	35.0	37.0	47.3
03'2005	53.9	33.2	40.0	40.2
03'2004	47.6	37.0	35.7	42.1
03'2003	45.0	37.3	43.8	33.8
04'2002	38.7	43.1	32.2	43.5
04'2001	33.1	35.4	25.3	31.8
04'2000	38.5	31.6	25.7	31.9
03'1999	39.1	31.0	21.8	32.6
09'1998	41.8	26.0	19.6	32.6
11'1997	43.7	21.0	25.4	24.1
X	**42.9**	**38.0**	**34.3**	**38.7**

Source: IISEPS

However, when we evaluate these indicators we should also take into consideration the fact that in Belarus people's trust in each other is low. Thus, responding to a question in the March 2013 IISEPS survey, "Can you trust most people or should you be very careful in relations with them?" only 23.1 percent of respondents chose the first option while 70 percent preferred the latter. This data supports Sztompka's conclusion about the crisis of trust in post-Soviet societies that transformed them into "atomized societies" in which trust is confined to small local pockets of inter-personal interaction."[26] In this context, the mass media remain one of the few institutions that provide many people some sort of "social grounding," i.e. values (for example, pro or contra Lukashenka, pro Russia

---

26   Sztompka, *Trust: A Sociological Theory*.

or the EU) shared by different parts of society, regardless of its nature.

Surprisingly, despite the fact that the actual ratio of state-run to independent media in Belarus is heavily tilted to the former, the ratio between their influences is quite comparable, and even exceeds the ratio of the constituent groups they rely on and represent. This data might indicate a chance for a gradual replacement of the state-run media sub-system with the non-state sub-system under favorable circumstances, i.e. real democratization of the existing regime.

6. Internal Media System Factors

There are various factors at play in the two media sub-systems, some of them are internal to the media system (journalism education and training, professional standards) while others are external. I will analyze two of them — one internal and the other external — to demonstrate how they affect the level of trust in the media.

The first factor is the interaction between the media and its audiences. For decades, Soviet media used audience feedback, such as letters and phone calls from readers, listeners and viewers, meetings with the audience, etc., not so much for widening the public space, but to strengthen the authorities' editorial discourse. After the collapse of the Soviet Union, independent media began restoring the long forgotten freedom of expression and forming a genuine public discourse. Today, approximately 10 percent of Belarusians express their opinions to the mass media, as the data in Table 5 indicate.

Table 5. Have You Ever Communicated with Mass Media (i.e. Sent Letters, Articles, and Answers to Various Competitions, Came to Editorial Meetings or Called Them by Phone)?

Options	Percent
Yes, several times	9.5
Yes, one time	11.0
No, never	78.5
DA/NA	1.0

Source: IISEPS September 2012 Poll

However, not all of the submissions to the media were published, and approximately a third did not get any response at all, as Table 6 shows.

Table 6. If You Communicated with Mass Media, What Was Their Reaction?

Option	Percent
My letter (or article) was published	7.0
I received a written reply from the editors	5.2
My letter (or article) was passed to the appropriate authorities for their reaction	2.0
My letter (or article) received no response from the editors	6.2
DA/NA	79.6

Source: IISEPS

Table 7 shows how media train the audience to address "in the right course." The more you follow "the right course" (i.e. cover "the right" issues and make "right comments"), the more you are published and the less your opinion gets "passed to the appropriate authorities" or receives no reaction at all.

Table 7. Editorial Reaction on Feedback Depending on Its Frequency, Percent

Frequency of Feedback	Letter Was Published	Received Written Reply	Letter Passed to Appropriate Authorities	Letter Received No Reaction
Several times	46.2	9.1	16.1	23.1
One time	21.0	10.2	28.7	34.1

Source: IISEPS

Table 8.   Trust in Belarusian Media, Percent

Type of Media	Sent Information to Media (20.5)	Sent Nothing to Media (79.5)
State Media		
Trust	30.9	35.6
Distrust	52.1	43.4
NA/DA	17.0	21.0
Non-State Media		
Trust	39.0	30.5
Distrust	39.3	41.2
NA/DA	21.7	28.3

Source: IISEPS

A comparative correlation analysis of the public trust in the media and the feedback experience reveals a different reality for the state and non-state media, as Table 8 shows. This table reveals the different mechanisms of response to audience's feedback by different media sub-systems. Those readers, listeners, and viewers who communicated with state-run media trust them less than before this experience, while those readers who communicated with the non-state media trust them more after communicating with them. This data supports the conclusion that different media sub-systems operate under different principles of interaction with their audiences. The state media, despite various advantages, tend to use public opinion in their own favor, reproducing the old social system. In contrast, non-state media, despite various disadvantages, tend to openly express public opinion, thus producing a new social system.

Another external factor that affects trust in the media is foreign influence. As Hallin and Mancini noted, "foreign influence seems much more central to the process of development of Eastern European media systems than to those of Western Europe. In the media sphere, both foreign ownership and the importation of professional models from outside the region clearly are major factors affecting the development of media systems."[27]

In the case of Belarus, the foreign factor in the media system's development and earning its public's trust is very specific. Due to

---

27   Hallin and Mancini, "Comparing media systems."

various restrictions—legal, political, and economic—foreign ownership is limited. For this reason, foreign ownership does not affect the media system significantly, like it does in other CEE post-Communist countries. Foreign media influence works in a different manner—not through ownership but, rather, through discourse (i.e. principles of coverage, like separation of facts and opinions, presentation of conflict opinions, issues selection), economic (funding, technology, educational and training programs), and moral-political support (awards, making political statements, invitations for various visits to foreign countries) from abroad.[28]

Foreign print media, i.e. socio-political periodicals, are not popular and do not have a significant influence. The total audience for a dozen Western radio stations that broadcast to Belarus during the last five years has decreased from 15 percent to just 5 percent. As Tables 9 and 10 show, television has a much more significant audience share. Russian TV, for example, attracts more than 91 percent of the audience.

Table 9. TV Audiences in Belarus ("What TV Channels Do You Watch"?)

TV Channels	Percent
Russian TV	91.2
Bearusian TV	89.6
Local TV	57.2
Satellite TV	28.1
Russian Service of Euro News (Lion)	22.1
Polish TV	10.0
Special RTVi Program for Belarus (New York-Moscow)	12.0
Independent TV Channel for Belarus BelSat (Warsaw)	9.8

Source: IISEPS March 2011 Poll

---

28 Oleg Manaev, "Foreign Media Influence on Belarusians," *Global Media Journal*, Polish Edition 1:4 (2008).

Table 10. Radio Audiences in Belarus ("What Radio Stations Do You Listen to?), Percent

Radio Stations	03/96	03/09	06/11
Radio Racia (Belostok)	3.4	2.4	1.6
European Radio for Belarus (Warsaw)	4.9	3.6	1.1
Belarusian Service of Radio Liberty (Prague)	3.2	1.6	0.7
Russian Service of Radio Liberty (Prague)	4.2	2.3	0.6
Belarusian Program of Radio Polonia (Warsaw)	4.5	3.1	0.5
BBC (London)	2.8	2.3	0.5
Baltic Wave (Vilnius)	2.8	2.2	0.3
VOA (Washington DC)	3.7	2.2	0.3
Radio Sweden (Stockholm)	1.4	1.1	-
Total audiences (listening in various combinations)	15.0	10.0	5.0

Source: IISEPS March 2011 Poll

According to an IISEPS June 2011 poll, the majority of Internet users choose foreign sources: 35 percent Russian, 13.3 percent European, 2.2 percent American, while just 33.3 percent choose Belarusian sources (see Table 11).

Table 11. Internet Usage in Belarus ("Do You Use Internet?"), Percent

Options	06/06	09/13
Yes, every day	5.1	31.5
Yes, some times a week	9.6	19.3
Yes, some times a month	8.4	7.0
Yes, some times a year	4.6	0.8
No	67.8	38.1
Do not know what it is	3.8	3.3

Source: IISEPS Jun 3 2011 Poll

In evaluating the role of foreign mass media, we should also keep in mind that during the last year only about 20 percent of Belarusians traveled abroad; a decade ago 15 percent did so. This means that for the majority of Belarusians, the media still are a major source of information about life abroad.

7. The "Islands in the Stream" Model

The discussion above leads us to important theoretical and practical questions. Can one define the different media subsystems which coexist (as well as social sub-systems that provide their support) as separate? Can one define this coexistence of different media subsystems as an "Islands in the Stream" model with its own nature, or just as a temporary period of transformation from one well-known model to another? What is the criterion for its definition?

I believe that the media system, as well as social and political development in Belarus, are not just an "atypical case" or a "deviation from the mainstream." While the state media subsystem gains support from the state and is trusted mostly by the "common majority," independent media gain support from abroad and are trusted mostly by the "advanced minority" who disagree with the leadership. The media strengthen "social capital" and "lubricate cooperation" in the two different parts of Belarusian society, contributing to their further coexistence. Moreover, the role of the media is not limited to simply contributing. As Gross argues, "the highly politicized, pluralistic, opinionated and judgmental journalism with neither shared standards nor a professional, democratic-minded culture that prevails in Eastern Europe not only represents civil society, but is civil society."[29] Both media sub-systems in Belarus not only reflect or represent their constituencies (the different parts of society mentioned above), but actually produce them.

The practical question in this regard that is frequently asked in the West is: When will the independent media in Belarus become sustainable and able to continue activities without support from

---

29   Peter Gross, *Entangled evolutions: Media and democratization in Eastern Europe* (Washington, DC: Woodrow Wilson Center Press, 2002).

abroad? Or, in other words: Will media in Belarus enforce democracy or reinforce authoritarianism?

There is no definite answer to this question yet. One could expect that because of the different, and sometimes contradictory social-political and cultural subsystems that coexist in Belarus due to its history, culture, and even geography, different media subsystems could coexist here for quite some time, not exactly replacing one another or converging in the end, but remaining natural for this nation and society. This social and media "duality" or "parallelism" could be broken in favor of either of the sides due to various internal and external factors.

The very existence of these two media systems—journalists, media outlets, ideas, technology, management, finance—indicates that in Belarusian society there is a demand for two completely different sets of values. One set of values appeals to one group of people, while the other appeals to the others. Expecting the "opening gateways" to quickly change the situation would be simplistic. It is not so much the media that shape the social reality as reality itself which shapes different forms of media. And it is not the specific people who work in these systems that are so important.

The two opposing media subsystems are constantly reproduced. I believe they will not go away for a long time, unless the different parts of the Belarusian society that generate a social demand for them disappear. Thus, one can confidently explain the reasons for the rapid decline of trust in state media. With the expansion of authoritarianism, they have to distort reality more. This alienates former supporters. But that does not mean that those who depart from "them" come to "us." They just go into consumerism, immersed in social apathy.

If at their origin (before the collapse of the Soviet Union), the non-state media displayed a more objective approach to reflecting reality—not only the present but also the past (the Grand Duchy of Lithuania, Bolshevik revolution, Belarusian People Republic, WWII, and so on)—now the range of discourse among independent media is much poorer. Objective information is increasingly giving way to the "promotion of democracy" and communication—to the "democratic mobilization" regardless of what it is about, whether education, culture, sports, or lifestyle.

The media include some extreme "black and white" and "our vs. not our" viewpoints. The system of "rejection" of their own and others (events, people, and opinions) operates in a tougher and more uncompromising manner. Those who are considered in the "wrong" are simply removed and discarded.

The combination of these factors explains the longevity of Belarus's model as a "hybrid regime" or "competitive autocracy," which more generally describes mixes of authoritarian and democratic elements that can coexist for a long time.[30] Similar processes—with their peculiarities—take place in Russia and Ukraine because of their similar social and cultural grounds.

Supporters of democracy should not mirror those who disagree with them—neither in politics nor in the media. Otherwise they become the same as the ones that they oppose. Many already have gone down this path. People see it and turn away. Of course, democrats should not forget about their principles. But they have to think about what to do in their own community. After all, the logical consequence of the myths that I mentioned eventually will be that when the democrats are eventually able to take power, they might be tempted to use authoritarian media methods in the name of democracy. Such actions would compromise the very purpose of democracy. The way out is not to ignore, not to alienate those "others." It is one thing to criticize the government for wrong policies, and quite another to criticize the other part of the people for their "wrong views."

The two different societies in Belarus will not go away in the foreseeable future. Those who are eager for democracy should move from the barricades philosophy to a philosophy of coexistence with their opponents—in politics, economy, culture, and in the mass media. After all, they are all one people—Belarusians.

---

30   See the above publications by Matsuzato, Corrales, Furman, and Dobson.

Mass Media Consumption in Post-Soviet Kyrgyzstan and Kazakhstan: The View from Below

Barbara Junisbai, Nazarbayev University; Azamat Junisbai, Pitzer College; and Nicola Ying Fry, Pitzer College

Much has been written in the literature on political communication about the social, economic, and political challenges that independent media in the post-communist region continue to face. While we have a good idea of how Western media experts and local practitioners view the media landscape, less is known about how media are perceived from the grassroots, that is, from the perspective of ordinary citizens. To fill this gap, we draw on original, nationally representative public opinion surveys conducted in 2012 to describe patterns of media consumption in Kyrgyzstan and Kazakhstan. Our work aims to shed light on two basic questions: What media sources do people go to for news and information about current events, and which of these sources are the most/least trusted? In interpreting survey results, we focus on how the two countries' national political trajectories influence media use and trust at the level of mass publics.

The data demonstrate that, overwhelmingly, television is the dominant source of information about current events in both countries. Radio and newspapers also play important roles, although these have a stronger presence for consumers of news in Kyrgyzstan than in Kazakhstan. Despite overall comparable patterns of media consumption, there are theoretically interesting country-level differences regarding trust in particular media sources. While trust in the Internet and radio are relatively similar across the two countries, magazines/journals, newspapers, and television enjoy higher levels of trust in Kazakhstan than in Kyrgyzstan—this, curiously, despite notably stronger media independence in the latter.

These and other findings are presented and analyzed below. First, we situate our study within the previous research on post-communist mass media. Thereafter follows a broad survey of the media landscape in the two countries under investigation. Next, after describing the research design and methods, we expand on our substantive interpretations of the survey results. This chapter is the first in a series that draw on this set of surveys to understand media use and their implications for political developments in Central Asia.

1. The Media as Political Intermediary: Potential and Constraints

For most people, mass media serve as the primary means for experiencing and interpreting the increasingly complex world around them. Media's role is particularly important for the political world, since rarely do ordinary citizens have direct access to the leaders or defining moments of our time, even at the local level. More often than not, it is via the mass media writ large—through television, news sites, radio, print media, and social media—that we have an opportunity to "get to know" government officials, "walk" the corridors of power, and "take part" in major political events. While the media's role in maintaining or usurping political power has been widely debated, one thing seems clear: For ordinary citizens, the media serve as a necessary link to otherwise remote political elites, parties, and the broader political system of which we are a part. In fact, the media have been described not only as intermediaries filtering cues up and down and back and forth along the chan of public opinion,[1] but also as self-interested political actors in their own right, complete with goals, biases, and policy preferences.[2]

Underlying most studies linking mass media, societal preferences, and political outcomes is the assumption that, irrespective of regime type, media can and should contribute to—if not ensure—quality governance, government accountability, and policy responsiveness. For some scholars, the future of established democracies is at stake; without an independent media acting as watchdog and channeling preferences from citizens to government and back again, liberal democracies cannot properly function.[3] For others,

---

1   Stephen Ansolabehere, Roy Behr, and Shanto Iyengar, *The Media Game* (New York: Macmillan, 1992); Paul Allen Beck, "Voters' Intermediation Environments in the 1988 Presidential Contest," *The Public Opinion Quarterly* 55:3 (1991): 371–94; Paul Allen Beck, Russell J. Dalton, Steve Green, and Robert Huckfeldt, "The Social Calculus of Voting: Interpersonal, Media, and Organizational Influences on Presidential Choices," *American Political Science Review* 96:1 (2002): 57–73; L. Lance Bennett and Robert M. Entman, *Mediated Politics: Communication in the Future of Democracy* (Cambridge: Cambridge University Press, 2001); Shanto Iyengar and Donald R. Kinder, *News That Matters* (Chicago: University of Chicago Press, 1987); Maxwell E. McCombs and Donald L. Shaw, "The Agenda-Setting Function of the Mass Media," *Public Opinion Quarterly* 36 (1972): 176–87; Thomas Patterson, *The Mass Media Election: How Americans Choose Their President* (New York: Praeger, 1980); Hing-Yuk Wong and Gary W. McDonough, "The Mediated Metropolis Anthropological Issues in Cities and Mass Communication," *American Anthropologist* 103:1 (2001): 96–111.

2   James Curran, *Media and Power* (London: Routledge, 2002); Benjamin I. Page, "The Mass Media as Political Actors," *PS: Political Science and Politics* 29:1 (1996): 20–24; Michael J. Robinson and Margaret A. Sheehan, *Over the Wire and On TV: CBS and UPI in Campaign '80* (New York: Russell Sage Foundation, 1983); Richard L. Rubin, *Press, Party and Presidency* (New York: Norton, 1981); Donald Shaw, "News Bias and the Telegraph: A Study of Historical Change," *Journalism Quarterly* 44 (1967): 3–12 and 31.

3   Paul Burstein, "The Impact of Public Opinion on Public Policy: A Review and an Agenda," *Political Research Quarterly* 56:1 (2003): 29–40; Bryan Caplan, *The Myth of the Rational Voter: Why Democracies Choose Bad Policies* (Princeton, NJ: Princeton University Press, 2007); Curran, *Media and Power*; Philip N. Howard, *The Digital Origins of Dictatorship and Democracy: Information Technology and Political Islam* (New York: Oxford University Press, 2010); Robert Waterman McChesney, *Rich Media, Poor Democracy: Communication Politics in Dubious Times* (Urbana-Champaign: University of Illinois Press, 2010); Robert I.

the central concern is not the health of existing democracies, but the potential democratization of as-of-yet-closed societies, as well as the factors that hinder its emergence.[4] In both cases, as Shafer and Freedman point out, the media can only carry out their prescribed functions under certain conditions. In their words:

> The existence of [media] freedom is essential for the dissemination of news, information, and varying viewpoints and perspectives on events and ... policy to the public. Predictability of the degree of [media] freedom is important for human rights and [media] rights advocates as they shape strategies to soften or overcome governmental constraints...[5]

Research on the connection between media freedoms and governance issues in the advanced industrial world (and especially the United States) can be traced as far back as the immediate post-WWII era.[6] Building on this foundation, research on the media's place in post-communist regimes has developed quickly over the past twenty years. A major impetus for the initial shift in geographic scope was, understandably, the collapse of the Soviet Union and the subsequent "transition" to a "normal" (i.e., democratic and capitalist) society, based on expectations among prominent Western scholars and policymakers of the region's eventual political and economic liberalization.[7] Pioneering works closely detailing the relative strengths and weaknesses of post-Soviet and post-communist media include Androunas (1993), Benn (1996), Brown

---

Shapiro, "Public Opinion and American Democracy," *The International Journal of Public Opinion Research* 75:5 (2011): 982–1017.

4   Marta Dyczok, "Was Kuchma's Censorship Effective? Mass Media in Ukraine before 2004," *Europe-Asia Studies* 58:2 (2006): 215–38; Matthew Loveless, "Understanding Media Socialization in Democratizing Countries: Mobilization and Malaise in Central and Eastern Europe," *Comparative Politics*, 42:4 (2010): 457–74; Eric McGlinchey and Erica Johnson, "Aiding the Internet in Central Asia," *Democratization* 14:2 (2007): 273–88; Katy E.Pearce and Sarah Kendzior, "Networked Authoritarianism and Social Media in Azerbaijan," *Journal of Communication* 62 (2012): 283–98.

5   Richard Shafer and Eric Freedman, "Press Constraints as Obstacles to Establishing Civil Societies in Central Asia: Developing New Models of Analysis," *Journalism Studies* 10:6 (2009): 866.

6   Joseph T. Klapper, "Mass Media and the Engineering of Consent," *The American Scholar* 17:4 (1948): 419–29.

7   Larry Diamond, "Promoting Democracy," *Foreign Policy* 87 (1992): 25–46.

(1995), Foster (1996), Łoś (1995), Rogerson (1997), Sajo (1995), and Wilson (1995).[8] Thereafter, it took another decade or so for studies of the media-political nexus in post-Soviet Eurasia to gain momentum, as researchers sought to explain the diffusion of democratic ideas and protest repertoires that were part of the color revolutions in Georgia, Ukraine, and Kyrgyzstan in the first decade of the 2000s. These were then followed by a third wave of studies documenting the official and *de facto* clamp-down on media by the region's leaders in response to threats from political challengers.[9]

As this overview suggests, much of the existing literature acknowledges the potential of post-Soviet media actors to fulfill their democratic function.[10] At the same time, studies realistically

---

8   Elena Androuna, *Soviet Media in Transition: Structural and Economic Alternatives* (Westport: Praeger, 1993); David Wedgwood Benn, "The Russian Media in Post-Soviet Conditions," *Europe-Asia Studies* 48:3 (1996): 471–79; Jeff L. Brown, "Mass Media in Transition in Central Asia," *International Communication Gazette* 54 (1995): 249–65; Frances H. Foster, "Information and the Problem of Democracy: The Russian Experience," *The American Journal of Comparative Law* 44:2 (1996): 243–91; Maria Łoś, "Lustration and Truth Claims: Unfinished Revolutions in Central Europe," *Law & Social Inquiry* 20:1 (1995): 117–61; Ken Rogerson, "The Role of the Media in Transitions from Authoritarian Political Systems: Russia and Poland," *East European Quarterly* 31:3 (1997): 329–54; Andras Sajo, "On Old and New Battles: Obstacles to the Rule of Law in Eastern Europe," *Journal of Law and Society* 22:1 (1995): 97–104; Laurie J. Wilson, "Communication and Russia: Evolving Media in a Changing Society," *Social Science Journal* 32:1 (1995): 109–20.

9   Hedwig de Smaele, "Mass Media and the Information Climate in Russia," *Europe-Asia Studies* 59:8 (2007): 1299–313; Scott Gelbach, "Reflections on Putin and the Media," *Post-Soviet Affairs* 26:1 (2010): 77–87; Barbara Junisbai, "A Tale of Two Kazakhstans: Sources of Political Cleavage and Conflict in the Post-Soviet Period," *Europe-Asia Studies* 62:2 (2010): 235–69; Sarah Kendzior, "A Reporter without Borders: Internet Politics and State Violence in Uzbekistan," *Problems of Post-Communism* 57:1 (2010): 40–50; Sarah Oates, "The Neo-Soviet Model of the Media," *Europe-Asia Studies* 59:8 (2007): 1279–97; Natalya Ryabinskaya, "Media Capture in Post-Communist Ukraine," *Problems of Post-Communism* 61:2 (2014): 46–60; Stephen White and Ian McAllister, "Did Russia (Nearly) Have a Facebook Revolution in 2011? Social Media's Challenge to Authoritarianism," *Politics* 34:1 (2014): 72–84; Ilya Yablokov, "Pussy Riot as Agent Provocateur: Conspiracy Theories and the Media Construction of Nation in Putin's Russia," *Nationalities Papers* 42:4 (2014): 622–36.

10 Svetlana V. Kulikova and David D. Perlmutter, "Blogging Down the Dictator? The Kyrgyz Revolution and Samizdat Websites," *International Communi-*

assess the significant limitations that persist on the ground.[11] Collectively, these works recount the continuing struggle of media forced to operate within a difficult—and sometimes impossible— political, economic, and social landscape.[12] Scholars do so from the perspectives of a wide range of actors, including that of Western practitioners and educators, independent journalists, Eurasian and Western human rights activists, international organizations, and donor organizations.

While these are certainly valuable contributions to our understanding of the resilience of the region's nondemocratic regimes and their prospects for political change, few studies to date ask basic questions about media use from the ground up—that is, from the consumers' point of view. In fact, we know little about how ordinary people, as opposed to experts and practitioners, utilize and assess the information resources and media options available to them. To address this gap, we draw on original, nationally representative public opinion surveys conducted in 2012 in Kyrgyzstan

---

cation Gazette 69:1 (2007): 29–50; McGlinchey and Johnson, "Aiding the Internet in Central Asia"; Cai Wilkinson and Yelena Jetpyspayeva, "From Blogging Central Asia to Citizen Media: A Practitioners' Perspective on the Evolution of the *neweurasia* Blog Project," *Europe-Asia Studies* 64:8 (2012): 1395–414.

11 Olivia Allison, "Selective Enforcement and Irresponsibility: Central Asia's Shrinking Space for Independent Media," *Central Asian Survey* 25:1-2 (2006): 93–114; Jonathan Becker, "Lessons from Russia: A Neo-Authoritarian Media System," *European Journal of Communication* 19:2 (2004): 139–63; Peter Gross and Timothy Kenny, "The Long Journey Ahead: Journalism Education in Central Asia," *Problems of Post-Communism* 55:6 (2008): 54–60; Timothy Kenny and Peter Gross, "Journalism in Central Asia: A Victim of Politics, Economics, and Widespread Self-Censorship," *The International Journal of Press/Politics* 13:4 (2008): 515–25; Richard Shafer and Eric Freedman, "Press Constraints as Obstacles to Establishing Civil Societies in Central Asia: Developing a New Model of Analysis," *Journalism Studies* 10:6 (2009): 851–69; Dinara Tussupova, "Mass Media and Ethnic Relations in Kazakhstan," *Problems of Post-Communism* 57:6 (2010): 32–45.

12 Andrei Richter, "Post-Soviet Perspective on Censorship and Freedom of the Media: An Overview," *International Communication Gazette* 70:5 (2008): 307–24.

and Kazakhstan. Using data from our two-country study, we compare and contrast patterns of media consumption and the reported level of trust associated with each type of media in both societies.

Responses to widely used and pre-tested questions provide a useful glimpse into the kinds of media that are used, what sources people trust, and patterns of relative frequency (i.e., comparing Internet, television, and print sources). In addition, this study compares results across two countries that share Soviet and pre-Soviet sociopolitical histories and, according to the widely used Freedom House and Polity IV indicators, continue to fall short of liberal democratic norms. Despite these broad similarities, important differences in their post-Soviet trajectories, it turns out, matter a great deal. In particular, variation in their political climates differentially structures patterns of media trust, sometimes in counterintuitive ways. These findings indicate that recent political history and current contexts influence individual perceptions, which, in turn, translates into varied patterns of trust in news sources in the aggregate.

2. Post-Soviet Media Landscapes: The Two Country Contexts Compared

As previously noted, despite shared histories, Kazakhstan and Kyrgyzstan have since independence followed divergent political trajectories. This split is, in part, the result of different natural resource endowments. Whereas Kyrgyzstan's small, mountainous territory contains few resources for export and trade (apart from gold and hydroelectric power), Kazakhstan is well-known for its oil, natural gas, light metals, and mineral resources, the revenues from which distinguish it as an economic powerhouse among the former Soviet republics. According to the World Bank, in 2013 Kyrgyzstan's per capita GDP was US$1,263.45. That same year, Kazakhstanis on average earned more than ten times that figure, with a per capita GDP of US$13,171.81.

Figure 1. Kyrgyzstan and Kazakhstan. GDP per Capita in Regional Context, 1991–2013

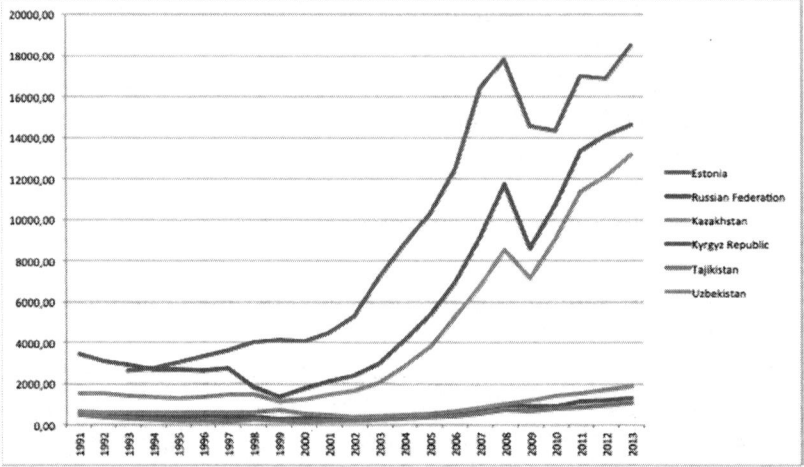

Source: World Bank (http://data.worldbank.org/topic/economy-and-growth)

To characterize the two countries within their regional context, Kyrgyzstan finds itself among the poorest of the post-Soviet states, along with Tajikistan and Uzbekistan, while Kazakhstan's earnings place it among the wealthiest countries in Eurasia, following the Baltic states and Russia (see Figure 1). From a purely economic standpoint, the contrast between the two could not be greater. While Table 1 demonstrates that Kyrgyzstan—along with Armenia and Georgia—is among the top economic reformers/privatizers in post-Soviet Eurasia, it nonetheless appears to have "lost" in the transition from Soviet rule. Kazakhstan, on the other hand, appears to have "won" economically speaking—even when inequality is taken into account.

Table 1.   Economic Variation in Eurasia,*
Circa 2012, Percent

Country	Estimated Private Sector Share of GDP, 2010
Armenia	75
Azerbaijan	75
Georgia	75
Kyrgyzstan	**75**
Kazakhstan	**65**
Russia	65
Ukraine	60
Tajikistan	55
Uzbekistan	45
Belarus	30
Turkmenistan	25

Sources: European Bank or Reconstruction and Development (ERBD), "Transition Indicators, 1991–2010," and "Structural Indicators, 2003–2010," both available at: http://www.ebrd.com/what-we-do/economic-research-and data/data/forecasts-macro-data-transition-indicators.html

*   Comparison only includes presidential and presidential-parliamentary systems; it excludes Moldova, which has been a parliamentary form of government since 2000.

If we shift our focus to the political context, however, the image of Kazakhstan's success becomes less clear-cut. Thanks to high oil and gas prices, Kazakhstan's long-standing president, Nursultan Nazarbayev, has managed to figure 1 — without inciting widespread public outrage — intermittent periods of political crisis, inter-ethnic clashes, public protest, and state-sponsored repression.[13] Regime

---

[13]   "Riots in Western Kazakhstan Could Destabilise the Country," *The Telegraph*, 19 December 2011, http://www.telegraph.co.uk/news/worldnews/asia/kazakhstan/8964991/Riots-in-western-Kazakhstan-could-destabilise-the-country.html; Joshua Kucera, "A Tale of Two Kazakhstans," *Slate.com*, 11 August 2011, http://www.slate.com/articles/news_and_politics/dispatches/features/2011/kazakhstan_rising/a_tale_of_two_kazakhstans.html; Joanna Lillis, "Rich-Poor Gap Fuels Tension in Kazakhstan's Commercial Capital," *Eurasianet.org*, 8 August 2006, http://www.eurasianet.org/departments/civilsociety/articles/eav080906.shtml; Joanna Lillis, "Kazakhstan: How Deep Does Ethnic Harmony Go?," *Eurasianet.org*, 19 May 2011, http://www.eurasianet.org/node/63513; Sean Roberts, "Bread, Circuses,

durability and political stability are results of selective coercion, targeted incentives, and the general legitimacy that President Nazarbayev and government institutions enjoy.[14] Legitimacy is reinforced via tightly controlled media and the existence of few independent or opposition outlets,[15] as well as through increased investment in the public sector and massive public construction projects, mainly in the capital, Astana. In addition, Kazakhstan's formal and informal political practices place high value on the outward appearance of elite cohesion. The constitution reserves extensive formal powers for the executive, and the dominance of the presidential party, Nur Otan, as the only game in town encourages elite consolidation under the president.[16] Informal practices, such as patron-client networks overseen by the president and elite and mass acceptance of Kazakhstan's first president as the nation's founding father, further create an image of intra-elite consolidation, political continuity, and great presidential strength.[17]

In sharp contrast to the staying power of the Nazarbayev regime, politics in Kyrgyzstan have been punctuated by extra-constitutional presidential turnover, high levels of open intra-elite contestation, public protest, and political violence, including ethnic violence.[18] The country's first two presidents, Askar Akaev and

---

and Automobiles in Kazakhstan: The Emergence of a Middle Class?," The Roberts Report on Kazakhstan and Central Asia, 17 November 2006, http://roberts-report.blogspot.com/2006/11/bread-circuses-and-automobiles-in.html; Tussupova, "Mass Media and Ethnic Relations."

14 Max Weber, *The Theory of Social and Economic Organization* (New York: The Free Press, 1947); Joel S. Migdal, "Researching the State," in Mark Irving Lichbach and Alan S. Zuckerman, eds., *Comparative Politics: Rationality, Culture, and Structure*, 2nd ed. (New York: Cambridge University Press, 2010), 162–92.

15 "Freedom of the Press: Kazakhstan," Freedom House, http://freedomhouse.org/report/freedom-press/2014/kazakhstan#.VB1kzSuSy6o.

16 Rico Isaacs, *Party System Formation in Kazakhstan: Between Formal and Informal Politics* (London: Routledge, 2011).

17 Henry Hale, "Regime Cycles: Democracy, Autocracy, and Revolution in Post-Soviet Eurasia," *World Politics* 58:1 (2005): 133–65.

18 Sally Cummings, *Understanding Central Asia: Politics and Contested Transformations* (London: Routledge, 2012); Barbara Junisbai, "Improbable but Potentially Pivotal Oppositions: Privatization, Capitalists, and Political Contestation in the Post-Soviet Autocracies," *Perspectives on Politics* 10:4 (2012): 891–916; Eric McGlinchey, *Chaos, Violence, Dynasty: Politics and Islam in Central*

Kurmanbek Bakiev, both fled after having alienated the domestic political and business elite and angered the masses as a result of rising prices, declining standards of living, and extensive political corruption. High levels of political competition following the demise of the second president led to the creation of a qualitatively different political regime through the introduction of a mixed presidential-parliamentary system. Freedom House has since labeled Kyrgyzstan "the most dynamic political system in post-Soviet Central Asia"—despite lingering issues, such as "endemic institutional weaknesses of national and local government agencies, the unreformed judicial sector, and the intermittent rule of law."[19]

In other words, while Kazakhstan and Kyrgyzstan were once similarly characterized as "soft" authoritarian regimes,[20] the political differences between them have only become magnified over time. Kazakhstan remains a highly personalist presidential regime in which the executive dominates all other formal institutions and elite groupings. Kyrgyzstan is, as of 2010, a hybrid political system in which executive powers specified in former iterations of the constitution have been curtailed. No longer, for example, does the Kyrgyz president have the power to appoint the prime minister or heads of local governments. These limits create a dual or divided executive that explicitly disperses both formal authority and elite loyalty between two national political figures rather than just one.[21] In addition, while Kazakhstan's Nur Otan dominates parliament and opposition parties are effectively marginalized, Kyrgyzstan's 2010 constitution prohibits any party from winning more than 65

Asia (Pittsburgh: University of Pittsburgh Press, 2011); Scott Radnitz, *Weapons of the Wealthy: Predatory Regimes and Elite-Led Protests in Central Asia* (Ithaca: Cornell University Press, 2010); Madeleine Reeves, "The Ethnicisation of Violence in Southern Kyrgyzstan," *Opendemocracy.net*, 21 June 2010, https://www.opendemocracy.net/od-russia/madeleine-reeves/ethnicisation-of-violence-in-southern-kyrgyzstan-0.

19 "Nations in Transit: Kyrgyzstan," Freedom House, http://www.freedomhouse.org/report/nations-transit/2014/kyrgyzstan#.VB1NyCuSy6o.

20 Edward Schatz, "The Soft Authoritarian Tool Kit: Agenda-Setting Power in Kazakhstan and Kyrgyzstan," *Comparative Politics* 41:2 (2008): 203–22.

21 Henry Hale, "Formal Constitutions in Informal Politics: Institutions and Democratization in Post-Soviet Eurasia," *World Politics* 63:4 (2011): 581–617.

seats in the 120-seat parliament and thus becoming the party of power.[22]

Table 2.   Political Variation in Eurasia,* Circa 2012

Country	System of Government	Freedom House Score, 2012		Polity IV Ranking, 2012
Georgia	Presidential	3.0	Partly free	Democracy
Ukraine	Presidential-parliamentary**	3.0	Partly free	Democracy
Armenia	Presidential	4.5	Partly free	Open anocracy
Kyrgyzstan	Presidential-parliamentary**	5.0	Partly free	Open anocracy
Kazakhstan	Presidential	5.5	Not free	Autocracy
Russia	Presidential	6.0	Not free	Open anocracy
Azerbaijan	Presidential	6.0	Not free	Autocracy
Tajikistan	Presidential	6.0	Not free	Closed anocracy
Belarus	Presidential	6.5	Not free	Autocracy
Uzbekistan	Presidential	7.0	Worst of the worst	Autocracy
Turkmenistan	Presidential	7.0	Worst of the worst	Autocracy

Sources: European Bank for Reconstruction and Development (ERBD), "Transition Indicators, 1991–2010," and "Structural Indicators, 2003–2010," both available at: http://www.ebrd.com/what-we-do/economic-research-and data/data/forecasts-macro-data-transition-indicators.html; "Freedom in the World 2015," Freedom House, https://freedomhouse.org/report/freedom-world/freedom-world-2015#.VOM_IrCUcok; and Polity IV 1946–2013, http://www.systemicpeace.org/polity/polity4x.htm

Notes: Freedom House ranks countries on a scale of 1 to 7, with 1 representing the most free and 7 the least free. Polity IV ranks countries on a scale of -10 to 10, which translates into autocracies (-10 to -6), anocracies (-5 to +5), and democracies (+6 to +10). Anocracies are hybrid regimes located in the gray zone between autocracy and democracy, and Polity IV further subdivides them into closed or open anocracy.

---

22   Shairbek Juraev, "Is Kyrgyzstan's New Political System Sustainable?," *PONARS Eurasia Policy Memo* No. 120, 2012, www.ponarseurasia.org/memo/kyrgyzstan's-new-political-system-sustainable.

*   Excludes Moldova, which has been a parliamentary form of government since 2000.
**   Ukraine's constitution was changed following the Orange Revolution, replacing the former presidential system with a presidential-parliamentary system in 2004. In 2010, another round of reforms under former President Yanukovych included measures that re-strengthened the executive. Kyrgyzstan's 2010 constitution specifies a mixed, presidential-parliamentary system, which replaced the country's previous presidential system.

As a result of dramatic constitutional changes in Kyrgyzstan and politics as usual in Kazakhstan, in 2012 (the year that our public opinion survey was administered), Freedom House declared Kyrgyzstan "partly free" and Kazakhstan "not free." According to Polity IV's analogous assessment, Kazakhstan was clearly an autocracy, while Kyrgyzstan was found to be an anocracy, a "mixed or incoherent authority regime" located closer to democracy than autocracy, but still falling short of the former. Nonetheless, Kazakhstan can still lay claim to being a more liberalized (or less autocratic) regime than many of its counterparts in the region. As Table 2 highlights, Kyrgyzstan, with a Freedom House score of 5.0 in 2012, is indeed more politically open and pluralistic than Kazakhstan. Yet, Kazakhstan's Freedom House score of 5.5 indicates that it, too, is more politically open and pluralistic than the other unfree/autocratic regimes in the region, including Russia.

Naturally, these differences in the political climate in Kazakhstan versus Kyrgyzstan are reflected in the two countries' media environments. Over the past two decades it is clear that Kyrgyzstan's media have — with a few exceptions — enjoyed greater freedom and played a larger role in political life than have their counterparts in Kazakhstan. The relatively better-off situation facing Kyrgyzstan's media comes into sharp focus if we look at trends over time. Table 3 summarizes the results of Reporters without Borders' Media Freedom Index for both countries from 2002, when the index was initiated, to 2012, when our survey was administered. The average score for Kyrgyzstan is about 11 points lower than that for Kazakhstan. This figure signifies that although neither can be considered to have a "free" mass media, the situation facing Kyrgyzstani media is closer to the ideal.

Table 3.   2002–2012 Media Freedom Scores, Kyrgyzstan and Kazakhstan compared

	2002	2003	2004	2005	2006	2007	2008	2009	2010	2011–12	Avg.
Kyrgyzstan	31.75	32	35.25	32	34	33.6	27	40	–	40	33.96
Kazakhstan	42	42.5	44.17	36.17	41	41.63	35.33	49.67	–	77.5	45.55

Source: "World Press Freedom Index," Reporters without Borders, http://rsf.org

Note: RSF scores countries on a scale of 0–100; scores closer to 0 indicate greater press freedom. Country scores are a composite of six indicators, including pluralism, media independence, environment and self-censorship, legislative framework, transparency, and infrastructure.

If we look at how sustainable independent media is as a business model, a similar trend emerges (Table 4). Although serious concerns about the media's long-term sustainability remain in both countries, Kyrgyzstan's average score during the period covered indicates that media have over time consistently been closer to "near sustainability" than in Kazakhstan. Undeniably, there have been constraints on Kyrgyz media freedom, but these take place alongside some progress toward "free-press advocacy [and] increased professionalism."[23] If we compare Kyrgyzstan's 2001 and 2012 scores, the degree of progress in a little over a decade is impressive: In 2001, the media were characterized as at the beginning stages of an "unsustainable, mixed system," but by 2012, as a whole media had come close to "near sustainability." Indeed, by 2014, Kyrgyzstan had reached "near sustainability," with a score of 2.11.[24] For the same years, Kazakhstan's scores fluctuated, but persistently stayed within the "unsustainable, mixed system" category, indicating little substantive change over time. It is only through understanding these overarching contexts that we can interpret citizens' media consumption and preferences. Before turning to our findings, however, we first describe the research design and methodology behind the study.

---

23   "Media Sustainability Index (MSI)," IREX, http://www.irex.
24   The Media Sustainability Index describes "near sustainability" as a score between 2 and 3. For more details see the notes associated with Table 4.

Table 4. 2001–2013 Media Sustainability Index Scores, Kyrgyzstan and Kazakhstan Compared

	2001	2002	2003	2004	2005	2006–07	2008	2009	2010	2011	2012	2013	Designation
Kyrgyzstan	1.29	1.62	1.84	2.08	1.78	1.97	1.78	1.93	1.92	1.62	1.89	1.79	Unsustainable
Kazakhstan	1.42	1.54	1.32	1.42	1.39	1.27	1.33	1.68	1.44	1.68	1.68	1.50	Unsustainable

Source: IREX, Media Sustainability Index, http://www.irex.org

Notes: IREX divides country scores as follows:

- Unsustainable, Anti-Free Press (0–1): Country does not meet or only minimally meets objectives. Government and laws actively hinder free media development, professionalism is low, and media-industry activity is minimal.
- Near sustainability (2–3): Country has progressed in meeting multiple objectives, with legal norms, professionalism and the business environment supportive of independent media. Advances have survived changes in government and have been codified in law and practice. However, more time may be needed to ensure that change is enduring and that increased professionalism and the media business environment are sustainable.
- Sustainable (3–4): Country has media that are considered generally professional, free, and sustainable, or to be approaching these objectives. Systems supporting independent media have survived multiple governments, economic fluctuations, and changes in public opinion or social conventions.

3. Methodology

Data

In fall 2012, the authors organized and oversaw nationally representative public opinion surveys in Kyrgyzstan and Kazakhstan. The questionnaire covers a broad range of socio-political and economic topics; in addition to our interest in media consumption, we incorporated other sets of questions that reflect theoretical and empirical debates in sociology, political science, and area studies. These include questions that tap into citizens' democratic (and "authoritarian") attitudes, perceptions of social and economic inequality, ideas about the role of government in the economy, attitudes toward religion and the role of religion in government, trust in institutions, and inter-generational social mobility. All questions were drawn from widely known and well-established surveys, including the International Social Justice Project (ISJP), the International Social Survey Program (ISSP),[25] the World Values Survey, and Afrobarometer. The use of pre-tested and commonly used questions was an intentional component of the study's design, as it both helps ensure reliable and valid measurement and enables theoretically intriguing comparisons of data collected in Central Asia to that collected elsewhere. Details of the research design and respondent selection follow below.

Research Design and Respondent Selection

It is important to note that efforts to organize nationally representative surveys in Central Asia must overcome formidable obstacles. Telephone-based surveys are not feasible because telephone coverage in most rural areas is scarce. As a result, face-to-face interviews must be conducted. However, the existing lists of residents, such as voter lists and address books, are outdated and incomplete. Thus, a sample of households, rather than a sample of individuals, is normally used. Yet, a comprehensive national list of households is not

---

25 Along with his keen encouragement, Dr. David Mason, who directed the ISJP effort in 13 countries during the 1990s, generously provided us with the English and Russian language questionnaires.

available in either country. Due to these constraints, the most widely used method for obtaining nationally representative data in both countries is a multistage stratified probability sample of households. This is the method utilized in the current study.

The first stage involved selection of cities, towns and villages from the existing list of settlements available from the State Statistical Agencies (*Goskomstat*) of both countries. To make the selection, all settlements were first classified into groups (strata) defined by region and population size. Both Kyrgyzstan and Kazakhstan are typically divided into five geographic regions: north, west, south, east, and central. Within each region, all settlements are classified into large urban (*oblast* capitals), other urban (other towns), and rural. This means that each of the five regions is further divided into three sub-strata. Within each region, a number of settlements from each sub-stratum were randomly selected. And within each settlement, the total number of interviews required was determined by the settlement's population size.

Following the selection of settlements and the determination of the number of interviews to be conducted, households were chosen using the random route sample method. Using this method, postal codes were first randomly chosen; similarly, streets within postal code areas were randomly selected; and, finally, actual households from each street were randomly selected. After a household was identified, respondents were chosen using the most recent/next birthday method. All adults aged 18 and older were eligible for participation.

Interviews in Kazakhstan were carried out by the Almaty-based BRIF Research Group. In Kyrgyzstan, the survey was conducted by the Bishkek-based El-Pikir Center for Public Opinion Research. Both organizations are recognized leaders in survey research in their respective countries and have extensive experience in conducting nationally representative surveys for domestic and foreign clients from the academic, government and private sectors. In addition, both have cultivated a network of trained interviewers for its data collection and employ comprehensive quality-control procedures to ensure valid responses.

A total of 3,000 face-to-face interviews were conducted with 1,500 interviews completed in each country. In Kazakhstan, 97 BRIF interviewers conducted the interviews in 150 sampling points covering all 14 oblasts. Average interview duration was about 45 minutes. The response rate for the Kazakhstan portion of the study equaled 60.1 percent. In Kyrgyzstan, 77 El-Pikir interviewers conducted the interviews in 153 sampling points covering all seven oblasts of the country. The average interview duration was about 50 minutes. The response rate for the Kyrgyzstan portion of the study equaled 89.6 percent. According to both survey research companies, these response rates are typical in their practice. The lower response rates in Kazakhstan are commonly attributed to growing weariness with survey researchers brought about by the recent proliferation of marketing studies. In Kyrgyzstan, fewer marketing studies take place due to a weak economy and, as a consequence, people are "unspoiled" by attention from researchers. Both companies reported some difficulty in accessing wealthy households, but this is a problem that is ubiquitous to survey research all over the world.

Measurement

We measure frequency of media consumption with the following question:

> *People learn what is going on in this country and the world from various sources. For each of the following sources, please indicate whether you use it to obtain information daily, several times per week, several times per month, monthly, less than monthly or never...*

The list of sources includes newspapers, magazines, television, radio, and the Internet. This question was followed by a second item asking respondents to indicate their *level of trust* for each of these sources on a scale of 1 to 5, where 1 stands for "completely mistrust" and 5 stands for "completely trust."

4. Results and Discussion

Convergence and Divergence in Media Consumption Patterns

In this section, we present survey results regarding frequency of media consumption by moving from the least to the most commonly used sources of news and information. As noted above, questions were asked about media usage across five categories: Internet, magazines/journals, radio, newspapers, and television (from least to most used, based on the survey results). For each source, respondents indicated a range of responses from "every day" to "never." In Kazakhstan, proportions of regular users of newspapers and the Internet (several times per week or more) are essentially tied at about 35 percent. In Kyrgyzstan, the Internet has yet to achieve parity with newspapers, as over 40 percent of respondents report using newspapers to learn about current events several times per week or more, while the corresponding number for Internet use stands at about 22 percent.

Of all five categories, the Internet is the only information source for which clear majorities of people in both Kyrgyzstan and Kazakhstan selected the option "never" (64.4 percent in Kyrgyzstan, and 53.3 percent in Kazakhstan). Approximately 34 percent of Kazakhstani respondents reported using the Internet for news and information several times per week or more, and this figure was much lower in Kyrgyzstan at about 22 percent. While the Internet as a source of information about news and current events seems to have progressed further in Kazakhstan than in Kyrgyzstan, its use for this particular purpose has yet to gain widespread acceptance in either society.

This finding is curious given the growth of the Internet in the region as a whole and, in particular, the strides that rates of computer ownership and Internet penetration have made in Kyrgyzstan and Kazakhstan. According to the World Bank, a little over half the population in Kazakhstan (or 54 out of every 100 people) and about 20 percent of the population in Kyrgyzstan (or 23.4 out of every 100 people) has access to the Internet, and this figure has increased from 17–18 users per 100 in both countries just five years ago.[26] In addition, a number of studies document the ways that artists, activists, and other grassroots groups are using the Internet in Kyrgyzstan to mobilize like-minded citizens behind similar causes and/or to disseminate information and news related to their cause.[27] One implication of these developments is that the Internet should be emerging as an important source of news and current events more broadly.

Our findings, in contrast, suggest that the overall growth in Internet use and expansion of specialized groups using social media might co-exist with a different dynamic taking place among the general population. On the one hand, it is evident that more and more people have access to the Internet each year and that certain social and political sub-groups/sub-cultures are Internet savvy in ways that facilitate political empowerment and information sharing, although perhaps in a limited way. On the other hand, our survey results highlight the fact that neither of these processes has, as of yet, had notable influence on societal patterns of Internet use. In other words, greater access and availability of locally generated content might not automatically translate into high levels of Internet use to obtain news and information. Instead, it is quite possible that the average user may be connecting to the Internet primarily for games and entertainment. Figure 2 shows the distribution of responses about use of Internet as a source of information about current events.

---

[26] "Internet Users (Per 100 People)," World Bank, data.worldbank.org/indicator/IT.NET.USER.P2.

[27] See, for example, Kulikova and Permutter, "Blogging Down the Dictator?"; Ramesh Srinavasian and Adam Fish, "Internet Authorship: Social and Political Implications within Kyrgyzstan," *Journal of Computer-Mediated Communication* 14:3 (2009): 559–80; and Wilkinson and Jetpyspayeva, "From Blogging Central Asia."

Figure 2. Internet Use, Kyrgyzstan and Kazakhstan Compared

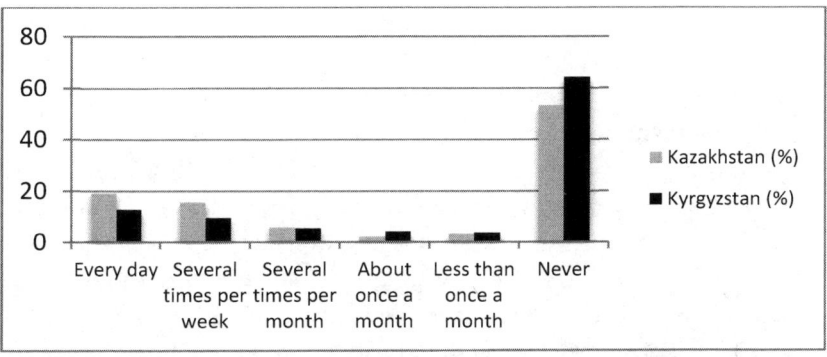

Source: Authors' data, 2012 Kazakhstan and Kyrgyzstan Survey

As is true of the Internet, magazines and journals are rarely read for their news content, and this is true in both countries. As Figure 3 shows, "never" was a modal response option in both countries at 39.4 percent in Kazakhstan and 47.9 percent in Kyrgyzstan. Because magazines are generally costly, target at a specialized (urban) audience, and/or tend to be geared more toward entertainment, this finding is not surprising. Instead, other, more widely available and affordable sources of information are likely to be tapped for news.

Figure 3. Magazine/Journal Use, Kyrgyzstan and Kazakhstan Compared

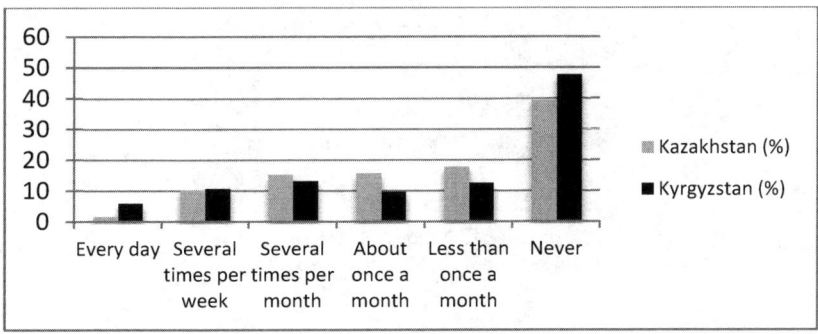

Source: Authors' data, 2012 Kazakhstan and Kyrgyzstan Survey

Survey results bear this out. In sharp contrast to the Internet and magazines/journals as news sources, people in both Kyrgyzstan and Kazakhstan are far more likely to refer to radio, newspapers, and television to learn about current events (see Figures 4 through 6). Turning first to radio in Figure 4, we see that reliance on this media format as a source of news and information differs considerably between Kazakhstan and Kyrgyzstan. Over one third of Kyrgyzstani respondents report daily use of radio, while the corresponding percentage in Kazakhstan stands at 16.5 percent. One might speculate that this is related to radio stations' news content. In Kyrgyzstan, for example, the *British Broadcasting Company* (*BBC*) and *Radio Azattyk* (the Kygyz Service of *Radio Free Europe/Radio Liberty*) have both been broadcast via radio and Internet instead of solely via the Internet, as is the case in Kazakhstan. In Kazakhstan, radio news tends to be limited to short hourly updates interspersed between other programming. This could also explain, at least in part, our finding that 37.1 percent of Kazakhstani respondents reported never turning to radio to learn about current events, while in Kyrgyzstan this response category was selected by 26.1 percent of respondents. Thus, it appears that radio is a more important source of news in Kyrgyzstan than in its larger, wealthier neighbor to the north.

Figure 4. Newspaper Use, Kyrgyzstan and Kazakhstan Compared

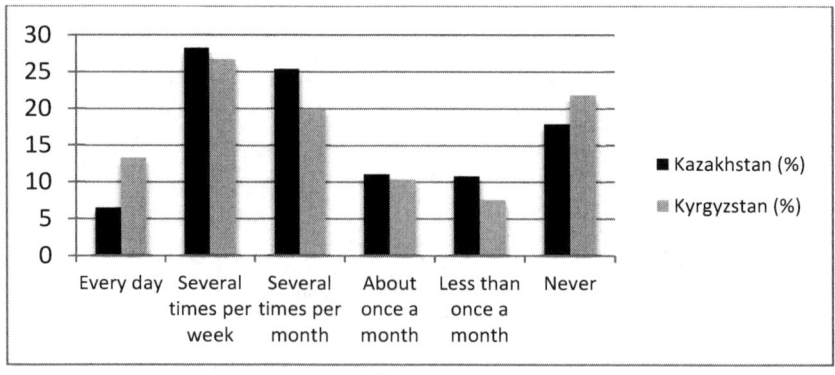

Source: Authors' data, 2012 Kazakhstan and Kyrgyzstan Survey

Even more so than radio, Kyrgyzstanis and Kazakhstanis in about equal measure readily turn to newspapers to learn about current events, as Figure 5 shows. Unlike patterns of radio use for informational purposes, patterns of newspaper use in the two societies are largely similar. In both countries, about 60 percent of respondents report reading newspapers at least several times per month. The only notable exception to the otherwise similar patterns of newspaper use in the two countries is the "every day" response category. In Kazakhstan, this response was chosen by 6.5 percent of respondents, while in Kyrgyzstan the share of daily newspaper readers jumps to 13.3 percent. Since most non-governmental newspapers are issued once or twice per week rather than daily—and sometimes are even more sporadically available for sale in stores and kiosks—it makes sense that fewer citizens are reading the news on a daily basis. Given a more independent press in Kyrgyzstan and the newspapers' association with particular political parties (or politically-minded owners), it also makes sense that newspapers would be a more robust source of information, debate, and opinion than their Kazakhstani counterparts.

Figure 5.   Radio Use, Kyrgyzstan and Kazakhstan Compared

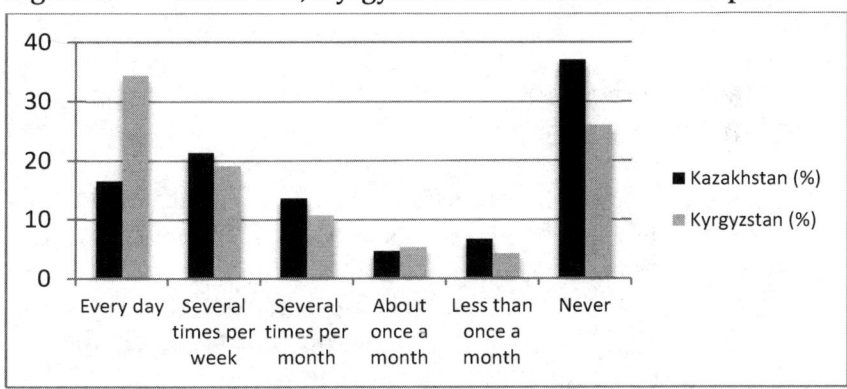

Source: Authors' data, 2012 Kazakhstan and Kyrgyzstan Survey

Finally, as Figure 6 demonstrates, the dominance of television in both countries' media markets is difficult to overstate. In Kazakhstan, 96.7 percent of respondents reported turning to television for news and information several times per week or more. In Kyrgyzstan the corresponding figure stands at 91 percent. Figure 6 shows the distribution of responses about use of TV as a source of information about current events.

Figure 6. Television Use, Kyrgyzstan and Kazakhstan Compared

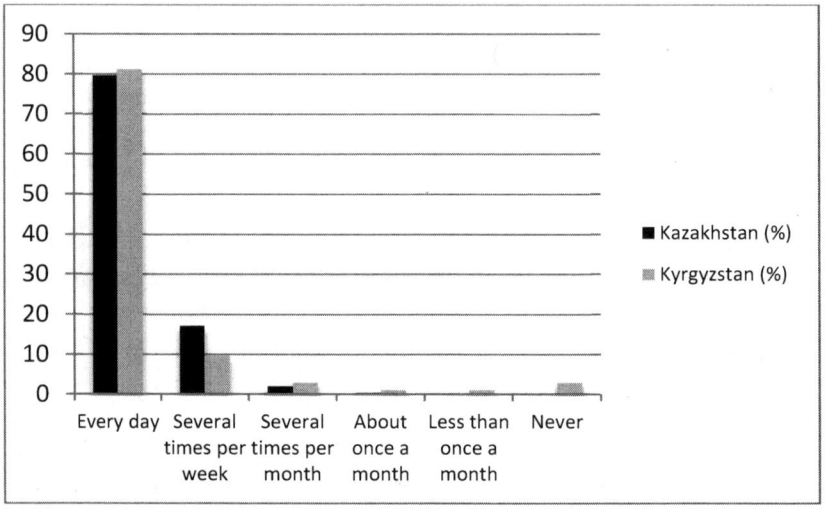

Source: Authors' data, 2012 Kazakhstan and Kyrgyzstan Survey

That television is the source of news and current events has positive and negative implications. On the upside, national television reaches rural areas, whereas other media forms such as print and Internet are often difficult to come by outside of major cities. Television thus has the power to create a unifying national narrative and to provide information to those who would otherwise be left uninformed. On the downside, state-owned television—and therefore state-sanctioned news—has by far the broadest reach. According to Freedom House, in Kyrgyzstan there are two state-owned television stations, both with national coverage. In theory at least, state-owned television is counterbalanced by the existence of independent regional television stations and the country's Public Broadcasting Corporation (PBC), which runs two national television stations. The PBC is overseen by a board whose members explicitly include "media experts, journalists, cultural figures, and civil society representatives," nominated by civil society, the president, and parliament, and subject to parliamentary approval.[28]

In Kazakhstan, however, opportunities for even limited diversity of views are made difficult by the pattern of media ownership there. As Freedom House explains, today all "[m]ajor broadcast media, especially national television networks, are partly or wholly owned by the state or by members or associates of the president's family."[29] It is worth noting that this was not always the case. During the 1990s and early 2000s there were a handful of independent regional (and national) media outlets that were unaffiliated with the center of power. Kazakhstan's relative media pluralism declined in the late 1990s and was finally eradicated around 2007. In a response to intra-elite conflicts that had periodically spilled over into the public sphere—and primarily via oligarch-owned media outlets—the Kazakhstani government by 2007 had renationalized or redistributed formerly independent television and radio outlets to close presidential allies.[30]

Finally, the dominance of televised news has an international component that cannot be ignored. Television stations and individual programming (both entertainment and news) from the Russian Federation are (re)broadcast in both countries. Because most television viewers continue to consume Russian-language news, viewers are heavily influenced by Russian perceptions of world and local events. Indeed, some reports find that Russian television stations and news programming are part and parcel of the Russian government's soft-power influence in the "near abroad," of which Kazakhstan and Kyrgyzstan are a central part.[31] The availability of Russian

---

28 "Freedom of the Press: Kyrgyzstan," Freedom House, http://www.freedomhouse.org/report/freedom-press/2012/kyrgyzstan-.VDJYaSmSy6o.
29 "Freedom of the Press: Kazakhstan," Freedom House, http://www.freedomhouse.org/report/freedom-press/2013/kazakhstan-.VDJY3SmSy6o.
30 Barbara Junisbai, "Oligarchs and Ownership: The Role of Financial-Industrial Groups in Controlling Kazakhstan's 'Independent' Media," in Eric Freedman and Richard Shafer, eds., *After the Czars and Commissars: Journalism in Authoritarian Post-Soviet Central Asia* (East Lansing, Mich.: Michigan State University Press, 2011).
31 Evgeny Troitsky, "UI Brief: Political Turbulence in Kyrgyzstan and Russian Foreign Policy," The Swedish Institute of International Affairs, http://ww

media means that news and current events tend to be biased toward pro-government perspectives, not only of the national governments in the capital cities Bishkek and Astana, but also in favor of interpretations proffered by an extra-national government located in Moscow. While these perspectives may at times be at odds with one another, it is nonetheless apparent that national and international state-owned mass media work in tandem to elevate officially sanctioned voices and agendas above the alternatives.

5. Convergence and Divergence in Patterns of Trust in Media

We now present the results regarding public trust in different media types, moving from least to most trusted sources of news and information. Table 5 depicts mean levels of trust in each source of media in the two societies (measured on a 5-point scale where 1="completely mistrust" and 5="completely trust"). The data demonstrate that magazines, newspapers, and television enjoy higher levels of trust in Kazakhstan than in Kyrgyzstan, while trust levels for radio and Internet are essentially tied. Respondents in Kyrgyzstan appear to be particularly skeptical about newspapers and magazines.

One way to interpret these differences is that Kyrgyzstanis have had more direct experience with and exposure to the rough-and-tumble world of political conflict, which has been covered to a much greater extent in the local media—and, more often than not, in newspapers, which tend to be highly politicized. It appears that open contestation—so often positively associated with a more pluralistic and democratic polity—may have a negative effect on public perceptions and thus reduce trust in Kyrgyzstan.[32] Due to ownership patterns and the dominance of state-owned or government-

---

    w.ui.se/upl/files/66217.pdf. See also Andrew E. Kramer, "Before Kyrgyz Uprising, Dose of Russian Soft Power," *New York Times*, 18 April 2010, http://www.nytimes.com/2010/04/19/world/asia/19kyrgyz.html?_r=0.

32   For a similar argument in the U.S. context regarding political conflict, public opinion, and trust in institutions, see John R. Hibbing and Elizabeth Theiss-Moore, *Stealth Democracy: Americans' Beliefs about How Government Should Work* (New York: Cambridge University Press, 2002).

affiliated media in Kazakhstan, open political conflict is far less likely to appear in any of the most commonly accessed news sources. Counterintuitively, because Kazakhstan's media are more tightly controlled and thus tend to shy away from coverage of political contestation, the resulting picture of a unified society may work to enhance overall public trust in the media as an institution.

Table 5. Comparison of 2012 Mean Rates of Trust in Media by Source

Source	Kazakhstan	Kyrgyzstan
Magazines	3.19	2.83
Newspapers	3.35	2.88
Radio	3.41	3.38
Internet	3.42	3.42
Television	3.73	3.45
Average Score	3.42	3.19

Source: Authors' data, 2012 Kazakhstan and Kyrgyzstan Survey
Notes: The question wording is, "How much do you personally trust the following sources of information...," followed by the list of media sources (magazine, newspapers, radio, etc.). Scores range from 1 to 5, where 1 stands for "completely mistrust" and 5 stands for "completely trust."

Another unexpected finding is highlighted in Table 5. Although the majority of respondents in Kyrgyzstan and Kazakhstan indicate that they never make use of the Internet as an information resource, they nonetheless place about as much trust in it as they do radio, a form of media that many people utilize on a regular basis. That the public trusts the Internet as much as they trust their two main news sources, radio and television, may signal a lack of differentiation between information resources.

Our results also indicate intriguing differences in how citizens perceive print versus electronic media. The public generally trusts radio and television at higher rates than they do the press (e.g., newspapers and magazines), and this pattern is predominant in Kyrgyzstan, where the mean for trust in print media is around 2.9 out of a maximum score of 5. These findings suggest that bias in television and radio programming tends to be more difficult for the average citizen to assess. As Nikolayenko's semi-structured interviews with adolescents in Russia and Ukraine reveal, respondents assume that it is harder to alter/doctor images than it is to manipulate newspaper coverage.[33] According to Nikolayenko, this assumption leads respondents to interpret televised images as more accurate and less biased than the text descriptions that appear in newspaper articles. A similar dynamic may be at play in Kazakhstan and Kyrgyzstan.

Additionally, if we recall the tight connection between politics and media in both countries, it makes sense that print media would be viewed with greater skepticism. That is, lower trust in newspapers is likely due to the fact that ownership patterns, political agendas, and party affiliations associated with print media are widely known and accepted realities on the ground. For example, certain print outlets are known to be associated with particular political parties in Kyrgyzstan and particular presidential associates in Kazakhstan.

As previously noted, Kazakhstan's electronic media tend to either be broadcast from the Russian Federation or are state-owned, which removes to some degree the sense that individual political players are "pulling the strings." Kazakh media ownership is further complicated because the true owners behind particular independent television and radio stations are not immediately transparent. According to one study of non-governmental media there, the opacity of ownership is a deliberate government strategy to keep nominally independent media under close unofficial control.[34] Ironically, such nuances may make it harder for average citizens to gauge bias in electronic media, and this more complex picture may be reflected in higher levels of public trust in television and radio.

6. Conclusions

In this chapter, we reported results from our survey of media consumption and levels of trust in Kazakhstan and Kyrgyzstan twenty years after the collapse of the Soviet Union. We found that in both

---

[33] Olena Nikolayenko, *Citizens in the Making in Post-Soviet States* (London: Routledge, 2011).
[34] Junisbai, "Oligarchs and Ownership."

countries television was the main go-to source for news and information about current events, while the Internet was least used. Despite these commonalities, relative trust in media differed between the two countries. Almost all media sources enjoyed lower levels of trust in Kyrgyzstan than in Kazakhstan, and the difference was especially pronounced in the case of print media. This finding was unexpected, since greater privatization, political freedom, media independence, and media sustainability in Kyrgyzstan are presumably associated with greater competition for readership/viewers. These factors should positively affect public trust in the quality of media sources due to improved journalistic professionalism, greater consumer choices, and improved access to alternative information.

To understand these differences in levels of trust in media, we look to differences in the overarching political climate. Competition among Kyrgyzstan's elite is public and at times fierce, and rival elites use independent and government media as a tool to sway public opinion. In Kazakhstan, in contrast, rarely is intra-elite contestation exposed in the official and nominally independent media. Paradoxically, open political competition and greater media independence in Kyrgyzstan may have a dampening effect on public trust, while in Kazakhstan behind-the-scenes political competition and controlled media appear to bolster it.

More generally, our survey results suggest that public trust in institutions may be lower in a polity characterized by greater political contestation and a more open and pluralistic mass media environment, in which media outlets are able to report and comment on contestation. Interpreted optimistically, it could be argued that a discerning and vigilant citizenry — one of the hallmarks of a democratic political culture — is emerging in Kyrgyzstan. As citizens gain more experience with democratic elections, debate, and related practices, they develop an appropriately critical outlook that scholars such as Larry Diamond and Robert Putnam argue to be crucial for consolidating and maintaining democracy.[35]

---

35 Larry Diamond, *Developing Democracy: Toward Consolidation* (Baltimore, Md.: Johns Hopkins University Press, 1999); Robert Putnam, *Bowling Alone: The*

However, survey results also indicate that the Kyrgyzstani public is not critical of media in equal measure. Similar to respondents in Kazaklucahstan, respondents in Kyrgyzstan are more likely to place their trust in image-based media (television and Internet) than they are to trust text-based media (newspapers and journals). If we recall that state-owned and/or Russian television broadcasts reach the widest audienceluca, a less optimistic view appears. That government and pro-government media are not only the primary sources of news and information, but also the most trusted sources, calls into doubt citizens' ability to respond critically to the officially sanctioned perspectives with which they are most frequently presented. In this way, less than democratic governments and (potential) autocratic leaders are well positioned to manipulate public opinion in their favor. As Morozov has demonstrated, governments around the globe use their media preeminence to entertain (and distract) the public, as well as ensure that the official version of events muffles alternatives.[36] Ironically, political leaders in both Kyrgyzstan's nascent democracy/"incoherent authority" regime and Kazakhstan's unfree/autocratic regime may in the end wield comparable influence over their mass publics, albeit by different mechanisms.

    Collapse and Revival of American Community (New York: Simon and Schuster, 2003).

36 Evgeny Morozov, *The Net Delusion: The Dark Side of Internet Freedom* (New York: PublicAffairs, 2011).

Networked Apathy: Georgian Party Politics and the Role of Social Media

Kornely Kakachia, Tbilisi State University; Tamara Pataraia, Caucasus Institute for Peace, Democracy and Development; and Michael Cecire, Foreign Policy Research Institute

Digital and Internet technologies are increasingly recognized as prominent tools for social and political mobilization.[1] The 2008 election victory of U.S. President Barack Obama appeared to signal a watershed moment as Internet technologies—particularly social media—likely played a uniquely pivotal role in marshaling citizen support and financial contributions.[2] The so-called "Arab Spring," a wave of people-power revolutions that swept across the Middle East and North Africa in 2010–2011, is often credited as another case study for the potentially powerful role of social media in social and political organization.[3] This notion is echoed in recent literature showing the potentially significant role that internet technology played in the outcome of multiparty democratic elections in Australia.[4]

---

1   The present study was conducted with the support of the Academic Swiss Caucasus Net (ASCN). The ASCN program is coordinated and operated by the Interfaculty Institute for Central and Eastern Europe (IICEE) at the University of Fribourg (Switzerland). It is initiated and supported by the Gebert Rüf Stiftung. The views expressed in this publication are those of the authors and do not necessarily represent opinions of the Gebert Rüf Stiftung and the University of Fribourg.

2   See David Carr, "How Obama Tapped Into Social Networks' Power," *New York Times*, 9 November 2008, http://www.nytimes.com/2008/11/10/business/media/10carr.html.

3   See, for example, Habibul Haque Khondker, "Role of the New Media in the Arab Spring," *Globalizations*, 8:5 (2011); and Ekaterina Stepanova, "The Role of Information Communication Technologies in the "Arab Spring", *PONARS Eurasia Policy Memo* No. 159, May 2011.

4   Rachel K. Gibson and Ian McAllister, "Do Online Election Campaigns Win Votes? The 2007 Australian 'YouTube' Election," *Political Communication* 28:2 (2011).

Studies of social media and political mobilization in post-communist Eurasia suggest that, in spite of levels of regional internet penetration at least generally comparable to those in the Middle East and North Africa, there is less evidence that internet technologies can currently play as significant a role as in the Middle East and North Africa or in liberal democratic societies. While the use of social media in the 2011 Russia protests highlights social media's ability to amplify discontent, the lack of apparent direct or indirect results undercuts hopes that the "Arab Spring" model of social media-based political mobilization is readily replicable.[5] In fact, internet technologies in some regimes appear to be increasingly as much a means of repression as liberation. "Networked authoritarianism," to borrow Rachel Mackinnon's description of social media-based repression in China,[6] is observed as an aspect of regime control, for example, in post-communist Azerbaijan.[7]

However, party politics in Georgia offers an altogether different type of test case. While it is a post-communist state with a profoundly personalized political system, Georgia has also historically inhabited the "middle ground" of regime typologies. Though there are indications that Georgia may be moving again toward democratization, it has generally fit the "competitive authoritarian" hybrid model proposed by Stephen Levitsky and Lucan Way.[8] And while post-independence Georgian regimes have consistently exhibited authoritarian tendencies to varying degrees, the country has also featured a degree of political competitiveness and pluralism that has set it apart from "classical" authoritarian regimes. Accordingly, Georgia would seem to offer an interesting milieu for the employment of Internet technologies and social media as tools for political mobilization.

---

5 Markku Lonkila, "Russian Protest On- and Offline: The role of social media in the Moscow opposition demonstrations in December 2011," *Briefing Paper* No. 98, The Finnish Institute of International Affairs, February 2012.

6 Rebecca MacKinnon, "China's 'Networked Authoritarianism'," *Journal of Democracy* 22:2 (April 2011).

7 Katy E. Pearce and Sarah Kendzior, "Networked Authoritarianism and Social Media in Azerbaijan," *Journal of Communication* 62:2 (April 2012).

8 Steven Levitsky and Lucan A. Way, "The Rise of Competitive Authoritarianism," *Journal of Democracy* 13:2 (April 2002).

This chapter considers the role of digital technology in Georgian party politics by examining social media activity related to the October 2012 Georgian parliamentary elections. The analysis focuses on the role of social media campaigns in the outcome of the election and how they contributed to the success of new actors emerging in the party system.

The methodology is primarily qualitative. We identified eleven prominent political parties in Georgia based on their political activities and successful electoral campaigns. We then analyzed and scored the parties' website and social media content for comparative purposes. Researchers examined information published on party websites regarding: ideology; internal management; strategies for recruiting new members; human resource management and career development policies; public relations strategies; capacity for political analysis; and the way in which political parties registered members, supporters, and their interaction with online users. The researchers also monitored the Facebook activity of the political parties and their leaders and carried out a comparative analysis of their social media campaigns during the 2012 parliamentary election. Finally, we conducted 75 in-depth interviews (55 before the election and 20 afterwards) with social media experts, bloggers, political scientists, and political party leaders.

The chapter proceeds in the following way. First, we provide an overview of Georgian party politics. Second, we survey the level of media freedom in Georgia. Third, we examine the state of the political parties' web sites. Fourth, we examine how politicians use social media. The conclusion examines the current impact of on-line strategies and their potential evolution.

1. Overview of Georgian Party Politics

In spite of near-universal support for democratization among Georgian politicians,[9] inexperience and the lack of a democratic political culture posed a challenge to Georgia's democratic consolidation.

---

9 S. Tsereteli-Stephens, "Caucasus Barometer: Rule of Law in Georgia — Opinion and Attitudes of the Population," CRRC-Georgia, http://crrccenters.org/activities/reports/.

These lacuna are particularly glaring in Georgian party politics. While the typical role of political parties in democratic systems is to articulate and aggregate group preferences — and hold elected officials accountable — a comparable, mature system does not currently exist in Georgia.

Georgian political dynamics appear to approximate that of many other post-communist systems in Eastern Europe, which feature relatively low voter turnout (46.6 percent in Georgia's 2013 presidential election), little interest in political parties, weak partisan loyalty, and minimal connection among parties and civil society.[10] The formal framework of multi-party politics is at odds with Georgia's profoundly personalized party politics, in which stable political constituencies have been traditionally absent. In fact, politics is so personalized that significant divergences in political opinion often go unnoticed.[11] The fact that almost all parties are founded on the basis of a personality or group of personalities helps to explain why there are more than 100 registered political organizations. This vast number of parties often causes the Georgian population to be more inclined to vote for candidates on the basis of personality and charisma — or, alternatively, to simply vote against the current government to express dissatisfaction — rather than because of political issues.[12]

A lack of members and loyal supporters makes it difficult for parties to articulate and aggregate preferences. Some commentators on Georgian politics argue that political parties have not grown out of social cleavages and thus do not represent large segments of

---

[10] For a detailed account on Eastern European party politics see: Gábor Tóka, "Political Parties in East Central Europe," in Larry Diamond, Marc F. Plattner, Yun-han Chu, and Hung-mao Tien, eds., *Consolidating the Third Wave Democracies: Themes and Perspectives* (Baltimore, MD: Johns Hopkins University Press, 1997), 93–134.

[11] Ilia Roubanis, "Georgia's pluralistic feudalism: a frontline report," OpenDemocracy.net, 3 July 2009, http://www.opendemocracy.net/article/georgia-pluralistic-feudalism.

[12] Konstantine Kandelaki, "Developing New Rules in the Old Environment: Local Government in Georgia," Local Government and Public Service Reform Initiative (Open Society Institute), http://unpan1.un.org/intradoc/groups/public/documents/apcity/unpan008027.pdf.

society—though they may articulate their sentiments—and are difficult to place on the left-right spectrum of classical political ideologies.[13] Charisma and populism fill the void left by the lack of party structures and programs. Competition among parties is often less about policies and primarily runs along a pro-government/anti-government fault line.

Moreover, Georgian political parties have persistently failed to satisfactorily perform functions that are associated with political parties in established democracies, such as representing groups in society, aggregating interests, or mobilizing voters.[14] The failure to express clear and consistent policies and the tendency to engage in populist action can also be explained by an inclination in Georgian politics towards a cult of personality.[15] As a result, many politicians appear to prefer an image of strength over reason or consistency. In general, this tendency has made presidential elections a poor stimulant for party politics, since competitions have historically been framed as contests of personality. Instead, parliamentary or local elections are the primary arenas in which political parties compete for votes.[16]

Many of the people we interviewed suspect that the weak links between parties and social and economic interest groups are to blame for parties' generally low level of popularity. Unlike in many western European democracies, for example, trade unions appear to lack widespread public trust in Georgia. According to regular surveys conducted by the International Republican Institute (IRI), levels of confidence in trade unions are consistently low, although there is a slight upward trend.[17] In the most recent survey,

---

13 Max Bader, "Fluid Party Politics and the Challenge for Democracy Assistance in Georgia," *Caucasian Review of International Affairs* 2:2 (Spring 2008).
14 Bader, "Fluid Party Politics," 84.
15 See George Welton, "Evaluating the Failure to Oppose: Political Opposition in Post-Revolutionary Georgia," GeoWel Research Georgia, http://www.geowel.org/index.php?article_id=20&clang=0.
16 For a detailed analysis of Georgian party politics, see Ghia Nodia and Alvaro Pinto Scholbach, eds., *The Political Landscape of Georgia: Achievements, Challenges and Prospects* (Delft: Eburon, 2006).
17 "Georgia Report: The Georgian Trade Union Movement," Transparency International, February 2010.

trade unions (with just 21 percent approval) are the second least trusted institution of the 16 included in the survey—beating only the mafia.[18]

2. Challenges to Media Freedom in Georgia

In Georgia, the right to access information without political censorship is enshrined in the Constitution as well as the law on Freedom of Speech and Expression, adopted by the Georgian parliament in 2004. The law brought the country closer to European standards because it decriminalized slander and shifted responsibility for the burden of proof entirely onto plaintiffs. However, it could not ensure editorial freedom for television broadcasters.

In the following years, and especially after 2007, the government made repeated attempts to enforce government control over private TV channels and other broadcasters in Georgia. These tendencies were reinforced after the Russia–Georgia war in August 2008, when the government introduced a strict information policy and strengthened its influence over the national broadcasters. During this period, national television companies came under increased pressure from the government, which sought to reduce critical reporting and silence opposition voices. However, smaller TV companies, which broadcast in a limited area, were able to continue their operations as usual, a fact that helped the Georgian government to maintain its image for protecting media freedom within the international community.

Until 2012, the National Communication Commission (NCC) was the government's primary tool to maintain political control over the media. However, it failed to adhere to the principle of political neutrality and abused its power by manipulating the media regulation process. For instance, several new pro-government TV channels (*Real TV, Region TV*) began to broadcast nationwide during this period even though they had no broadcasting licenses. At

---

18   The church, by contrast, enjoys 91 percent trust and parliament 41 percent. The 2009 figures are a relative improvement. According to the June 2005 survey, Georgians were more likely to consult local mafia bosses for help than their trade union, which appeared at the bottom of the survey.

the same time, the NCC denied several license applications from private TV companies. Political influence on the NCC can also be seen in the fact that the NCC chairman had business interests in one of the pro-government TV companies and in an advertising company that had exclusive rights to produce and run TV commercials.

Between 2009 and 2012, Georgia's foreign partners (the USA and the EU) and international organizations (OSCE, NATO) as well as national and international non-governmental organizations (NGOs) repeatedly called for media reforms. Thanks to their efforts and advocacy, Georgia made numerous amendments to Georgian legislation in 2008–2012, including changing the law on broadcasting on April 8, 2011. However, in 2012, Freedom House reported that national television "is widely perceived as biased in favor of the government." The report also noted that TV channels with a limited broadcasting area supported the opposition. The 2012 developments confirmed that the government was not ready to reverse its media policy decisions as it made continued attempts to increase control over information delivered to the Georgian public. Immediately before the election campaign started, the most popular and largest cable TV operators (their owners were widely viewed as being government supporters) excluded pro-opposition channels from their portfolio, significantly curbing access to pro-opposition media for a considerable number of Georgian citizens. In response, several Georgian civil sector organizations launched a large-scale campaign, entitled "This Affects You Too." The popularity of the campaign and international pressure in support of media freedom before the elections led to important amendments to the legislation. Namely, on June 29, 2012, parliament adopted the so-called "must carry, must offer" principle, which obliged all cable TV operators to broadcast all Georgian TV companies for 60 days before the election.

These reforms seemed to have some impact. According to reports published in September 2012 by two international organizations—the Parliamentary Assembly of the Council of Europe (PACE) and the OSCE's Office for Democratic Institutions and Human Rights (ODIHR)—the pre-election media environment in Georgia prior to the parliamentary elections on 1 October 2012 was "competitive," albeit "polarized." PACE welcomed the endorsement of "Must Carry" rules that improved pluralism in the country's media environment. The OSCE/ODIHR interim report, covering the period between August 22 and September 5, 2012, found that Georgian media outlets were polarized according to political outlook and lacking in independent editorial policies.[19]

Politicians in Georgia understand the level of influence traditional media retains in the formation of public perceptions. This influence is especially relevant for Georgia where television remains the main source of news for about 80 percent of Georgian citizens residing in the capital and 92 percent of the rural population. Even in Tbilisi, just 11 percent of people surveyed in 2011 said that the Internet represents their main source of information.[20] The 2011 media survey data also indicates that a large portion of the Georgian public is critical of the current state of affairs in the media, as about 42 percent of the Georgian adult population said they thought there was no freedom of speech in Georgia as opposed to 34 percent who said that there was (25 percent did not know or refused to answer).[21] At the same time, there are indications that public sentiment is shifting on this count. In a November 2012 poll conducted by the National Democratic Institute, 43 percent of respondents reported that freedom of speech was improving since October 2012. Another 49 percent said the press freedom had stayed the same. Only 1 percent said the situation was getting worse; 6 percent responded that they did not know.[22]

Nonetheless, open questions remain over the freedom of the media in Georgia. Under such circumstances, unrestricted access to the Internet and the free dissemination of online news are especially

---

19   "CACI Analyst," Central Asia Caucasus Institute, http://www.cacianalyst.org/?q=node/5843.
20   "Media Survey 2011," Caucasus Research Resources Centre (CRRC), http://caucasusbarometer.org/en/me2011ge/codebook.
21   "Media Survey 2011," Caucasus Research Resources Centre.
22   "Public attitudes in Georgia, November 2013," National Democratic Institute, http://www.civil.ge/files/files/2013/NDI-November2013-Survey.pdf.

important. The Internet provides traditional media and news agencies with an opportunity to disseminate their information online more freely and bypass traditional barriers.

Access to social networks is unrestricted in Georgia and the Georgian government does not censor the Internet. This was a contributing factor to Freedom House's decision to upgrade Georgia's Internet freedom ranking from "partly free" in 2011 to "fully free" in 2012. Internet freedom was a subject of heated public debate in Georgia in 2011–2012. One of the most actively debated disputes was a lawsuit against the Georgian parliament brought to the Constitutional Court in 2011 by the Georgian Young Lawyers Association (GYLA), a domestic human rights NGO. GYLA appealed against the newly adopted law that gave the authorities the power to monitor all Internet activities, including private online communication, without a court warrant. GYLA argued that such monitoring was a blatant infringement of the right to privacy guaranteed by article 20 of Georgia's Constitution. After hearing the case on October 24, 2012 (immediately after the new government came to power following the 1 October parliamentary elections), the Constitutional Court ruled in favor of GYLA, emphasizing that the law did not provide any mechanisms to ensure the protection of the right to privacy and prevent unauthorized monitoring of internet activities, including private online communication, by law-enforcement bodies without a court warrant.

Overall, few media outlets provided diversified and politically neutral news for Georgian citizens prior to the 2012 parliamentary elections. Among these relatively free sources were the Internet and a number of private newspapers with central and regional coverage, which had editorial independence but limited circulations (2 percent of the population). Accordingly, the next section analyzes some statistical data to show how actively Georgian citizens were engaged in social media prior to the October 2012 parliamentary elections.

3. Internet and Social Media in Georgia

According to official statistics, Georgia's population is estimated to be 4,497,600 people,[23] more than 1,300,000 of whom had access to the Internet by August 2012.[24] A 2011 report by the NCC[25] found that the number of internet users is increasing by 3 percent-5 percent every year. If this trend continues unabated, in several years, the internet will likely have a noticeable impact on Georgian public life. Experts claim that when at least 50 percent of a country's population—the amount described as a critical mass—obtains access to the World Wide Web, the internet will have sufficient influence to shape public opinion.[26] This is not yet the case in Georgia, where the number of internet users was approximately 29 percent of the country's population in 2012.[27]

Despite the growing number of Internet retail subscribers in Georgia, a limited number of people use the Internet every day and are actively engaged in social media. According to the Caucasus Research Resource Centre (CRRC) survey, *Caucasus Barometer 2011*, less than 25 percent of the Georgian adult population uses the Internet on a daily basis. Moreover, 49 percent of the population has never used the Internet, and 6 percent has no idea what the Internet is (see Figure 1).[28]

---

23 For further details, see "Main statistics: Population," National Statistics Office of Georgia, http://geostat.ge/index.php?action=page&p_id=152&lang=eng.
24 "Georgia," Internet World Statistics, http://www.internetworldstats.com/asia.htm#ge.
25 "Annual Report 2011," Georgian National Communications Commission, http://www.gncc.ge/files/3100_2949_314871_1.pdf.
26 Nick Anstead and Andrew Chadwick, "Parties, election campaigning and the internet," in Andrew Chadwick and Philip N. Howard, eds., *Routledge handbook of Internet politics* (London: Routledge, 2009), 56.
27 "Georgia," Internet World Statistics.
28 "2011 Caucasus Barometer," Caucasus Research Resource Centers, http://www.crrccenters.org/caucasusbarometer/.

Figure 1. Frequency of Internet Use in Georgia in 2011, Percent

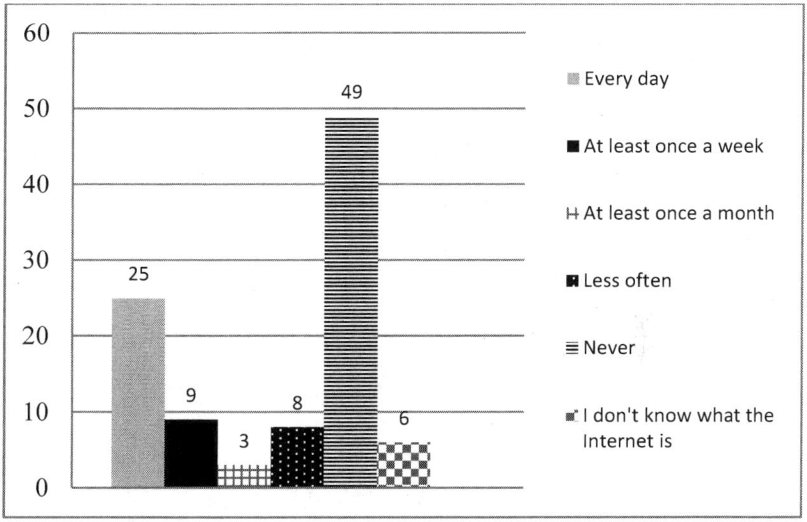

Category	Percent
Every day	25
At least once a week	9
At least once a month	3
Less often	8
Never	49
I don't know what the Internet is	6

Source: Caucasus Research Resources Centre (CRRC)

Further assessment of the same survey results shows that 34 percent of the Georgian adult population has regular opportunities to use the Internet. Taking into account the official 2012 figures that put the number of Georgia's adults aged 18 and over at 3,433,000,[29] it can be concluded that approximately 800,000 users access the internet often, and approximately half of that number surf the web from time to time (once a week or once a month). Among regular Internet users (daily or once a week), who constitute 34 percent of the country's adult population, 26 percent said that Facebook was their first choice for socializing online (Figure 2). Thus, approximately 330,255 adult internet users spend most of their online time on Facebook.

---

29   "GeoStat data 2012," National Statistics Office of Georgia, http://www.geostat.ge/?action=page&p_id=151&lang=geo.

Figure 2. Most Frequent Internet Activities — Use of Facebook, Percent

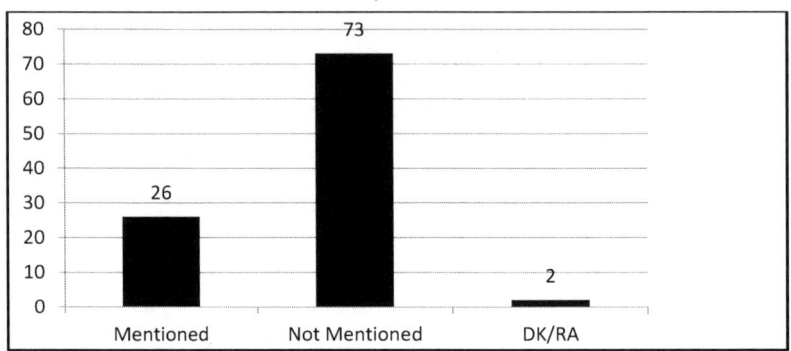

Source: CRRC, Caucasus Barometer 2011
(The question was asked to respondents who use the Internet)

The above data allows us to develop a general view about Internet usage tendencies in Georgia and suggests that Facebook is the most popular social network in Georgia. One of the main reasons of its popularity is that it offers a Georgian language interface created for and used by native speakers (the language barrier limits the Georgian public's interest in the internet for other purposes, such as eBay, YouTube, and other sites, though Internet banking services are widely accessed by the public). The share of active Facebook users in Georgia is not high. They represent only a tiny fraction of all Internet users. Of these, approximately 251,000 are from the 18–35 age group and around 76,000 are in their 50s.

Figure 3. Relative Numbers of Internet Users

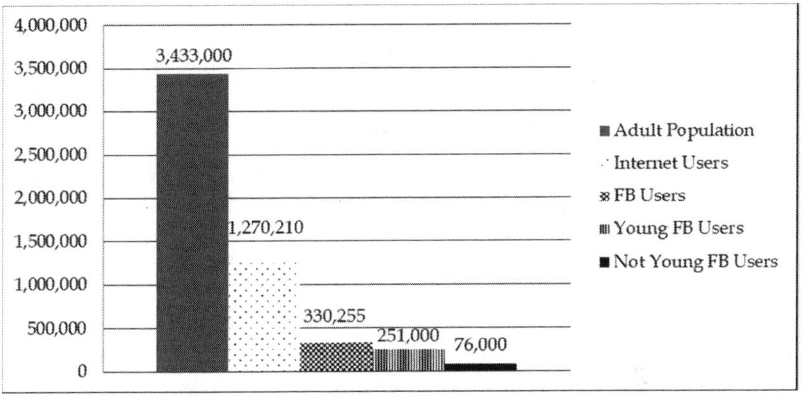

- Adult Population: 3,433,000
- Internet Users: 1,270,210
- FB Users: 330,255
- Young FB Users: 251,000
- Not Young FB Users: 76,000

Source: CRRC, Caucasus Barometer 2011

CRRC's Caucasus Barometer 2011 allows us to identify the reasons why the majority of the Georgian adult population remains offline (Figure 3). According to the survey results, the main reason is that a considerable number of Georgian residents do not have computers and most of them also lack computer knowledge and skills. In addition, the lack of reliable Internet access remains a problem for many Georgian residents, especially for those who reside in rural areas.

Another social network, Twitter, has fewer users in Georgia. In the last two years, only Beeline, a mobile operator with the poorest coverage in Georgia, had mobile Twitter support. In 2012, the top two Georgian mobile operators, Geocell and Magti, followed suit and offered this service. As a result, Georgian customers are now able to send free-of-charge SMS messages via Twitter to multiple recipients simultaneously. However, Twitter does not recognize Georgian fonts, so it has rather low popularity in Georgia.

A comparative analysis of the Twitter accounts of the Georgian president, the leader of the former ruling party, and his opponent, the opposition leader and now prime minister, in the post-election period (after October 2012) can help to assess the popularity of Twitter in Georgia. The Georgian president's account has only 7,221 friends and 59 followers, and most of them add comments in English—there are few comments in Georgian (as of 1 May 2013).

Prior to April 2012, the Georgian president had published only 776 Twitter messages that were commented on by some of the followers. In contrast, the Georgian prime minister's Twitter account has 22,132 followers, although it had not been updated since November 2012 (as of 1 May 2013). Before the elections, the former Prime Minister Bidzina Ivanishvili (then the leader of the opposition) had published only some 870 Twitter messages, most of them in English. This means that neither the president nor the current prime minister consider Georgian Twitter users their main target audience. The prevalence of English messages suggests that both tend to use their Twitter accounts to promote their views and ideas abroad rather than at home. As one of the popular party PR group members noted, through tweets, Georgian political parties "target their international partners and foreign friends more than Georgian followers and party supporters."[30] The Georgian experts who are active in social media and who were interviewed during the research suggested that given its first mover's advantage in 2010-2011, few other social networks will be able to challenge Facebook's popularity in Georgia.

4. Political Parties on the Internet Prior to the 2012 Parliamentary Elections

Well before the October 2012 parliamentary elections in Georgia, it was no longer a novelty for political parties to have websites. In fact, our survey results show that, by early 2012, the best established political parties all maintained functional websites. Only one major political party, the Georgian Dream party, had no official website at that time as it had not yet been officially founded (it was founded on April 19, 2012).

The survey of political parties' websites revealed that parties tend to publish mostly static and general information on their websites which does not need regular updating. The websites were not helpful in understanding what ideological differences exist be-

---

30   Interview conducted with G. P., male, 29 April 2013.

tween the parties. The sites generally limited themselves to publishing mission statements and a rather general description of the party's objectives and priorities. But generally, there were no policy declarations that reflected the party's ideology or specific program. The Free Democrats stood out among the political parties in that they specified at least some of their sectoral political programs. Beyond that, the Republican Party was the only party to publish its election program online for the 2008 parliamentary elections. In 2006, the site had published a "Republican Choice" policy paper.

While many campaign websites now routinely include interactive features, a survey of Georgian political party websites showed that the Georgian parties are usually passive online and do not use their websites to communicate with members and supporters efficiently. The websites did not provide information about the results of public meetings and sometimes did not offer any opportunity to submit feedback at all. In most cases, the websites provided only a party email address and telephone number as a means of communication, leaving it unclear who was responsible for communicating with potential supporters and members. The website of the former ruling party, the United National Movement, was a clear example of such one-sided communication. As a rule, users were able to send their greetings, but there were no feedback opportunities for questions and complaints.

Levels of participation in online polls were also rather low. Political parties rarely included such features on their websites. For instance, only about 900 users took part in an opinion poll on the Labor Party's website in February 2012. The National Forum conducted another poll with a single question: "Do you think it is necessary to change the election law?" which garnered responses from only about 1,600 users.

Only four out of ten political parties provided online party membership application forms on their websites. These parties were the National Forum, Free Democrats, Labor Party, and Christian Democrats. None of them offered registration for supporters and none, including the former ruling party, published information about the number of members and supporters by city or region. Only the websites of the United National Movement, and to a lesser extent, the Labor Party and New Rights had information about the location of their regional offices. All of these features indicate that most Georgian political parties have not viewed information and communication technology as a means of attracting additional supporters.

Parties have not tried to make the donation process more transparent through their websites, which do not provide much data on fundraising. Only the United National Movement and Christian Democrat websites provide data about the names and addresses of donor companies and the amount of each donation. It is noteworthy that financial declarations of Georgian political parties are freely available—they are published annually on the internet and can be accessed by everyone. However, some political parties prefer not to publish such information on their websites. For instance, six member parties of the Georgian Dream coalition received a combined total in donations of 4,607,000 GEL in 2012 (except August–September), while the United National Movement raised 13,434,000 GEL; the Christian Democrats received 961,000 GEL, and the Labor Party was given 337,000 GEL.[31] (The 2012 Georgian budget totalled 7 billion GEL (4.3 billion USD), while GDP amounted to 26.1 billion GEL). A breakdown of the expenditure shows that the political parties directed most of their funds to pay for office rent, communication costs, advertising, and wages. Political associations allocated the biggest chunk of their money, 81 percent on average, to TV political ads, while online ads were at the bottom of their priorities. In fact, only two political parties—he Free Democrats and United National Movement—used Internet ads, but on a limited scale.[32] This data indicates that political parties do not pay much attention to their activities on the Internet and they do not think that it is worth paying for online advertising in their campaign. According to several well known politicians, and verified

---

[31] "Georgia: Finances of Political Parties 2012," Transparency International, http://transparency.ge/post/report/akhali-angarishshi-politikuri-partieb is-finansebi-12-4-13.

[32] "Georgia, Finances of Political Parties 2012," Transparency International.

through regular polling, the internet in Georgia is still only accessed by a limited proportion of the population.

Thus, by the beginning of 2012 almost all Georgian political parties had their own websites, but, after examining them, it was impossible to define which was more sustainable in terms of institutional and financial resources The content of all the sites was largely static, general and ideologically vague. The websites were rarely updated or used for the distribution of information.

5. Political Parties on Facebook

Social media was especially important during the run-up to the October 2012 parliamentary elections in Georgia because the level of media independence in Georgia fell short of international standards during this period. Almost all the political parties that participated in our survey clearly intended to present their programs to a wider audience with the help of social media and social networks. The level of political party leaders' activity on Facebook was also quite high and they followed communication strategies similar to those of their political parties. It was evident that Georgian political parties preferred to promote the personalities of their leaders rather than their political programs, ideologies, or policies. These leaders also have personal Facebook accounts which they use to lead campaigns on behalf of their political parties. This is indicative of the personalized nature of politics in Georgia (Figure 4).

Figure 4. Politics is Highly Personalised in Georgia (Number of Likes, 09/18/2013)

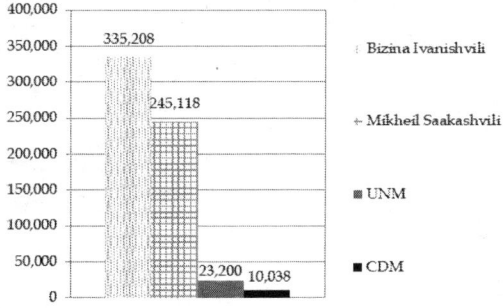

Source: Author's own calculation

The two most well-known leaders on the political scene, Mikheil Saakashvili (United National Movement) and his main political opponent Bidzina Ivanishvili (Georgian Dream coalition), both had active and well-maintained Facebook accounts: content was regularly updated, campaign tours were extensively covered and photo materials provided. Other political actors—Irakli Alasania (leader of the Free Democrats), Davit Usupashvili (leader of the Republican Party), Davit Gamkrelidze (New Rights Party), Gubaz Sanikidze (National Forum), and Zviad Dzidziguri (Conservative Party) also had active Facebook accounts. As the monitoring showed, the parties with youth-dominated governing bodies appeared to be more aware of the advantages of social media and more motivated to overcome the negative consequences of limited access to traditional media sources. Parties governed by older generation leaders lacked this knowledge and their attitudes were different.

As one interviewee put it: "We, members of the youth wing, pay significant attention to social media, because we think that this is the most flexible and fast way to communicate with young people."[33]

Another expert interviewed during the research noted that Georgian political parties were seen not as organizations with a certain ideology and agenda, but as groups of popular leaders. Financially strong political parties have unlimited access to all available traditional media sources and dominate the market, which gives additional impetus to less well financed political parties to be interested in social media:

> [Facebook] is necessary to disseminate ideas; this is especially true in the Georgian context. Here we have propaganda channels. The [traditional] mass media is controlled by either the government, or an oligarch. Thus, social media is especially important for others, which helps them to share their views and propagate ideas.[34]

In short, political parties, which have limited access to traditional media, "try to publish news on Facebook and communicate with

---

33 Interview conducted with T. Z., male, 1 June 2012.
34 Interview conducted with G. G. male, 28 April 2012.

the public through the youth."³⁵ According to political party representatives interviewed during the research, it is not common for Internet users to join political parties via social media. Most newcomers to politics make their choice based on their involvement during electoral campaigns. Social media is more useful for political parties in opening up communication channels with the wider public and strengthening contacts among existing party members.

Information on the campaigns of political parties is usually planned and published by a couple of network administrators working in party structures. Most of them limit their involvement to the publication of news reports/photos of political party events or live stream reports on press-conferences that involve the appearance of political leaders in social media.³⁶

Because Internet services are quite expensive and less accessible in many rural regions of Georgia, political parties are motivated to develop a more active campaign and help young people residing in Georgian villages to become more actively involved in social networks, including mobile services. Said one interviewee: "We have a project in which we teach youth how to use modern technologies and receive alternative information."³⁷

Political party representatives admitted that the reason why political parties have become more actively engaged in social networking is partly due to the fact that foreign experts have promoted the idea among political parties and encouraged them to be active in social media. In recent years, foreign donors have worked actively on capacity building among Georgian political parties. Various democracy promotion organizations, such as the National Democratic Institute (NDI), the International Republican Institute (IRI), and the Netherlands Institute for Multiparty Democracy (NIMD) have been involved in the development of democratic institutions in Georgia within the framework of EU and US state assistance programs.

---

35   Interview conducted with I. J., male, 1 May 2012.
36   Interview conducted with I. K., male, 1 May 2012.
37   Interview conducted with T. Z. male, 1 June 2012.

According to the assessment of these donor organizations, political parties in Georgia face several continuous challenges, including restrictions on media independence and a shortage of funds. Accordingly, they aim to help parties develop structures and capacities that will enable them to improve their performance and to function at a high level. Georgian politicians, members of different political parties, and representatives of youth wings had opportunities to attend trainings, seminars and discussion meetings organized by donors and devoted to social media, blogs, and networking. They were given the chance to establish new communication channels utilizing social media, help the public to receive alternative information, and express their critical views in the social media.

Georgian politicians interviewed during the research admitted that, had they received stronger financial support, almost all political parties would have been interested in establishing much more intensive and viable contacts with voters. One of the experts interviewed also noted that:

> Saakashvili and Ivanishvili have well paid consultants working not only on the Georgian [social media] market, but they [Saakashvili and Ivanishvili] pay a lot of money to write articles in foreign newspapers.[38]
> I know that the president's [Saakashvili's Facebook] page, whether you believe it or not, works very well. They have brought in foreign experts, consultants, who lead (election) campaigns and conduct strategic planning. This is not necessary in the Georgian context, because we have experienced people in Georgia, who have the same level of experience as foreigners. But we have a tendency in Georgia to trust foreigners more than local experts...and it works well.[39]

6. Online Feedback, Live Stream, Conferences, Ads, and Likes

An analysis of the political parties' Facebook accounts revealed that the Georgian political parties rarely utilized feedback mechanisms afforded by social media. Parties almost never used social networks for opinion polls. Moreover, they often deleted negative comments

---

38 Interview conducted with T. B. male, 30 May 2012.
39 Interview conducted with S. L., male, 2 June 2012.

on Facebook without responding to them. "[Negative feedback] may be removed, but information is received and reviewed. After we solicited questions for Bidzina Ivanishvili, the received questions were collected, and responses were prepared later,"[40] explained one respondent.

The review of the politicians' performance also showed that in response to any criticism directed at a political party, supporters would immediately set up fake or real accounts on forum pages or Facebook to unleash their rage on the critics. In the words of one interviewee:

> If you open, for example, the wall of Georgian Dream and write something which is unacceptable for someone, supporters will 'stone' you. They would certainly remove your comments, and this is true for both sides (for presidential supporters and opposition leader supporters). If comments are not removed, you will be stoned.[41]

During the survey interviews, politicians reported being especially interested in reading negative comments. They said that they all read these comments and only then allowed Facebook page administrators to remove them.[42] However, they were not very active and did not enter into interactive dialogue with their subscribers, even during the electoral campaign for the October 2012 parliamentary elections. Political leaders' Facebook pages used a limited number of applications, such as petitions and online forums. The most popular activities on the Facebook pages of political parties were postings of photos and sharing information from materials broadcast in traditional media. These types of information were formal and official. Accordingly, the most numerous statuses and shared info were on the political subjects that dominated in the traditional media. Political parties devoted limited human and material resources to conducting comprehensive election campaigns through social media. Many political leaders admitted that electoral campaigns conducted through social media were new experiences for them

---

40   Interview conducted with T. Z.
41   Interview conducted with E. P., female, 2 June 2012.
42   Interview conducted with N. S., female, 17 May 2012.

and that they learned to achieve political objectives through Facebook and other social media platforms' applications only during the campaign.

The procedures followed by organizers during political party leaders' online conferences did not significantly differ from similar conferences organized in traditional media outlets, where moderators would immediately delete negative feedback from personal accounts. Georgian politicians use different platforms for conducting online conferences, but they often faced technical problems that make communication more difficult for the public. For example, a Labor Party representative complained about the low quality of services provided by the Ustream.com platform. Because of technical difficulties and low traffic speed, only approximately 100 participants managed to watch and participate in the online conference conducted in 2012.[43]

In general, experts did not see many changes in the approaches to the Internet used by Georgian politicians. Until 2008, internet forums Forum.ge, Batumi discussion club, and Planeta.ge were the most active and frequently accessed organizers of online conferences among Georgian social websites. In 2007–2008, they hosted a conference with prominent politicians representing major political parties (Republicans, United National Movement, etc.) every week, providing live streaming and feedback services. However, this practice came to an end in 2012, giving way to a different format of conferences. For instance, Bidzina Ivanishvili preferred to hold press conferences. Accordingly, the Internet newspaper *Netgazeti* hosted live stream conferences twice in 2012 that allowed politicians to communicate interactively with the public.[44]

Political parties with well-organized and efficient press services followed suit. Former President Saakashvili, Free Democrats leader (and now Defence Minister) Irakli Alasania, and Tbilisi Mayor Gigi Ugulava took part in conferences organized by and hosted on the website of the pro-UNM Tabula magazine. The conferences were aired on television. Likewise, former Parliament

---

43 Interview conducted with I. K.
44 Interview conducted with K. S., male, 2 June 2012.

Speaker David Bakradze himself hosted online conferences on his Facebook account.

In spite of the relative affordability of social media advertising, not all active political parties ran advertisements on Facebook. For instance, the experts interviewed claim that, in Georgia, such ads cost several hundred Georgian lari and can attract 2,000–3,000 users, on average. It is a constant communication tool; the ad is displayed constantly on Facebook pages and targeted to Georgian users. However, the politicians interviewed during the survey noted that the number of users was not high enough to justify the purchase of Facebook ads during the election campaign.

> Most individuals registered on Facebook have already made up their political decision. A Facebook campaign does not make any difference for political parties as more than 80 percent of their [Facebook] users had already made a decision [six months before the elections] whom to support. Those who receive information from the internet are politically active individuals.[45]

Thus, using Facebook ads were seen as being tantamount to "preaching to the choir."[46]

"Likes" are not reliable indicators of popularity. According to interviewed experts, in the Georgian context, fake profiles make it easy to generate fake likes. For instance, during a famous online competition between the personal pages of President Saakashvili and his main opponent, Ivanishvili, each of them received 4,000–5,000 likes every day, which is odd for a country like Georgia, which only has approximately one million active Internet users. In reality, the likes count for nothing unless there is a real user behind each account. It seems to be a common practice for Georgian politicians to generate fake likes. According to some Georgian experts, several American and Chinese companies are known for selling "likes" on the Internet. Thus, "likes" should not be regarded as dependable indicators of popularity.

---

45   Interview conducted with L. V., male, 17 May 2012.
46   Pippa Norris, "Preaching to the Converted? Pluralism, Participation and Party Websites," *Party Politics* 9:1 (2003): 21–45.

In addition, according to some media reports, in 2012, public servants and employees of state-run organizations were ordered by their superiors to establish at least ten accounts each to generate a large number of likes for the president's page. In the same vein, when Speaker Bakradze launched a virtual election of the parliament speaker, according to media reports, students of at least one Georgian school were asked by officials to visit and "like" Bakradze's page. As a result, this campaign received negative feedback and lost users' trust.[47] Similar cases were reported by the experts interviewed during the survey. Most of these experts shared the view that "likes" do not define the degree of popularity of Georgian politicians and do not characterize the performance of politicians.

As explained by one interviewee,

> The government ordered civil servants to 'like' certain Facebook pages [several years ago] ... I am worried because we are talking about 'liking' not institutional FB pages but individual ones. For example, [civil servants were ordered] not to like the FB page of the Ministry of Education but education minister Dmitri Shashkin's page.[48]

Several experts also recalled an example in which Georgian politicians used children for political purposes. This mainly occurred in the framework of the ruling party's activities. Usually, political party members ask children to create fake pages and "like" one particular page, as in the above mentioned Bakradze case.[49]

7. Discussion and Conclusion

Georgian political parties seem to prefer Facebook to any other social network available in Georgia. However, data on social media monitoring shows that parties do not use the potential of social media efficiently. The results showed that GD and the UNM, the two largest political parties, used social media features and platforms more than other political actors. Despite this finding, there were no clear signs that parties used social media as an established political

---

47 Interview conducted with S. L., male, 2 June 2012.
48 Interview conducted with D. K., female, 24 April 2012.
49 Interview conducted with A. T., female, 5 July 2012.

communication strategy. Interviewed political elites reported being skeptical of the role of social networks and their potential to help win more supporters and increase their ratings. Some parties claimed that online political activity, either on Facebook or other social networks, was simply a waste of resources because it could not and would not help to win more votes. Television and visits to constituencies to speak directly to the people were identified as the only efficient ways to sway neutral voters.

The empirical investigation demonstrated that Georgian political parties fail to utilize the full range of application options for communication offered by social networks. Parties use social media mainly to distribute information rather than generate new voters through communicative styles that engage discussion and dialogue. However, social media's lack of observable effects on the election may be a consequence of the primarily passive manner by which social media are employed by political parties in Georgia.

While Internet technologies did not appear to have any marked direct effect on the 2012 elections, the use of social media and the Internet may have contributed indirectly to GD's upset victory. For the first time, a critical mass of opposition-leaning literature and opinion was readily available, in clear international English, for journalists, analysts, and opinion-makers abroad to examine a more nuanced perspective of the internal political situation.[50] Given the outsized influence that Western official opinion plays in Georgian internal politics, this may have contributed to both the electoral upset and the relatively peaceful transfer of power. In some ways, Georgia's experience in 2012 somewhat tracks with Michael Xenos and Patricia Moy's observation of the limited direct, but more marked contingent, effects of internet use on the 2004 U.S. presidential elections.[51]

---

[50] Michael Cecire, "Georgia's 2012 Elections and Lessons for Democracy Promotion," *Orbis* 52:2 (2013).

[51] Michael Xenos and Patricia Moy, "Direct and Differential Effects of the Internet on Political and Civic Engagement," *Journal of Communication* 57:4 (2007).

The likely advantage conferred to GD through increased use of internet technologies, even if indirectly, may illustrate the potential for social media to play a more prominent role in Georgian politics for smaller, less well-resourced political parties than GD or the UNM. Rachel Gibson's observation of the Green Party's force-multiplying use of internet technologies in the 2008 Australian elections would appear to lend further credence to this notion.[52] Although not discussed by informants, political parties' and activists' reticence to make greater use of social media may be related to concerns about press freedom. Revelations following the 2012 election showed that the Interior Ministry had erected a robust surveillance apparatus that monitored phone, text, and internet traffic.[53] The existence of such a system was widely rumoured ahead of the 2012 election, which may have depressed public and opposition inclinations to utilize internet technologies more fully in the election campaign.

Nonetheless, Georgian political parties appear to use internet technologies and social media as a matter of course rather than as a proactive means to appeal to the public. And when social media is utilized by political parties, it is done so in a way that is largely passive and fails to take advantage of the interactive potential of social networking. This would seem to largely echo the use of political social media practices in post-communist Ukraine, where political parties' use of internet technologies are assessed to be mostly passive.[54] This is significant, considering Ukraine's relatively comparable hybrid regime model, although Ukraine appears to be on a downward trajectory, as Georgia would appear to be progressing in important respects. Further investigation of the Georgian case looking at the October 2013 election and, potentially, the upcoming 2014 local elections—which will likely assume more meaning with

---

52 Gibson and McAllister, "Do Online Election Campaigns Win Votes?"
53 See Civil Georgia, "Interior Ministry Called to Remove 'Black Box' Spy Devices from Telecom Companies," *Civil.ge*, 25 May 2013, http://www.civil.ge/eng/article.php?id=26111.
54 Tetiana Katsbert, "Social Media and Ukrainian Presidential Elections," *Digital Icons* 1:2 (2009).

ongoing decentralization reforms—could illuminate the relationship between social media usage in democratizing hybrid regimes. Further studies of social media usage in Georgian politics would also benefit from the use of automated analytical tools to better quantify social media metadata, such as through the use of keywords, metatags, and "hashtags," to name a few.

II. Television

Coercion or Conformism? Censorship and Self-Censorship among Russian Media Personalities and Reporters in the 2010s

Elisabeth Schimpfossl, The University of Liverpool; and Ilya Yablokov, The University of Manchester

Television is the primary, and most effective, tool employed by the political regime to influence its people, and the federal television networks are critical elements of the political system in Putin's Russia.[1] Eighty-eight percent of the Russian population use television news as their prime source of information, 65 percent regard the news reporting as objective, and 51 percent trust television as an information source.[2] What the Russian viewers see on state-aligned television is strongly shaped by the Kremlin. Particularly during Putin's third presidential term, news reporting has become more propagandistic.[3] Often without being told what to do, journalists, reporters and television hosts are usually keen to get it right and do what they think that the authorities want them to do. Yet at the same time they are also individuals with their own characters and ideas.

This chapter will explore processes around media governance on federal television networks during Putin's third presidential term, in particular the question of self-censorship among presenters, reporters and media personalities. It will discuss the ways in

---

[1] This article was produced as a part of the AHRC-funded project "Mediating Post-Soviet Difference: An Analysis of Russian Television Representations of Inter-Ethnic Cohesion Issues," carried out by Professor Stephen Hutchings and Professor Vera Tolz at the University of Manchester.

[2] See results of the poll conducted June 20–24, 2013: "Otkuda rossiyane uznayut novosti," Levada Center, http://www.levada.ru/08-07-2013/otkuda-rossiyane-uznayut-novosti.

[3] Stephen Hutchings and Vera Tolz, *Nation, Ethnicity and Race on Russian Television: Mediating Post-Soviet Difference*. Monograph in progress.

which the media adapts how news is made and framed to the expectations of the authorities. It will make comparisons between renowned media personalities and less or little known "rank-and-file" reporters.

Questions around censorship and self-censorship are familiar to Russian reporters[4] and have attracted a fair degree of academic attention, especially from social scientists working on Ukraine and Central Asia.[5] As Sarah Oates concluded from the study of the television coverage of Russian elections, reporters chose to adjust the message their reports deliver to the position of their political masters.[6] Censorship, the outright prohibition, alteration or suppression of thoughts in media outlets or other forms of public expression, is usually linked to coercive tactics imposed upon those not complying. Self-censorship implies a self-inflicted restriction of free expression, also arising from subordination to the political interests as well as fear of superiors.[7] We argue that many reporters act out of conformism. "Conformism" is a difficult notion, as it can mean both opportunism and routinized willingness to accept unquestioningly the usual practices or standards, which were originally imposed through coercion. The latter case was typical for the Soviet Union; first, coercion forced reporters and public activists to suppress their thoughts, which, later, became the silently accepted norm of behavior to get by without trouble. The term *adekvantnost'* which was used by a number of the reporters who agreed to speak

---

[4] "Razgovory o media: Maksim Koval'skiy i Mikhail Zygar'," *Afisha*, 3 August 2012, http://gorod.afisha.ru/archive/media-kovalski-zygar/; Robert W. Orttung and Christoper Walker, "Putin and Russia's Crippled Media," *Russian Analytical Digest* 123 (21 February 2013): 2.

[5] Marta Dyczok, "Was Kuchma's censorship effective? Mass media in Ukraine before 2004," *Europe-Asia Studies* 58:2 (2006): 215–38; on Central Asia, see Timothy Kenny and Peter Gross, "Journalism in Central Asia: A Victim of Politics, Economics, and Widespread Self-censorship," *The International Journal of Press/Politics* 13:4 (October 2008): 515–25.

[6] Sarah Oates, *Television, Democracy and Elections in Russia* (London: Routledge, 2006), 194.

[7] Masha Gessen, "Fear and Self-Censorship in Vladimir Putin's Russia," *Nieman Reports* (Summer 2005), http://www.nieman.harvard.edu/reportsitem.aspx?id=101154.

to us, but without attribution, appeared to combine the two differing concepts of conformism.

The issue of conformism in news making was studied by Olessia Koltsova. Among other things, she analyzed the role of censorship and self-censorship in the day-to-day practices of Russian journalists, as well as how they conformed to their superiors' wishes. According to Koltsova's study, rank-and-file journalists in the mid-2000s were not particularly interested in the political aspects of their management's decision making. They would have agreed anyway, which gave them leeway to express their own thoughts.[8]

With regards to self-censorship, we will draw on Koltsova's *News Media and Power in Russia*. However, we will shift the focus from local channels examined in her study to Russia's federal television channels. In Putin's third presidential term, massive changes have taken place in the television landscape. A close examination of the reporters currently active in Russia will allow us to determine whether self-censorship has remained one of the most significant elements of media governance.

This chapter challenges the view that self-censorship, if understood as a concept based on fear, is the main regulator in Russian media governance. Instead, we argue that media personalities and reporters on Russian federal television channels do have the option to avoid reporting news which contradicts their own political convictions. Those media personalities and reporters who work in positions which involve direct promotion of Kremlin positions usually have chosen to do so, and do it deliberately.

1. Methodology and Empirical Data

We were particularly interested in whether Russian media governance is based on coercion or whether media personalities and reporters primarily conform to the ideas and values promoted by the current regime. To learn more about how media personalities and reporters perceive policies imposed by their editors and how they

---

8   Olessia Koltsova, *News Media and Power in Russia* (London: Routledge, 2006), 138–42, 148.

assess their own role, we conducted interviews with renowned media personalities as well as "ordinary" reporters.

We attempted to interview reporters, presenters and anchors from the widest possible political spectrum covered by the federal television channels. Those opposed to the Putin regime who have openly raised issues of censorship were excluded, as their opinion is publicly available. Instead, we were keen to interview reporters, presenters and anchors affiliated to state-aligned television who do not usually talk about issues of censorship and self-censorship. Also, we sought to find interviewees at different stages of their careers and on different hierarchical levels. We eventually conducted interviews with 13 media personalities and reporters between January and August 2013 in Moscow. Eight have been used for this analysis; 4 famous media personalities and 4 rank-and-file reporters. These individuals were chosen in order to represent an even spread within the ranks of the broadcasting companies. We were therefore afforded the opportunity to analyze at two different levels how these individuals assess self-censorship.

The four famous media personalities (Dmitriy Kiselev/then *Rossiya,* later appointed by Putin as head of *Rossiya segodnya*), Arkadiy Mamontov/*Rossiya,* Maksim Shevchenko/*Pervyy kanal (Channel One)* and Anton Krasovskiy/formerly *NTV*) allowed us to refer to them by name. These four individuals represent a relatively wide political spectrum, from deeply conservative to relatively liberal, both in a political and economic sense. Given their present or past affiliation with the Kremlin, we need to take into consideration that their responses could be toeing the line.

The second set of interviewees consists of relatively unknown reporters who work for important prime-time news programs on major television channels. *Pervyy kanal* is Russia's main television channel, commanding a 14.4 percent market share, 75 percent of which is controlled by the state. *Rossiya*, the second most popular television channel with 13.2 percent market share, is part of the state-owned media holding *VGTRK* (All-Russia State Television and Radio Broadcasting Company). *NTV* and *REN TV* are privately owned television channels with audience shares of 12.1 percent and 5.2 percent, respectively. The main shareholders enjoy close links to the Kremlin. Overall, these four channels cover 44.9 percent of all Russian television viewers.[9]

In these interviews we focused on more technical questions related to everyday journalistic practices and procedures: how agendas are set, how decision-making mechanisms operate, and how hiring practices work. Except for one case (the *REN TV* reporter), our incognito reporters represent the same channels as the renowned media personalities. However, they are at the lower end of the internal company hierarchies. Interviewing journalists at the higher and lower end of the spectrum allowed us to gain an insight into two different levels of media governance and editorial hierarchies. These lower-level interviewees preferred to remain anonymous.

In our analysis, we focused on the media personalities' and reporters' career trajectories, political views and the power relations expressed in their narratives, both between them and media authorities as well as between them and their audience. Our aim was to reconstruct contemporary television governance on the basis of our interview analysis and the contextualization of the collected narratives within information gathered from openly available sources, including academic analyses.

We will first discuss the responses given by our four well-known interviewees regarding censorship and self-censorship. Then we will look into the narratives and self-perception of the incognito reporters. These two sets of interviews are used as the basis for our main argument that media personalities and reporters perceive self-censorship in contemporary Russia under Putin's third term as being, first, deliberately applied, i.e. out of conviction and, second, free of coercion. Hence, conclusions drawn from their narratives are that, instead of being repressed individuals, they have sufficient opportunities to choose not to write or articulate things they disagree with.

---

9   All audience shares are given according to the TNS Gallup poll conducted between October 21–27, 2013, http://www.tns-global.ru/rus/data/ratings/tv/index.wbp?tv.action=search&tv.regionId=9B17541D-53F1-4092-BD51-83041DDAB639&tv.startDate=21.10.2013&tv.endDate=27.10.2013&tv.raitingNameId=0FE4F395-898A-4187-B3BB-3DC1C077622E.

2. Renowned Media Personalities: Career Trajectories, Political Views and Censorship

The famous media personalities enjoy their celebrity status for different reasons; they are characters, often sharp, witty, provocative and non-conformist. The television networks' need to keep ratings up means that management has to give in to the occasionally complex, vain and erratic nature of their most famous television hosts, pundits and anchors. Hence, notwithstanding the state's attempt at stricter media control, consumers of state-aligned television can still enjoy listening to a broad range of politically provocative and non-orthodox ideas. At the same time it is absolutely clear to these individuals who has the final say and to whom they have to subordinate. Since the start of Putin's third presidency, it has become more difficult to balance these dichotomies.

Career trajectories

Dmitriy Kiselev (*Rossiya*) was appointed by Putin as the head of the state-owned news agency *Rossiya segodnya* in December 2013. Until 2012, he served as the deputy director of the state-owned media holding *VGTRK*. During the time of the interview in March 2013 he was author and presenter of *Vesti nedeli,* the second most popular weekly Sunday news program.

Arkadiy Mamontov from the *Rossiya* channel is the author and host of the talk show *Spetsial'nyy korrespondent*. The show raises topical and controversial political issues. Their aim is to spread the Kremlin line among the public. The experts and guest speakers are chosen in order to provoke heated discussions. A number of Mamontov's shows even caused diplomatic scandals.[10]

---

[10] The government of Tajikistan, for example, raised sharp criticism of a hate campaign in a series of television shows in spring 2013 directed at Central Asian migrants. Mamontov's *Spetsial'nyy Korrespondent* took an active part in this campaign. "MID RT: Rossiya nachala shirokomasshtabnuyu informatsionnuyu kampaniyu protiv Tadzhikistana," *Avesta.tj*, 24 April 2013, http://www.avesta.tj/goverment/18037-mid-rt-rossiya-nachala-shirokomasshtabnuyu-informacionnuyu-kampaniyu-protiv-tadzhikistana.html.

Maksim Shevchenko (*Pervyy kanal*) is the former host of the talk shows *Sudite sami* and *V kontekste*. He became acclaimed for his sharp and witty discussion style in *Sudite sami*. Shevchenko's public activities extend to political activism. For example, he took part in election campaigns, supporting Kremlin-loyal politicians.[11]

Anton Krasovskii was formerly presenter on the Kremlin-sponsored online channel *Kontr TV*. Prior to this, he worked on *NTV* from 2010 to 2012 as editor and host of the popular talk show *NTVshniki* which discussed current political affairs and was closed down in summer 2012. In between his employment at *NTV* and his post at *Kontr TV*, Krasovskii made a name as a presenter on *NTV* and briefly as a campaign manager for the oligarch and 2012 presidential candidate, Mikhail Prokhorov. Lately, Krasovskii has published articles in *The Guardian* and other Western European newspapers on homophobia in Russia.

Political views

These four media personalities are, or at least used to be, loyal to the government. They act as executors of state policies. Despite their loyalty to the Kremlin, they are also bold and vain characters, whose showmanship and partly radical views are crucial to keep viewer ratings up, and the audience entertained.

Kiselev is a militant defender of the Putin regime. In 2013, *The Economist* labeled him "Russia's chief propagandist."[12] In the interview with us, he declared the growing "Islamic threat" one of his personal priority topics.[13] In the West, Kiselev has become known for his homophobic statements, his anti-Western stance and, lately, for his ferocious support of Putin's Ukraine/Crimea policies, for which his name appeared in the list of individuals targeted by EU

---

11 For example, Shevchenko was an official supporter of Moscow's mayor Sergey Sobyanin during the summer 2013 electoral campaign in Moscow. Ilya Azar, "Sobyanin po proiskhozhdeniyu—korennoy evraziets," *Lenta.ru*, 30 July 2013, http://lenta.ru/articles/2013/07/30/shevchenko/.
12 "Russia's chief propagandist," *The Economist*, 10 December 2013, http://www.economist.com/blogs/easternapproaches/2013/12/Ukraine.
13 Dmitriy Kiselev. Interviewed by Elisabeth Schimpfossl, Moscow, 27 March 2013.

sanctions.[14] In the 1990s Kiselev was a strong advocate of liberal views and unconditionally defended the rights of the Fourth Estate. His program *Okno v Evropu* (Window onto Europe) promoted a cosmopolitan view of the world. In a discussion in 1999, Kiselev claimed that a reporter has no right to be a propagandist.[15] Since then his position has taken a U-turn and he considers it to be one of a reporter's primary tasks to produce new values, educate the Russian people, and establish new norms.

Mamontov is as radical in his patriotic conservatism as Kiselev. He is notorious, in particular, for his views on migrants, and his crude approach to journalism. One reporter we talked to called him "a symbol of propaganda."[16] Mamontov became famous as a war reporter on *NTV* in the 1990s, a time when the news channel was known for its critical coverage of the military conflict in Chechnya. (After Gazprom took over the network following Putin's rise to power, it supports the Kremlin's position). Mamontov's stance changed in 2000, after he joined the state-owned *VGTRK*, from being critical of the regime into being highly critical of Russia's "enemies," both within and outside the country. In the 2000s he began to play a major role on behalf of the Kremlin to trigger events which resulted in the justification for the repression of political oppositionists. [17]

A common reference point for these two media personalities is the first post-Soviet decade. They look at the 1990s resentfully. Mamontov remembered:

> 1993 [when El'tsin crushed the parliament by force] had great influence on me. I was in the White House [the parliament] and saw everything. I began to understand that they betrayed us. They were not democrats, but swindlers, who looted my country pretending to be democrats. They looted it

---

14 Peter Spiegel and Christian Oliver, "EU adds new names to visa bans," *The Financial Times*, 21 March 2014, http://www.ft.com/intl/cms/s/0/315b890 a-b090-11e3-8058-00144feab7de.html#axzz2xp7wCLcA.
15 "Dmitriy Kiselev o zhurnalistike (1999 g.)," YouTube, https://www.y outube.com/watch?v=6yhrKB7sr6I.
16 Anonymous interviewee. Interviewed by Elisabeth Schimpfossl, 2013.
17 Svetlana Meteleva and Aleksandr Raskin, "Spetskor upolnomochen zayavit'," *Russkiy Newsweek* 4:17, 30 January 2006.

and carried the money to the West. Eighty percent of my country thinks like this.[18]

Also, the former liberal Kiselev looks back at the 1990s as a dark decade and highly approves of Putin's turn to anti-liberalism:

> We can't rely on Western liberalism... By 2000 Russia was close to falling apart. Entire regions did not pay taxes, we had a war, and one region after the other declared its independence from Moscow. Putin put everything back together, found the political will and saved the country.[19]

The U-turn these two media personalities made from being staunch liberals to anti-liberals probably partly explains the ferociousness of their present stance. However, this does not mean that their former liberal outlook was any less conformist than their new anti-liberal outlook. In the 1990s it was fashionable to be a liberal and today it is fashionable to be an anti-liberal.

In contrast to Mamontov and Kiselev, Shevchenko represents a later generation of pro-Kremlin pundits. His generation of media personalities did not go through a transformation from liberal to conservative, but was formed by the Putin administration in the 2000s. As public intellectuals of the new millennium, representatives of this generation articulated the various ideological concepts which the presidential administration had developed. In addition, they went along with the policy changes the presidential administration undertook. Despite this fealty to the authorities' changing positions, ironically, these younger media personalities enjoy more legitimacy both in public and in journalistic circles. In contrast to the older generation, they never collaborated with the Yeltsin regime, which became increasingly discredited in the late 2000s, often by those who supported it in the 1990s. The older generation had entered a treaty with the "devil" when supporting Yeltsin's presidential campaign by participating in a propaganda campaign which led to his re-election in 1996.[20] The fact that Shevchenko was

---

18 Arkadiy Mamontov. Interviewed by Elisabeth Schimpfossl, Moscow, 28 March 2013.
19 Kiselev. Interviewed by Elisabeth Schimpfossl.
20 Ivan Zassoursky, *Media and Power in Post-Soviet Russia* (Armonk: M.E. Sharpe, 2004), 64–79.

not involved in it makes his criticism of Russia's neoliberalism and the pro-Western attitudes, which the political establishment of the 1990s advocated, more credible.

Being popular for his provocative statements and sharp criticism of the West, Shevchenko combines contradictory views in a blend which polarizes and at the same attracts audiences, ensuring his popularity. He entertains his audiences with political statements which oscillate between the left and the far right. As he explained in the interview with us and often states publicly, Shevchenko favors a strong state which opposes the West.[21] He advocates a return to some socialist elements in education. He justifies Stalin's terror as well as the Soviet campaigns against Jews and identifies with, for example, Austria's right-wing on the issue of immigration.[22]

Shevchenko frequently presents himself as standing in opposition to the regime, which in occasional statements consists of bureaucrats and criminals. In one interview, he even demanded that the authorities should not treat political prisoners too harshly.[23] Nevertheless, he is considered to be loyal to the Kremlin. Paradoxically, this apparent inconsistency makes him extremely useful as an official media personality. Political flexibility and the ability to quickly adapt his political identity to the regime's changing line afford Shevchenko the opportunity to stay within the bounds of what the authorities consider acceptable. For this reason, he enjoys far more freedom and leeway to make critical statements against the regime than many of his colleagues.

Anton Krasovskii was the only media celebrity who did not toe the Kremlin line. Only a few weeks prior to our interview he lost his job on *Kontr TV* for announcing live on air that he is gay. Like Shevchenko, Krasovskii represents the post-2000 generation. Many of them are extremely cynical about the current state of

---

21   Maksim Shevchenko, "My ne Evropa? I slava bogu!," *Moskovskiy komsomolets*, 11 February 2013, http://www.mk.ru/specprojects/free-theme/article/2013/02/10/810258-myi-ne-evropa-i-slava-bogu.html.
22   Maksim Shevchenko. Interviewed by Elisabeth Schimpfossl, Moscow, 3 April 2013.
23   Ilya Azar, "Sobyanin po proiskhozhdeniyu — korennoy evraziets."

things in the country and lack general trust in democracy, including the democratic demands which the opposition movement put forward.

"Like Stolypin, my aim is a Great Russia. The liberals aim at destroying and looting Russia. Nobody can change my opinion. I know many of them [liberal opposition] personally. They are not the best people. Any average member of Putin's United Russia [*Edinaya Rossiya*] is much closer to me than any Aleksey Navalny," Krasovskiy argues.[24]

Despite being banned from work on state-aligned television in Russia because of his public criticism of the authorities, Krasovskiy still approves of the current regime and sharply criticizes the Russian opposition movement.[25]

Views on censorship

In his prominent position, Kiselev is as much censor as the censored: "I write my own texts and nobody reads them in advance, i.e. there is no censorship whatsoever."[26] In the interview with us, he stressed freedom of opinion and diversity as being important aspects of his program: "Our reporters represent a wide range of views and political opinions. We have conservative ones, and we have liberals. I am myself an enlightened conservative, a moderate conservative."[27]

Kiselev's tolerance of political diversity has clear limits. It ends where political views are not in accordance with the current regime, in particular with Putin. The rationale here is simple and clear; every reporter who is opposed to the government should find a medium not financed by the government to work for. Due to his pow-

---

24 Anton Krasovskiy. Interviewed by Elisabeth Schimpfossl, Moscow, 26 March 2013.
25 Sergey Korzun, "Bez durakov," *Radio Ekho Moskvy*, 21 September 2013, http://echo.msk.ru/programs/korzun/1159140-echo/#element-text.
26 Kiselev. Interviewed by Elisabeth Schimpfossl.
27 Kiselev. Interviewed by Elisabeth Schimpfossl.

erful position in the media hierarchy, Kiselev influences how information policies are shaped: "In general, being a well-known reporter, I make politics. I am in a strong position to do so."[28]

However, Kiselev sees his role far beyond the task of news making:

> I act as God, as Jesus Christ. On television, I have a role as the creator. This is not because I want it. This is because since the Soviet era only 20 years have passed... If English reporters found themselves in such a situation, they would have done the same [as us]. One hundred percent. We are obliged to colonize our own country, and the English are excellent colonizers. They imposed their values in many parts of the world.[29]

Here, references to the West serve to legitimize the missionary vocation.

In sharp contrast to Kiselev, Mamontov named the lack of freedom of speech as one of the most pressing issues in Russia today: "We need freedom of speech as much as we need air to breath. We need it to be able to talk about corruption. To uncover it and to talk about it. We need to be able to say who is a crook and who is a thief."[30] However, this cannot be interpreted as an expression of criticism of the current media governance.[31] Instead, Mamontov cleverly turns the tables. He takes up burning issues which have been frequently raised by the opposition movement, such as corruption, migration policies, and widening social inequality in the country. He then flips them to support his own agenda, thereby neutralizing the opposition.

Mamontov's framing of the origins of self-censorship shows a certain cunning. Being an important actor of Kremlin media policies, he does admit that there is self-censorship, something everybody suspects anyway. However, he does not point a finger at the

---

28 Kiselev. Interviewed by Elisabeth Schimpfossl.
29 Kiselev. Interviewed by Elisabeth Schimpfossl.
30 Mamontov. Interviewed by Elisabeth Schimpfossl.
31 Neither was it a rare statement. Instead, he has frequently taken up similar issues. See, for example, "Mamontov Arkadiy Viktorovich. Master–klass 18.05.2011," YouTube, 18 May 2011, https://www.youtube.com/watch?v=dcY1i9NgWNc.

government, or the media elite, for why censorship and self-censorship have prevailed. Instead, he blames the backward Russian people for it: "Freedom of speech does exist, but is not supported by the people's mentality. Its mentality is different; it is still Soviet."[32]

Mamontov includes himself when attempting criticism; "I censor myself at times, after all I am a Soviet person."[33] To illustrate this, Mamontov cited a corruption scandal, which erupted in 2012 around the Minister of Defense Anatoliy Serdiukov and his lover Evgeniia Vasil'eva "who adored luxuries."[34] Serdiukov's departure from the government was, among other things, triggered by the documentary which Mamontov produced for his show. The documentary described the scale of corruption among Serdiukov's close circle. Mamontov explained: "We could have said much more about her [the lover], but we decided not to… I was afraid that it would annoy people too much."[35] This self-censorship, as Mamontov further elaborated, is related to two things. First, there is a lack of a culture of speaking out and articulating criticism. Second, Russian newsmakers are reluctant to say what they think for fear of unexpected consequences.[36]

Similarly to Kiselev, Shevchenko ferociously defended his channel's governance by claiming journalistic and editorial freedom:

> There is no self-censorship; we have a normal editorial policy. This is not any different to what any reporter from the *Frankfurter Allgemeine* or the *Kurier* experiences… If I put my money into a channel or a newspaper, why should I be forced to like everybody? This is why there is such a thing as editorial policy. If the state invests money in a media outlet, it has the right to demand that it follows the state's policy.[37]

Compared to the celebrity hosts we discussed previously, Krasovskii's statements about censorship and self-censorship were more

---

32 Mamontov. Interviewed by Elisabeth Schimpfossl.
33 Mamontov. Interviewed by Elisabeth Schimpfossl.
34 Mamontov. Interviewed by Elisabeth Schimpfossl.
35 Mamontov. Interviewed by Elisabeth Schimpfossl.
36 Mamontov. Interviewed by Elisabeth Schimpfossl.
37 Shevchenko. Interviewed by Elisabeth Schimpfossl.

explicit. He admitted that direct censorship existed at his workplace. At the same time he saw great freedom of expression which he referred back to geographical factors, among other things. Whenever reporters transgress acceptable boundaries, the time zones in Russia enable the authorities to stop such disagreeable programs. It will simply be taken off air:

> A program first appears on screen in the Far East, and nobody watches it. The population there is small, they are not interested and many don't even have a TV set. You can show them whatever you want. Then, if some program doesn't find approval, it is simply taken off the screen. Anyway in Irkutsk, nobody will see it.[38]

This distinctive feature also demonstrates the flexible nature of media control in Russia: in many ways it does not need coercive mechanisms, whilst still affording reporters their creative freedom.[39]

Self-censorship was, according to Krasovskii, no issue in the television projects he participated in. These include the liberally inclined television shows *NTVshniki* and *Tsentral'noe Televidenie*. They were notorious for their occasionally scandalous approach and attempts to report on issues which were excluded from the programs on other federal channels. However, these two shows, together with a few others on federal television, are rare exceptions enjoying significant freedom to report on cutting edge issues without being subject to censorship.

By contrast to these individuals who demonstrate solid loyalty to the regime, most of Russia's major (free-thinking) media personalities disappeared from television screens in the 2000s as soon as they made open and honest statements.[40] One of Russia's most successful political reporters, Leonid Parfenov, lost his job on *NTV* in

---

38   Krasovskii. Interviewed by Elisabeth Schimpfossl.
39   "Na NTV syuzhet o pokhishcheniyakh lyudey v Chechne vyrezali iz peredachi 'Tsentral'noe televidenie'," *Gazeta.ru*, 3 October 2011, http://www.gazeta.ru/news/lenta/2011/10/31/n_2076166.shtml.
40   Most of those who stayed on television throughout the 2000s were made redundant during the editorial purges at the beginning of Putin's third term. For more, see, for example, Arina Borodina, "Pavel Lobkov: ne podnimu tost ni za zdravie, ni za upokoy NTV," *RIA Novosti*, 10 October 2013, http://ria.ru/interview/20131010/968861350.html#ixzz2hgsjJlfD.

2004 because he ignored the prohibition on reporting the war in Chechnya.[41] His removal was the first major act of censorship by a federal television company owner in the 2000s. In 2010, Parfenov publicly stated that reporters had become bureaucrats unwilling to criticize top-ranking politicians and that political journalism had degraded into merely praising the political leadership.[42] Up to now, he has remained persona-non-grata in political programs on state-aligned television. His political unpredictability makes him one of the most visible examples of censorship in the history of post-Soviet television.[43] The fact that Parfenov has been allowed to keep one film a year on *Pervyy kanal* (on Russian culture and history) is a clever move of the regime; by still allowing Parfenov to appear on screen, they can claim that freedom of information does exist. Another highly acclaimed television reporter, Vladimir Pozner, managed to keep his programs at the state-aligned *Pervyy kanal*, despite openly admitting that the head of the channel interfered with who he was allowed to invite onto his show.[44]

Pozner and Parfenov clearly have different political positions compared to most of the media personalities we talked to. One must assume that, indeed, the state exerts pressure on media personalities and reporters whose views diverge from those of the Kremlin. However, these two individuals also illustrate differences in how they are managed by the state. Parfenov's unpredictability caused the authorities to remove him from political programs on state-aligned television. By contrast, the regime has come to terms

---

41   Afanasiy Sborov, "Kto uvolil Leonida Parfenova," *Kommersant"-Vlast'*, 7 June 2004, http://www.kommersant.ru/doc/480909.
42   "Vystuplenie Leonida Parfenova na tseremonii vrucheniya premii imeni Vladislava List'eva," *Pervyy kanal*, http://www.1tv.ru/sprojects_edition/si5817/fi6319.
43   "Leonid Parfenov ob izgnanii iz raya, proroke Dzhobse i krivom kaftane," *RBK*, 20 March 2013, http://top.rbc.ru/viewpoint/20/03/2013/849970.shtml.
44   Vladimir Pozner, "Chto izmenilos' na televidenii," *Afisha*, 1 March 2012, http://gorod.afisha.ru/archive/new-politics-tv/.

with Pozner, who agreed with the channel's head, Konstantin Ernst, not to invite a number of prominent opposition figures.[45]

This also indicates why an apparent political rebel like Shevchenko is acceptable for, if not welcomed by, the authorities. However provocative he appears, his statements remain within the boundaries of the Kremlin's agenda. Predictability, and loyalty the regime can rely on, are crucial to survive on state-aligned television. These are, however, vague categories which need to be internalized by media personalities. By contrast to well-established Western state broadcasting companies, such as the *BBC*, who provide clear guidance to their staff, in Russia, reporters, pundits and anchors are confronted with unwritten rules. The logic behind this rule of the game became most apparent in the statements made by the rank-and-file reporters we talked to.

3. Rank-and-File Reporters on Censorship

All the other reporters we interviewed universally agreed that with regard to censorship one must not report negatively about Vladimir Putin. The state-aligned networks even hire teams of special reporters to manage Putin's whole news agenda. This goes back to the early 2000s when the federal channels developed the image of Putin as the sole leader of the nation.[46] If a private television channel resorts to cautious criticism, as *REN TV* has done occasionally, the term "president" is replaced with "power" [*vlast'*].[47]

The existence of the taboo for any critical assessment of Putin's work tends to be accepted as fair and right by our interviewees:

---

45 Oleg Kashin, "Vladimir Pozner: Ernst skazal, chto soglasen s kazhdym moim slovom," *Colta.ru*, 26 February 2013, http://www.colta.ru/articles/media/355.

46 For further discussion on that, see Stephen Hutchings and Natalia Rulyova, *Television and Culture in Putin's Russia: Remote Control* (London: Routledge, 2009), 33-35.

47 Interview with the *REN TV* reporter. The existence of relative freedom on *REN TV* is still an issue to be discussed among the experts. It is most probably explained by the need to be seen to have at least one major source of balanced information. For details, see Anna Kachkaeva, "Kak sobytiya stanoviatsya ili ne stanoviatsya sobytiyami televizionnymi," 26 January 2013, http://www.svoboda.org/content/transcript/482102.html.

"There is a clear boundary. We are not allowed to cover certain topics, as is the practice on any channel. Just like in every family, the children are not allowed access to the family budget. There are boundaries everywhere. There is a special team who works on, with and for the president."[48]

Apart from this taboo, the reporters we interviewed denied any censorship, arguing that, in fact, "everything goes."[49] They claimed not to have experienced any direct interference or any instructions to cut out parts from reports or withdraw them. On the contrary, they insisted that their editors and bosses do not exert the slightest hint of coercive control. This can be partly explained by these individuals' specific positions. Most of them have consciously distanced themselves from covering political issues, working in fields that are politically less sensitive, which allows them much greater freedom.[50]

Another reason for the freedom our interviewees claimed to have enjoyed might be related to the fact that television channels need to sustain viewers' interest in the programs. As one of our interviewees explained, *Pervyy kanal* cannot aim solely at brainwashing viewers because their viewers will become bored and will stop watching the channel. The need to keep viewers' interest ensures that the state-aligned channels keep the level of information censorship within certain limits.[51]

Censorship and self-censorship tend to risk making reports dull and boring, whereas a reporter's creativity usually does the opposite. The opinions and interests of many reporters often overlap with those of their viewers, and a reporter's personal background and experiences will significantly influence the content of a report and the slant it will take. This partly explains the appearance of shows and reports with anti-migrant, sexist or homophobic content. As our interviewee from *NTV* admitted:

---

48   Interview with the *NTV* reporter.
49   Interview with the *NTV* reporter.
50   Interview with the *Pervyy kanal* reporter.
51   Interview with the *Pervyy kanal* reporter.

> I don't like migrants [*priezhzhikh*], even though I myself moved here. But at least I'm not from another country... If you take them individually, put them in a corner and talk to them, they all are good people. But if they are in masses, they become unmanageable, they turn into bad people.[52]

In short, unless a reporter's views run counter to their employers' editorial policies, they might indeed be granted great freedom in their work.

There are, however, clear mechanisms for ensuring informational discipline and loyalty. Almost all of our interviewees identified *adekvatnost'* — literally "adequacy", but better translated as the right instinct combined with adroit appropriateness and a portion of wiliness — as the main trait required for potential candidates to be hired by a federal television channel. One reporter defined *adekvatnost'* as "the ability to react appropriately to the conditions in which you find yourself."[53] It is assumed that reporters should understand the specific character of their job and avoid violations of unwritten laws (which could be changed without any explicit notification). A reporter from *NTV* stated: "You understand what you are allowed to do and what not. It is basically on a subconscious level that you understand what to do... Although you can suggest whatever you like. If you present it appropriately [*adekvatno*], there is no problem."[54]

Adekvatnost' as a reporter's characteristic is neatly tied to self-censorship. In many cases it is straightforward. When experts are consulted or guests invited to the studio, each reporter has their own contacts who are selected according to the principle of *adekvatnost'*. As a reporter explained, "anyone can be included in such a list. It is not a prescribed list from the Kremlin... Of course, every reporter looks for experts who are likely to conform to the policy of the channel."[55] It is assumed that every reporter who is up-to-date

---

52   Interview with the *NTV* reporter.
53   Interview with the *Pervyy kanal* reporter.
54   Interview with the *NTV* reporter.
55   Interview with the *Pervyy kanal* reporter. Russian television experts and journalists publicly confirmed that several people banned from participating in television programmes. See Irina Petrovskaia, "Televidenie. Krizis zhanra,"

with political developments in the country is able to decide for him- or herself whom to include on their individual list of banned people. This requires intervention from supervisors only in exceptional cases.

Unexpected and rapid political changes, however, can turn self-censorship into a challenge. One interviewee told us a story about when they had invited a writer who fell out with Putin on the very day when the interview was scheduled to take place:

> We asked ourselves: maybe we should not have him [the writer] here anymore? And without any instruction from above our team decided to cancel the interview. Our producer gave him [the writer] some lame excuse that some technical equipment broke down here in the studio or something. The program is pre-recorded, so we could have actually just cut out some bits if necessary, but we wanted to cover our backs... He [the writer] instantly wrote about it on *Twitter*, and in the end we had a scandal.[56]

The need for a reporter to sense what is appropriate at a particular moment in time, might lead to insecurity and overly cautious approaches.

Overall, however, our interviewees claimed to enjoy fairly unlimited freedom in their journalistic practice. An *NTV* reporter stated that "even on federal channels you can find a compromise with your conscience. If you are cultured and educated, you can easily find your way."[57] Moreover, reporters have the freedom to suggest topics they wish to cover as long as they entertain the viewers, guarantee high ratings and are relevant to current developments.[58] To enjoy the freedom to hold views which diverge from those of the government usually implies not being involved in the broadcasting of political news. This rule of the game, however, also means that if a reporter is keen to report on political topics, he or she will choose this path consciously, being well aware of all the limitations.

Fond Liberal'naya missiya, 17 November 2011, http://www.liberal.ru/articles/5493; "Pozner rasskazal o 'stop-listakh' Pervogo kanala," *Lenta.ru*, 24 February 2011, http://lenta.ru/news/2011/02/24/pozner/.

56 Interview with the *Rossiya-24* reporter.
57 Interview with the *NTV* reporter.
58 Interview with the *REN TV* reporter.

4. Conclusion

Our interviews with both celebrity media personalities and rank-and-file reporters indicate that coercion is not an aspect which concerns journalism on federal television channels. Self-censorship is euphemistically described as *adekvatnost'*, a term which is vaguely defined, but definitely seen as a virtue and expression of professionalism. A close look at the practices of Russian reporters, pundits, anchors, editors and managers with regard to self-censorship reveals that they have developed their own sophisticated mechanisms to execute Kremlin policies, without ever making this process too explicit. It would be wrong to assume that the images broadcast by television were initiated by the Presidential Administration and imposed coercively onto media personalities and reporters. In many respects television reports and talk shows disclose at least as much, if not more, of a media personality's or reporter's personal characteristics than of explicit political pressure and interference.

All the media personalities and reporters we interviewed showed complete understanding of this form of regulating and governing media and information policies. Many of them hold the view that, if a media personality and reporter does not agree with the editorial policy of one media organization, he or she is free to change to another organization. As in Koltsova's study of reporters working for regional channels in the mid-2000s, our interviewees also seem to freely promote their masters' view. In the case of state-aligned channels, this is the Russian government's. This conclusion does not imply that all the media personalities and reporters we interviewed are cynics. It does imply, however, that those who practice political journalism do so consciously and deliberately. Whoever is happy to play, will play hard.

Wherever celebrity media personalities admit to "regulatory mechanisms" (usually described as editorial policy), they refer to Western editorial practices, stating that the latter are in no way better. As in many spheres of life, Western practices decisively legitimize Russian practices, which our interviewees ferociously defended. In general, however, renowned media personalities, such as Mamontov and Kiselev, deny censorship as such and argue that neither censorship nor self-censorship is the decisive tool of media governance regulating the daily news agenda on screen. And indeed, proximity to the decision-making centers allows them to speak freely and disseminate their ideas without being censored. Instead, they are part of the process of news production: Being important public mouthpieces for the Kremlin, Mamontov and Kiselev mediate the discourse produced by the Kremlin and, at the same time, partake in its production.

The Russian political puzzle became even more complicated after 2012, as the future of the political regime now looks much more unpredictable than at any previous time of Putin's rule. This challenge makes the political elite keep their eye on federal television as a main pillar of their informational power. As our analysis shows, media personalities and reporters are ready to employ whatever means they have to ensure stability and the maintenance of Putin's regime. The large majority of media personalities and reporters who work in state-aligned television seem to regard their principal role in defending the status quo. They see themselves as important agents of ensuring stability in the country by means of their programs. Their mission is to impose an order which stands in sharp contrast to the turbulence and the chaos of the 1990s. Especially well-known media personalities perceive themselves as far more than simply reporters, pundits or anchors. They serve the country by simultaneously being (and having the right and vocation to be) media professionals, educators and politicians.

The "Russian Idea" on the Small Screen: Staging National Identity on Russia's TV

Marlene Laruelle, The George Washington University

Television remains the most widely disseminated media in Russia today, and a majority of the population believes that it provides reliable information. Even if the internet is starting to challenge this supremacy, television continues to shape public opinion, which sees in it not only a means of information, but also a form of entertainment accessible to all segments of the population. Television thus contributes both to reproducing and shaping cultural and political consensus in Russian society. Topics that create consensus among society are scarce, but national identity is assuredly one of them. While there is no unanimity on the content making up Russia's national identity, the notion that it is an important topic to which the authorities should pay a lot of attention is largely accepted. It frames an understanding of domestic evolutions and international affairs for the majority of citizens, and disseminates a culture that is based on the Soviet legacy — the lowest common denominator, but the most broadly shared. This chapter hypothesizes that television is a central driver of Russia's national identity debates.[1]

The role of cinema and television in the Kremlin-backed revival of the patriotic mood in Russia has been the topic of many studies. They have mainly concentrated on the production of fiction rather than on the role of historical documentaries or talk shows. This latter aspect, little of which is known, is the focus of the present investigation. In the following sections, I argue that the tradition, born in the nineteenth century, of discussing the topic of the "Russian idea" (*Russkaya ideya*) through the genre of *publitsistika* is now successfully delivered through television. The empirical works

---

1   I am grateful for the anonymous reviewers' comments.

draws from Russia's main patriotic channels, mostly *Rossiya-K* (formerly *Kul'tura*), but also, to a lesser extent, *Zvezda* and *Spas*, which offer a unique lens for the televisual staging of the "Russian idea."

From a quantitative sociological point of view, the choice of *Rossiya-K* as the focus of the content of Russian television may seem questionable. The channel has a relatively small audience, only 1.7 percent in 2012 (14th position), with the three main channels — *NTV*, *Pervyy kanal*, and *Rossiya-1* — occupying 43 percent of the ratings.[2] *Rossiya-K* appeals to a particular subset of the television audience that does not identify with post-Soviet cultural transformations and rejects the "invasion" of foreign, especially American, programs on the country's airwaves. Its core audience is older and well educated: 40 percent are aged 45–64 and 35 percent are over 65 years of age; more than 90 percent have at least a median education and 43 percent have a higher education (the highest rate of all Russian networks).[3] Statistically speaking, then, *Rossiya-K* is not representative of the Russian media landscape as it targets a specific group, the intelligentsia. Yet it reflects a quasi-ideal debate about Russia's national identity, one that took shape in the 2000s and led to something of a cascade effect by conveying a symbolic repertoire to a mass audience.

In the first part of the chapter, I define the notion of the Russian idea and the major role of the *publitsistika* genre in it, and then explore briefly the "visualization" that has been ongoing for several decades, transforming the Russian idea from a written concept to a visual one, relayed by painting, cinema, and television. In the second part, I discuss *Rossiya-K* programming strategies and investigate how the program "Who are we?," launched in 1992 and presented as "the first program devoted to Russian (*russkaya*) civilization," contributes to "reloading" the Russian idea by offering a consensus narrative based on empathy and non-critical thinking.

---

[2] "Reyting populyarnosti rossiyskikh kanalov," *Vedomosti*, 4 February 2013, http://www.vedomosti.ru/library/news/8690401/rejting_populyarnosti_rossijskih_telekanalov.

[3] See statistics at "Kul'tura — reklama na telekanale," http://www.startmarketing.ru/media/tv/channel/kultura.

1. The Russian Idea and the *Publitsistika* Genre

The term "Russian idea" conventionally refers to an impressive body of texts discussing the "essence" of Russia's national identity.[4] It emerged at the end of the nineteenth century, but now is used to encompass nearly two centuries of debates, whose thematic framework is shaped by two main questions: the relationship with Europe (whether Russia is part of Europe, part of Asia, straddles both worlds, or is separate from both),[5] and the relationship between the state and its population (whether Russia is a nation-state, an empire, or a multinational federation, with a political nature that is autocratic, democratic, or ideocratic). The body of texts established the atemporal traits of the nation's "essence," in various ways combining messianism (the myth of Moscow as the Third Rome), Orthodox spirituality, the sense of the collective (*sobornost'*), and of the person (*lichnost'*), the belief in a central role for the state and/or the autocrat in guiding the people, the worship of the peasant masses as bearers of the "original" culture, and the idea that Russia and its imperial margins constitute a separate world and unique civilization that the West does not understand or respect.[6]

Similar to the other European states, national identity became a topic of discussion starting in the second half of the eighteenth century. The idea of a specific path (*Sonderweg*) inspired by the Germanic example was counter-posed to the claimed universalism of both the French royal model and the republic. This idea spread throughout Russia, both in university milieus and aristocratic circles.[7] In the 1830-1840s, the Slavophiles (Aleksey Khomyakov and

---

[4] On contemporary texts on the "Russian Idea," see Wendy Helleman, ed., *The Russian Idea: In Search of a New Identity* (Bloomington: Slavica Publishers, 2004).

[5] Edward C. Thaden, *Interpreting History: Collective Essays on Russia's Relations with Europe* (New York: Columbia University Press, 1990).

[6] Andrzej Walicki, *The Slavophile Controversy. History of a Conservative Utopia in Nineteenth-Century Russian Thought* (Notre Dame, Ind.: University of Notre Dame Press, 1989).

[7] James Billington, *Russia in Search of Itself* (Washington, DC: Woodrow Wilson Center Press, 2004).

his disciples), glorifying the Slavic identity and the authentic culture of the rural people, opposed the Westernizers, who were looking westward, but also the supporters of state nationalism, grounded in the dynastic fidelity to the Romanovs (Sergey Uvarov, Konstantin Pobedonostsev). In the 1860-1880s, the Panslavists tried to reconcile both Slavophiles and state nationalists by focusing Russia's foreign policy on Balkan issues, but also by supporting the conquest of Central Asia and a more assertive policy in Asia. At the end of the century a new trend of *pochvennichestvo* or "return to the soil" (Konstantin Leontev, Vladimir Soloviev, Nikolay Fiodorov and Nikolai Berdyaev) emerged, which insisted on religious and philosophical values and viewed modern ethnic nationalism with suspicion.[8]

The theme of the Russian idea did not disappear during the decades of Soviet rule. It survived among émigrés and reappeared in the Soviet Union in the mid-1930s, during Stalinism, when the regime moved toward a Russian-centric mass culture promoting a form of "national-bolshevism."[9] After the shock of the twentieth CPSU Congress and the realization of its full magnitude in the 1960s, the famous "village prose" idealized a peasant life on the verge of disappearing.[10] Khrushchev's atheist campaigns and new industrialization wave raised the alarm among intellectual circles on the preservation of natural and cultural heritage. Village prose reached its apogee in the 1970s, when its main writers — Viktor Astafiev, Vassili Shushkin, and Valentin Rasputin — were awarded

---

8   See Wayne Dowler, *Dostoevsky, Grigor'ev and Native Soil Conservatism* (Toronto: University of Toronto Press, 1982); Linda Gerstein, *Nikolai Strakhov: philosopher, man of letters, social critic* (Cambridge: Harvard University Press, 1971); Stephen Lukashevich, *Konstantin Leontev: A Study in Russian "heroic vitalism"* (New York: Pageant Press, 1967); Stephen Lukashevich, *N. F. Fedorov, a Study in Russian Eupsychian and Utopian Thought* (Newark: University of Delaware Press, 1977).

9   David Brandenberger, *National Bolshevism: Stalinist Mass Culture and the Formation of Modern Russian National Identity, 1931–1956* (Cambridge, Mass.: Harvard University Press, 2002); Katerina Clark, *Moscow, the Fourth Rome: Stalinism, Cosmopolitanism, and the Evolution of Soviet Culture, 1931–1941* (Cambridge, Mass.: Harvard University Press, 2011).

10 Kathleen Parthé, *Russian Village Prose: The Radiant Past* (Princeton, NJ: Princeton University Press, 1992).

the most prestigious Soviet prizes, ensuring that each of their works would have several million copies published,[11] and benefited from the support of a portion of the Soviet establishment, the so-called "Russian Party."[12]

Debates on the Russian idea belonged to the long tradition of *publitsistika*. This term defines a specific genre of publications that includes philosophical essays, journalistically inspired political texts, and more literary works, all which have in common debating major national issues. The absence of press freedoms in imperial Russia gave a noble pretense to this literary genre. The great figures of Russia's intellectual life used the so-called *thick journals*, which were literary publications restricted to the intellectual elites in the capital and emerging cultivated classes in the provinces, to discuss the nation's future. The Soviet era saw the same scheme replicate itself. The major journals of the 1960s, 1970s, and 1980s — mainly *Nash sovremennik, Molodaya gvardiya, Moskva*, and *Volga* — served as the forum for debates on the Russian idea, and their print runs increased by more than 100 percent between 1971 and 1982.[13]

In post-Soviet Russia, the Russian idea has again become a subject of public debate. Although he is usually blamed for having broken with patriotic values, Boris Yeltsin nonetheless sought rapidly to reconcile with Russian patriotism. On 12 June 1996, the date of the national holiday to celebrate the adoption of Russia's Declaration of Sovereignty of 1990, he claimed that "the most important issue for Russia is to seek out a national idea, a national ideology."[14] The government newspaper *Rossiyskaya gazeta* launched a competition around a new Russian idea and collected hundreds of slogans sent in by readers. If Vladimir Putin rejected all ideological references during his first term in office and concentrated on restoring

---

11   Yitzhak M. Brudny, *Reinventing Russia: Russian Nationalism and the Soviet State, 1953–1991* (Cambridge, Mass. and London: Harvard University Press, 2000), 103.
12   Nikolai Mitrokhin, *"Russkaya partiya": dvizhenie russkikh natsionalistov v SSSR 1953–1985 gg.* (Moscow: NLO, 2003).
13   Brudny, *Reinventing Russia*, 103.
14   "El'tsyn o natsional'noy idee," *Nezavisimaya gazeta*, 13 July 1996, 1.

the "vertical of power," his second term saw the structuring of different ideological wings within United Russia, with explicit references made to conservatism and patriotism. This tendency intensified during his third mandate. In his presidential address at Valdai on 20 September 2013, Putin officially made national identity a topic of concern for the Kremlin:

> Today we need new strategies to preserve our identity in a rapidly changing world, a world that has become more open, transparent and interdependent. (…) For us, questions about who we are and who we want to be are increasingly prominent in our society. (…) It is evident that it is impossible to move forward without spiritual, cultural and national self-determination.[15]

The national identity promoted by the Kremlin remains without explicit content, and is above all based on Soviet nostalgia, which transcends all social and ideological divisions, and even, albeit more moderately, all age brackets. The contemporary *Russkaya ideya* debate is heavily influenced by this Soviet—and militarized—patriotism advanced by the Kremlin, but the topics discussed extend far beyond it.

If freedom of the press is partly limited in post-Soviet Russia, freedom of book publishing is not. The means of diffusion diversified, but the *publitsistika* genre was able to adapt to the changes underway. Today bookstores, as well as public and university libraries display large specialized collections, especially from Eksmo, which, with 20 percent of the market, is Russia's largest publisher. Eksmo publishes works from authors of the late Soviet period (Igor Shafarevich, Vladimir Chivilikhin, Vadim Kozhinov), authors who have been established for the last twenty years (Aleksandr Prokhanov), and new names that have appeared in the post-Soviet period (Sergey Kara-Murza, Natalia Narochnitskaya, Maksim Kalashnikov, Yuri Mukhin, etc.). Added to this list are dozens of reissues from major authors of the nineteenth century and the main representatives of the Silver Age of Russian philosophy (Vladimir Soloviev, Nikolai Berdiaev, Sergei Bulgakov, George Florovsky) and au-

---

15   See the transcript of the speech at http://en.kremlin.ru/events/presiden t/news/19243.

thors from the early twentieth century like Ivan Il'in, who were relatively unknown previously, but are enjoying growing popularity. The presidential party United Russia also entered the fray in 2005, when it created its own publishing house Evropa, which sponsors pro-Kremlin *publitsistika*.

The *publitsistika* tradition has also moved to the Internet. Since the beginning of the 2000s, online journals have flooded Runet, the Russian-speaking Internet. A former dissident and until recently Russia's foremost image maker for Boris Yeltsin and Vladimir Putin, Gleb Pavlovsky, played a central role in putting the "Russian idea" tradition online, by launching *Russkiy zhurnal* [The Russian Journal][16] as early as 1997, and many other sites, such as *Kreml.org*, *strana.ru*, *SMI.ru*, *gazeta.ru*, *lenta.ru*, and *vesti.ru*, which shape and reshape public opinion. The "national-democrats," a new generation group led by Konstantin Krylov that calls for a democratic ethno-nationalist Russia, launched another online journal, *Voprosy natsionalizma* [*Questions of Nationalism*].[17] Hitherto this remains the only scholarly journal about Russian nationalism published by Russian nationalists. Finally, blogs and livejournals are becoming a venue for information and debate that all groups, regardless of political persuasion, use to contribute to narratives on the Russian idea.

2. The Russian Idea Becomes Visual

Although writing remains the main mode of diffusion for the canons of national identity, visual means are not far behind. Under the umbrella of Socialist messianism, Soviet propaganda played a crucial role in forging the visual stereotypes of "eternal Russia," popularizing the faces of its national heroes (Alexander Nevskiy, Dmitry Donskoy), and creating an image of *Rodina-mat'* [The Homeland Mother]. Soviet history textbooks were richly documented with images, and the Tretyakov Gallery has been almost entirely dedicated to the Russian idea. In the last decades of the Soviet Union, the rediscovery of painters such as Mikhail Nesterov (1862–1942), whose

---

16   *Russkiy zhurnal*, http://russ.ru/.
17   *Voprosy natsionalizma*, http://vnatio.org/.

canvases of an endless Russia of rivers, birch trees, and shrines, deeply shaped representations of Russianness. Designers such as Ivan Bilibin (1876–1942), whose sketches became the standard illustrations for Russian fairy tales and legends, brought a new shape to the debates on the Russian idea. Ilia Glazunov (1930), the champion of Russian nationalist painting — he received the distinguished title of USSR national artist in 1980, despite the anti-Semitic character of some of his paintings — also greatly contributed to reframing a visual ideal of Russia's identity. The national theme continues to inspire artists from younger generations, such as Aleksey Belyaev-Gintovt (1965), who received the Kandinsky prize in 2008 and is probably one of the best representatives of the "second modern" art movement in Russia.[18]

More so than painting, however, it is cinema that plays the leading role in providing a medium for the staging of Soviet and post-Soviet Russia's national identity debates. The national theme occupied one of the first films of the post-Soviet period, *The Russia that We Lost* (1992), by Stanislav Govorukhin, who rehabilitated the imperial past.[19] However, it was not until the first post-Soviet blockbuster, the *Barber of Siberia* in 1999, by Nitika Mikhalkov, that the Russian movie industry and especially the genre of patriotic film was rehabilitated. Since then, the combination of Hollywood techniques and national themes has ensured contemporary Russian cinema's commercial success and has played a decisive role in shaping public opinion.[20] A Fund for the Support of Patriotic Cinema, created in 1996 and financed by various charitable organizations linked to the military,[21] offers exclusive financing and distribution to directors who work on patriotic themes or play up Soviet

---

18 Maria Engström, "Neokosmizm, imperiya i aktual'noe iskusstvo: Aleksey Belyaev-Gintovt" (paper presented at the International Conference "Russian Aviation and Space: Technology and Cultural Imagination," University of Leeds, Leeds, UK, 28–30 October 2010).

19 For more details on the main post-Soviet films, see Peter Rollberg, *Historical Dictionary of Russian and Soviet Cinema* (Lanham, Toronto, and Plymouth: Scarecrow, 2008).

20 Stephen Norris, *Blockbuster History in the New Russia: Movies, Memory, and Patriotism* (Bloomington: Indiana University Press, 2012).

21 See its site, http://www.patriotfilm.ru.

nostalgia. From 2009, the Education Ministry has received special financing to enable it to commission films based on "ideas of humanism, of spirituality, of patriotism, and of other traditional values of the peoples of Russia."[22] Many productions are devoted to World War II, while others focus on the conflicts in Afghanistan and Chechnya, presenting reflections of the contemporary state of the country in metaphoric form.[23] Staging the Russian idea in cinema became one of the main genres of what Mark Lipovetsky refers to as *post-sots* (post-Socialism).[24]

The cinema industry also greatly invested in producing high-quality television series, the viewership of which burgeoned through the 2000s.[25] Largely controlled by the Kremlin, television remains the principal means for the state to spread its patriotic message, especially the rehabilitation of everything military. Television channels have been broadcasting series devoted either to the police, the army, and the secret services,[26] or to national history, with melodramatic stories inspired by events from medieval, imperial, or

---

22 Aleksandra Zaytseva, "Novoe kino Rossii: patriotizm za gosden'gi," *BBC Russia News*, 6 November 2008, http://news.bbc.co.uk/hi/russian/russia/newsid_7712000/7712514.stm.
23 Birgit Beumers, "Myth-making and Myth-taking: Lost Ideals and the War in Contemporary Russian Cinema," *Canadian Slavonic Papers* 42:1–2 (2000): 171–89; David Gillespie, "Confronting Imperialism: The Ambivalence of War in Post-Soviet Film," in Stephen L. Webber and Jennifer G. Mathers, eds., *The Military and Society in Post-Soviet Russia* (Manchester: Manchester University Press, 2006), 80–93.
24 Mark Lipovetsky, "Post-Sots: Transformations of Socialist Realism in the Popular Culture of the Recent Period," *The Slavic and East European Journal* 48:3 (2004): 356–77.
25 See Peter Rollberg's article "Peter the Great, Statism, and Axiological Continuity in Contemporary Russian Television" in this volume.
26 During the 2000s, the audiences of these series increased, as an indication of the popular interest in military fiction. Examples include *The Special Services* (2002), a series about elite troops fighting the Chechens and their Islamist allies; *The Code of Honor* (2002–2003), which takes up the various military exploits of special units; *Sarmat* (2004), which is based on the story of a professional soldier of Cossack origin who served in Afghanistan and then Chechnya; *The Saboteur* (2004), a series celebrating the sacrifice of an elite unit of the Soviet army operating in Nazi Germany; *The Criminal Battalion* (2004), which emphasizes the cooperation between the Orthodox Church and the Red Army during World War II; *The Cadets* (2006), which recounts the adventures

Soviet Russia, as well as to television adaptations of major novels of the nineteenth century or of the Soviet Thaw. This reloaded history, not interested in historical accuracy, displaying above all feeling and characters, plays a major role in reshaping views of national identity, in both the literal and figurative senses.[27]

Television channels do not just produce fiction series. They contribute to diversifying the genres by which identity is staged by rebroadcasting historical commemorations,[28] and patriotic concerts, which are something of a genre in their own right since Soviet times. Concerts systematically accompany the professional celebrations of the different military corps, days of Russia's military glory, and other major national holidays, such as February 23, May 9, June 12, and November 4. They are also organized for the jubilee days of large companies that, like Gazprom, symbolize the country's success and occupy the prime evening time slot on *Pervyy kanal*. Historical commemorations and concerts share similar ritual features: pompous opening speeches, ceremonial gestures such as a moment of silence, patriotic and military objects as symbolic backdrops, and the presence of major political figures and variety singers (*estrada*). Again, the themes that are drawn upon during these events are closely linked to the supposed ethnic Russian identity and include folk groups in Slavic peasant and Cossack dress, stylized represen-

---

of young members of the Suvorov Military Institute; and *Soldiers* (2006), which is based on multiple adventures and humorous anecdotes in the daily lives of conscripts and officers.

27   Elena V. Prokhorova, "Flushing Out the Soviet: Common Places, Global Genres and Modernization in Russian Television Serial Productions," *Russian Journal of Communication* 3:3–4 (2010): 185–204; Birgit Beumers, "The culture of serialization, or the serialization of culture," in Birgit Beumers, Stephen Hutchings, and Natalia Rulyova, eds., *The Post-Soviet Russian Media: Conflicting Signals* (London: Routledge, 2009), 159–77.

28   Stephen Hutchings and Natalia Rulyova, "Commemorating the past/performing the present: Television coverage of WWII victory celebrations and the (de)construction of Russian nationhood," in Beumers, Hutchings, and Rulyova, *The Post-Soviet Russian Media*, 134–155.

tations of the Russian countryside, and recurrent allusions to Orthodoxy. The Soviet past is also present through well-known films and songs.[29]

Numerous "authors' programs," and talk shows regularly debate national identity as well. Vladimir Solovyev's talk shows on *Rossiya-1*, *Poedinok* (which has existed since 2002 as *K bar'eru*), in which two individuals go head-to-head on current political issues, and *Voskresnyy vecher*, are one example. Mikhail Leontev's shows (*Odnako* and *Bolshaya igra*) are another. Well-known ultranationalist publicists such as Alexander Prokhanov and Vadim Kurginian, as well as more controversial figures such as Eurasianist geo-politician Alexander Dugin and his Islamic acolyte Geydar Dzhemal, and major cultural figures such as Nikita Mikhalkov, appear on them. They offer cultural interpretations of current political events, based on the Russian idea's canons.

In 2005, two channels appeared which openly displayed patriotic agendas: *Zvezda*, launched by the Ministry of Defense, and *Spas*, created by the Orthodox Church. Both the army and the Church constitute the main "armed wing" of the Kremlin in its promotion of patriotism, and each channel cultivated possible ranges for the "Russian idea."

Named in reference to the Soviet army newspaper *Krasnaya zvezda*, *Zvezda* was launched for the sixtieth anniversary of the victory against Nazism. Mentioned in the first State Program for Patriotic Education in 2001, Zvezda is funded by advertising revenue and therefore exists on the basis of commercial support. However, it aims to become "an instrument of preservation for the national heritage and of patriotic education for the new generations (…) for the sake of the motherland."[30] For its executives, "only a man sincerely dedicated to his country is capable of living in harmony with

---

29   Vera Zvereva, "Televizionnye prazdnichnye kontserty: ritorika gosudarstvennogo natsionalizma," in Marlene Laruelle, ed., *Sovremennye interpretatsii russkogo natsionalizma* (Stuttgart: Verlag-Ibidem, 2007), 318–35.
30   "Patrioticheskiy kanal "Zvezda" nachnet veshchanie s mul'tfil'mov, muzyki i kino," *Media-online.ru*, 16 February 2005, http://www.media-online.ru/ind ex.php3?id=7286; "I ne nado gorovit' o tuposti voennykh," *Novaya gazeta*, 7

the interests of the state, defending his country, and having an informed understanding of contemporary realities."[31] The former Minister of Defense, Sergey Ivanov, who played a key role in launching the channel, defined its mission as follows: "This entire channel works on the patriotic education of Russian citizens, those in uniform and those not. Both children and young people more generally happily view good old Soviet films."[32] The ideological shortcut between "patriotic education" and "cinema" is striking. At its launch, the president of the new channel stated that it would show very few Western productions, especially of a violent or sexually explicit nature, nor any "depicting Russians as barbarians and bandits."[33]

The channel dedicates around 10 percent of its airtime to the army itself, by playing documentaries and showing archival images, mainly in relation to Soviet commemorations and professional days. The remaining time is divided between reruns of Soviet cinema classics—in the main films related to war and re-enactments of war—musical events, and cartoons.[34] This schedule of programs reproduces, without innovation, what the Kremlin considers to be cultural norms, namely the Soviet legacy, without updates: programs on military topics, and broader topics related to Russian history, with a clearly formulated conservative agenda in terms of values, family, and mores; and a classic definition of what is the core of Russian identity, the state great power. *Zvezda* has only authorized a single cultural import from American television, which I call the "Discovery" model. Following the example of the *Discovery channel*, *Zvezda* airs many documentary films on world aviation,

---

       April 2005, http://2005.novayagazeta.ru/nomer/2005/25n/n25n-s37.shtml.
31   "About," *TVZvezda.ru*, http://www.tvzvezda.ru/tv/about/.
32   Vladimir Sungorkin and Viktor Baranets, "Sergey Ivanov: My s Putinym poznakomilis' v razvedke...," *Komsomol'skaya pravda*, 5 March 2013, http://kem.kp.ru/daily/26041/2955749/.
33   "Patrioticheskiy kanal "Zvezda"."
34   Steven Lee Myers, "Red Star Over Russian Airwaves: Military TV Network," *New York Times*, 11 February 2005, A4; Jeremy Bransten, "Russia: Patriotic TV Channel Nearing Launch, But Will Anyone Watch?," *RFE/RL Newsline*, 16 February 2005, http://www.rferl.org/reports/mm/2005/02/5-240205.asp.

navy and weapons history, techniques and know-how, and conspiracy-minded explanations of world events.

Spas occupies another, even narrower television niche. Funded by the Moscow Patriarchate, it reproduces the Church's narrative by contributing to "the creation of a world view and values system necessary for the effective development of the state based on actual Orthodox values; and the reinforcement of the spiritual foundations of the Russian state."[35] Orthodox catechism takes up about 10 percent of airtime, while one-third goes to the promotion of Orthodox culture, and more than half to broader cultural topics, always with a moral angle. Unlike Zvezda, Spas has developed its televised *publitsistika* tradition via many talk shows. At least three of them give voice to contemporary conservative thinkers and promote nineteenth-century authors that are considered heralds of Russian conservatism.[36] Vsevolod Chaplin, chairman of the Synodal Department for the Cooperation of Church and Society and one of the principle ideologues of the Patriarchate, has his own program, *Vechnost' i vremya* (*Eternity and time*), through which he propagates his philosophical viewpoints in a similar way to his own written works.

3. *Rossiya-K*: No Culture without National Identity, and Vice Versa

Through painting, cinema, and television more generally, debates on Russia's national identity have gone beyond the narrow field of written and online *publitsistika*, "democratized" and reached the broader public. *Rossiya-K* (called *Kul'tura* until 2010) is part of this trend. It offers an elite-oriented range of television culture that is largely based on the Soviet legacy. As in the *publitsistika* tradition, "culture" is represented as an inescapable element of "national identity" and vice versa: the notion of being a *kul'turnyy chevolek* (a cultured person, with culture being understood as involving not only

---

35   "O kanale," *Spastv.ru*, http://www.spastv.ru/history.html.
36   *Rossiya i mir* [Russia and the world], *Konservativnyy klub* [The conservative club], *V poiskakh smysla* [In search of meaning].

knowledge, but also values and mores) encompasses the idea of being a responsible citizen and a true patriot.

Rossiya-K is part of the *All-Russia State Television and Radio Broadcasting Company (VGTRK)*, which also controls several important state channels, such as *Rossiya 1*, *Rossiya 2* and *Russiya 24*. Entirely state owned, *Rossiya-K* remains the only national channel without advertisements. It was created in 1997 by a presidential decree, at a time when the political atmosphere in Russia had started to change. An increasing number of voices were calling for a "recovery" of the Russian state and centrist figures, such as Aleksandr Lebed, Yevgenii Primakov, and Yuri Luzhkov, "set the mood" for the new political scene. The failure of Yeltsin's first years of liberalism also affected the cultural domain. Patriotism was being rehabilitated since the May 1995 commemorations of the end of the Great Patriotic War.[37] *Rossiya-K* is reminiscent of this period — as is the Fund for patriotic cinema — and a symbol of the authorities' will to reinvest in the cultural domain and promote a consensus vision of the past.

Rossiya-K presents itself as Russia's cultural channel and cultivates this unique brand. Since its creation, the channel has benefitted from the support of many major cultural figures. The "faces of the channel" [*litsa kanala*] have included Dmitri Likhachev, who is often described as the guardian of national culture and Russia's conscience, cellist and conductor Mstislav Rostropovich, filmmaker Karen Shakhnazarov, and writer Daniil Granin.[38] In 2002, when Vladimir Putin was bringing the independent channels controlled by oligarchs back under state control,[39] the functions of the board of *Rossiya-K* — some thirty figures from the cultural world — were

---

37   For more on this issue cf. Marlene Laruelle, *In the Name of the Nation: Nationalism and Politics in Contemporary Russia* (New York: Palgrave MacMillan, 2009), 120-33.

38   http://old.tvkultura.ru/news.html?id=2212&cid=376.

39   J. A. Dunn, "Where did it all go wrong? Russian television in the Putin era," and Samuel A. Greene, "Shifting media and the failure of political communication in Russia," in Beumers, Hutchings, and Rulyova, *The Post-Soviet Russian Media: Conflicting Signals*, 42-55 and 56-70 respectively.

transferred to the Council for Culture and Arts under the Presidency, confirming the recentralization of television production.[40]

Similar in many respects to the French-German channel *Arte*, *Rossiya-K* offers high-quality programs and documentaries with a broad spectrum of what is included in "culture"—literature, cinema, theater, classic and modern music, opera, dance, painting, sculpture, religion, science, education, and history. The programming alternates between the channel's own productions and rebroadcasts of major Soviet cinema classics, including cartoons for children. This Soviet cinema element was at the core of the channel's brand at its inception in 1997, but now is less specific to it, as the reemphasis on national productions has given greater visibility to Soviet era films on all networks. *Rossiya-K* offers, nonetheless, some unique programming, such as *Smekhonostal'giya* (Nostalgia laughter), a fascinating retrospective on the different genres of humor during the Soviet period, based on the idea that today's generations need to know "what made us laugh twenty or forty years ago, what were the jokes of our parents and grandparents."[41] Globally, *Rossiya-K* has reoriented its programming toward documentaries and talk shows dedicated to culture, as well as historical television series.

The channel does not limit itself to offering a frozen definition of culture based on past achievements. It sees culture as a living process and tries to celebrate contemporary art and culture as well. This courageous decision opened a space for polemics, which goes to show just how much cultural processes are interpreted within the framework of the national identity debates. For instance, in 2013 one of the channel's shows, *Bolshoy dzhaz* (Big jazz), was at the center of a social media debate about the place of cultural imports into

---

40   "Telekanal Kultura: istoriya sozdaniya i rukovodstvo," *RIA Novosti*, 19 November 2009, http://ria.ru/culture/20091119/194532918.html#ixzz2rhrJN0 t1.

41   See "Smekhonostal'giya," *TVkultura.ru*, http://tvkultura.ru/brand/show/b rand_id/20884. See also Ellen Mickiewicz, "The conundrum of memory: Young people and their recollections of Soviet television," in Beumers, Hutchings, and Rulyova, *The Post-Soviet Russian Media: Conflicting Signals*, 125–37.

national culture. *Bolshoy dzhaz* broadcasts a competition for young musicians in which they have to play, among other things, American jazz classics. Some members of the jury resigned, stating that they did not want to participate in the selection of "American clones" and the "assassination" of Russia's national roots.[42] Among participants in the social media discussion, two camps stood opposed, those that consider playing American jazz to be treason against Russian culture and its ability to produce its own national jazz, and those who think that Russian culture needs to integrate itself into its international context. The debates on national identity therefore can arise as a detour on nearly any cultural subject that the channel takes on.

They are also at the center of many discussions on the channel's two main talk shows, *Tem vremenem* (*In the meantime*) and *Chto delat'?* (*What is to be done?*[43]), where scholars and figures from the cultural and intellectual realms debate current matters that divide Russian society. The first talk show deals regularly with topics linked to identity issues: the future of the Russian language abroad, the Kremlin's goal of writing a single textbook on the history of the twentieth century, defining traditional values, the role of religion in public life, and evolutions of the intelligentsia. It regularly gives its airtime to schools and universities. The channel also devotes a great deal of its schedule to historical subjects. The knowledge of the past is a "cultural" element that is traditionally valued. Historical reports are numerous. Some are organized around a classic topic (a historical event), while others have a more original approach. One example is *Vazhnye veshchi* (*Important things*), which constructs a historical narrative around an object such as a Suvorov manuscript, Fidel Castro's hat, or Pushkin's chair. By providing a history of objects, the program participates in promoting the museological patrimony

---

42   Susanna Al'perina, "Ne zhurite i zhurimy budete. Na teleproekte kanala Kul'tura "Bolshoy dzhaz" razgorelsya skandal," *Rossiyskaya gazeta*, 13 May 2013, http://www.rg.ru/2013/05/13/skandal-site.html.

43   The title is borrowed from Nikolay Chernyshevskiy's book, *Chto delat'?* (What is to be done?), written in 1862–1863, a manifesto of Russian philosophical materialism and radicalism, which deeply influenced Russian revolutionary movements in the last third of the nineteenth century.

of the country; the main museums in Moscow and St. Petersburg are involved in the making of the show.

Rossiya-K is not a shelter from the polemics that stir the Russian academic world in relation to history. The boundary between science and para-science is particularly blurry in Russia, a legacy of decades of Soviet rule during which what was "true" and what was "false" could shift based on the political needs of the authorities. The widespread attraction to alternate history, often with a nationalist coloration,[44] is echoed by the—unassumed—influence of the *Discovery channel* model, which offers a large window to "conspirological" views on historical events and seeks to promote a sensational reading of world history. Two of the channel's programs feed Russian society's appetite for alternate history. *Po sledam tayny*[45] (*On the traces of secrecy*) and *Iskateli*[46] (*Seekers*) exploit the sensational success of Dan Brown's *The Da Vinci Code*-style stories. The first focuses on paranormal activities, eschatological predictions of the end of the world, mysteries of ancient civilizations from Egypt to the American Indians, including the Atlantis myth, unidentified flying objects (UFOs), and pre-historical human races. The second focuses on the unknowns of Russian history: unsolved murders, cases of espionage, secret Nazi trips to the Soviet Union, and the discovery of the Holy Grail in the Caucasus. In 2012, the show announced that it had discovered the skulls of a race of giants in the Caucasus, which drew official protests from researchers at the Institute of Archaeology.[47] A similarly blurry line between academic scholars and *publitsistika* figures has sometimes marked the program *Akademiya* (*Academy*), which reproduces lectures for students in a fictitious classroom. Although major names of science come to present a di-

---

44 Marlene Laruelle, "Conspiracy and Alternate History in Russia: A Nationalist Equation for Success?," *The Russian Review* 71:4 (2012): 656–80.
45 See "Po sledam tainy," *TVKultura.ru,* http://tvkultura.ru/brand/show/brand_id/28975.
46 See "Iskateli," *TVKultura.ru,* http://tvkultura.ru/brand/show/brand_id/20907.
47 Aleksandra Borisova, "Kul'tura verit v velikanov na Kavkaze," *Gazeta.ru*, 14 May 2012, http://www.gazeta.ru/science/2012/05/14_a_4582405.shtml.

verse array of topics, from the genesis of the brain to the interpretation of a historical text, one also can find more questionable figures on it, such as the fascist publicist Alexander Dugin, who taught a course on the sociology of the imagination.

4. Reloading the Russian idea

Rossiya-K thus seeks to articulate the different ways to promote "culture" and to include within it elements deemed proper to the national culture. The channel explicitly devotes at least three broadcasts to Russian national identity. Each of them corresponds to various timeworn criteria of the debate, and explores a particular way of framing Russia's multifaceted national identity: through the West's eyes, through the *kraevedenie* tradition, and through the *publitsitika* one.

Rossiya, lyubov' moya (*Russia, my love*[48]) corresponds to a long tradition of the Russian idea, that of the outside gaze from the West. This tradition insists on the country's national diversity. In the show, a French person who has been living in Russia for twenty years narrates and promotes the folklore of the different peoples of Russia. It is one of the only programs where the focus is placed on non-ethnic Russians, in purely folkloric fashion: old women in traditional costumes singing and dancing, Buryat shamans performing rites, and reindeer herders working in the far north. All the clichés of Russia as a multinational country are displayed in an empathic view, with no comments about the socio-economic realities surrounding them. The fact that the narrative comes from a Westerner contributes to a kind of "self-orientalizing" that marked Russia's ethnographical knowledge already in the nineteenth century.[49]

"Letters from the provinces" [*Pis'ma iz provintsii*[50]] is directly inspired by the "village prose" tradition. It "de-centers" Russia from

---

48 See TVKultura.ru, "Rossiia, liubov' moia," http://tvkultura.ru/brand/show/brand_id/43908.
49 On this question, see the regular debates in *Ab Imperio*, and, among others, Nathaniel Knight, "On Russian Orientalism. A Response to Adeeb Khalid," *Kritika: Explorations in Russian and Eurasian History* 1:4 (2000): 701–15.
50 See "Pis'ma iz provintsii," *TVKultura.ru*, http://tvkultura.ru/brand/show/brand_id/20920.

Moscow and St. Petersburg by stating/staging that the authentic Russia is the provincial one. It thus revives the tradition of *kraevedenie*, the knowledge about Russia's regions that animated elites in the provinces and two capitals in the nineteenth century, constituting its own genre of amateurs.[51] The show is a hymn to rural life, with an offstage voice using an intimate tone, intersected with traditional Russian songs and bard melodies. The focus is on local cultural life, with an emphasis on writers and artists from the region, on the renewal of religious life, and the lives of villagers and those who seek to revive traditional crafts. The geographical distribution is indicative of the spatial self-projection of contemporary Russia, with a particular emphasis on the north (the concept of "*Russkiy Sever*," the Russian North, is en vogue), European regions, the edges of the Volga, and Siberia from the Altay to Buryatia and Tuva. The rest of the country—southern Russia, the North Caucasus, Far East, Arctic region, and Urals—is largely absent from this mental atlas. The show promotes a very folkloric national introspection. It synthesizes a form of permanence of "Russianness," rehabilitates a vanished past, glamorizes lifestyles that are fading away, and enhances "traditional" values.

However, *Rossiya-K*'s most famous program on Russian national identity remains *Kto my? (Who are we?)*. The oldest on Russian television, it was created in 1992 and originally aired on the first channel. In constrast to the two programs described above, it aims at a more ideologically structured debate around the concept of the Russian idea. Its producer, Feliks Razumovskiy, a historian by training, has conceived and presented the show since its very inception. *Kto my?* presents itself as being devoted to "Russian [*russkaya*] civilization," and discusses "our traditions, manners, habits, saints, and chimeras, those of which we can be proud and those that bring sorrow." Paradoxically, the program refers to Petr Chaadaev (1794–1856), whose *Lettres philosophiques* (1836) opened the debates

---

51   On *kraevedenie*, see D.S. Likhachev, "Kraevedenie kak nauka i kak deyatel'nost'," in L. P. Mariupol'skaya, ed., *Russkaya kul'tura* (Moscow: Iskusstvo, 2000), 159–73, http://www.lihachev.ru/pic/site/files/fulltext/russ_kultura_12.pdf.

between Slavophiles and Westernizers, but who was always very dismissive of everything Russian, considering Russia could not do better than to learn from Europe. The program chose to insist on another aspect of Chaadaev's narrative, according to which "history is the key to understanding peoples." The show claims to belong to the *publitsistika* tradition and seeks to answer the questions of "who are we" and "on what path do we find ourselves."[52]

In a 2009 interview, Razumovskii proposed a kind of new manifesto for the Russian idea debates. He describes the permanent search for "Russia's national self-consciousness" [*russkoe natsional'noe samosoznanie*] in terms that nineteenth-century Slavophiles would not have rejected. He proclaims that Russia lost its national consciousness under Peter the Great due to the shock of a violent Europeanization. Since then Russia has been searching for her own identity but could not find it because it is borrowing its thoughts, techniques, and references from another culture:

> All our intellectual activity in the humanities heavily depended and still depends now on Western Europe and more specifically on Western science. But we have lost sight that (...) all that Western researchers have discovered—concepts, methods—is thought for their civilization, but is often not suitable for ours. (...) From this comes the mission to overcome the habit of using a common template for issues of national consciousness.[53]

Kto my?, therefore, aims to build this new "national self-consciousness" by systematizing a narrative on Russia's history and identity. The show is organized into large thematic cycles divided between six to twenty episodes. All of the major classical topics of Russian history have been covered: the first Slavs, the opposition between Novgorod democracy and Moscow autocracy under the Mongol yoke, the Time of Troubles, the relationship between the tsar and the Duma, between the intelligentsia and the bureaucracy, the Silver Age, relations with Poland, and so on. The show offers a cozy

---

52 See "Kto my?," *TVKultura.ru,* http://tvkultura.ru/about/show/brand_id/21144/.
53 Feliks Razumovskiy, "My utratili znaniya o samikh sebe," *TVKultura.ru,*, 4 March 2009, http://tvkultura.ru/article/show/article_id/30898.

ambiance, designed for an elite already familiar with national history. Feliks Razumovskiy appears in a sweater and slacks to provide context to the places in the story: in front of a landscape of plains and rivers when discussing the arrival of the first Slavic populations, in front of churches when debating the destruction of the Orthodox clergy by the Soviet regime, and in the apartments of major figures of Russian history. The program combines long narrations by Razumovskiy himself, archival images, and historical reenactments by costumed actors.

A *derevenshchiki* atmosphere shapes the overall narrative: the dehumanization of Russia's soil by the Soviet regime, and the destruction of the landscape [*landshaft*] have led to the spiritual impoverishment of the Russian nation and its descent into depression. An entire series, *Istoriya, raspyataya v prostranstve* [History strewed in space] focused on the impact of Russia's territorial vastness on national identity. Classic precepts of the "Russian idea" endorse the idea that space is more important to national identity than the political nature of the state. Razumovskiy states that Russians are better than any other people to work the earth, conquer new spaces, and occupy the territory [*osvoenie*]. In this logic, he thinks the Russian empire cannot be compared to a classic colonial empire and sees the comparison as a "historical lie." He legitimates the Russian empire through several arguments: Russia paid a heavy toll, both human and financial, to develop its peripheries, saved the Baltic region from Germanic assimilation, and brought Enlightenment to the peoples of Central Asia.[54]

The program's tone is one of consensus and the national history is captured in terms of its long duration and continuity. The Soviet experience is fully integrated into imperial history, even though there is a measured anti-Soviet slant. Two specific series have been dedicated to the violence of the twentieth century: one to the destruction of the peasant world, *Krov' na russkoy ravnine* (*Blood on the Russian plain*), and one to the liquidation of the Orthodox Church, *Russkaya golgofa* (*Russian Golgotha*). The series on the revolutions, called *Prem'era russkogo absurda* (*The premiers of the Russian*

---

54   See http://old.tvkultura.ru/page.html?cid=5924.

absurd), is a good example of the prevailing logic of historical continuity. In it, Razumovskiy puts in parallel view the revolutions of 1905 and 1917 and those of 1990–1991, and concludes that "revolutions must not be analyzed as political events, but spiritual ones in which the people expiate their sins and express their grief."[55] Similarly, the long series devoted to political violence, *Kaznit' nel'zya pomilovat'* (*Execute Never Pardon*) intensively psychoanalyzes Russian leaders from Ivan III to Stalin and compares the executions that the latter perpetrated against the old Bolshevik guard to an ancient Russian tradition of divisions and competition between emotionally fragile figures and obscure political games.

National history as told by Razumovskiy is consensus based, but only for those who recognize themselves as a part of the ethnic majority. The program gives minorities little space to tell their own versions of events; neither Tatars, nor North Caucasians, nor Siberian peoples are recognized as full-fledged actors in Russia's history.

Three series of *Kto my?* focus on those who have embodied, or currently embody, "otherness" in Russia: Jews, Georgians, and North Caucasians. The series *Evreiskiy vopros, russkiy otvet* (*Jewish question, Russian answer*) rehashes, to a certain extent, the ambivalences of Alexander Solzhenitsyn in *Two Hundred Years Together* (2001).[56] It does not deny the existence of historically rooted anti-Semitism in Russia, but it also does not deconstruct it as a social or political phenomenon. The first show of the series insists on the under-played, original historical link between Orthodoxy and the Holy Land, and affirmed that the "Russian soul" owes much to Palestine. The following ones review centuries of exchanges between "Russians" and "Jews," from accusations of heresy in the Middle Ages to the *pogroms* of the nineteenth century and the anti-Semitic policies of the Soviet Union under Stalin. The broadcast message is largely depoliticized. Razumovskiy reiterates that Russian masses were "disoriented" and "crushed" by the socioeconomic changes of

---

55 See http://www.youtube.com/watch?v=y8IDEcayWx4, YouTube.
56 See Nathan Larson, *Aleksandr Solzhenitsyn and the Modern Russo-Jewish Question* (Stuttgart: Ibidem-Verlag, 2005).

the last third of the nineteenth century, which explains *pogroms*, and that anti-Semitism has come back in post-Soviet Russia because the country is "spiritually and morally weak." But the series' conclusion remains ambiguous as it indirectly validates the existence of two distinct cultural essences. Razumovskiy states that "there is no need to deny the existence of a 'Jewish question'," affirms that "Russia accumulated centuries of experience in trying the settle the 'Jewish question'," and that "today it is necessary to construct friendly relations but without illusions."[57] Thanks to these ambivalences, each viewer is able to conclude that the program has confirmed his or her own view of history.

The two series on the Caucasus are based on similar ambiguities. *Gruzinskaya pesn' Rossii* (*The Georgian chant of Russia*) insists on the intensity of historical, religious, and cultural links between Russians and Georgians, and complains of the "nationalist diseases"[58] that have become a post-Soviet epidemic. The series is done without almost any reference to the political and geopolitical character of the tensions between the two countries. The series *Rossiya na Kavkaze* (*Russia in the Caucasus*) is probably one of the most interesting discursive reconstructions. It does not deny the conflicts related to Russia's conquest of the Caucasus and describes in detail the wars of the nineteenth century. However, it heavily emphasizes the criminal nature of many Caucasian resistance groups, drawing an explicit parallel to the contemporary situation. Razumovskiy recalls, for example, "Chechen society functions according to an archaic structure, and the criminal world is founded on the same types of structures."[59] According to him, the military conquest was legitimate: he highlighted the specialization of Chechens and their neighbors in kidnapping Russian travelers and selling them at slave

---

57 See http://www.youtube.com/watch?v=Y9EFTviz9is, YouTube.
58 See "Gruzinskaya pesn' Rossii 05," YouTube, http://www.youtube.com/watch?v=dSe85gU-pak.
59 See "Rossiya na Kavkaze 06," YouTube, http://www.youtube.com/watch?v=ykuueMwv8XA.

bazaars, concluding that "for Russia it was not possible to reason with bandits [because] they only understand the use of force."[60]

However, the central message of the series is more sophisticated. The goal is to deconstruct the ethnic identity of the North Caucasus and redraw the region as a part of greater Russia by insisting on a central theme: that the North Caucasus has a second, often forgotten, identity: the Cossack one, which must be rehabilitated. Memory wars thus rage within the show, which assigned a place of pride to the Cossacks in order to Russify the North Caucasus. For instance, Razumovskiy proclaims that Stalin's deportations of "punished peoples," the violence of which he does not deny, are meaningless unless they are seen in the context of preceding events, namely the liquidation of the Cossack world by the Bolsheviks. The North Caucasian drama is thus reformulated as a Russian drama, in which the North Caucasian people are relegated to a secondary status and their memorial and identity claims are absorbed into a pan-Russian context.

The aim of *Kto my?* is to offer a reconciled and consoling view of the major moments of Russian history: the Tsarist empire is rehabilitated; the Soviet Union is decried for its ideology but integrated into the nation's continuity and traditions, and valorized as far as its status as a great power and its culture are concerned; ethnic minorities are not denied but consigned to a second-rank status. The overarching pathos is that of a suffering nation, decimated by pathologically unstable leaders and frantic masses and by a significant loss of the sense of values and identity. To create this powerful narrative, *Kto my?* uses a simple but effective mechanism: it bypasses difficulties related to ideological opposition, tensions in interpretation, and disagreement of sources by insisting on a subjective perspective on Russia's history. Each actor is given his own emotional logic; and the "people," the "soil" and "space" are all depicted as living historical actors. Although devoted to history, the program does not feature on-camera interviews with external con-

---

[60] See "Rossiya na Kavkaze 01," YouTube, http://www.youtube.com/watch?v=IXrQz9Ckxqc.

tributors: the goal is not to offer a platform for discussion to historians and their scholarly questions, but rather to reconstruct a narrative that is plausible for all. History is thus read through empathy and emotions, which makes it possible to avoid having to take sides in conflicts of interpretation and thus having to choose one side against another.

5. Conclusion

The role of the small screen in society can be discussed in Russia as anywhere else in the world: does it educate citizens or entertain them? In the Russian televisual landscape, entertainment is clearly the option that has been taken: the educational option could potentially mobilize against the regime, and the Kremlin is not at all interested in undermining the status quo. *Rossiya-K* distinguishes itself from the majority of channels by its clearly educative and elitist character. Its talk shows are of a high quality and offer a broad overview of perspectives. Its cultural programs match the standard of Arte and encompass modern and international expressions of art. But its broadcasts on Russian identity are part of a far more traditional framework and leave almost no room for a more modern and globalized version of the national identity debate, one that would put into question primordialist interpretations.

In this domain, *Rossiya-K* has its roots in the country's mainstream. It participates in performing a conventional reading of national identity and national history, which subtly combines a dose of nostalgia for the Tsarist empire, a still influential Soviet legacy — with emphasis placed on the Great Patriotic War and the revival of all the "golden funds" [*zolotoy fond*] of Soviet culture, from literature to cinema — and a resigned acceptance of the changes underway. In this overview, consensus is created through three elements: historical continuity of Russia beyond political ruptures; a collective mourning of the lost past (the peasantry, Orthodoxy, rural life, the great cultural heroes of the past…); and an emotional pathos that pushes aside the political and social stakes in order to concentrate on lived experience and the feelings of individuals. The consensus is therefore not created on the doctrinal content of the Russian idea — which remains subject to polemic — but on the container, the frame: styles of speech, voice, rhetoric, screening respond to deeply rooted cultural expectations that are shared by a large majority of the population. In this regard, *Kto my?* is a success: it legitimizes the very principle of the Russian idea, that of a frame of debate that creates harmony beyond any explicitly formulated doctrinal content.

Rossiya-K has a limited audience rating, but it demonstrates the political authorities' conscious strategy to feed the intelligentsia and to respond to its requests for a cultural channel with no advertising and high quality broadcasting. Some of the channel's audience is critical of Putin's political choices, expresses more cosmopolitan views than the general public, but often remains sensitive to national identity issues.[61] The channel thus offers a balanced product to suit the varying sensibilities of the intelligentsia. *Rossiya-K* is also likely used as a way of getting a sophisticated narrative on the nation to "trickle down." In other words, it works as a "testing" platform for reshaping the identity consensus, since what it proposes is then offered in a diluted form to less educated mass audiences through formats that are closer to sitcoms and talk shows than to the *publitsistika* tradition. For instance, the more popular talk shows of *Rossiya-1*, such as those of Vladimir Solovyev, largely overlap thematically with *Rossiya-K* staging on national identity.

One might wonder whether the formula so successfully propagated by *Rossiya-K* for almost twenty years now is challenged today. Demographically speaking, the channel's viewership is becoming older and its narrative on Russian identity, based on elite cultural references and modes of expression inherited from the Soviet era, is probably gradually losing its meaning for a newer generation of Russian citizens. One example of the channel's "disconnect" with the new set of identity frames is the lack of any xenopho-

---

61   See, for instance Samuel A. Greene and Graeme B. Robertson, "The Uses and Abuses of Identity and Nationalism in Russian Popular Politics" (paper presented at the PONARS Eurasia D.C. Workshop, Washington, DC, 21-22 March 2014).

bic atmosphere, massively broadcast on all other channels. Xenophobia has become a key element of the social consensus in today's Russia—between 70 and 80 percent of the population express xenophobic feelings in one way or another[62]—but is absent from the channel's repertoire. Newer generations continue to display nostalgia for a reconstructed Soviet past but grant less importance to amateur knowledge in the arts and culture as being a major part of national identity. They recognize themselves more easily in narratives emphasizing material wellbeing, xenophobia, and Russia's European path—a combination that Alexei Navalny, among others, has come to embody.[63] The channel's future will thus depend on the way in which the new generation of the intelligentsia thinks about culture and history in shaping the national identity debate, and how television adapts to the growing competition coming from the internet world.

---

62 "Levada-Tsentr ob otnoshenii rossiyan k migratsii i mezhnatsional'noy napryazhennosti," SOVA, 25 November 2013, http://www.sova-center.ru/racism-xenophobia/discussions/2013/11/d28452/.

63 Marlene Laruelle, "Aleksey Navalny and challenges in reconciling 'nationalism' and 'liberalism'," *Post-Soviet Affairs* 30:3 (2014).

Peter the Great, Statism, and Axiological Continuity in Contemporary Russian Television

Peter Rollberg, The George Washington University

Mass media are fundamental for all modern societies. For autocracies, however, controlling and manipulating the national mass media is nothing less than vital, particularly when these autocracies claim for themselves the status of democracies.

In today's Russia, television as the mass medium with the widest audience reach is a key element for maintaining political stability and social functionality. This purpose blends seamlessly with television's enormous profitability. Thus, Russia's mainstream television reflects precisely the political-economic model upon which the Russian autocratic neo-capitalist society is founded. Mainstream television's characteristic blend of uncritical fictional and non-fictional content enables the current political structures to reproduce themselves without fear of being challenged.

The hugely popular genre of miniseries, which appeals to tens of millions of viewers, plays an important role in conveying and spreading values that are aligned with the current political status quo. Quality miniseries that are produced with considerable state investments—including literary adaptations and historical dramas—legitimize the current power structures by invoking the legacies of cultural classics and legendary, albeit controversial, political leaders such as Ivan the Terrible, Peter the Great, and Iosif Stalin. Such quality miniseries are especially important since they target the intelligentsia, a stratum that traditionally holds a negative view of mass media, and of television in particular.

This chapter analyzes the—rather limited—debates surrounding the Russian state's engagement in television and tests some of the assumptions expressed by their participants. A close viewing of the miniseries *Peter the First: The Testament* (2011) allows for an analysis of the values that are promoted by state-supported quality television in today's Russia, in other words, the state's "axiological strategies" and the extent to which these values represent a continuation of Soviet values.

1. What Is the "Correct Kind of Television"?

In February 2011, the journal *Cinema Art* (*Iskusstvo kino*) published excerpts from a roundtable discussion entitled "Why Do I Not Watch Television?"[1] The debate gave voice to oft heard complaints about the dismal quality of contemporary mass media, but also shed light on the mechanisms that solidify the current status quo in the relationship between state, society, and media business in Russia. *Cinema Art*, one of the few respected Russian publications that consistently address concerns about the country's television, usually allows for a high degree of pluralism. However, this roundtable was unusual insofar as it featured a combination of media celebrities, public intellectuals, and influential businessmen. Daniil Dondurey, *Cinema Art*'s editor-in-chief, described television as the main instrument for the production of national culture and templates for individual behavior, calling it "an institution for unifying into one entity the people inhabiting a common territory. [Television networks] are invisible secret services for the management of the country, the economy, human capital, and for guaranteeing national security."[2] Inspired by such hyperbole in regard to the immense power of present-day television in Russian society, participants began to express their frustration about mainstream channels, primitive formats, transparent bias in presenting news, sub-par language, and repetitive plots. Then, rather unexpectedly, the litany was interrupted by an interjection that gave the debate an entirely new turn. Petr Aven, chairman of the board of directors of the company "STS Media," unceremoniously asked whether the roundtable had any practical purpose, causing momentary irritation. He then pushed the discussion from self-righteous displeasure and wishful

---

1 Daniil Dondurey, "Pochemu ya ne smotryu televizor?," *Iskusstvo kino* 2 (February 2011): 5–23.
2 Ibid., 5.

thinking toward a sober assessment of who the decision-makers in today's Russian media are, whose interests they represent, and what they will and will not do in their programming. With unabashed directness, Aven described the real communication between private businesses and the Russian state apparatus that he views as fundamental for the creation of the kind of television that could be both quality-oriented and profitable, formulating the following goal: "Which instruments and structures can we build when communicating with the state so that, on the one hand, we won't lose money and on the other, this will be the correct kind of television [*pravil'noe televidenie*]."[3] The latter formulation is conspicuous in its ambivalence, begging the question: who will decide what the "correct kind of television" is, and whose worldview and values determine the "correctness" and legitimacy of media in Russia?

The roundtable discussion reflected the profound transformations that Russian mass media underwent in the two post-Soviet decades. The dynamics of these processes were shaped by economic, political, and, to a lesser degree, internal cultural factors. During the first fifteen years of neo-capitalism, the interaction between the Russian state apparatus, private businesses, cultural elites, and civil society was often dramatic, indicating major shifts in the media sphere, including a decrease in the relative importance of print media, a switch from private to state dominance, and the exponential growth of social media. Yet, despite these shifts and the new media's increasing impact, especially among the young, "the most dominant media outlet is television in Russia."[4] The numbers are staggering—"national television networks reach over 90 percent of the Russian population of over 140 million people."[5] Nine out of ten Russians older than age four watch TV for almost four hours

---

3   Ibid., 17.
4   Sarah Oates, "The Neo-Soviet Model of the Media," *Europe-Asia Studies* 59:8 (December 2007): 1286.
5   Masha Lipman, "Constraint or Irrelevant: The Media in Putin's Russia," *Current History* (October 2005): 320. This number has not changed much; data from 2013 suggest that 90–105 million people regularly watch television. Cf. Daniil Dondurey, "Telereyting kak vospitatel' natsii," *Iskusstvo kino* 4 (April 2013): 5.

daily, five days per week; the audience of television is three times larger than that of the Internet.[6] Indeed, Russia represents "one of the most television-addicted cultures in the world."[7] At the same time, television has become the most reviled medium—efficiently controlled by the central administration and cynically exploited by corporate business. In Dondurey's view, television, under the cover of a "provider of free of charge information and entertainment," supplies audiences with value systems, norms, behavioral examples, and codes of reaction to any type of situation and problem in all spheres of real life.[8]

It is revealing for the worldview of Russia's oligarchic elite that, in the discussion, Aven consistently reduced the problem of quality to an assumed contradiction between undefined "positive social goals" and profitability. Based on this logic, he called for a stronger financial engagement of the Russian state in matters of media so that companies' potential financial losses could be absorbed by the state. Aven explicitly bemoaned his assertion that the Russian government does not spend money on achieving its social goals, whereas "for us it [i.e., operating media companies] is nothing but a business, and it cannot be otherwise." He claimed that the goals of his channel will under no circumstances be political in nature—"Our bylaws state that we do not engage in politics."[9] At that point, the debate entered the axiological[10] sphere: what kind of values does Russian television embrace, and which values does it oppose or ignore? When several speakers complained that Russian society is "xenophobic and homophobic" and that, if television began to present foreigners and sexual minorities in a favorable light this could help remedy the pathetic state of affairs,[11] Aven retorted: "I am certainly not opposed to any kind of minority, but we and the

---

6   Lipman, "Constraint or Irrelevant," 320.
7   Elena Prokhorova, "Fragmented Mythologies: Soviet TV Miniseries of the 1970s" (Ph.D. Dissertation, University of Pittsburgh, 2003), 2.
8   Dondurey, "Telereyting kak vospitatel' natsii," 5.
9   Dondurey, "Pochemu ya ne smotryu televizor?," 18.
10 The term axiological is used here in a rather general sense, denoting ethical values and their derivatives (from the Greek *axiā*, "value").
11 Dondurey, "Pochemu ya ne smotryu televizor?,"19.

people who are in charge of our television (...) believe that such plots will not increase our ratings—and that's all there is." To Kseniia Sobchak's objection that an active engagement on behalf of minorities would fulfill precisely the educational mission of television, Aven responded: "But we do not have such a mission. (...) Currently we believe that this is not profitable for us. If it becomes profitable, we will do it. All other questions should be addressed to the state."[12] He then clarified that his channel could replace its profits stemming from commercials by state funds, using them for more socially useful purposes.[13] Thus, rejecting any responsibility for the values promoted by his channel (except for political values that are excluded by definition), the media tycoon redirects the issue of socially useful values to the Russian state, whereas for Russian corporate media businesses, the only criterion of assessing values is their profitability. As a matter of fact, such convenient axiological abstinence goes hand in hand with the oligarch's proclaimed political abstinence.[14] However, the conversation participants failed to mention that the Russian state is already engaged in direct funding for the media, and always has been, purportedly to enable culturally useful projects.

It is important to note that discussions such as the one described here are the exception, not the rule, in today's Russian media discourse. In general, despite its status as the most influential institution shaping human capital,[15] television rarely is the subject of public debate. This lack of analysis applies particularly to its fictional content. The current hopelessly stable status quo makes the scholarly analysis of how exactly television as the most powerful mass medium in post-Soviet Russia spreads its messages particularly relevant. However, "[the content] of Russian television is rarely the object of study for experts on modern culture," as media

---

12 Ibid.
13 Ibid., 20.
14 Axiology is here understood as the general concept of what is defined as *good* and *right* in individual and social matters.
15 Dondurey, "Tereleyting kak vospitatel' natsii," 6.

expert Vera Zvereva observed.[16] Indeed, "Television is a 'totalitarian dream,' offering infinite potential for the central control of meanings."[17] One of the most peculiar characteristic features of television—the seamless combination of fictional and non-fictional content—can serve as a tool for cognitive disorientation, making it hard to distinguish one sphere from the other. In this regard, the dominant Russian television genre of the past fifteen years—the miniseries[18]—plays a precarious role by disseminating sociopolitical and ethical values in a pleasurable, often hard-to-notice form, complementing carefully crafted and controlled news segments and other non-fictional content.

2. Miniseries as the Lead Genre in Russian Television

In the 2000s, the Russian Federation became the leader in broadcasting television miniseries (*serial'nye formaty*), currently producing between 2,500–3,000 hours of miniseries per year. In 2009, on average of five hours of evening primetime TV, three hours and 40 minutes were occupied by miniseries.[19] Characterized as "almost the only instruments of explaining life for the great majority of people," miniseries have a hard-to-measure, yet profound, impact on their audiences that is likely derived from their orientation toward the subconscious: sexual desire, expectation of violence, fear of death, sense of anonymity and isolation, etc.[20] Miniseries' enormous impact warrants rational and analytical reflection on the part of scholars studying Russia's political system. Yet, while observers of contemporary Russian media do devote considerable attention

---

16   Vera Zvereva, "Vozvrashchenie 'Bol'shogo stilya'? Zakon i kulak: 'rodnye militseyskie teleserialy," *Novoe literaturnoe obozrenie* 4 (2006): 305–23.
17   Birgit Beumers, Stephen Hutchings, and Natalia Rulyova, eds., *The Post-Soviet Russian Media: Conflicting Signals* (London and New York: Routledge, 2009), 6.
18   The term "miniseries" here denotes a narrative format on television with a limited number of episodes.
19   Daniil Dondurey, "Maksim Stishov—Dmitriy Fiks: 'Otstaem let na tridtsat'," *Iskusstvo kino* 11 (November 2010): 125–37.
20   Dondurey, "Maksim Stishov—Dmitriy Fiks."

to political programs, fictional content attracts considerably less attention, even though its influence on popular perceptions runs deep and its effects are likely long-lasting.[21] The present chapter's focus is on one specific figure — Peter the Great — and its representation in a state-funded miniseries,[22] with the goal to discern and contextualize its inherent range of values. While the insights gained from a specific thematic analysis are limited by definition, the underlying assumption is that further application of a diachronic comparative methodology to similarly significant, identity-defining historical figures (Aleksandr Nevskiy, Ivan the Terrible, Catherine the Great, Nikolas II, Joseph Stalin, etc.) and to genres other than historical drama, including war and espionage films, will help expand this chapter's findings.

Media debates such as the abovementioned reflect the dilemma of today's Russian intelligentsia vis-à-vis mass media under neo-capitalist conditions: the 1990s are seen by many intellectuals as a lesson on the blatant abuse of private media ownership and are regarded as just as intolerable as the 2000s, when the Russian administration replaced media oligarchs such as Vladimir Gusinskiy and Boris Berezovskiy with its own minions. The long desired alternative, namely, establishing and protecting mass media as an independent fourth estate that represents and promotes civil society, seemed to be in reach after the break-up of the Soviet Union but today appears merely like a utopia.[23] Critical elite journals such as

---

21 A noticeable exception is Nancy Condee's analysis of Vladimir Khotinenko's 2005 historical miniseries *Death of an Empire* [Gibel' imperii] in the article "Perezhivaya chuzhuyu katastrofu: imperiya smotrit 'Gibel' imperii'," *Pro et Contra* 4:33 (2006): 29–37; for a discussion of methodological aspects of her study cf. 34–36.

22 Just as Petr Aven suggested in the aforementioned roundtable discussion, to enable the production of *Peter the First: The Testament*, a branch of the Russian state stepped in: even prior to the film's credits proper, the viewer sees the announcement "Made with the Support of the Administration of Saint Petersburg and of the Legislative Assembly of Saint Petersburg." Not only is this announcement factually accurate — it is part of one of the film's conceptual lines: genuine, legitimate culture benefits from active state engagement.

23 On February 18, 2013, the Presidential Council for the Development of Civil Society and Human Rights held a meeting devoted to "The Problem of Plu-

Iskusstvo kino have a very small circulation—at best, they can keep alive a resemblance of critical discourse on Russian media at a time when the mass media themselves avoid such debate at all cost. But even in elite outlets there is no doubt that all media-related issues are decided between the state and corporate businesses; intellectuals representing civil society are no longer part of the decision-making structures. This exclusion means that the Russian intelligentsia as a value-producing and value-negotiating stratum has de facto been excluded from mainstream mass media; its role can be marginal and symbolic at best. Obviously, the lack of critical reflection on the effect of television on individuals and society as a whole is part of its successful functioning: television producers and those whose agenda they represent "are not interested in a debate on the

---

ralism of Modern Television and Civil Self-Consciousness." Parts of the transcripts were published in *Iskusstvo kino* (D. Dondurey and N. Zarkhi, "Plyuralizma net. Vlast', obshchestvo, televidenie: preodolim li konflikt?," *Iskusstvo kino* 4 (2013): 16–25). In his opening remarks, the well-known TV journalist Leonid Parfenov stated: "We once used to a have public television channel (...): ORT. It was quasi-state-run and became fully state-run in one minute (...) after a critical report about the catastrophe of the "Kursk," Dorenko's next program was taken off the air. And everybody understood the ramifications right away. From that point on, nothing has changed. (...) When we talk about excessive state influence on the ether—and let me say that the ether is entirely in the hands of the state in regards to editorial policies, regardless of ownership—[now] it would be reasonable to expect the reverse process: the disengagement of the state from the first three federal networks." Calling the situation of Russian television today a "national embarrassment," Parfenov compared it to Ukraine and Moldova that look more positive than "our depressing state of affairs à la the Central Committee of the CPSU." Without naming concrete names, Parfenov pointed out that the supreme censor is the first deputy of the Administration of the President. Activist Maksim Shevchenko echoed Parfenov's assessment by stating that "the establishment holds absolutely all leadership positions in television." And well-known TV personality Vladimir Pozner quoted from his conversation with president Putin: "He who has the power orders the music." The irony of the situation is reflected by the fact that the very council holding the meeting is part of the President's administration. Interestingly, a number of participants expressed concern that a disengagement of the state could lead to a repetition of the situation of the mid-1990s, when television channels were owned by oligarchs who used them to politically influence audiences for or against president Yeltsin. Also noteworthy is a statement by Irina Khakamada, who emphasized the role of self-censorship as a factor no less powerful than the direct or indirect intrusion of the state.

technologies that are at work, therefore minimizing or tabooing the results of its work."[24]

The miniseries did not become the dominating genre on Russian television overnight.[25] After a period of socio-cultural disorientation lasting until the late 1990s, Russian television producers cautiously returned to the tradition of Soviet miniseries that were a significant cultural phenomenon of the 1960s and especially the 1970s.[26] Series such as *The Adjutant of His Excellency* [*Ad'yutant ego prevoskhoditel'stva*], 1970, *Seventeen Moments of Spring* [*Semnadtsat' mgnoveniy vesny*], 1973, *The Meeting Place Cannot Be Changed* [*Mesto vstrechi izmenit' nel'zya*], 1979, and *The Eternal Call* [*Vechniy zov*], 1973, shared, despite their thematic and qualitative variance, a number of features. First, they enjoyed unprecedented popularity, literally emptying the streets at night and maintaining this effect during numerous reruns. Second, they became an integral part of cultural mass consciousness, including numerous jokes lampooning these miniseries' plot clichés, character constellations, and repetitive utterances. Third, their popularity never extended beyond Soviet borders—one had to be part of the cultural community in order to fully appreciate this type of entertainment and successfully decode their messages and allusions. After the breakup of the Soviet Union, Russian television networks showed little interest in the continued production of such serials, both for conceptual and financial reasons. Importing Mexican series was much cheaper and more profitable than trying to respond to the rapid transformation of tastes and viewing habits of a culturally confused neo-capitalist society. However, in the late 1990s, Russian television reacted to a noticeable oversaturation of foreign fare and, especially after the financial crisis of 1998, an economic situation that encouraged and even necessitated the production of domestic serials. Among the

---

24   Dondurey, "Telereyting kak vospitatel' natsii," 5.
25   For a detailed historical survey of post-Soviet miniseries, see Birgit Beumers, "The Serialization of Culture, or the Culture of Serialization," in Beumers, Hutchings, and Rulyova, eds., *The Post-Soviet Russian Media*, 159–68.
26   For a profound discussion of the peculiarities of Soviet miniseries, see Prokhorova, "Fragmented Mythologies."

available genres, crime became the first choice, reflecting a powerful trend in commercial literature whose boom had begun with cheap thrillers by authors such as Aleksandra Marinina and Darya Dontsova. *The Streets of Broken Lanterns* [Ulitsy razbitykh fonarey], 1998, was the new trend's first real hit, signaling an increasingly surefooted engagement in domestic television entertainment. Shot in St. Petersburg, it capitalized on features that are vital for the crime genre: suspenseful plots, recognizable milieus, and social and psychological motivation. These miniseries also conveyed a common yearning for order and justice that was addressed by investigators who were portrayed as ordinary, relaxed, and empathetic individuals. In subsequent years, the exploitation of nostalgic feelings toward the Soviet past proved to be even more successful.[27] But in the first year of the new millennium the miniseries that enjoyed unprecedented success was again within the crime genre, only with a radically changed axiology: *The Brigade* [Brigada], 2002, marked the transition from identification with the law to identification with the lawless. The fact that four young, clever criminals lacking any moral qualms were elevated to the status of national superheroes can be interpreted as a shift in audience perception and even mentality. Dondurey sounded the alarm: in an article in *Izvestiya*[28] he pointed out that the roughly 200 hours of miniseries offered weekly by various channels were for the most part dealing with criminals and their victims. Calling Russian television a "tear factory" (*fabrika slez*, a pun derived from the Russian term for "dream factory"—*fabrika grez*), Dondurey was particularly concerned about the fact that in this "new generation of miniseries," private business is portrayed as criminal by its very nature. "This is another Russian paradox: our television's aggressive fight against

---

27 David MacFadyen has analyzed the specific impact of genres in current Russian television miniseries in his monograph *Russian Television Today: Primetime drama and comedy* (London and New York: Routledge, 2008), including soap operas, costume dramas, and criminal series.
28 Daniil Dondurey, "Ekstremal'noe TV. Seriynye ubiystva stali serial'nymi," *Izvestiya*, 12 July 2002, 9.

the market (...) while being funded by the latter's favorite offspring-advertising."[29]

Post-Soviet Russian miniseries generally are situated in a framework of conflicting critical hierarchies. On the one hand, there are pure entertainment criteria oriented toward the lowest common intellectual denominator in order to gain maximum profits and solely measured through commercial rankings: the more viewers watch a program, the greater the numbers that can be manipulated in their role as consumers. On the other hand, there is a competing intellectual-cultural hierarchy which uses quality standards inherited from earlier periods of Russian history. Despite Russian television's profound commercialization, professional critics and culturally discriminating segments of the viewership continue to assess the quality level of fictional television production on a continuum ranging from purely commercial (low-brow) to predominantly intellectual (high-brow). In the early 2000s, competing with the openly commercial type of television miniseries that often adapts Western formats, genuine quality television made a significant comeback, particularly in the genre of literary adaptation.[30] This was possible due to increased financial opportunities that a stabilized Russian economy created in the second post-Soviet decade, as well as the realization by parts of the media establishment that a referral to traditional values represented by classical literature could be both prestigious and profitable.[31] The new trend, in clear opposition to the exploitation of crime and violence, began with Vladimir Bortko's ten-part *The Idiot* [*Idiot*], 2003, faithfully adapted from Feodor Dostoevsky's novel, which was celebrated as a national event. The film's outstanding cast, historical authenticity,

---

29   Dondurey, "Ekstremal'noe TV," 9.
30   Soviet television in the 1970s and 1980s did produce several superb miniseries that were quite successful with audiences, for example, *The Life of Klim Samgin* [*Zhizn' Klima Samgina*] from Maksim Gor'kiy's novel, *A Raw Youth* [*Podrostok*] adapted from Feodor Dostoevsky's 1874 novel, and *Red and Black* [*Krasnoe i chernoe*] from Stendhal.
31   Russia is not alone in this emphasis on its literary tradition: the literary adaptation has been a mainstay of such powerful television conglomerates as the *BBC*.

and skillful narration all contributed to its success that clever producers immediately tried to replicate by adapting other Russian classics. It is typical of Russian literary adaptations that they stay close to the text. However, they are by no means axiologically and politically neutral or entirely defined by the literary classic's worldview. Bortko's adaptation is distinct in its selective emphasis on the novel's anti-Western elements rather than Dostoevsky's bitter depiction of a deformed and defunct Russian society—an emphasis that apparently went unnoticed by viewers and reviewers when the miniseries was first aired but that in hindsight appears significant for axiological trends in Russian television as a whole. Indeed, non-ethnically defined patriotism, juxtaposing values of the Russian nation to those of the West (Russian compassion and transcendence of class barriers vs. Western greed and hypocrisy) increasingly appears as a characteristic feature of both literary adaptations and historical epics.

From a strictly aesthetic point of view, it is convenient and to a certain degree legitimate to raise objections against the vast majority of Russian miniseries.[32] However, as a whole, the genre represents a lively cultural stratum with rich quality gradations and a wide range of themes. While it is the quantity of miniseries output that most impresses—and disturbs—outside observers, the different quality levels, covering the entire spectrum from trash to art, deserve particular attention. The Russian state predominantly supports high-brow productions, either through central funding from the Ministry of Culture or through a regional administration such as the Moscow municipality. Invoking the demands for greater state involvement quoted at the beginning, it is legitimate to ask what values such miniseries espouse. A highly indicative example is *Peter the First: The Testament* [*Petr Pervyy. Zaveshchanie*], 2011. Adapted from a novella by Daniil Granin and directed by Vladimir

---

32   For a discussion of Russian television genres in relation to their Western counterparts, see chapters 6 (sitcoms) and 7 (game show) in Stephen Hutchings and Natalia Rulyova, *Television and Culture in Putin's Russia: Remote Control* (London and New York: Routledge, 2009).

Bortko, it is representative of post-Soviet Russian quality television and value-oriented miniseries with a direct engagement of the state.

3. Peter the Great and the State Theme

Already during his lifetime, Peter the Great (1672–1725) acquired a semi-mythical stature that only grew in the following centuries and shaped the tsar's depiction in historical fiction, cinema, and even opera. The first cinematic portrayal of Peter the Great was released as early as 1910.[33] The two-part Soviet epic *Peter the First* [*Petr Pervyy*], 1937–1938, opened the genre of monumental biopics as a mainstay of Stalinist cinema, marking a sharp turn from a class-based to a personality-centered assessment of history.[34] Seventy years later, the prestigious miniseries *Peter the First: The Testament* offers a post-Soviet interpretation of this historical figure — a "Peter the Great for our time." It consists of four one-hour episodes, the first of which provides the narrative exposition introducing all macro- and micro-plots and conceptual themes. Naturally, any film that deals with well-known historical figures such as Peter the Great is facing an uphill battle to generate suspense because the audience is already familiar with the essential facts, a problem that distinguishes historical drama from other television genres. In order to awaken viewers' interest despite the known ending, filmmakers are forced to pay increased attention to the psychological plausibility of characters so that their development and interaction become intriguing in themselves. *Peter the First: The Testament* reveals from the very beginning that it was made by experienced professionals who are dealing with this obstacle in a solid manner. The narrative is composed so that that the viewer is eager

---

33   *Peter the Great* [Petr Velikiy], also known as *The Life and Death of Peter the Great* [Zhizn' i smert' Petra Velikogo], directed by Kai Hansen and Vasiliy Goncharov.

34   This change was initiated by the Communist Party, beginning with a decree issued on 16 May 1934, "On the Teaching of Civil History in the Schools of the USSR," followed by editorials in *Pravda* criticizing "unpatriotic" films and theater plays. For a discussion of this trend, see *Istoriya sovetskogo kino: 1931–1941*, vol. 2 (Moscow: Iskusstvo, 1972), 228–31, and Peter Kenez, *Cinema and Soviet Society 1917–1953* (Cambridge: Cambridge University Press, 1992), 161.

to learn how it will unfold, even though it is clear that Peter is inevitably going to die—indeed, the title itself leaves no doubt about the ending.

From the start, the film presents the viewer with a prematurely aged and visibly ailing tsar who is still trying to rule with an iron grip, fighting rampant corruption and disloyalty. Peter's court notices the unmistakable signs of weakening prowess and secretly negotiates varying alliances for the time after his passing. To protect his legacy—a robust centralized state that continues to modernize Russia—Peter needs a male heir. Since his wife, Ekaterina, can no longer give birth, his devoted second-in-command, the sly Prince Menshikov, searches for a new spouse and seems to succeed: when attending the wedding of Moldovan Prince Dmitriy Kantemir, Peter is enchanted by the host's nineteen-year old daughter from his previous marriage, Maria, who performs an exotic dance. Father Kantemir is not opposed to a liaison with the Russian ruler, the more so as it could help him return to Moldova's throne. But Maria, an unusually educated and emancipated young woman who prefers libraries to court functions and who dreams of loving and marrying an intellectual equal whom she can respect as a true partner, is put off by the idea of living with a man thirty years her elder whose behavior often comes across as vulgar and outrageous. In the meantime, the ailing Peter is tormented as much by kidney stones as by scheming courtiers. The schemers hope to maintain their influence once Ekaterina succeeds her husband on the throne, expecting her to protect them from the wrath of Peter's grandson, Petr Alekseevich, who is feared to revenge his father's execution. To the courtiers' dismay, Maria ultimately acquiesces to Peter's advances and eventually develops genuine feelings for the state ruler [*gosudar*]. He, in turn, proves his virility and impregnates her—but Ekaterina's henchmen instigate a miscarriage. At the end, Peter dies in horrible pain and without a male successor.

On the level of primary plot, the film intrigues the viewer with the question of how the tsar's amorous plans will unfold. Focusing on this private issue is particularly effective because few people know about Peter's purported affair with Maria Kantemir, a story that is scarcely documented and likely comes as a novelty even to historically well-versed viewers.³⁵ While it must be clear to any minimally educated viewer from the beginning that Peter will not be able to hand his legacy to a male heir since he was succeeded by his widow, suspense is generated by the question of how exactly his plan will fail—an excellent pretext for historical drama. The secondary plotlines also make continued viewing worthwhile, fleshing out the relations between competing courtiers whose characters are drawn out quite deftly by prominent performers, as well as the deterioration of spousal relations between Peter and Ekaterina and the progression of the tsar's illness. But it is the film's conceptual plane that offers the most intriguing questions engaging the viewer on a level far beyond simple entertainment. It is represented by the following themes:

1. *Autocracy*: The ruler's principles of how to efficiently govern the Russian empire are systematically illustrated and verbalized in the vast majority of scenes. The theme of autocracy, which is traditional for most fictional works dealing with Peter the Great, is introduced at the beginning when the insomniac tsar has visions of

---

35 Maria Kantemir (1700–1757) was the daughter of Moldovan ruler [*gospodar'*] Dmitriy Kantemir who lost his country after Peter the Great's unsuccessful 1711 Prut campaign against the Ottoman Empire. Prince Dmitrii lived in St. Petersburg since 1720, actively participating in the court's life. However, his second wife and his daughter Maria were not fond of the many festivities and abstained, citing illness as the reason—this fact angered the tsar, who ordered an investigation. The affair between Peter and Maria began in winter 1721 and, according to some sources, lasted until the tsar's death. Maria, just like Peter's wife Ekaterina, accompanied the tsar during his 1722–1723 Persian campaign, where she had a miscarriage. She later was part of Moscow high society but never married. The main source of information about Maria Kantemir and her liaison with Peter is an article by the influential historian Leonid Maykov (1839–1900), "Knyazhna Mariya Kantemirova [sic!]" that appeared in the journal *Russkaya starina* 89:1 (1897): 49–69; 89:3 (1897): 401–17; 89:6 (1897): 425–51; and 89:8 (1897): 225–53, and was part of a monograph on Maria's famous brother, satirist Antiokh Kantemir (published in 1903). Maikov cites sources such as the correspondences of the French ambassador to Russia, de Campredon, and the collection of anecdotes about Peter by Scherer. However, Maikov's textological methods have been repeatedly criticized (cf. M. D. El'zon, "Maykov Leonid Nikolaevich," in *Russkie pisateli 1800–1917. Biograficheskiy slovar'*, vol. 3 (Moscow: Nauchnoe izdatel'stvo Rossiyskaya entsiklopediya, 1994), 462–63. Conspicuously, Maykov's article has inspired works of fiction rather than academic scholarship.

violence during the 1682 Streltsy revolt[36] (shown in black-and-white), and continues with scenes of Peter's interaction with the Senate and individual courtiers. Conspicuously, Prince Kantemir's teenage son, Antiokh, presents Peter with a Byzantine imperial belt in anticipation of the tsar's elevation to the rank of emperor; the allusion to Byzantium serves as a reminder of Russia's claim to be the Third Rome, which gives Peter a metaphysical stature and a mission transcending common standards of tsarist rule.

2. *Corruption*: This phenomenon is depicted as a deep-rooted feature of Russian society. The first scene following the credits shows the interrogation and torture of the former vice-governor of Yaroslavl, Poptsov, in which Peter personally participates. The theme is further developed through Poptsov's execution, followed by a scene in which the methods of high-level thievery are depicted directly: the seasoned prince Kurbatov, responsible for the treasury, nonchalantly inflates the costs of a masquerade ball so as to take the extra cash for himself; he, too, is later executed. At one point, Peter accuses Menshikov openly of being the greatest thief of them all, to which he responds with a smile "This is true — but I am one of us."

3. *Expansionism*: Russia's territorial expansion is presented as a geopolitical and civilizational necessity and a matter of course. Peter is informed that Sweden has finally been defeated and that, after 18 years of war, the Swedish fleet has been driven from the Baltic Sea, to which he comments in lionesque manner: "From now on, Russia will forever be a part of Europe," followed by another crucial remark: "unless the people succeeding us will mess it up," which implicitly refers to Russia's post-Soviet geopolitical dilemmas. Paradoxically, the expansionist theme is complemented by culturally pro-European attitudes; thus, Menshikov declares, "Europe is our teacher and example." Russia's subsequent expansionist wars are repeatedly referred to as the natural course of events.

4. *Multinationalism*: The Russian empire is shown to be multinational by nature and mission. In one scene, Ukrainians (*malorossi-*

---

36   Streltsy were guardsmen armed with firearms; after a 1682 revolt, Peter the Great gradually dissolved their units.

yane) complain to the senate about their harsh treatment by the central state, a petition that is brushed off by the tsar. Moldova, according to Kantemir, aspires to join the Russian empire because it is a Christian power. A Lezgin,[37] one of Kantemir's servants, saves the tsar's life during an assault, and Peter hires him on the spot as a member of his guard.

5. *Populism*: The connection between the Russian people and their ruler is depicted as vital. A peasant by the name of Efim Nikonov purports to have invented a submarine. During its practical demonstration in a pond, the device sinks, to the laughter of courtiers. The only one not laughing is Peter. He takes the peasant's idea seriously and orders the continuation of his experiments.

All five themes are essentially statist. Furthermore, all are mutually dependent and reinforcing, forming a semantic nexus: Russia is an empire in need of a strong ruler in order to fight its innate corruption, to advance its geopolitically vital expansion and multinational mission which are naturally promoted by the ruler's connection with common folk and his appreciation of their talents. All five statist themes are introduced in the first episode and consistently developed in subsequent installments. As a matter of fact, it is the ongoing struggle between the Russian state doctrine embodied by Peter the Great and the particular interests of the courtiers that generates a psychological and intellectual suspense no less powerful than the erotic plotline. Thus, in *Peter the First: The Testament*, the viewer is overtly and subconsciously encouraged to identify with the ruler's perspective, i.e. understand and evaluate the events from the viewpoint of the autocratic state, its functioning and its sustained vitality as embodied by Peter. This effect is furthered by the fact that the major and minor plotlines are closely intertwined with the five conceptual themes and derive their motivational logic from them.

For the discriminating viewer whose socialization took place in the Soviet period, *Peter the First: The Testament* offers an addi-

---

[37] Lezgin, or Lezgian: a member of an ethnic group in Southern Dagestan and Northern Azerbaijan.

tional intellectual challenge — the comparison with preexisting fictional renditions of the legendary historical personality, particularly Aleksei Tolstoy's hugely popular novel (1929-1945) and Vladimir Petrov's two-part biopic (1937-1938) whose larger-than-life portrayal of the tsar became canonical since its release. Because the latter has been regularly shown on television, Petrov's film is still on many Russian viewers' minds; in particular, Nikolai Simonov's interpretation of the title character has remained emblematic.[38] The underlying issue of political, cultural, and axiological continuity and discontinuity is decisive for the understanding of contemporary Russian society. Television miniseries, as the currently most popular of all cultural forms, are significant indicators for the interpretation of socio-cultural perceptions and trends. The often articulated hypothesis of a seamless continuity between Soviet and post-Soviet culture can be tested by comparing the Stalinist epic to Bortko's miniseries.

The production of the *Peter the First* was begun at Lenfilm studio in 1935, a massive undertaking both logistically and artistically. The unprecedented investment in the recreation of period buildings, vessels, and costumes, together with an all-star ensemble gave the film an authenticity that supports its ideological message, the propaganda of statist values with particular emphasis on autocratic methods. A lot was at stake: this was to be the first biopic to visualize a new, essentially non-Marxist concept of history as created by "great men." Peter is shown as a passionate giant — both physically and intellectually — who forces internal and external foes, including his son Aleksei, to accept his state consolidation agenda or perish. The film opens with a low point in Peter's career — his shameful defeat by the Swedes in the battle of Narva and the betrayal of his son who wishes to roll back his father's reforms and even sides with Russia's foreign enemies, and the constant opposition and sabotage

---

38   Vladimir Bortko admitted that "we all imagine the actor Nikolay Simonov in that role." C.f. Oleg Pochinyuk, "Zaveshchanie Velikogo Petra," *Krasnaya zvezda* 85, 18 May 2011, 24.

of reactionary boyars. But the larger-than-life Peter is able to overcome the setbacks; moreover, he is egalitarian in his approach and intuitively understood and loved by common folk.

The three-hour long epic was released in two parts, the first in 1937, the second in 1938, and became an immediate hit. Based on a screenplay by Aleksei Tolstoy, an author with a long-standing interest in historical fiction and particularly in Peter the Great, *Peter the First* depicts the tsar as a genius whose will was decisive in determining Russia's future as a geopolitical superpower. Stalin personally met with Tolstoi and Petrov and approved their concept of an enlightened autocrat who rises above the limitations of his time, putting an end to controversies surrounding the film.[39] "Everything was conceived in breadth, there was no time for pity," exclaims the tsar in the film, a statement that was later ascribed to Stalin himself. Contemporary audiences viewed *Peter the First* both as a fascinating period piece and as a political statement addressing their own time and their own supreme leader, creating the impression of continuity through the ages.

Of the five statist themes that form the axiological foundation of *Peter the First: The Testament*, the first (autocratic principles), the third (expansionism), the fourth (multinationalism), and the fifth (populism) are all prominently present in the 1937–1938 epic. These commonalities confirm the hypothesis of considerable continuity between the 1930s and the 2010s. However, the Stalinist rendition completely leaves out the second theme, Russia's intrinsic corruption.[40] Instead, it emphasizes the incompetence and downright stupidity of the boyars as a reactionary class that is ready to side with Russia's foreign enemies — an implicit justification for autocratic methods to neutralize high-ranking "enemies of the people" in the 1930s. It is noteworthy that the boyar theme is absent from Bortko's post-Soviet miniseries. Furthermore, the Stalinist epic repeatedly shows Peter's rejection and mockery of the Orthodox Church and

---

39 Cf. Marina Kuznetsova, "Petr Pervyy," in *Shedevry rossiyskogo kino* (Moscow: Andreevskiy flag, 2000), 204.
40 There is one scene in which Peter catches his favorite Menshikov stealing and punishes him on the spot; however, this is a far cry from Bortko's miniseries where thievery is shown consistently as a systemic problem in Russia.

her values; this anticlerical theme, too, is absent from Bortko's miniseries — the post-Soviet portrayal of the tsar endows him with a piety that is unimaginable in the Stalinist biopic. Thus, in Episode Two of the miniseries, Peter prays and speaks to an icon, asking forgiveness for having killed his own son and having shed so much blood, but also justifying his deeds before God by claiming that he did it all to give the Russian nation dignity. The Soviet film portrays Peter in his prime, being surrounded by devoted friends who help him carry out his ambitious plans; the only person he distrusts is his own son, whose firm Orthodox faith and conservatism are coupled with a lack of patriotic loyalty.[41] In the post-Soviet miniseries, Peter the Great is a lonely genius surrounded by collaborators appearing as interchangeable, negligible characters whose importance evaporates when the ruler is absent.[42]

The analogy between Peter the Great and Stalin, both of whom supposedly had no choice but to act ruthlessly for the good of their nation, was an ever-present subtext in the Stalinist period. Later films about Peter the Great, especially Sergei Gerasimov's dilogy *Peter's Youth* [*Yunost' Petra*] and *In the Beginning of Great Deeds* [*V nachale slavnykh del*], 1980, carry on implicit polemics with the Stalinist interpretation of Peter's rule, instead emphasizing his openness to the West and his support of education. But the director of the 2011 miniseries, Vladimir Bortko, once again — and explicitly! — likened Peter the Great to Stalin, stating that both leaders "radically changed the destiny of our country and of the world as a whole."[43] Since Peter the Great traditionally symbolizes the idea of "enlightened" autocratic statehood and embodies both its reformist potential and personal vulnerability, the viewer of the miniseries increasingly becomes an object of persuasion of the crucial role that the

---

41   A much more differentiated interpretation of the relationship between Peter and his oldest son and their underlying differences was the theme of *Tsarevich Aleksey* (1997), a little seen feature film by Vitaliy Mel'nikov whose implied polemics against the Stalinist picture was typical of the 1990s.

42   Marina Suranova, "Rezhisser Vladimir Bortko: To, chto segodnya v televizore — eto antikhudozhestvenno i amoral'no," *Novye izvestiya* 82, 20 May 2011, 1.

43   Ibid.

ruler's personality plays for the future of the nation. This is another common element of Bortko's portrayal in the 2010s and Petrov's in the 1930s: the destiny of Russia's statehood is claimed to depend on the success or failure of one man.

Overall, a comparison between the Soviet and post-Soviet film allows the conclusion that axiological continuity between the 1930s and 2010s can be detected on the level of fundamental statist themes, rendering the functionality and mission of the state and autocratic principles of rule into central axiological criteria.[44] However, there is no continuity regarding the themes of class tension and spirituality.

Some subplots of the miniseries contribute to human interest in a manner that is only indirectly associated with statist themes, for example, the competition between the powerful yet aging Ekaterina and the young Maria for Peter's sexual attention. A theme that is unique to the post-Soviet portrayal of Peter the Great is that of an aging potentate whose days are numbered and who is forced to realize the uncertain outcome of his projects and his legacy.[45] However, any human aspects proper are dominated by the themes specifically related to the Russian state. While on the surface, the film appears as a lavishly executed historical drama, making it attractive for large target audiences, its underlying and all-pervasive focus is Russian statehood, its builders, supporters, and foes.

Bortko has always demonstrated a rare ability to sense the Russian zeitgeist and respond to it both on the big and small screens, beginning with the mildly anti-Soviet Bulgakov adaptation *Heart of a Dog* (1989) that shot him to national fame. *Peter the First: The Testament* shares with Bortko's previous works (that also include a solid if somewhat pedestrian *Master and Margarita*, 2005) a

---

44 Bortko's explicit and implicit didacticism is also part of his miniseries' connection with fundamental assumptions of Soviet cinema as a cultural institution.
45 Bortko stated that the film project for him started with the image of an old man with a cane running through the city and still trying to accomplish something when nobody is obeying him and nobody is afraid of him anymore. Pochinyuk, "Zaveshchanie Velikogo Petra," 24.

meticulous approach to mis-en-scene, a dramatic script, an outstanding cast uniformly delivering excellent performances, and a gripping score with memorable leitmotifs — all evidence of the filmmaker's high degree of professional mastery and essential marks of quality television.[46] His controversial Gogol adaptation *Taras Bulba* (2009), which was criticized for its overt anti-Polish message, was one of the costliest Russian films in whose financing the state had a stake. Following global financial crisis, however, Bortko experienced considerable difficulties in getting his feature film project on Peter the Great funded. In an interview, he described the efforts that the author Daniil Granin undertook to help the project, approaching government officials at the highest level, to no avail.[47] Apparently, the failure to secure funding for a feature film led to the project of a miniseries, a format that Bortko himself at some point mentioned as the only profitable one in Russia today, likening it to prostitution, weapons trade, and drug trafficking.[48] (On another occasion, however, he also stated that only a miniseries can fully capture the complex narrative structures of a novel.[49]) Ultimately, it was the administration of St. Petersburg that provided essential financial support. Whatever the initial artistic considerations may have been, the format of a miniseries shown on prime-time television secured Bortko's film a maximum number of viewers, incomparably higher than even the most successful feature film would have had.

4. Ideological Messages in Historical Disguise

Regarding the ideological underpinnings of *Peter the First: The Testament*, its numerous references to Russia's contemporary situation are particularly intriguing. While Bortko's miniseries can certainly be seen as a serious, albeit controversial, contribution to the discourse on Russian statehood and the conditions under which its

---

46   Bortko's *Peter the First* is certainly superior to the 1986 U.S. miniseries starring Maximilian Schell.
47   Vladimir Zheltov, "Vladimir Bortko: My ubili kino sobstvennymi rukami," *Nevskoe vremya* 58, 6 April 2010.
48   Ibid.
49   Cf. Pochinyuk, "Zaveshchanie Velikogo Petra," 24.

continuity can be secured, the film never questions the Russian state's legitimacy as such. This curious lacuna is key to the understanding of the film's underlying axiological framework and its relation to Russia's current situation. Surely, Granin's story about "Peter the Great's last love" is not firmly corroborated by mainstream historiography, even though the plot, while arguably tending toward the currently popular genre of "alternative history," does present a plausible hypothesis. But that is beside the point— after all, neither the novella nor the film were meant as scholarly treatises.[50] Rather, moving the idea of a male heir as a condition to secure state continuity to the narrative center is indicative of the miniseries' goal to get a mass audience interested and involved in the film's axiological foundation. In other words, as soon as the viewer is hooked on the court intrigue about Peter's desperate need for a son, the film has achieved its major incentive: engaging the audience in the statist themes. What is both problematic and revealing for this approach is the fact that Bortko, while capturing the sad final days of a self-proclaimed mega-reformer, leaves out what exactly he was reforming. As a matter of fact, Bortko takes the concentration on the statist theme even further than his Stalinist predecessor, in which an important subplot illustrates the plight of a fugitive serf who is tortured by a boyar and exploited by a capitalist but appreciated by the tsar. The 2011 film does not question, or even address, the inherent importance of Peter's policies for the Russian people—their benevolence is taken for granted, as if legitimate per se. What Bortko conveys to the viewer is not an analysis of the nature of the Russian state and its institutions and laws, but the urgency to protect them and secure their survival.

It is remarkable how little attention the constructive side of Peter's rule receives as opposed to his authoritarian decisions, gestures, and speechifying. Peter is right and righteous from beginning to end; there is not one serious opponent who would dare to probe the legitimacy of his autocratic policies at any point. Instead, even those characters who are intellectually on par with him, such as Dmitriy Kantemir and his daughter, share his statist goals and do

---

50 Conspicuously, the credits do not list the usual "expert consultants."

their utmost to advance his autocratic agenda. Bortko shows Peter the Great as a ruler without alternative, whose viewpoints still seem sound and modern and who selflessly fulfills a historical mission whose true dimensions are visible to him alone. While the cruel practices of Peter's administration are not concealed, they are not critiqued either—nor is any alternative to them ever even mentioned. Thus, an entire historical discourse debating Peter's rule and legacy that took place in the 19th and early twentieth century is excluded. Just like Petrov's portrayal in the 1930s, Bortko's film approves unconditionally of autocratic principles as the only reasonable policies for Russia. The main arguments for this approval are the external threats to Russia's integrity from competing empires and the internal threats of rampant corruption and shortsighted group interests. Corruption is purported to be a specifically Russian problem. Not coincidentally, Bortko's film opens with the aforementioned scene in the torture chamber, where a jailed official is forced to admit his bribery. The tsar, frustrated by his inability to root out the problem, exclaims "Why don't the Germans take bribes, why don't the Dutch—and why do the Russians?" The film never provides an answer, simply taking corruption in Russia as a given that every ruler has to face. Peter's fight against it is merciless, yet even his closest allies are fallible to the temptations of riches. To the question of why under Peter thievery was so common, Bortko responded: "Thievery always blossomed in Russia, for a thousand years. Nobody was ever able to do anything about it."[51] Thus, the miniseries' entire anti-corruption theme is intended to prove that only an independent autocrat is able to take on this phenomenon.

Peter the First: The Testament makes it abundantly clear what the tsar is fighting *against*, but not what is he fighting *for*. Except for the scene in which the wooden submarine is tested and a discussion on whether it is reasonable to furnish a naval expedition to find a possible connection between Asia and America, Peter's creative activities are never put on display. However, merely enforcing laws and acting violently is not sufficient for either improving matters in a country or for state-building. As a matter of fact, reducing Peter

---

51   Irina Tumakova, "Zaveshchanie Petra," *Izvestiya* 21, 8 February 2011, 10.

the Great's practice to endless interrogations and executions supports precisely what his opponents had been accusing him of all along: that his rule was more totalitarian than enlightened. The Russian people, in whose name the draconian measures are carried out, appear in the miniseries too rarely to prove that they benefit from the autocratic system. If at all, their reward lies in a nebulous notion of "Russian dignity" and "progress" and is projected into an imaginary future. This oversight is not coincidental; it lies at the heart of Bortko's and Granin's worldview and values: it is not the actual Russian people who gain from a stable power structure — it is the state itself that appears as an absolute value. State stability and continuity are consistently invoked as values per se, needing no further legitimization. This priority of the state's protection and survival as a supreme value even overshadows Peter's actual policy of promoting meritocracy which should have been observed by his successors and rarely was. Conspicuously, both Aleksei Tolstoi's novel and Vladimir Petrov's film did make upward mobility and meritocratic decisions important elements of their subplots, likely because they were seen as pillars of the new classless system in the Soviet Union. Bortko's film, made in a time period that no longer promotes classlessness, instead emphasizes Peter's insistence on his absolute entitlement, which is shown as an indispensable part of successfully ruling Russia. In an interview prior to the film's premiere, Bortko explicitly stated his interest in the political aspects of the story which, according to him, is about the decision-making of the highest ruler of the state, "regardless of what it is called: Father-Tsar, General Secretary, or President." [52] Further developing Granin's sufficiently speculative hypothesis,[53] Bortko's film suggests that after Maria lost Peter's child due to court schemes, the anointment of her younger brother Antiokh Kantemir as the future

---

52 Tat'yana Shipilova, "Vladimir Bortko: Ne tol'ko pro lyubov'," *Sovetskaya Sibir'* 83, 12 May 2011.
53 The male successor was not a condition sine qua non in Russia — after all, Peter's wife Ekaterina succeeded him on the throne. Had he really intended to elevate a more educated and moral person to the highest position in Russian society, he could have divorced Ekaterina, married Maria Kantemir, and declared the latter his successor.

tsar was a realistic option. Indeed, that would have given the Russian crown to one of the most advanced minds of his time – in other words, it would have put an intellectual on the throne. Such wishful thinking was characteristic of enlightenment and echoed by the communist reformist intellectuals of the 1960s, the so-called *shestidesyatniki*; obviously, it is still alive among post-Soviet intellectuals.

5. Conclusions

Peter the First: The Testament premiered 14 and 15 May 2011, on the *Russia* [*Rossiya*[54]] network. If ever there were any doubts, in interviews given prior to the premiere, Bortko expressed his sincere belief in legitimate authoritarian statehood as the only model that works for Russia. Surely, he shares this view with numerous Russian intellectuals past and present, including some former dissidents, extrapolating it to the current Russia, whose successful future is not at all a given. In *Peter the First: The Testament*, Bortko chose a bold move to visualize this need for statist continuity: at the end of Episode Four, in 1725, when Peter's collaborators carry the open casket with the dead tsar, their procession continues into modern-day St. Petersburg with its blinding streetlights and endless lines of cars. Referring to the fact that Peter did not leave a testament, Bortko stated polemically: "But he did leave a testament to you and me! He left us a country, the city of Petersburg, and whatever is going to happen to all that depends on us."[55] Thus, the testament of the film's title makes its way into contemporary Russia, as if to remind today's citizens to not squander what the great ruler had left them three hundred years ago. Such a metaphor concludes the line of implicit and explicit references to the future – i.e., to Russia's present and its autocratic state model – and appeals to twenty-first century audiences, both of which are indicative of the film's didactic mission. Needless to say, the direct appeal to the audience

---

54 *Rossiya* is a state-owned channel founded in 1991.
55 Shipilova, "Vladimir Bortko: Ne tol'ko pro lyubov'." In a similar vein, Bortko formulated: "During his reign, the ministries were formed, the industry, science, and to whom did he leave all that? To us." Cf. "Petr Pervyy: poslednie uroki," *Rossiyskaya gazeta* 96, 5 May 2011, 15.

is a feature characteristic of Soviet cinema, too — another element of cultural and axiological continuity. The symbolic ending leaves no doubt as to how Bortko and those who financed this large-scale miniseries interpret Peter the Great and his relevance for contemporary Russia. It also points to a partial axiological consensus of current Russian elites when calling for a stronger involvement of the Russian state in shaping Russian mass media, particularly television. It is not the fight against currently popular attitudes toward foreigners and minorities that the state funds — it is the proclamation of the vital importance of the state itself.

Both in Soviet and post-Soviet cinema, Peter the Great has been an object for projections, with different authors prioritizing certain aspects of his rule in order to claim historical precedents and thus continuity. While the two compared interpretations of Peter's rule are devoted to a distinct time period — Petrov's 1937–1938 picture focuses on the years of power consolidation, Bortko's 2011 *Peter the First: The Testament* on on the final four years — both share the positive portrayal of Peter the Great as the "chosen" enlightened autocrat.[56] Neither of them pay attention to the plight of the tens of thousands of serfs who perished during the building of the new capital, or to the profound contradiction between the raison d'ètat promoted by the ruler and its horrific consequences, thus ignoring the alternative interpretation of Petrine rule from Pushkin's *Bronze Horseman* to Merezhkovskiy's *Peter and Aleksei*.[57] This selectiveness is remarkable in itself, but also stands as a sign of axiological continuity: both in Soviet and in post-Soviet media, the success of Peter as the imperial statist per se trumps humanist considerations.

---

56   An interesting counter-image is given in Yury Il'enko's Ukrainian film *A Prayer for Hetman Mazepa* [*Molitva za getmana Mazepu*], 2002, where Peter, shown from the point of view of desired Ukrainian independence, appears as a ruthless powerbroker and pervert.

57   One of the most recent, and profoundly revisionist, contributions to the debate on Peter the Great's role in Russian history is a book by the controversial popular historian Andrey Burovskiy, *Petr Okayannyy: palach na trone* (Moscow: Eksmo, 2013).

In Search of Kazakhness: The Televisual Landscape and Screening of Nation in Kazakhstan

Marlene Laruelle, The George Washington University.

Television is the most widespread form of media in Kazakhstan, as well as the most trusted.[1] This confidence in television cannot be explained only by the political authorities' control over it. Television is trusted also because it offers cheap entertainment and a mirror in which the nation can project itself as an "imagined community." It creates shared social touchstones among viewers, emphasizes common cultural denominators, minimizes socioeconomic gaps, sets family rhythms according to the schedules of news and primetime shows, and influences collective fashions and values. Television thus plays a critical role in building and shaping nationhood and citizens. However, Kazakhstan's authorities waited a long time before investing in the small screen and cinema. In the 1990s, they gave priority to changing urban landscapes and toponyms, and in rewriting history textbooks.[2] Using visual tools to celebrate the nation began only in the 2000s, through some blockbusters, such as *Nomads*,[3] but also through investments in television programming. While cinema has already been the subject of several

---

[1] See in this volume, Barbara Junisbai, Azamat Junisbai, and Nicola Ying Fry, "Mass Media Consumption in Post-Soviet Kyrgyzstan and Kazakhstan: The View from Below," and Olena Nikolayenko, "Youth's Media Consumption and Perceptions of Electoral Integrity in Kazakhstan and Kyrgyzstan."

[2] Alexander Diener, "National Territory and the Reconstruction of History in Kazakhstan," *Eurasian Geography and Economics* 43:7 (2002): 565–583.

[3] Rico Isaacs, "Nomads, Warriors and Bureaucrats: Nation-Building and Film in Post-Soviet Kazakhstan," *Nationalities Papers* 43:3 (2015): 399–416. Investing in cinema also emerged as a response to the success of *Borat*. See Robert A. Saunders, "In Defence of *Kazakshilik*: Kazakhstan's War on Sacha Baron Cohen," *Identities* 14:3 (2007): 225–255.

studies, the small screen has so far been left out of scholarly analysis.[4]

As with print media, the authorities sought to assert control over television since the mid-1990s, when it became evident that the political opposition could use media as a tool against the ruling elites. The example of the Khabar media empire, controlled by President Nursultan Nazarbayev's daughter Dariga and her husband Rakhat Aliyev until he fell into disgrace in 2007, is the most revealing example of the state re-taking the media world under its wing.[5] However, media control by oligarch circles close to the regime or state-run structures should not obscure the authorities' relative lack of investment, until recently, in television as a soft power tool to communicate with their citizens. The fact that the principle station, *Pervyy kanal "Evraziya"*(*Channel One-Eurasia*), airs mainly Russian programs is a good example of this general disinterest. However, change has been underway for several years now: the authorities have understood the need to make better use of this powerful media. The current context of strengthening economic and strategic links with Russia in the framework of the Eurasian Economic Union and the Collective Security Treaty Organization constitutes a "push factor" for many Kazakh senior officials to invest into tools that reinforce Kazakhstani/Kazakh cultural autonomy.

It is in this context that this chapter examines how the nation is presented and staged on the small screen. The place and influence of Russian media in the Kazakhstani landscape and the lack of a local state response that presents a Kazakh point of view have been discussed in Kazakh media and think tank circles over the last several years, and more acutely since the beginning of the Ukrainian crisis.[6]

---

[4] I am grateful to Diana Kudaibergenova for fruitful discussions on earlier versions of this article.

[5] Barbara Junisbai, "Oligarchs and Ownership. The Role of Financial-Industrial Groups in controlling Kazakhstan's 'Independent Media'," in Eric Freedman and Richard Shafer, eds., *After the Czars and Commissars: Journalisms in Authoritarian Post-Soviet Central Asia* (East Lansing, Mich.: Michigan State University Press, 2011), 35–58.

[6] See, for instance, discussion of the Aspandau club, "Informatsionnaya bezopasnost' Kazakhstana—v poiskakh ob"ektivnoy istiny," http://aspanda

In the first section of the chapter, I give a brief overview of the Kazakhstani televisual landscape and its recent evolutions in ownership, language, and audience ratings. I then move on to examine documentary films as a reflection of official historiography, noting that the films have the same emphasis and "blank pages" as the official history and that they reflect the same hesitation about stressing the "Kazakhness" of Kazakhstan.[7] I then decrypt the broadcast *Signs. Legends of the Steppe*, which encapsulates a new genre I name "patriotic entertainment," a more entertaining version of Kazakh history, adapted from reality shows, to discover national heritage through a combination of patriotism and entertainment. I conclude that the Kazakh state will increasingly rely on this and other innovative methods of presenting Kazakhstan's past in response to Russia's more assertive foreign policy and a desire among Kazakhs to learn more about their own history and traditions.

1. Profiling Kazakhstani Television Channels

Kazakhstan has a well-developed media market that bears more similarities to its Russian neighbor than the rest of Central Asia. It offers fourteen channels and more than ninety Internet and cable television operators. Despite this large diversity, seven channels attract most viewers: state-run *Pervyy kanal "Evraziya,"* which alone accounts for 25 percent of the audience; *KTK*, launched in 1991 as the first private channel; *NTK*; *Kazakhstan*, which first broadcast in 1958 and was known in Soviet times as *KazTV*; *Kharbar*, created in 1995 as the channel of the information agency of the same name and famous for having been the center of the media empire of Rakhat Aliyev; *Kanal 31 (Channel 31)*, which is private and started in 1992;

---

 u.kz/ttc/informacionnaya-bezopasnost-kazahstana-v-poiskah-obektivnoy-istiny.

7 On Kazakhness and Kazakhstanness, see, among others, Marlene Laruelle, "The Three Discursive Paradigms of State Identity in Kazakhstan: Kazakhness, Kazakhstanness and Transnationalism," in Mariya Omelicheva, ed., *Nationalism and Identity Construction in Central Asia: Dimensions, Dynamics and Directions* (Lanham: Lexington Books, 2014), 1–20.

and *Sed'moy kanal* (*Channel 7*), the newest one, launched in 2009.[8] Many other satellite channels, available for a small fee, target specific segments of the audience with dedicated music, sports, or regional programming.[9] Worth mentioning is *Asyl Arna*, an Islamic channel started in 2007 that mainly broadcasts in Kazakh, but also in Russian in order to bring its programs on Islamic values and the Koran to the Muslim diasporas of Kazakhstan (e.g. Chechens, Dagestanis, Tatars, Bashkirs, Uyghurs).[10]

Figure 1.   Kazakhstani Television Channel Ratings in 2013

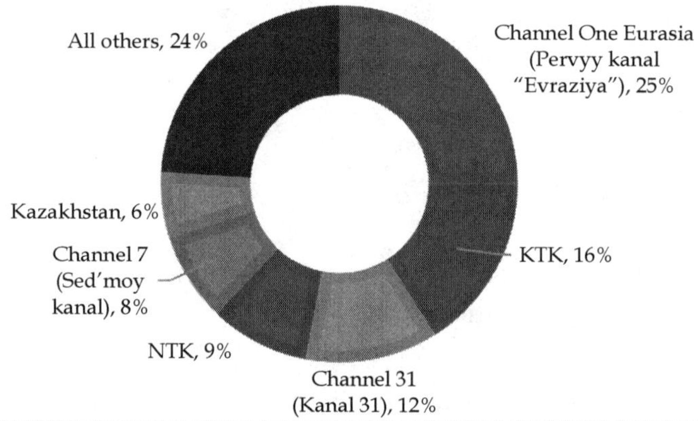

- Channel One Eurasia (Pervyy kanal "Evraziya"), 25%
- KTK, 16%
- Channel 31 (Kanal 31), 12%
- NTK, 9%
- Channel 7 (Sed'moy kanal), 8%
- Kazakhstan, 6%
- All others, 24%

Source: "Televizionnyy rynok Kazakhstana", 2014, http://www.tvmedia.kz/tv/

According to a 2014 study by J'son & Partners Consulting, 53 percent of the programming on the main channels available for free to every Kazakhstani viewer is nationally produced, versus 47 percent being foreign (mostly Russian).[11] However, this number should be

---

8   "Televizionnyy rynok Kazakhstana," *TVMedia.kz*, http://www.tvmedia.kz/tv/.
9   "Populyarnye onlayn tv v kategorii 'Kazakhstan'," Vefire.ru, https://vefire.ru/category/kazakhstan/.
10   See its website: "Home Page," *Aslyarna.kz*, http://www.asylarna.kz.
11   "Obzor rynka televizionnogo kontenta v Respublike Kazakhstan," J'son & Partners Consulting, http://json.tv/ict_telecom_analytics_view/obzor-rynka-televizionnogo-kontenta-v-respublike-kazahstan.

relativized: this quantitative majority is not correlated with the viewers' preferences. In terms of what people actually watch, Russia-produced contents still dominate, as I will show below.

The same goes for the language used on television—Kazakhstani programs can be in Russian or in Kazakh. Debating the place of the titular language in the republic's media is nothing new. Until the early 1960s, *Radio Kazakhstan* aired more than half its programming in Kazakh, a figure that fell to one-third under Nikita Khrushchev, with another radio station, Shargar, partially offsetting the difference with Kazakh language broadcasts. Local Soviet television only broadcast for three hours per day in Kazakh. As William Fierman has noted, in Soviet times Kazakh-language programs were targeted for rural audiences, with topics mostly focused on agricultural life. In the cases of both radio and television, material produced in Moscow and in Russian was more appealing and varied.[12] Paradoxically, the situation evolved little since Kazakhstan's independence in 1991. Russian-language domination of Kazakhstan's television market lasted through the 1990s and 2000s. The 1999 law on language in state media mandated that, at a minimum, Kazakh must be used at least as much as all other languages combined;[13] however, these levels were not possible to enforce. In 2013 it was decided that each Kazakhstani channel should broadcast at least 35 percent in Kazakh, a number updated to 50 percent in 2015.[14] But the majority of channels circumvented the law by broadcasting in Kazakh language at night so as not to lose their audience share.

---

12 William Fierman, "Reversing Language Shift in Kazakhstan," in Harold F. Schiffman and Brian Spooner, eds., *Language Policy and Language Conflict in Afghanistan and Its Neighbors: The Changing Politics of Language Choice* (London and Leiden: Brill, 2012), 140–141.

13 "Zakon Respubliki Kazakhstan ot 23-go iyulya 1999 goda No. 451-1 "O sredstvakh massovoy informatsii"," Online.zakon.kz, http://online.zakon.kz/Document/?doc_id=1013966.

14 Gul'mira Ileulova, ed., "Obzor kazakhstanskogo rynka teleindustrii na primere sravnitel'nogo analiza videokontenta telekanalov KTK, 31 kanal, Khabar," *spik.kz*, 28 June 2015, http://www.spik.kz/articles/kult-tur/2015-05-28/issledovatelskiy-proekt-obzor-kazakhstanskogo-rynka-teleindustrii-na.

Some channels, such as *Pervyy kanal "Evraziya"* and *Sed'moy kanal*, draw a distinctly Russian-speaking audience. *Pervyy kanal "Evraziya"* is a specific case because it mainly rebroadcasts programming from Russia's *Pervyy kanal (Channel One)* (called *ORT* before 2001). Kazakhstan's premier station is a joint project controlled 20 percent by Russian *Pervyy kanal* and 80 percent by the Kazakh state. *Pervyy kanal "Evraziya"* is a rare case where a state channel is partially owned by another state. The small channel *Mir* (and its news channel *Mir-24*) form a similar case of ownership partly based in Russia. *Mir* began in 1992 based on a CIS mandate, and reaches most post-Soviet states as well as Central Europe and Germany, where its primary audience is Russian-speaking diasporas. The channel broadcasts in Russian and targets audiences sympathetic to the Soviet past, with programs dedicated to the cultures of Eurasia and political discourse that supports regional integration.[15] Some other channels are aimed more openly at the Kazakh-speaking public. The most obvious example is the Kazakhstan state channel, which also airs in neighboring countries with Kazakh minorities (Uzbekistan, Kyrgyzstan, Russia, Mongolia, China) and by government decision, became officially entirely Kazakh-language in 2011.[16] The effect of this decision is mostly symbolic because the channel ranks only sixth in viewership, with less than 10 percent of the audience. Other examples include *Khabar*, which broadcasts in both languages but attracts few Russian speakers, and two smaller channels, *Astana* and *El Arna*.[17]

The study of the Kazakhstani televisual market commissioned in 2014 by the TV Media Advertising Agency gives us a relatively complete overview of the viewership.[18] In terms of age groups,

---

15   See its website, MirTV, "About," http://www.mirtv.ru/about/.
16   "O telekanale," *Qazaqstan*, http://kaztv.kaztrk.kz/ru/view/channel/page_1221_pervyi-natsionalnyi-telekanal-kazakstan. See also James Killner, "Kazakh state TV station ditches Russian language broadcasts," *The Telegraph*, 8 September 2011, http://www.telegraph.co.uk/news/worldnews/asia/kazakhstan/8750245/Kazakh-state-TV-station-ditches-Russian-language-broadcasts.html. Nevertheless, I watched a Russian-language broadcast on that supposedly 100 percent Kazakh channel in June 2015.
17   "Televizionnyy rynok Kazakhstana," *TVMedia.kz*.
18   Ibid.

some channels reach younger audiences (*Kazakhstan*, *Kanal 31*, *NTK*) with an average age around thirty years or less, while others aim for older viewers (*Pervyy kanal, Rakhat, Sed'moy kanal*) closer to their forties. Some channels stand out as having an even older audience, such as *REN TV*, *RTR Planeta*, and *NTV Mir*. *NTV*, *Khabar*, and *Kazakhstan* have more male viewers. Yet others attract men and women in equal numbers, or mainly women, who in 'Western' societies traditionally tend to watch more television. Other sociological criteria conventionally used to analyze television viewership are not relevant for Kazakhstan, such as education, which does not seem to affect the reach of the main channels (around 50 percent of viewers have secondary education, 25 percent tertiary, and 15 percent primary). Indeed in the former Soviet space, these education categories do not reflect professional realities. A small difference can be seen with channel *Kazakhstan*, which has more viewers with only a primary education, likely because it targets a rural audience.[19]

In terms of content, Khabar sets itself apart for its emphasis on news, which accounts for one-third of its airtime as compared to 12 percent for other channels. *Pervyy kanal* and *KTK*, the two main channels, devote half their airtime to films and series, and one-sixth to entertainment. Meanwhile *Khabar* and *Kazakhstan*'s broadcasts are one-third films and series and less than 10 percent other forms of entertainment. In turn, they offer more in the category called "social and political programming," which is less visible at *Pervyy kanal* and *KTK*. This ambiguous term often covers programs that give a voice to mid-level officials to promote state actions.

The Kazakhstani television market reproduces many characteristics of its Russian neighbor. In 2014, 44 percent of the whole broadcasting time was devoted to series.[20] Private channels are commercial above all and finance themselves through advertising. They specialize in profitable programs, which are mostly entertainment: music, sports, films, series, and talk shows—usually clones of Russian productions, which themselves copy Western ones. The

---

19 "Televizionnyy rynok Kazakhstana," *TVMedia.kz*.
20 "Obzor rynka televizionnogo kontenta," J'son & Partners Consulting.

channels often form parts of powerful media groups that also own newspapers, radio stations, and websites, and which are under the control of oligarchs close to the government. The most well-known case is that of the *Khabar* media holding, which has long been officially private but in reality was controlled by Dariga Nazarbayeva and her husband Rakhat Aliyev. Since his fall from grace in 2007, control has passed to the Ministry of Culture and Information. Khabar had been behind several innovative media projects, including the launch of Caspionet in 2002, the country's first satellite service, now renamed Kazakh-TV.

The two main state channels, *Pervyy kanal "Evraziya"* and *Kazakhstan*, reflect the duality of Kazakhstan's position on identity issues. The former rebroadcasts programs from Russia and is largely Russian-language; the latter is entirely Kazakh-language and targets a more rural audience. *Pervyy kanal "Evraziya"* is the main engine for spreading Russian perspectives on world news and Russian cultural products in Kazakhstan, and puts the country in the situation of consuming "foreign" cultural products. By contrast, via channel *Kazakhstan* the state is trying to disseminate productions that are both Kazakh-language and "made in Kazakhstan." But success is not a foregone conclusion.

The TV Media Advertising Agency study of the Kazakhstani television market confirms this analysis and provides precise figures.[21] On *Pervyy kanal "Evraziya,"* the most-watched programs in 2013 in Kazakhstan were largely Russian: the X-Factor music competition and main miniseries of the time (*Gyulchatay, Rusalka, Znakharka, Dom malyutki*, etc.) Only a speech by Kazakhstan's president attracted enough viewers to make it into the top six. The first Kazakh miniseries, *Kasym*, which describes the adventures of a young Kazakh hero during the Second World War, came in seventh. On *Khabar*, a Turkish series about Suleyman the Great had the most viewers of any show in 2013, followed by the Nazarbayev speech and several Russian series. On *Kazakhstan*, the entirely Kazakh-language channel, *Kelin*, a Kazakh miniseries, came out on top, followed by entertainment programs, concerts, and talk shows.

---

21 "Televizionnyy rynok Kazakhstana," TVMedia.kz.

The channel *KTK* set itself apart from the others, as all of its top shows are "Made in Kazakhstan" and include local news broadcasts on various issues, including corruption, and interviews with public figures.

The entertainment blockbusters from Russia draw the largest audiences on Kazakhstani television, and only a few local productions, news, concerts, and to a lesser extent miniseries, can compete with Russian cultural products. One of the key reasons for this misbalance is income from advertising. As former *KTK* director Arman Shurayev pointed out: "To produce one hour of a good miniseries, one can easily spend about $200,000 in Russia (…) Here in Kazakhstan, for the same hour, I can spend maximum $10–15,000."[22] The Kazakh-speaking market for advertising will never be profitable enough to provide sufficient private revenues for production companies to produce quality shows, and they will therefore continue to rely on state support. This is the paradox of Kazakhstani television: while it is largely regime-controlled and promotes official policy, the channels do not have a captive audience. The most enticing cultural products win and, in this race for viewers, Russian channels are much more competitive. This situation has recently begun to raise concerns among state officials and the Kazakh-speaking part of the population, and is now propelling a more active state policy in producing "made in Kazakhstan" programming.

2. Educating the Kazakhstani Public on Kazakh National History

In early March 2014 the presidential administration reorganized the Ministry of Culture and Communications, which became only a Ministry of Culture, while the communications section was upgraded into a State Agency for Communication and Information,

---

[22] Arman Shuraev, "90 protsentov otechestvennykh serialov nel'zya pokazyvat'," *meta.kz*, 2 March 2012, quoted in Ileulova, ed., "Obzor kazakhstanskogo rynka teleindustrii."

not attached to the government, but functioning as a central executive organ.[23] This change of administrative status was decided a few weeks before Russia's annexation of Crimea and it is difficult to affirm whether it was related to the Ukrainian crisis. Nonetheless, it is probable that since the country's entry into the Customs Union and then the Eurasian Economic Union, the Kazakhstani authorities were interested in strengthening their national media. In June 2014 the government published a "Strategic Plan of the State Agency for Communication and Information for 2014–2018" that calls for modernizing the Internet infrastructure, but also for reinforcing national production on television.[24] It remains difficult to identify who are the main decision-makers who oversee the role of television and the contents of local production, though many of my local informants mention the name of State Secretary Marat Tazhin. We know a little bit more about those who push for a state policy of commissioning historical documentaries.

The first figure is former Minister of Culture and Information Mukhtar Kul-Mukhammed, one of the members of the intergovernmental study group on national history [*Mezhvedomstvennaya gruppa po izucheniyu natsional'noy istorii*].[25] This intergovernmental group was created in 2013, under the leadership of Tazhin, to oversee all activities linked to the "rebirth of national historical memory," including "the study of blank pages."[26] Kul-Mukhammed is an influential politician close to Nazarbayev who repeatedly has held the posts of minister of culture and communications and of state secretary. He was born in Xinjiang and was one of the Kazakhs

---

23 "Ukaz 'O dal'neyshey sovershenstvovanii sistemy gosudarstvennogo upravleniya Respubliki Kazakhstan'," Akorda, 7 March 2014, http://www.akorda.kz/ru/page/page_216086_ukaz-.

24 "O strategicheskom plane Agenstva Respublika Kazakhstan po svyazi i informatsii na 2014–2018," *Tengrinews*, 6 June 2014, http://tengrinews.kz/zakon/docs?ngr=P1400000621.

25 "V Kazakhstane snyaty masshtabnye istoricheskie fil'my," *Headline.kz*, 26 September 2013, https://news.mail.ru/inworld/kazakhstan/society/14927393/.

26 "Sostoyalos' III zasedanie Mezhvedomstvennoy rabochey gruppy po izucheniyu natsional'noy istorii," *Nomad*, 26 September 2013, http://www.nomad.su/?a=3-201309260037.

of China "repatriated" to Kazakhstan in the 1960s. Many of them advocate for a more nationalist vision of Kazakhstan, driven by the memories of Stalinist repressions, forced collectivization, and emigration to China. Kul-Mukhammed defended a thesis on Alash Orda and runs several groups in charge of identity issues: a terminological and onomastic commission, which oversees the Kazakhization of place names and official terms; a commission on relations with co-ethnics abroad, the Oralmans; and a commission supervising language policy.[27]

The second figure is film director Anvar Mamraimov, who also serves as the director of the press-service of the Institute of Archeology and is author of several monographs popularizing ancient history of the steppe world and the Silk Roads. He began his career in the 1980s, with a first film about the mausoleum of Ahmed Yassavi in Turkestan, which was censored in Almaty, but finally found acceptance by central television in Moscow.[28] Since then he has become the champion of Kazakh historical films, with more than 200 broadcasts to his credit, of which twenty have been documentary films released with the state studio *Kazakhfilm*.[29]

The first historical documentary films commissioned by the Ministry of Education were part of the Cultural Legacy program [*Kul'turnoe nasledie*], which Nazarbayev launched in 2003 and ended in 2011. The program collected thousands of archival documents about the history of the steppe world from various world capitals, kicked off new archaeological excavation campaigns, restored historical monuments, republished editions of the main texts of Kazakh literature for popular circulation, and did the same for the classics of traditional Kazakh music.[30]

---

27 See the biographical page available at http://online.zakon.kz/Docume nt/?doc_id=30105657.
28 "Anvar Mamraimo: Ia—mnogostanochnik," *Antenna*, http://antennakz.c om/znay-nashich/anvar-mamraimov-ya-percentE2percent80percent94-mn ogostanochnik.html.
29 See his biography on his Facebook page, https://www.facebook.com/in-starch/posts/774937529193301.
30 "Gosudarstvennaia programma 'Kul'turnoe nasledie Kazakhstana'," Madeni Mura, http://www.madenimura.kz/ru/president-speech-madenimura/.

Just before the program closed, in 2010–2011, *Kazakhfilm* received a commission to produce twenty documentaries on national history. Although this number is mentioned in several documents, fewer than a dozen can be found online and it is likely that the rest were not released. An analysis of the ones that were filmed allows for a better understanding of the historical and cultural elements that the state wished to emphasize: Korkut, who created one of the most famous epics of the Turkic world, and traditional Kazakh music; the mausoleum of the founder of the Sufi order, Ahmed Yassavi, in Turkestan; the Tamgaly petroglyphs; and the Zharkent mosque, famous for its Chinese style. The only episode to deal with more contemporary history looked at the few pre-revolutionary buildings (the Tsarist officers' headquarters) still in place in the former capital Almaty. These documentaries are filmed in a conventional style and are probably boring for a non-specialist audience. They feature steppe landscapes and extras playing historical figures on parade (with a voice-over, in Russian), regularly interspersed with interviews with specialists on the topic — museum curators, historians, archeologists. The narrative tone is emphatic, celebrating the wisdom of the steppe world. The entertainment value is reinforced with a series of "new age," colorful portraits of the figures being celebrated.

The documentary on Korkut is particularly interesting because Korkut is also the national hero of Azerbaijan and many of the experts interviewed are Azeris.[31] The narrative does not argue against the "Azerization" of Korkut and displays pan-Turkic tones; it succeeds in drawing Korkut toward the Kazakh world by insisting that he was born in the Syr-Daria region, and by reminding the audience about his critical role in creating traditional Kazakh music on the dombra kuy, which UNESCO declared part of mankind's cultural heritage.[32] In 2013, channel *Kazakhstan* was chosen by the

---

31 "Korkyt—istoriya kiuya," YouTube, https://www.youtube.com/watch?v=jFpWSDGxd74.

32 Dinara Urazova, "UNESCO recognizes Kazakh yurt and kuy as cultural heritage of humankind," *Tengrinews*, 8 December 2014, http://en.tengrinews.kz/people/UNESCO-recognizes-Kazakh-yurt-and-kuy-as-cultural-heritage-257701/.

authorities to release three new historical films on the Sakhas, Huns, and Usuni, the steppe peoples who formed the first protostate structures on the territory that would become Kazakhstan.[33] The same year the channel premiered an eight-episode series marking the 300th anniversary of Abylay Khan (1711–1781), who unified the three hordes and was recognized by Russia and China as the leader of a unified Kazakh world. It is worth noting that it was the only fully Kazakh-language channel that was selected to air these new documentary films, an important symbolic gesture, but one which reduced the films' ability to reach the majority Russian-speaking viewers.

In choosing subjects for these state-sponsored historical documentaries, priority was given to the region's ancient history. Kazakhstani television seemed content to stage the less controversial aspects of national history—namely ancient and medieval figures that already had been celebrated during the Soviet period—and has long avoided sensitive subjects. It was not until the end of the 2000s that television finally reached for more contemporary issues, namely the integration into the Russian world. The channel Khabar took the courageous initiative of a bolder approach by commissioning and airing a film about Alash Orda,[34] the modernist Kazakh elites from the early twentieth century who constituted a provisional Kazakh government from December 1917 to August 1920. Many Alash Orda members, among them their main leaders Alikhan Bukeikhanov (1866–1937), rallied to the Bolshevik regime and formed the first generation of National-Communists, who were progressively repressed in the 1920s and then massively at the end of the 1930s. The film promotes Alash leaders as true democrats fighting for Kazakh statehood.

However, one must note the timidity with which Kazakhstani television approaches the "blank pages" of national history linked to interaction with the Russian world. With the exception of the film on Alash and several short documentaries on its members, and a

---

33 "V Kazakhstane snyat ryad istoricheskikh fil'mov," *Nur.kz*, 25 September 2013, http://www.nur.kz/283279.html.
34 Available at VKontakte, http://vk.com/docukz.

film about Mustafa Chokay replayed many times, Kazakhstani television largely avoids Soviet history. Moreover, these films often are aired only in Kazakh and thus remain accessible to a minority of the population, when the aim should be showing Kazakh views of Soviet history to the Russian-speaking population. This small screen policy thus reflects the hesitations of the current political regime, which descended directly from the Soviet elites, and tries to avoid opening painful memories of the Soviet era. The *Madeniet* (Culture) channel, launched in early 2014, screened many historical and cultural documentaries, but like its Russian equivalent *Kul'tura*,[35] targets a limited cultured audience.

More recently the Kazakhstani authorities decided to prioritize the nationalization of the shared Soviet history and focus on the most consensus-based period of it, the Second World War, known locally, as in Russian, as the Great Patriotic War. In 2013, *Khabar* devoted a four-episode series to the only Kazakh general in the Soviet army, Bauyrzhan Momyshuly (1910–1982), based on Alexander Bek's novel, *Volokolamsk Highway* (1944). Momyshuly's career trajectory reveals the ambiguities of Soviet policy on promoting minorities. A platoon commander in the Central Asian Military District's 315th Regiment, Momyshuly was sent to the front in 1941 and tasked with defending the highway passing through the city of Volokolamsk. Momyshuly gained recognition for his military exploits, but also was known for his nationalist views since the 1930s, which prevented him from receiving the Hero of the Soviet Union title whilst alive. It was bestowed on him posthumously in 1990, at the insistence of Nazarbayev, who was then chairing the Supreme Soviet of the Kazakh republic. The series honors his Kazakh identity more so than his loyalty to the Soviet regime. In 2014, Talgat Bigeldinov, twice a Hero of the Soviet Union and celebrated for his achievements in Soviet aviation, became the subject of another documentary, *To Rise in the Air! [Podnyat'sya v vozdukh!]*.[36] Preparations for the seventieth anniversary of the end of the Second World War,

---

35 See chapter in this volume.
36 "V Astane prezentovali fil'm 'Podniat'sia Podnyat'sya v vozdukh!," *Bnews.kz*, 5 May 2015, http://bnews.kz/ru/news/post/202636/.

in 2015, led to the release of several films. They include a production on the Panfilov division, which took part in the defense of Moscow against Nazi Germany and consisted mostly of soldiers from Kazakhstan and Kyrgyzstan, a film celebrating the role of Kazakh soldiers in the liberation of Kiev,[37] and a series commemorating Kazakh hospitality in welcoming deported peoples and Russian soldiers during the war.[38]

Tensions around the 2014 Ukrainian crisis have reinforced the will of the Kazakh authorities to invest in stimulating national history. At the Selinger youth camp in August 2014, Putin answered a question about the growth of nationalist feelings in Kazakhstan with an ambivalent statement. He celebrated Nazarbayev, who "has performed a unique feat" because "he has created a state on a territory where there has never been a state. The Kazakhs never had a state of their own, and he created it. In this sense, he is a unique person in the post-Soviet space and in Kazakhstan."[39] The statement stirred Kazakh public opinion, especially among young, nationalist-minded elites. In response to it, Nazarbayev announced that 2015 would be the 550th anniversary of the birth of the Kazakh state, embodied by the Kazakh khanate created by Kerey and Zhanibek in 1465. He posits: "It may not have been a state in the modern understanding of this term, within the current borders. ... [But] it is important that the foundation was laid then, and we are the people continuing the great deeds of our ancestors."[40]

---

37 "Posol'stvo Kazakhstana na Ukraine prezentovalo fil'm 'V ogon' za rodinu'," *Tengrinews*, 22 October 2014, http://tengrinews.kz/sng/posolstvo-kazahstana-ukraine-prezentovalo-film-v-ogon-rodinu-263890.
38 Mikhail Korchevskiy, "Seriya sotsial'nykh rolikov zapuskaetsya na kazakhstanskikh kanalakh," *KTK.kz*, 26 March 2015, http://www.ktk.kz/ru/news/video/2015/03/26/58499.
39 "Seliger 2014 National Youth Forum," *Kremlin News*, 29 August 2014, http://eng.kremlin.ru/news/22864.
40 "Kazakhskoy gosudarstvennosti v 2015 ispolnitsya 550 let—Nazarbayev," *Tengri News*, 22 October 2014, http://tengrinews.kz/kazakhstan_news/kazahskoy-gosudarstvennosti-v-2015-godu-ispolnitsya-550-let---Nazarbayev-263876/.

In 2014, as every year, December 16 independence festivities were an occasion for muscular discourse on patriotism. Nazarbayev recalled:

> Independence was hard won by many generations of our ancestors, who defended our sacred land with blood and sweat. (...) Independence is the unflinching resolution of each citizen to defend Kazakhstan, their own home, and the motherland to the last drop of blood, as our heroic ancestors have bequeathed us.[41]

A few days later in his address to the nation, Nazarbayev insisted on the need to develop patriotism among the younger generations, who no longer learn about history from books, and therefore should have it delivered through public commemorations and media.

Even in a period of economic crisis, the authorities allocated a significant budget to the festivities for the half millennium of Kazakh statehood: 3 billion tenge, or 16 million dollars, will be invested in exhibitions, video productions, conferences, and archeological expeditions, as well as in a large historical reenactment planned for the fall of 2015.[42] Television is one of the premier methods for communicating this revived patriotic message. On Nazarbayev's order, a new series on the history of the Kazakh khanate started production in January 2015.[43] Originally planned for twenty episodes, it was reduced to ten episodes, probably for planning reasons (it had to be written urgently for broadcast by the end of the year), but then was coupled with a series of documentary films and an animated movie.[44] Rustem Abdrashev, known abroad for his

---

[41] "Den' nezavisimosti prazdnuet Kazakhstan," *Tengri News*, 16 December 2014, http://tengrinews.kz/Kazakhstan_news/den-nezavisimosti-prazdnuet-kazahstan-266983/.

[42] "Tri milliarda tenge vydelyat na prazdnovanie 550-letiya Kazakhskogo khanstva i 20-letiya ANK," *Tengri News*, 19 November 2014, http://tengrinews.kz/kazakhstan_news/milliarda-tenge-vyidelyat-prazdnovanie-550-letiya-kazahskogo-hanstva-20-letiya-265489/.

[43] "Serial o Kazakhskom khanstve snimut v Kazakhstane," *Tengri News*, 4 November 2014, http://tengrinews.kz/cinema/serial-o-kazahskom-hanstve-snimut-v-kazahstane-264593/.

[44] "Tri seriala k 550-letiyu Kazakhskogo khanstva snimut v Kazakhstane," *Times.kz*, 16 February 2015, http://timeskz.kz/6219-tri-seriala-k-550-letiyu-

Gift to Stalin, was chosen to direct the series, probably in recognition for his directing a film celebrating Nazarbayev's youth, *The Path of a Leader*. The new mini-series will cover three centuries of history, beginning with Kerey and Zhanibek, who refused the rule of Khan Abulkhair Sheibanid (associated to Uzbeks) and moved to the Seven Rivers region, near Almaty, in the southeastern part of the present-day Kazakhstan, to create an independent khanate, and will end with Kenesary, the last khan who tried (and failed) to resist Russian advances in the steppes in the first half of the nineteenth century.

3. Entertainment, Religiosity and Patriotism: The Series *Signs: Legends of the Steppe*

The documentary films described above are official productions that state authorities commissioned. Whatever the quality, they only reach a limited audience, which sees them as a state narrative. Other approaches allow viewers to familiarize themselves with national history in a more entertaining way, and to identify more directly and personally with the distinctiveness of their country. An in-depth analysis of Kazakhstani-produced miniseries and their role in staging the national "us" is still lacking in the scholarly landscape. For this chapter, I selected only one series that, I believe, renewed the genre: the thirty-episode *Signs: Legends of the Steppe* [*Znaki. Stepnye legendy*], screened on *Sed'moy kanal* since 2013.[45] During informal interviews conducted in Kazakhstan on the topic of the media landscape, many of my local informants mentioned *Sed'moy kanal* as being the most innovative channel, since its dynamic team offers slightly different cultural products. Many other miniseries are worth studying, but in this chapter I focus only on *Signs*.

---

kazahskogo-hanstva-snimayut-v-kazahstane.html; "Serial o Kazakhskom khanstve sokrashchen s 20 do 10 seriy," *Nomad*, 23 January 2015, http://www.nomad.su/?a=14-201501230009.

45   About 15 series are available on YouTube: http://www.youtube.com/watch?v=7zmyir2NH1Q.

The setting is the same for each episode. One of the channel's most famous journalists Nuriddin Bidosov, dressed in a relaxed way in jeans, t-shirt, and a cap, travels all over Kazakhstan to visit some thirty historical and religious sites. The staging is modern, inspired by reality shows such as "Survivor." The narrative promotes adventures and technical feats, such as crossing more than 10,000 km of Kazakh steppe in an SUV, often on unpaved roads, in the desert, far from any urban center. It also focuses on human exploits: the journalist and interviewed people recount how they reached "their limits" in overcoming supernatural, physical and spiritual challenges.

Indeed the originality of the series is in offering a trip that is simultaneously geographical, historical, and spiritual. Distinctive landmarks set the pace for the journey: the journalist's route stops at every famous shrine [*mazar*] to which locals make pilgrimages and where they often engage in healing practices. These sites are the tombs of saints, typically spiritually elevated ascetics from Sufi mystical orders, but also mythical figures linked to the Prophet's family.[46] This tradition had been partly obscured during the Soviet era, but the regime never directly repressed it; it was seen as a national tradition and relic [*perezhitki*], not as a religious practice threatening official atheism. This practice of pilgrimage has taken on an unprecedented scale since Kazakhstan's independence.[47] The authorities fund the rehabilitation of these shrines not because of their religious values, but in order to "kazakhify" the national territory and show a national, Kazakh footprint on it, with the indirect goal of avoiding any territorial contestations with Kazakhstan's neighbors, especially Russia. Some of the chosen locations are natural landmarks, such as Charyn canyon, a cave with supposed magical springs, lakes with curative powers, or mythical places from local legends; the others celebrate famous knights [*batyr*] as in the case of the cave of Konyr-Aulie, the supposed hidden tomb of

---

46   See Kenneth Lymer, "Rags and rock art: the landscapes of holy site pilgrimage in the Republic of Kazakhstan," *World Archaeology* 36:1 (2004): 158–72.
47   Ulan Bigozhin, "State, Shrine, and Sacred Lineage in Post-Soviet Kazakhstan" (paper presented at the CERIA seminar, George Washington University, 3 February 2015).

Genghis Khan. The program also visits the graves of great national figures (Bidosov calls them "great men" [*velikie lyudi*]), such as the founder of the Sufi order Ahmed Yassavi,[48] writer Abay, and poets and folk singers [*akyn*] Suyunbay Aronuly and Zhambyl Zhabaev.

At each site visit Bidosov recounts the local legends. The custodians of the shrines give color to the lives of those buried there and explain different rituals linked to the sanctity of the place. They read Koran verses to visitors, and introduce them to sacred lineages, promoting a discourse of "rediscovery" of "authentic" Kazakh values forgotten during the Soviet era.[49] But they also sometimes act as fortune-tellers, or blessing mediators.[50] Bidosov inserts himself in these rituals and attends prayers. The "evidence" of the holiness of the site most often resides in cases of miraculous healing: for example a young boy who had never spoke a word until crossing the shrine of Suyunbay Aronuly, or a paralyzed person who regained use of his limbs by drawing water from the sacred spring of Charyn canyon. The revelation also can be of a more intimate nature: for example a poet who found inspiration by visiting the shrine of Abay, or an infertile woman who finally became pregnant after visiting the mausoleum of Aisha-bibi. In each new place, the star reporter speaks to people who experienced dramatic changes in their lives' trajectories during their visit to the shrine. Many of them could be defined as *born again*, claiming to have undergone spiritual regeneration following their visits to the shrine, which allowed them to end bad habits and become respectable men or women. Shrines, healing, and morality thus go hand-in-hand, as in the rest of Central Asia.[51]

---

48   Devin DeWeese, "Sacred places and 'public' narratives: The shrine of Ahmad Yasavi in Hagiographical traditions of the Yasavi Sufi order, 16th-17th centuries," *The Muslim World* 90:3-4 (2000): 353-76.

49   On the question of legitimacy around the shrine, see Krisztina Kehl-Bodrogi, "Who owns the shrine? Competing meanings and authorities at a pilgrimage site in Khorezm," *Central Asian Survey* 25:3 (2006): 235-50.

50   See Pawel Jessa, "Aq jol soul healers: religious pluralism and a contemporary Muslim movement in Kazakhstan," *Central Asian Survey* 25:3 (2006): 359-71.

51   See Maria Louw, "Pursuing 'Muslimness': shrines as sites for moralities in the making in post-Soviet Bukhara," *Central Asian Survey* 25:3 (2006): 319-39.

In most cases, deceased family members have visited the interviewees during their dreams, inviting them to make the trip to the shrine. In the nomadic Central Asian tradition, ancestral spirits (called *arbaks*) interact with humans and are worshipped in order to gain favors and benefit from their protection. Since they form the link with the world of the dead, they also symbolize the social and ethnic continuity of the nation.[52] Bidosov emphasizes the eminently national character of these shrines. He recalls the historical content in which a saint or historical figure lived, mentions that ancient Turkic-Mongol peoples believed in heaven, Tengri,[53] celebrates the popular devotion that at any time would surround these national figures, and recites verses or songs to commemorate their exploits, always done "for the good of the people" [*na blago naroda*].

The program is not content to rehabilitate Sufi spirituality or the *arbaks*. It links the places visited to extreme spiritual experiences. Many people Bidosov encounters describe sensations that can be defined as "extra-sensory" in their encounters/confrontations with the spirits of the place. Some say the spirits have physically challenged or injured them. For instance the Ukash-ata shrine, supposedly containing the tomb of a soldier of Prophet Mohammed, can "punish" those lacking pure souls by injuring them physically. Others have seen the spirit in human form or via the unexplained movement of objects, or been saved at the final moment from a mortal situation through inexplicable coincidental circumstances. The production alternates the narratives of the custodians and interview excerpts with dramatic reconstructions (done with actors) of these encounters with forms of "higher" conscience. At the

---

52　On the notion of arbak, see, for the Kyrgyz case, Svetlana Jacquesson, "Power play among the Kyrgyz: State versus Descent," in Isabelle Charleux et al., eds., *Representing Power in Ancient Inner Asia: Legitimacy, Transmission and the Sacred* (Belligham, Wash.: Center for East Asian Studies, Western Washington University, 2010), 221–44.

53　On Tengrism, see Marlene Laruelle, "Religious Revival, Nationalism and the 'Invention of Tradition': Political Tengrism in Central Asia and Tatarstan," *Central Asian Survey* 26:2 (2007): 203–16.

end of each episode, Bidosov gives viewers some concluding remarks about the need for spirituality, morality, national awareness, and for respecting ancestors.

The series is a successful merging of genres. It uses as its model American adventure and "unexplainable phenomena" shows, drawing on the same set of staging techniques using lighting and special effects. It also borrows from similar shows on Russian channels, but offers a specifically Kazakh national take. The series combines the revival of Islamic piety and reflects the growth in the country of "religious tourism" via pilgrimages to shrines. It also cultivates a fashion—present since the years of stagnation throughout the Soviet Union—for "extra sensory" phenomena, from UFOs and mysterious civilizations that have vanished to the practices of energetic healing, Asian medicine, Oriental-inspired philosophies, and so on. In this the program is an accurate reflection of Kazakhstani citizens' contemporary spiritual quests, marked by religious mash-ups—elements of "traditional" Islam combined with New Age atmosphere. The individual initiation received by visitors is apprehended as the main legitimizing elements to explain the sanctity of the shrines.

The program is also an innovative way to impart patriotic feelings on to its viewers. The latter discover new, often remote, places in Kazakhstan and enjoy a fun and patriotic journey in getting to know their own country and its forgotten corners. The program sketched a new geography of Kazakhstan, focused mostly on the southern areas of the country (the region most famous for its shrines and historical monuments) as well as central Kazakhstan around Kzyl-Orda and eastern Kazakhstan around Semei. In all the episodes available on YouTube, there is a noticeable absence of northern and western Kazakhstan, correctly reflecting the general symbolic marginalization of the latter in spatial representations of the country. The program plays on regionalist clichés. In Shymkent for instance, Bidosov appears with a cowboy hat and Western film music—the region often is called the Texas of Kazakhstan[54]—but

---

54   Nathalie Koch and Kristopher D. White, "Cowboys, gangsters, and rural bumpkins: Constructing the 'other' in Kazakhstan's 'Texas'," in Marlene

never mentions the different Kazakh hordes and clans, a sensitive issue in public opinion. In each episode Bidosov insists on the fact that visitors from "all regions of Kazakhstan" visit these holy sites, in order to stage the country's unity.

Signs: Legends of the Steppe displays a fascinating subtext about Kazakh identity. The program is entirely in Russian, and when some interviewees speak Kazakh, they are translated. Almost all participants in each episode are ethnic Kazakhs, although some Russians appear in secondary roles (it is only in one show that a young Russian woman is the main interviewee). All the places visited are linked to Kazakh identity; nothing in the landscape or discourse is reminiscent of the Soviet past or links to Russia. The program celebrates rural life, a rarity in the Kazakh cultural arena that is more focused on the urban world. The show is a far cry from the Emirati-style buildings of the new capital Astana and its avant-garde architecture,[55] or from the opulent apartments of the upper-middle classes which are the setting for many Kazakh miniseries.[56] Everyday heroes of the series are often young people, but they encounter older generations [*arbaks*] and shrine custodians—dressed in "traditional" clothes and wearing a Muslim hat. Paradoxically the steppe world is not actually celebrated in the series. Ancestral transhumance, adopted for the needs of grazing cattle and symbolized by the yurt, are not a part of the displayed repertoire, whereas the nomadic theme has become widespread in pop music.[57] On the contrary, because the program focuses on pilgrimage sites, it insists on

---

Laruelle, ed., *Kazakhstan beyond Economic Success: Exploring Social and Cultural Changes in Eurasia* (Lanham, Md.: Lexington Books, 2015).

55 On Astana, see Bernhard Köppen, "The Production of a New Eurasian Capital on the Kazakh Steppe: Architecture, Urban Design, and Identity in Astana," *Nationalities Papers* 41:4 (2013): 590–605; Natalie Koch, "The 'Heart' of Eurasia? Kazakhstan's Centrally-Located Capital City," *Central Asian Survey* 32:2 (2013): 134–47; Nathalie Koch, "The Monumental and the Miniature: Imagining 'Modernity' in Astana," *Social and Cultural Geography* 11:8 (2010): 769–87.

56 On Kazakh miniseries, see, in this volume, Peter Rollberg, "The Birth of a Nation on Screen: *Astana My Love*".

57 Megan Rancier, "Resurrecting the Nomads: Historical Nostalgia and Modern Nationalism in Contemporary Kazakh Popular Music Videos," *Popular Music and Society* 32:3 (2009): 387–405.

the sedentary heritage of the Kazakh nation—in accordance with official Kazakhstani historiography since independence.[58]

Bidosov often emphasizes the importance of people attaining a better knowledge and understanding of "Kazakh mentality." The program summarizes this way of thinking as shaped by the spiritual legacy [*dukhovnoe nasledstvo*] of the Kazakh ancestors, who could be Islamic religious figures, military heroes, or carriers of Kazakh culture (folksingers, poets, writers.) This spiritual legacy has some religious motives, but it cannot be understood as Islamic. Islam is present across the shrines, prayers, and sacred lineages linked to the Prophet or Sufi saints. But it is associated with beliefs that refer to the region's Tengrist and shamanic past—which celebrates the spiritual forces coming from nature, e.g. stones, lakes, springs—and "New Age" beliefs that incorporate various healing practices, and the supernatural as integral elements of the individual spiritual quest. Spiritual legacy also includes knowledge of one's own national past, respect for the pantheon of national heroes, and awareness of oneself as a product of this past. Values that embody this Kazakhness are pride of the national past, generosity and sharing, responsibility and respect. In a sense, *Signs: Legends of the Steppe* offers a Kazakh version of the famous *Russian soul*, embodying core human values, combined with a revalorization of so-called traditional Islam.

4. Conclusion

Television is both a window on public opinion and an inventive way to shape it. It operates in both directions, first by incorporating political obligations in terms of official newspeak, forbidden and permissible topics, and cultural values, and then by taking into account the tastes of a decreasingly captive public that is able to turn

---

58 On historiographical debates in Kazakhstan, see among others, Yuriy Malikov, "The Kenesary Kasymov rebellion (1837–1847): A national-liberation movement or 'a protest of restoration'?," *Nationalities Papers* 33:4 (2005): 569–97. More broadly, and for the Soviet period, see Diana T. Kudaibergenova, "'Imagining Community' in Soviet Kazakhstan: An Historical Analysis of Narrative on Nationalism in Kazakh-Soviet Literature," *Nationalities Papers* 41:5 (2013): 839–54.

to other media sources, including those available online or via foreign satellite channels. Kazakhstan is a good example of this dual role of television. Although the authorities see it as a core means of communicating with their constituencies, the channels also rely on ratings and advertising, which form the basis of their economic viability. The televisual landscape in Kazakhstan is thus plural in the sense that it retransmits official state discourse—one can see that Nazarbayev's speech gained a large share of viewers—but also offers entertainment, most of which is produced outside the Kazakhstani state's control, in Russia.

With the exception of the new cultural channel *Madeniet*, Kazakhstani television offers few quality educational programs on nationhood and is relatively un-invested in such programs. To represent the new nation, preference was given to a forward-looking vision captured by the architecture in Astana and its symbolism rather than a better understanding of a controversial past. The blank pages of Kazakh history, namely relative to Russia in general and the Soviet Union in particular, remain difficult to assess in a consensual way. The political will to avoid creating cultural gaps between the Russian minority, which represents still a quarter of the population, and the Kazakh majority, but also between the Russian-speaking, urban Kazakh population, and the rural, Kazakh-speaking one, probably plays a critical role in the absence of these sensitive historical moments. Even commemorating the victims of the Soviet regime speaks only to part of the population, explaining why Alash Orda was not erected at the founding historical element of independent Kazakhstan. But having to determine the responsibility of the Soviet elites, whether they were federal ones based in Moscow or republican ones based in Alma-Ata, would spur tensions and create new ideological divisions. Television productions have thus remained reluctant to address those troubled times, and have not been affected by the growing trend among young social activists and ethno-nationalist groups to campaign against the Soviet regime and the role of Russia in the Kazakhstan's history.[59]

---

59 Marlene Laruelle, "The Rise of Ethnonationalism in Kazakhstan: Decolonizing on Internet," in Laruelle, ed., *Kazakhstan beyond Economic Success*.

Still staging the nation may take multiple forms—more popular, less official, and more innovative in branding the country than the rigid state-mandated vision—and television emerges as a perfectly malleable tool to frame the nation. Hence the emergence of patriotic entertainment programs like *Signs*, which succeeds in blending different social phenomena: the revival of interest in the Kazakh past and in knowledge of the nation's vast territories, the rise in domestic tourism and especially in healing pilgrimages, the supernatural being in vogue, and the celebration of the Kazakh mentality and so-called traditional Islam. *Signs* thus sketches an alternate Kazakhness that is less official and more fluid, innovative, and in tune with global trends. This new genre of patriotic entertainment—already fully established in Russia—is probably destined to grow and mature: the authorities want to revive patriotic fervor in order to avoid pressure from Moscow following the Ukrainian crisis, and younger, increasingly Kazakh-speaking, post-Soviet generations display a greater pride in the country's past and in the celebration of Kazakhness.

Small Screen Nation-Building: *Astana — My Love*

Peter Rollberg, The George Washington University.

On 21 June 2010, the president of the Republic of Kazakhstan was officially presented with a television miniseries titled *Astana — My Love*, two episodes of which were screened on this occasion.[1] The newspaper *Kazakhstanskaya pravda* reported from the Central Concert Hall "Kazakhstan" in Astana, where the ceremony took place, that these episodes "already allow us to predict that the miniseries will evoke great interest and find its audience. In order for this to happen, the film has all the necessary qualities: an intriguing plot, dramatic turns, and a fine cast. But its main accomplishment is that it is filled with love and kindness."[2] At the ceremony, Kazakhstan's Minister of Culture pointed out that such a large-scale project could only be carried out due to the economic growth that Kazakhstan had achieved under the leadership of President Nursultan Nazarbayev.

It is hard to imagine a comparable ceremony greeting with such fawning commentary in a Western context — the premiere of a television miniseries attended by the country's leading dignitaries and celebrated as a national event. Indeed, what was so special about *Astana — My Love* that it merited a demonstration of official endorsement? Who were the creators of the film and who the influ-

---

[1] I would like to express my gratitude to Erlan Karin for providing primary materials, Marlene Laruelle for recommending important secondary sources and critiquing an earlier version of the article, Evan Alterman for finding and translating Turkish sources, and the anonymous reviewers for helpful suggestions.

[2] Adiya Rakhmetullaeva, "'Astana — lyubov' moya'," *Kazakhstanskaya pravda*, 22 June 2010. *Ahiskapress*, a Turkish-language news portal for Meskhetian Turks, also reported on the event; cf. "Cumhurbaşkanina Kazak-Türk Yapimi 'Astana, Aşkim Benim' İsimli Dizinin," *Ahiska Press*, 21 June 2010, http://ahiskapress.com/?p=1913.

ential forces behind them? What was their sociopolitical and cultural agenda, and how did it translate into the fabric of the final product?[3] When film events in authoritarian societies are assigned a political-representational role, the genre of choice is usually the documentary, claiming to reflect the splendid "reality" of the society in question; specifically, feature-length documentaries were preferred for regime celebrations in various historical periods.[4] However, this is not the case with *Astana – My Love*, an unabashed melodrama.

This chapter presents a close reading of a television miniseries that was produced and released as a blend of entertainment and propaganda. *Astana – My Love* follows most standard procedures of television miniseries in regards to character constellation and plot development, but also contains some elements that are unique — these are indicators of Kazakhstan's ongoing debates about its national identity and strategies for the future. In the following discussion, I analyze the image of the past offered by this miniseries, the role of the president, allusions to desirable allies in the present and in the future, and ethical and cultural values in a neo-capitalist authoritarian environment presented as positive. This approach helps pioneer the understudied role of television in Central Asian societies, going beyond methodological challenges (among others the inability to get viewership data) and offering some important insights from one particular miniseries, its text and its context.

---

3   Just one year earlier, the twelve-part miniseries *City of Dream* [*Gorod mechty*], 2009, had been released. Directed by the experienced Kyrgyz filmmaker Ernest Abdyzhaparov, its title also refers to Astana and most of its episodes take place in the capital. However, the image of Astana is far less glamorous, and the characters go through genuine crises when moving from Almaty to the new capital. This series was given no official endorsement and vanished quickly.
4   The textbook example is German documentary filmmaker Leni Riefenstahl whose visual grandiosity defined fundamental totalitarian aesthetics — the premieres of her films were turned into official state events. In the Soviet Union, directors such as Roman Karmen, Ilya Kopalin, and Lidiya Stepanova were recognized with numerous Stalin and State Prizes and enjoyed exceptionally long careers; their documentaries, too, were treated as highly relevant for the formulation of state policies.

1. *Astana—My Love*: Popular Entertainment and Political Indoctrination

The plot of *Astana—My Love* resembles a fairy tale rather than a documentary: In 1985, on a Turkish Airlines plane flying over Kazakhstan, the wife of an influential Turkish entrepreneur gives birth to a daughter. The assisting physician is a Kazakh woman whose son was born a little while before. In celebration of this coincidence, the two mothers promise to marry their children to each other once they are grown up. But years later, the Turkish woman dies, and the vow eventually is forgotten. Then, in 2009, the girl Inju—now an ambitious young lady working as a television journalist—visits Kazakhstan's new capital Astana, and the boy Erlan—a promising architect currently working as a cab driver—gives her a lift to the hotel. Neither of them is aware of their fateful background, but that, of course, will change in the course of the twelve-hour series. Conspicuously, the representation-by-documentary tradition is not completely neglected: while *Astana—My Love* leaves no doubt about the fictitious nature of its story, the series does add elements that make the unbelievable more realistic, resorting to subplots involving professional and business competition, spousal disloyalty, and crime. More importantly, in the final episodes, Kazakhstan's president himself makes repeated appearances via documentary footage, simultaneously watched on TV by several characters of the miniseries. Thus, the documentary genre that is so popular with authoritarian officialdom made its entry through the backdoor of those "television in television" scenes and provides the melodrama with a quasi-documentary dimension.

Communication scholars often treat miniseries synonymously with soap operas,[5] although technically the two genres are distinct.[6] They do share a large number of episodes, the fact that—if commercially successful—they are continued for one or more seasons, have

---

[5] For a non-academic Kazakhstani reflection of this view, cf. Asel' Mukanova, "Kino na 'mylo'!," *Kazakhstanskaya pravda*, 17 October 2008.

[6] For a substantial discussion of the terminology and its implications, see Ien Ang, *Watching Dallas: Soap Opera and the Melodramatic Imagination* (London and New York: Methuen, 1985), 52–55.

a linear continuous main plotline and a relatively stable cast. However, with few exceptions, the cultural prestige of soap operas, which usually take place in the same sets year after year, is lower than that of miniseries—after all, the latter have increasingly attracted important directors, screenwriters, and performers who would never agree to work on regular soap operas, such as *Days of Our Lives*.[7] And still, in post-Soviet societies, even successful miniseries are not seen as legitimate parts of national cultural memory, which is defined by the standards of traditional high culture. Kazakhstani critics rarely afford television miniseries serious attention, pointing out that even the most quoted native miniseries—*The Crossroad* [*Perekrestok*], 1996–2000,—did not lead to a subsequent cult or regular reruns.[8] However, similar to most post-Soviet societies, television miniseries, especially from Latin America, have enjoyed enormous popularity in Kazakhstan, despite their relatively low prestige among professional critics.[9] They played a particular role in the renaissance of national culture at the end of the tumultuous 1990s, when *The Crossroad* was launched with British funds and, during the first season, realized with direct technical and creative assistance from the *BBC*—an experience aptly called by one of the involved specialists a "Marshall Plan of the Mind."[10] At the time

---

7 Martin Scorsese and Steven Spielberg have directed miniseries; David Lynch made one of the most artistically interesting ones, *Twin Peaks* (1990–1991). The budgets of some *HBO* miniseries such as *Rome* or *Boardwalk Empire* are comparable to those of medium-level feature films.

8 However, in recent years there has been a shift in the attitudes of cultural criticism toward television miniseries, in part due to quality products such as *The Sopranos*. The reputable journal *Iskusstvo kino* devotes entire issues to the miniseries phenomenon; one analyst even went so far as to call miniseries "the main chroniclers of humanity" and claim that TV serials "prepare an internet nation." Cf. Andrey Bystritskiy, "Serialy gotovyat internet-narod," *Iskusstvo kino* 11 (2014): 133–40.

9 Because of the fundamental difference in status, television miniseries that are currently produced in Kazakhstan and other post-Soviet countries should not be put in the same category as feature films whose prestige is distinctly higher; comparisons between television and cinema films tends to neglect the specific production and reception conditions of each of them.

10 For an insightful account of the working conditions and the specific problems that British television producers, writers and other colleagues were facing in

of Kazakhstan's severe economic crisis, this was a project that gave employment to many forlorn writers and performers and laid the groundwork for the necessary professionalization of television feature production in the country. That miniseries also pursued a goal that could be defined as "social pedagogy" — "to help the viewer become familiar with the new realities of life, and to see and understand the social changes that are unfolding in Kazakhstan"[11] — in other words, assist them during the transition from a communist to a capitalist economy.

The success of *The Crossroad* can be considered "natural" due to its freshness and closeness to Kazakhstani reality; no official influence was necessary to engineer its popularity.[12] The situation was different for *Astana — My Love*: the exceptional fanfare accompanying its premiere clearly indicated that its significance went far beyond that of a regular television product and its success was not left to chance or normal free media market competition. A closer look at its content and context will shed light on the cultural components of neo-authoritarian governance in Kazakhstan's post-Soviet framework and lead to a deeper probe of the substance of its encoded messages as well as its production and marketing strategies.

Astana — My Love consists of twelve one-hour episodes. At the beginning of each episode, prior to the title and credits, for several seconds a quotation fills the screen:

> "Cities create a country, the capital creates a nation."
> - Nursultan Nazarbayev

Kazakhstan, cf. Ruth Mandel, "A Marshall Plan of the Mind," in Faye D. Ginsburg, Lilia Abu-Lughod, and Brian Larkin, eds., *Media Worlds: Anthropology of New Terrain* (Berkeley: University of California Press, 2002), 211–28.

11 Raushan Shulembaeva, "Letopis' nezavisimosti. God 1996-y. Sbyvayutsya zavetnye mechty," *Kazakhstanskaya pravda*, 2 November 2011.

12 Still, that project, which ran for five years with altogether 465 episodes, was endorsed by President Nazarbayev at the time; cf. Amos Owen Thomas, "Franchising culture for Kazakhstan television: producers' ambivalence and audiences' indifference," *Jump Cut* 52 (2010), http://www.ejumpcut.org/archive/jc52.2010/thomasKzakstanTV.

The fact that an epigraph precedes a miniseries is highly unusual for the genre, supplying *Astana – My Love* with an authoritative weight that distinguishes it from regular television serials. Furthermore, the epigraph contains an explicitly ideological – indeed teleological – message, intended to provide an interpretive framework to its viewership.[13] Beginning with the president's quote, the introductory episode leaves no doubt about three key aspects of the miniseries as a whole: 1. The plot is not meant to depict everyday reality in the strict sense of the term; the ritualistic promise of a boy and a girl to each other due to the circumstances of their birth is more characteristic of fairy tales and foundational myths. 2. The girl's Turkish and the boy's Kazakh nationality signify a special relationship between Kazakhstan and Turkey that gives the love story a symbolic and geopolitical dimension. 3. Repeated references to the fact that the girl's birth happened in the skies over Tselinograd – in other words, over the future Astana – suggest that the location holds a particular meaning for the characters and what they symbolize; in addition, the miniseries' title itself leaves no ambiguity in regards to the conceptual role of the location. In this context, the Nazarbayev quotation implicitly suggests a parallel between the birth of the female lead and the birth of a nation.

2. The Producers

It is easy to see that *Astana – My Love* was conceived as a prestige project, furnished for the anniversary of the founding of Kazakhstan's new capital and in preparation of the 20th anniversary of the country's independence in 2011. Produced by *Kazakhfilm* studio *Shaken Aimanov* and the Turkish company Eurasia Film Production,

---

13   In their discussion of Michel Foucault's concept of "governmentality" as applied to Uzbekistan and Kazakhstan, Laura Adams and Assel Rustemova refer to the work of Mitchell Dean who uses the notions of *telos* and "national idea" within the framework of a country and its culture – this has direct significance for officially endorsed miniseries such as *Astana–My Love* that verbalize and visualize a teleological dimension, i.e., "the city of the future." Cf. Laura Adams and Assel Rustemova, "Mass Spectacle and Styles of Governmentality in Kazakhstan and Uzbekistan," *Europe-Asia Studies* 61:7 (2009): 1252.

with participation of the Turkish Radio and Television Corporation, it was first shown on Kazakhstan's popular *Khabar* channel in July 2010. Even before the project's completion, the producer announced that the series could potentially reach 200–250 million viewers and was negotiating sales to Turkey and Arab states.[14] The stakes were so high that a genuinely critical debate about the film's merits and shortcomings in official Kazakhstani media was out of the question.[15] Instead, *Astana – My Love* was immediately included in Kazakhstan's lavish 2011 jubilee DVD edition celebrating the country's cinematic legacy: of the 20 DVDs representing the best achievements of 50 years of Kazakhstani cinema, six (each DVD containing two episodes) were given to this serial that had just been released. Moreover, *Astana – My Love* is the only television miniseries in the entire edition and concludes it both chronologically and by design. The prestige position assigned to it indicates that its production was planned and carried out on the highest government level.[16]

While the exact background of its conception, financing, and realization will likely remain opaque, it is clear that two Kazakhstanis played decisive roles in creating this project: the then-Minister of Culture, Mukhtar Kul-Muhammed, and the producer, Gulnara Sarsenova. As the credits state, *Astana – My Love* is based on an idea of Kul-Muhammed. A prominent member of Nazarbayev's inner circle,[17] a brief look at his career allows for some insight into

---

14 Galina Shimyrbaeva, "Dolgaya istoriya lyubvi," *Kazakhstanskaya pravda* 22, 2 February 2010.
15 The exceptions were some online venues that are discussed in this article; official newspapers were all positive in their response to the miniseries.
16 The history of its production and release indicate that *Astana–My Love* presents a vision of the nation of Kazakhstan and its future that has been implemented in a top-down manner. However, as Rico Isaacs has argued, there exist more than one narrative "pertaining to the notion of the Kazakh nation and identity in film." Cf. Rico Isaacs, "Nomads, Warriors, and Bureaucrats: Nation-building and Film in Post-Soviet Kazakhstan," *Nationalities Papers* 43:3 (2014): 2.
17 In her study of the Kazakhstani elites, Sally Cummings lists the presidential advisers as members of level 3 of the Institutional Ranking of Influence (of seven) and the Ministry of Information of Information and Social Accord as

the origins of the project's underlying concept.[18] Born in 1960 in the Uighur Autonomous region of China, Kul-Muhammed's family immigrated to Kazakhstan in the late 1960s. Kul-Mukhammed defended a thesis on Alash Orda, the prominent Kazakh nationalist movement of the early twenty century, and since the 2000s has been in charge of many state commissions dealing with national identity issues.[19] Kul-Muhammed's academic expertise indicates an interest in the philosophical aspects of statehood, including its origins and specific conditions of development, that can be tied to the conceptual underpinnings of *Astana — My Love*, including the role of the leader of a nation, its capital, and its architecture.

The producer of the miniseries, Gulnara Sarsenova, belongs to the same generation as Kul-Muhammed. Born in 1961, she also graduated in journalism from Kazakh State University in Almaty. In addition, Sarsenova studied at the Soviet State Film Institute VGIK in Moscow where one of her teachers was Tat'iana Lioznova, creator of the legendary Soviet miniseries *Seventeen Moments of Spring* [*Sem'nadtsat' mgnoveniy vesny*], 1973.[20] A successful businesswoman, Sarsenova is the owner of *French House* [*Frantsuzskiy dom*], a chain of luxury goods stores, and is credited with founding the newspaper *New Generation* and the magazine *Revue*. As a film producer, she has helmed international coproductions such as the historical blockbuster *The Mongol* (2007), which was nominated for an Oscar as Best Foreign Picture, and projects such as *Tulpan* (2008) which enjoyed international success on the art-house circuit. Her

---

part of level 5. Cf. Sally N. Cummings, *Kazakhstan: Power and the Elite* (London: I.B. Tauris, 2005), 40.

18 "Muktar Kul-Muhammed," Wikipedia, http://ru.wikipedia.org/wiki/Mukhtar_Kul-Muhammed.

19 See the biographical page available at http://online.zakon.kz/Document/?doc_id=30105657.

20 The fact that Sarsenova regularly mentions her apprenticeship with Tat'iana Lioznova is an indicator for the high esteem in which Soviet miniseries are still held by many Kazakhstanis. The 1970s were the decisive decade for the genre in the Soviet context; cf. Elena Prokhorova, "Fragmented Mythologies: Soviet TV Miniseries of the 1970s" (PhD diss., University of Pittsburgh, 2003).

semi-documentary musical film "My Star" (2012) features the president's daughter, Dariga Nazarbayeva, a fact that confirms Sarsenova's proximity to the highest echelons of Kazakhstan's elite.[21]

The biographies of Kul-Muhammed and Sarsenova suggest that *Astana – My Love* was the product of established and ambitious members of Kazakhstan's elite whose worldview and values are close to, if not identical with, a number of ideological concepts of that elite in the Nazarbayev era, and who found it advantageous to convey basic assumptions of this ideology through the format of a popular television miniseries, as well as to openly demonstrate their loyalty to it. Surely, the internal discussions about the Kazakhstani nation's development are difficult to pinpoint for outside observers and much is left to speculation; however, given the generous financial support of the project by the state it seems safe to conclude that at least influential segments of the Kazakhstani elites were aligned with the series' underlying ideology.

Yet, the people behind *Astana – My Love* must also have been aware that Kazakhstanis hardly watch television to be lectured for twelve hours about the country's shining future. The danger of an epigraph together with the name of its author burden the subsequent viewing experience with the expectation of political gravitas, of a small screen sermon to the people of Kazakhstan. As if to counter this impression, the producers chose as the miniseries' promotional slogan a very different line: "Love, schemes, betrayal, power struggle, ambition [*more drayva*], and love again." In other words, there are two verbal messages associated with *Astana – My Love*: one situated in the most prominent spot, at the beginning of each episode, and the other used for advertising the miniseries for mass consumption through the media. Together, these strategies represent the ambiguous blend of authoritarian self-representation and commercial appeal that is typical of the project and Kazakhstan's state-supported culture as a whole.

---

21   Marina Khegay, "Ee zvezda," *Karavan*, 24 February 2012, http://www.caravan.kz/article/41835.

The director, Ermek Shinarbaev,[22] began his career with serious, sensitive feature films adapted for television from stories by Russian-Korean author Anatoliy Kim (*My Sister, Liusia*, 1985; *Stepping out of the Forest onto the Meadow*, 1987; *The Revenge*, 1991). He was part of the team that created the innovative *The Crossroads* in the late 1990s and subsequently made a number of feature films and documentaries devoted to music and fine art, often coproduced with French companies. Shinarbaev's films can be characterized as middle-brow and largely apolitical; unlike some other directors of his generation, he has never been interested in controversy or social criticism. Still, his reputation prior to *Astana – My Love* was that of a serious artist—a standard to which the miniseries, despite a few minor artistic achievements, certainly does not live up. Be that as it may, *Astana – My Love*, while purporting to reflect the "mission" of Astana and its loving inhabitants, presents an extremely selective image of society.

3. The Rich and the Beautiful

The miniseries' central plot line is the love between the Kazakh architect Erlan and the Turkish television journalist Inju; however, immediate complications arise from the fact that Inju is already engaged to Kemal, a promising Turkish entrepreneur, while Erlan has a serious relationship with Laura, a ballet dancer who is also the lover of aging architect Alibek. Erlan has just returned from study abroad in the United States. He is depicted as honest, loyal, dependable, and forthright. Most importantly, Erlan is genuinely gifted—his project of a representational building for Astana is reputed to add another gem to the capital's impressive ensemble of palaces. However, Erlan's friend and fellow junior architect, Abzal, betrays him, stealing the project in order to solidify his position in the construction company of Alibek, whose daughter Marzhan he is dating. This blatant betrayal of friendship sets in motion a number of

---

22   In some publications his name is transliterated as Shynarbaev.

dramatic clashes that are the substance of the following ten episodes. Only in episode 11, Abzal is finally eliminated, clearing the way for the triumphant episode 12.

Almost without exception, the characters of *Astana – My Love* are architects, surrounded by entrepreneurs, media celebrities, doctors, and elegant housewives. The occupation and wealth of the dramatis personae leaves no doubt as to the series' milieu: the upper crust of the Kazakh and the Turkish establishment. Alibek is obviously a multimillionaire, whereas Inju's father is repeatedly referred to as "a billionaire."[23] This choice of milieu of the "rich and beautiful" is typical both for producers and regular audiences of television miniseries worldwide, allowing the viewer a temporary distraction and relief from annoying everyday banality and trivial problems, be they social or financial, justifying the focus on interpersonal issues: love, trust, hatred, ambition, competition, and betrayal that are supposedly the same in all social strata. Both Kul-Muhammed and Sarsenova inhabit this world, and likely millions of regular Kazakhs would like to be part of it, too. If *Astana – My Love* were merely a regular product of the television dream factory, there would be nothing objectionable in such exclusiveness. However, the miniseries was conceived and presented as a dramatization and visualization of ideological and cultural officialdom. Therefore, its deliberate ignoring of any genuine social difficulties,

---

23   It should be noted that the secondary plot lines are rarely pursued with any consequence. For example, Alibek's amorous adventures that seriously threaten his marriage in two episodes are resolved at a speed indicating that no deepening of this conflict is desirable, perhaps because it could be perceived as a hint at some high-ranking officials' own escapades. As is common in miniseries, sudden turns abound (for example, Kemal gives Inju a horse and a few seconds later she is injured by it when she rides it the first time, etc.). The fact that these turns are unmotivated by any rational factors is usually accepted by those viewers who are satisfied by minimal plausibility and do not expect psychological analysis or realistic causality for each event— these plot turns mainly function as fillers, creating short-lived suspense and an equally quick denouement. But they also produce a collateral effect when, in the overarching fight of good versus evil these sub-conflicts are temporarily won by the forces of darkness. While those victories are just as short-lived as the conflicts from which they result, they can increase the viewer's human interest in the good characters who otherwise may appear all too bland.

its elimination of any element that does not fit its image of wealthy urban perfection conveys a strategy that goes beyond principles of entertainment. The consistently featured upper class milieu gives the film a surface of political and social homogeneity, providing the entire miniseries with an air of intentional political unawareness. The only political entity explicitly mentioned is the president who, as the film suggests, is a unique phenomenon and belongs to a higher order.[24]

But the choice of milieu in *Astana—My Love* is not simply based on genre clichés, political opportunism, and social ignorance. After all, oil executives, diplomats, or pop artists also would have been legitimate candidates for a representative Kazakh miniseries, producing the same glamour effect on screen. However, it is the architects who are most closely connected to the declared mission of creating a new nation through its capital. They represent the one professional group that turns the presidential vision of Astana as the center of nation-building into reality, much more directly than oil executives who oversee the production of the country's riches or diplomats who represent it to the outside world or pop singers who praise it. Had the producers and directors chosen, say, genuine city administrators as characters, it would have been much harder to ignore social reality and its unpleasant and hard-to-resolve conflicts. But architects, from the point of view of official state ideology, are members of the very professional cast that carry out the will of the supreme nation-builder whose omnipresence is signaled in the miniseries from its opening. Architects are engaged in creating a livable future; past or present are much less relevant for their work and in the case of Astana, as a city created from scratch, not relevant at all. Thus, the choice of this professional milieu is logically connected to the film's epigraph. Furthermore, the world of privilege in which the architects and their families live can be construed as the justified reward for the central role they are playing in making

---

24   For an in-depth discussion of the Nazarbayev cult in Kazakhstan, see Rico Isaacs, "'Papa'—Nursultan Nazarbayev and the Discourse of Charismatic Leadership and Nation-Building in Post-Soviet Kazakhstan," *Studies in Ethnicities and Nationalism* 10:3 (2010): 435–52.

the president's vision of Kazakhstan's future reality. Watched in this light, the function of the characters as carriers of values and the implied normative ethics acquire a new meaning as well: only those who are morally firm have the right to participate in the creation of a new nation through its capital and, ipso facto, its architecture. Moreover, these creators inhabit their own product, living in the self-designed parts of the city, not in the old Soviet quarters that are never shown at all.

Kazakhstan's neo-capitalist upper class is blatantly visible in every episode; however, the system on which it is based is never explicitly addressed, let alone questioned. The fact that Kazakh society includes a social stratum of privileged citizens living in huge mansions and driving expensive cars is presented as a matter of course and normal. This fact is also not historicized, which can only be justified by the characters' youth: unlike the relatively balanced age representation in the groundbreaking miniseries *The Crossroad*, the majority of performers in *Astana – My Love* is young; indeed, many of them were hired as students from acting classes. Furthermore, none of the characters is genuinely old—the oldest one is the senior architect and businessman, Alibek, a man in his fifties. This demonstrative emphasis on youth and youthfulness in connection with Kazakhstan's young capital is one of the miniseries' implicit messages. The vast majority of the characters grew up in the independent Kazakhstan and have no reason to refer to the Soviet past, whereas the few older characters apparently have eradicated it from their memory.

The series consistently purports that there is upward mobility for everybody, metaphorically formulated as "realizing one's dreams." The methods to move up in this class system vary and depend on each character's moral outlook. Both Erlan and his rival Abzal, representing good and evil in its pure form, want to succeed. The difference is that Erlan is not interested in moving upward per se—for him, promotion and wealth in the future are the natural and just gratification for his hard work, talent, and dedication in the present. Abzal, on the other hand, pursues his goal regardless of the costs, including through lies, betrayal, and crimes. In order to satisfy his ambitions, the carrier of evil has to resort to unethical and finally illegal methods, finding allies among corrupt officials and criminals. The schemes that they engage in have a whiff of reality but are not allowed to fully evolve or dominate any episode. In the end, the police arrest all the crooks, their masters who play billiards in shady restaurants, and other denizens of an underworld that has no connection to the bright Astana in which good people are busy realizing their dreams. Evil can only slow down the process of realizing the predestined Kazakh national utopia; the harm inflicted by evil is temporary and is corrected with relative ease by forthright characters such as Erlan in conjunction with the police who unfailingly arrive in *deus ex machina* manner.

It is fundamentally important for the character constellation of *Astana – My Love* that the good characters are also the gifted ones. However, this leaves the viewer with a dilemma: if talent by definition is destiny—what are the lesser gifted or ungifted supposed to do? Accept their rightful place at the bottom (which is excluded from the film's space)? In this regard, Abzal once again represents an interesting case. He clearly understands that Erlan is superior to him as an architect—and that this is a result of "destiny," a given. Initially, he befriends Erlan so as to profit from his talent. But when the competition for upward social mobility begins in earnest, Abzal is not willing to accept destiny's choice and let Erlan move faster. Instead he engages in scheming, lies, and downright fraud to neutralize his talented competitor, faking his own non-existent talent to the outside world. The fact that the film rejects ruthless methods that are typical of free market societies points to the existence of an assumed system of justice in Kazakh society. Aberrations such as Abzal's behavior have no place in the city of the future, and even Abzal ultimately must realize this.

In regard to the Kazakhstani class system, the most revealing plot elements are those associated with money and power, including the competition for multi-million-dollar contracts and the price of surgical procedures. However, *Astana – My Love* consistently demonstrates that in the long run none of the individual decisions can change the overall outcome of the predetermined process, namely, Astana's and Kazakhstan's ascension to a glorious future. The real decision-making power is beyond the characters' reach; it lies with destiny and those who understand its direction. This metaphysical dimension is alluded to from the beginning: human beings can move in accordance with their fate or in resistance to it, but they cannot change it in principle. This explains the soothing effect of such television products on viewers who accept the metaphysical assumption of destiny in the first place. But such fairy-tale-like soothing also produces one of the sociopolitical effects that make miniseries such as *Astana – My Love* attractive for a political establishment interested in the consolidation of existing power structures. It encourages trust in the grand design underlying the nation's trajectory, regardless of possible aberrations caused by "evil forces." Miniseries such as *Astana – My Love* encourage an acceptance of society as it is. Not surprisingly, they rarely, if ever, feature characters who question destiny's plan on a national scale or for themselves. Rather, in the vast majority of cases, miniseries favor characters who actively work toward the grand design's maximum realization.

4. A Future without Past

Given the representational function of *Astana – My Love*, the country's history is mentioned surprisingly rarely. In regard to Astana itself – arguably the central character of the miniseries, just like Dallas in its legendary predecessor – destiny's grand design is associated with the city's steady growth in the present, but not its past.[25] Apart from the Nazarbayev epigraph, an implicit conceptual indicator is the theme song, "Astana" and the fascination with the city's wellbeing that is shared by those characters who are destined for happiness: Erlan's innermost desire is to create another impressive building for the capital, while Inju is working on a documentary about Astana that will be shown on Turkish TV. This "documentary within a fairy tale" is a venue that breaks with the film's principle of conveying its underlying ideological concepts in an implicit manner. Carefully alternated with romantic scenes, Inju's reports

---

25 For a discussion of the real perceptions of Astana among Kazakhstanis, see Natalie Koch, "The 'Heart' of Eurasia? Kazakhstan's Centrally Located Capital City," *Central Asian Survey* 2:32 (2013): 134–47.

about Astana provide the pretext for brief but explicit lectures. Thus, in episode 5, she meets with a family in which the sons are named after legendary Kazakh heroes. The naming is based on the belief that the qualities of those heroes will transfer onto the current carrier of the name: Ablaikhan,[26] Kabanbai,[27] Otegen,[28] Karasai,[29] and Kenesary.[30] This is the first time that some minimal historical context is established in a film that otherwise focuses exclusively on the present and the future. Another such rare occasion happens when one of the characters polemicizes against the common view of the Kazakh people as nomads. His counterargument is that what now is Astana is located on the Silk Road and that Kazakhs in the past also were craftsmen, artists, and preachers.[31] A third historical reference is contained in episode 10, titled "The Land of Nomads and Dreamers." Kemal, the young Turkish businessman who has fallen in love with Alibek's daughter Marzhan, accompanies her to the mountains were the two witness a folk festival featuring traditional competitions, including *kuresi* (wrestling) and *baiga* (horse racing). This experience takes place near the miniseries' culmination, at which point the forces of darkness are removed through the

---

26 Ablai Khan (1711–1781) was a Kazakh ruler who fought for a strong centralized state; in recognition of his valor in fighting the Dzungars he was named a *batyr* (hero). The 2005 blockbuster *Nomad* is based on his life.
27 Kabanbai was an eighteenth century military leader who is also called a *batyr*. In May 2014, on the Kazakhstani holiday, Day of the Defenders of the Homeland, a monument to Kabanbai that cost about one million dollars was dedicated in Ust-Kamenogorsk.
28 Otegen Otegululy (1699–1773) was a *batyr* who for many years fought against the Dzungars. Interestingly, he opposed the peace deal with China brokered by Ablai Khan.
29 Karasai Altynaiuly (1698–1671) became known as Karasai *batyr*; his clan comes from the area of Akmolinsk.
30 Kenesary Kasymov (1802–1847) was a Kazakh ruler; the grandson of Ablai Khan who led a war for national independence against Russia during which he was captured and executed by Kyrgyz warriors.
31 Due to the crisis in Ukraine and Russia's annexation of Crimea, the issue of Kazakhstani state history and the integrity of its borders has become more pressing since 2014, which is reflected in the plans to celebrate the 550th anniversary of the Kazakh state. Cf. Marlene Laruelle, "Kazakhstan's Posture in the Eurasian Union: In Search of Serene Sovereignty," *Russian Analytical Digest* 165, 25 March 2015.

arrest of the criminals, the death of the hired killer, and the self-removal of the traitor Abzal—the road to harmony is finally free.

However, the scarcity of references to Kazakhstan's ancient history is exceeded by far by the virtual absence of references to Kazakhstan's Soviet period. Based on watching *Astana – My Love*, it is inconceivable that prior to 1991, i.e., a mere twenty years earlier, the development of Kazakhstan as part of the USSR was interpreted from a strictly Marxist-Leninist (and, for some thirty years, Stalinist) viewpoint, ascribing the role of the leader to the "older brother" Russia. In the miniseries, Russia is hardly ever mentioned.[32] Although the characters communicate in Russian, they receive their education in New York and London, not Moscow or St. Petersburg. Their professional and personal aspirations are directed toward Turkey and the West, not Russia—and not China. Regarding Russian characters in the film, they are extremely rare and secondary at best. One character in particular, Rita, a friend of Erlan's mother, plays a rather irritating role, for her smothering "care" causes more problems than it resolves. Interestingly, the miniseries was shot in Russian and dubbed into Kazakh, and the viewer of the DVD can choose between the two language versions. The title song "Astana" is sung in Kazakh during the opening credits and in Russian at the end. However, it is highly conspicuous that toward the film's conclusion, when President Nazarbayev answers Inju's question, he does so in Kazakh, giving a speech lasting several minutes that is eagerly watched and apparently understood by all characters on

---

32   Astana has been conceived as a truly Kazakh project, as opposed to Almaty that is seen as more Russian. "The change of capital, announced in 1994 and accomplished in 1997, has often been interpreted as a gesture in favor of its Kazakhness (...). However, Nazarbaeyv's project goes much further: the point is to anchor Kazakhstan within the international community and to plot a bright future for it, embodied by the futuristic appearance of the new capital." Marlene Laruelle, "The Three Discursive Paradigms of State Identity in Kazakhstan: Kazakhness, Kazakhstanness, and Transnationalism," in Mariya Omelicheva, ed., *Nationalism and Identity Construction in Central Asia. Dimensions, Dynamics and Directions* (Lanham, Md.: Lexington Books, 2014), 1–20.

TV — without any Russian translation for the characters or the viewers.[33]

Another aspect of reality that is virtually absent from the entire film is religion. None of the characters is ever seen praying or referring to religious practices. *Astana — My Love* depicts Kazakh and Turkish society as modern and secular: both women and men, youths and parents make their own decisions about love and labor; these decisions are debated but ultimately accepted by those around them. The underlying guiding principle, however, is not the individual's self-determination. Neither is it a divine authority or its representatives on Earth. In *Astana — My Love*, the guiding principle, which the characters recognize and obey, is *destiny*. For the Kazakhstani elites, in whose name the miniseries was made and who officially endorsed it, destiny acts a post-Soviet replacement for history that, in a Hegelian cum Marxist-Leninist framework, was interpreted as that which evolves with the inevitability of a law of nature.[34]

5. Destiny Replaces History

The association of President Nazarbayev with a television miniseries fashioned as a modern fairy-tale[35] could have easily been construed as sacrilegious by dogmatic watchdogs. Certainly, from their

---

[33] Here, the film indirectly reflects the ongoing debate about the status of the primary language in Kazakhstan, which has divided the country and its elites. One news item refers to the fact that the miniseries was shot and first aired in Russian in July 2010 and only several months later in Kazakh; the article's title—"The Characters of the Kazakh-Turkish Series 'Astana–My Love!' Have Begun to Speak in the State Language"—has a sarcastic ring to it. "Geroi kazakhstansko-turetskogo seriala 'Astana — lyubov' moya!' zagovorili na gosudarstvennom yazyke," *BNEWS KZ*, 14 September 2010, http://bnews.kz/ru/news/post/37908.

[34] The functional similarity of the traditional notions of "destiny/predestination" and "history" as the realization of eternal laws deserves further exploration.

[35] The makers of the series tried to diffuse the negative connotations of the term "fairy tale" in relation to a film that is focused on the president's pet project: "This is a story that could only happen in this blessed and wondrous place as is the new capital of Kazakhstan, Astana. Only because of the new miraculous energy that fills the air does the story of the two young heroes resemble

inception, television miniseries have used fairy-tale master plots and character archetypes to draw viewers in. But this consideration must have been outweighed by the implicit expectation of a happy ending for all fairy tales that is suggested in Episode 1 of *Astana – My Love*, which coincides with the teleological nature of the message expressed by the Nazarbayev quote, namely, the successful creation of a nation through its capital, embedding the private story in a wide-ranging political and historical context. Furthermore, the set-up is a clear indicator that this girl and this boy are meant for each other, as are their respective nations. Thus, the driving force behind the plot of this film is neither psychological nor social logic but *destiny*. Destiny as a metaphysical category imposing its will on humans regardless of their intentions or individual understanding does not operate in a linear, transparent, or rationally explicable manner. It is thus ideally suited as the supplier of conflict: despite the optimistic promise in Episode 1, the audience can also indulge in a variety of obstacles, misunderstandings, clashes, and complications before the central characters whose marriage is literally made in heaven will finally be united. The emerging Turkish-Kazakh alliance creates a related expectation of intercultural dealings as a source of tension and pleasure. But the geopolitical gravitas that enters the miniseries through this aspect at the same time also strengthens the declared predetermination: with the symbolic weight on their shoulders, ultimately the two lovers are destined to find each other, no matter what hindrances may come their way. Another aspect connects the plot of *Astana – My Love* to the Nazarbayev quote from the opening: since the Turkish girl's birth took place in the skies above the future capital Astana, the success of the national project is predestined just as the happiness of the future lovers is; initiating personal and national destiny in heaven is equivalent to the notion of "the right constellation of stars" in astrol-

---

a fairy tale." Cf. "Astana Lyubov' Moya," gulnarasarsenova.kz, http://gulnarasarsenova.kz/pages/astana.

ogy and evokes quasi-divine connotations. Consequently, the nation's leader is presented as a chosen one who is aligned with a higher destiny.[36]

Within the context of *Astana – My Love*, the notion of "destiny" has replaced that of "history," which used to explain the evolution of the Kazakh nation as part of the Soviet project. Now, predetermination stands in lieu of any sort of social theory. Destiny is the driving force on all levels: in private life and professional advancement; in the existing class system; in the evolution of Kazakh society, which is reflected in the miraculous growth of its capital; and in the geopolitical dimension, represented by the "natural" alliance between Kazakhstan and Turkey. Destiny is a profoundly metaphysical notion that has the advantage of not being debatable in a factual-scientific framework while connecting current thinking about the nation's mission to age-old traditions and deeper layers of a mentality that emerged through millennia. Thus, a seemingly harmless, fairy-tale-like miniseries bears important markers of Kazakhstan's sociopolitical program. Ingrained in the ups and downs of a romantic story are the proposed values of a self-conscious, tradition-based Eurasian type of modernity.

As a result, what may appear as a heavy-handed narrative scheme requiring the audiences' deliberate suspension of disbelief is in essence a perfect construction uniting individual happiness with the positive development of two nations carried out through the vision of Kazakhstan's supreme leader who, one is led to believe, has been chosen by destiny no less. It can be assumed that this construct was meant to appeal to general viewers' interest in soap-opera-style entertainment while at the same time conveying fundamental elements of Kazakhstan's twenty-first-century state doctrine. A consequence of this idealized combination is the characters' role as carriers of values. Within the proposed symbol-laden historical, geopolitical, and metaphysical framework any sort of individual psychology is largely irrelevant. What matters is the consistency

---

36 · For those familiar with President Nazarbayev's biography, his personal connection to Astana/Tselinograd, where he worked prior to the country's independence, establishes another important factor of "destiny."

of the characters' value-driven behavior. Moreover, because of the openly demonstrated quasi-official and representational nature of the miniseries, a number of details acquire a significance that goes far beyond that of a regular "soap opera," providing room for doctrinal and ideological interpretation instead.

While Abzal fulfills the usual role of the "bad guy" that is considered a requirement for miniseries, the specifics of his demise present a noteworthy deviation from Western stereotypes. Prior to his violent death, in episode after episode, Abzal lies ruthlessly and betrays people to whom he had sworn loyalty. A slick young cynic without remorse, Abzal takes two-facedness to perfection, deceiving his fiancée, his boss and soon-to-be father-in-law, his lover, and his friends. Only when his actions unintentionally lead to the death of his mother, the foundation of Abzal's personality breaks, causing a stunning transformation from stock character to a genuinely suffering individual. The trauma he experiences changes his perception—everything he had regarded as valuable suddenly loses its meaning. As a consequence, not only does Abzal try to repent to the extent possible by making up to Erlan and Kemal some of the damage that he had inflicted on their companies, but he also apologizes to Marzhan right before a hired killer stabs him—a finale that he himself apparently was trying to bring about. This moralistic turn is highly unusual for the miniseries genre in general and for *Astana—My Love* in particular. Not only do the Kazakh filmmakers never completely deprive Abzal—the stereotypical carrier of negative values such as greed, lust, and cynicism—of his humanity: in the end, they provide him with an opportunity for genuine redemption and his former friends with a chance to mourn him. Thus, careerism and sociopathic disposition are not declared to be unchangeable elements of the human condition that must be fought out, as Western miniseries demonstrate ad nauseam, but are depicted as choices that can be reversed. Had *Astana—My Love* offered more such subversions of miniseries clichés, it could have become an artistic phenomenon rather than a political one. Alas, this one episode of forgiveness is a solitary element in an otherwise predictable, cliché-ridden, albeit socio-culturally insightful television product.

The social impact of miniseries such as *Astana – My Love* within the media culture of Kazakhstan is hard to gauge with any degree of exactitude: opinion polls are not being conducted, and viewer ratings for 2010 are unavailable. Publicly available ratings for television broadcast became available only after 2013. Clearly, the fact that a television project of this stature has been so openly promoted and endorsed does not mean that audiences have accepted it. Thus, one article, published in July 2010, took a very critical stance, asking why the unprecedented amount of three million dollars was spent on an artistically low-quality product: "For what kind of audience was this series conceived? For the Kazakh? But we know almost everything about Astana as is."[37] In response, a number of online visitors shared the critic's viewpoint, bemoaning the wasting of the nation's funds on a miniseries: "The bureaucrats of the Ministry of Culture have suddenly discovered their passionate love for Astana! And, as luck would have it, that love unexpectedly coincided with the 70th birthday of the President of the Republic of Kazakhstan. In this case, it is no sin to waste even more than 3 million dollars." Another visitor expressed a nationalist notion: "I did not like this film because it was shot in Russian. When will we shoot normal films in Kazakh? We have been independent for so many years, and still we speak only Russian."[38] However, while one can conclude that such critical attitudes may be representative of larger segments of the population, at this point it is impossible to prove. Therefore, what remains noteworthy and beyond doubt, are the sociopolitical and cultural intentions of the makers of *Astana – My Love* as indicators of trends in the Kazakhstani elites.

6. Conclusion

Kazakh and foreign film scholars have interpreted the return of recognizably national, commercially viable film production as part of

---

37 Bakhyt Seiten, "'Astana–lyubov' moya': povod k neveselym razmyshleniyam," old.camonitor.com, 9 July 2010, http://old.camonitor.com/archives/503.
38 Seiten, "'Astana–lyubov' moya'."

nation-building.[39] Television is harder to analyze within this paradigm because of the overwhelming quantities of content that must be included in an analysis of general trends. Still, the influence of television on society cannot be overestimated.

Astana — My Love is easy to dismiss as a twelve-hour commercial for Kazakhstan's president and his policies. But the main motivation for this miniseries is contained in the manner in which it seamlessly integrates sociopolitical values in a melodramatic story, making the intended indoctrination largely painless since it is delivered in an entertaining fashion. If the ideas visualized and verbalized in this miniseries seem to be a relatively accurate reflection of state ideology, it is difficult to gauge how effective they are. What can be said without a doubt is that *Astana — My Love* was an officially launched contribution to the discourse on Kazakh identity and a forward-looking nationhood whose significance is underlined by the personal appearance of the president and his public endorsement of the project.

---

39   Cf. Gulnara Abikeyeva, "Cinematic Nation-Building in Kazakhstan," in Michael Rouland, Gulnara Abikeyeva, and Birgit Beumers, eds., *Cinema in Central Asia* (London: I.B. Tauris, 2013), 163–74.

III. Social Media

Glasnost 2.0

Sarah Oates, University of Maryland

Does the Soviet experience with glasnost teach us that even if Russians don't have media freedom, media dissonance can lead to social upheaval? The diversification of media voices via the rise of the Internet in Russia may not be media "freedom" as we know it in the West, but it can still signal change as it amplifies divisions in society. Western analysts, scholars, and arguably even the Soviets themselves missed the significance of that dissonance in accelerating political change almost three decades ago during the glasnost period. Today, there is evidence that Russia stands on the threshold of political upheaval again, with the online sphere broadening and amplifying a type of "Glasnost 2.0" effect. Not only is there a diversification of media voices and evidence of fracture within the central message as there was in the late 1980s, but now there is the augmentation of this dissonance via online social networks. This has the potential to broaden, deepen—and perhaps most significantly—accelerate change in Russia.

Currently, analysts look more toward other countries rather than to the Soviet past to consider the possibility for change in Russia. Do the events of the Arab Spring signal a step-change in the ability of online communication to challenge authoritarian regimes, particularly in the way that social action linked to digital communication can travel across country lines? This is a question that has galvanized the attention of post-Soviet analysts, citizens, and leaders alike as Russia experienced wide-scale street demonstrations less than a year after the collapse of Hosni Mubarak's regime in Egypt. What is significant and useful about the Arab Spring vis-à-vis the Russian case is understanding how media dissonance functions in non-free states. In particular, a closer reading of the elements of glasnost in the late Soviet period can help us to understand how changes within a communication ecosystem, even if they are not intended as freedom of the press, can mimic media freedom to the point that it has the same effect. Is the type of information shift that accelerated the end of the Soviet regime already under way in contemporary Russia? Are we failing to perceive it in the same way that virtually everyone was surprised by the abrupt collapse of the authority of the Communist Party of the Soviet Union?

This chapter argues that a careful consideration of changes in media diversity, as opposed to the introduction of media freedom, is key. This reframing of the argument will create a far more useful and nuanced understanding of information and political trajectories in present-day Russia than attempts to weld "liberation technology" arguments onto the Russian case. At the same time, this highlights the need to place the effect of communication technology within historic and national contexts instead of searching heedlessly for a type of globalized Internet "effect."

Analyzing the relationship between media diversity and political protest in Russia takes a new interest and urgency in the wake of the Ukrainian crisis in early 2014. What social and political forces are unleashed by the Internet in non-democratic regimes? This chapter argues that the inability to identify centralized points of permanent protest does not mean that people are not learning and changing their tolerance of authoritarianism through the rising diversity of information and interaction fostered by the digital sphere. In addition, this chapter is being completed as Russian intervention in Crimea widens on a daily basis, highlighting that emergent networks of media freedom are easily overwhelmed by waves of patriotism during armed conflict.

1. The Democratizing Features of the Internet

The Internet has several features that transform the media landscape, which forces us to ask the question of whether the Internet represents mere media evolution or complete media revolution. Specifically, the Internet converts the transmission of news from almost exclusively one-to-many to a many-to-many model. Traditional forms of mass media remain influential in media systems as they are key creators of content; however, these legacy media outlets have lost their monopoly on information creation and dissemination. The same distributive and economic forces of the online sphere that undermine traditional forms of mass media have created a vibrant infosphere that includes social networking, blogging, alternative news sites, direct information from sources via websites, Email campaigns, and more. This creation and sharing of content takes place largely outside of government regulation (in most countries). It is both instantaneous and inexpensive in most places. The rise of smartphones and the burgeoning of wearable communication technology (such as Google Glass) make information even more immediate, portable, and integrated with the individual.[1] The nature of the Internet also collapses barriers among economic, social, and political activities, such as enabling discussions about citizen rights in parenting forums in Russia.[2]

Key factors of the online sphere, such as immediacy, lack of controls, speed, many-to-many communication, as well as the affordance of political discussions outside traditional politicized channels, suggest that digital technology can subvert the censorship found in authoritarian states. This finding has led to the idea of "liberation technology," i.e. that the Internet can play a key role in overthrowing dictatorship.[3] This concept has gained particular currency in the United States, where the phrase has been used by the State Department as a key policy in terms of supporting citizens in foreign countries who wish to challenge regimes considered repressive by the United States. Such positive associations are countered by fears that naïve use of the Internet by dissidents—or even just curious citizens—in non-free states could lead to identification and backlash by these governments. These concerns are voiced to a

---

1   For an overview on current thinking about the individual, society, and the internet, see a report by a European Commission expert group: Onlife Initiative. *The Onlife Manifesto: Being Human in a Hyperconnected Era* (Brussels: European Commission, 2012), https://ec.europa.eu/digital-agenda/sites/digital-agenda/files/Manifesto.pdf.
2   Sarah Oates, *Revolution Stalled: The Political Limits of the Internet in the Post-Soviet Sphere* (New York: Oxford University Press, 2013).
3   Larry Diamond, "Liberation Technology," *Journal of Democracy* 21:3 (2010), 69–83.

mild degree by Diamond, but to a far greater extent by Evgeny Morozov.[4] Both hopes and fears about liberation technology should be bounded by the fact that although online communication has universal features, those elements will be significantly shaped by national systems. For example, almost all nations have state broadcasting systems. In some countries, such as the United Kingdom with its British Broadcasting Corporation (*BBC*), the national broadcasting system strives to provide an informative balance for citizens. In Russia, the main state-run broadcaster *Pervyy kanal (Channel 1)* deliberately attempts to frame or distort information to keep the Kremlin elite in power. Thus, no one would call television in and of itself a "liberation technology," although it could function as one in the right situation (and indeed it did in 1991 in Russia, as discussed below).

A reasonable argument would be that television can be controlled relatively easily by the state, whereas the Internet cannot be so easily subverted. Television can be kept in check either directly via firings and purges or less directly (and more effectively over the long term) by setting norms and self-censorship in service to the regime, as is the case at the *Pervyy kanal* and journalists in general in Russia.[5] Meanwhile, the Internet is built on the concept of networks, constantly changing and controlled by no one central authority. While the online sphere has choke points, such as the ability to shut down specific Internet service providers or arrest dissident bloggers, the Internet can fairly readily be "re-wired" for new platforms or bloggers to take up the dissenting role. Yet, what both of these arguments leave out is the audience. In order for television to dominate the information heights, it must resonate with its audience. In order for the online sphere to serve as both an effective communication system and a possible foil to state-dominated media interests in a repressive regime, it also must have an engaged

---

[4] Diamond, "Liberation Technology"; Evgeny Morozov, *Net Delusion: The Dark Side of Internet Freedom* (New York: Public Affairs, 2011).

[5] Svetlana Pasti, "Two Generations of Contemporary Russian Journalists," *European Journal of Communication* 20:1 (2005): 89–115; Katrin Voltmer, "Constructing Political Reality in Russia: Izvestiya — Between Old and New Journalistic Practices," *European Journal of Communication* 15:4 (2000): 469–500.

audience. Thus, the audience—often neglected and overlooked in communication studies—is a key factor in terms of the efficacy of media outlets.

2. Features of the Soviet and Post-Soviet Media Environment

Even before the wide adoption of the Internet, the contemporary Russian media landscape appeared significantly different from that of the Soviet media. The Soviet media was staid, controlled, and dominated by frames and language that reflected Communist messages.[6] The Soviet media worked in the service of the Communist Party with its mission to indoctrinate the population in the tenets of communism and maintain a constant campaign of pro-Party propaganda. This "Soviet Communist" model is described in Siebert et al.[7] and contrasted with the role of the media in other political systems (including democracies and even authoritarian regimes that linked control to individuals rather than communist philosophy). The Soviet Communist model is not only a useful description of media throughout much of the Soviet regime (a description that grows ever more important as we educate students who were born after the collapse of the Soviet Union), but also describes the entire typology of a media system. The question here is whether the underlying nature of the system in which the media serve political masters rather than the public interest has continued to this day in the Russian media. The contemporary Russian media both remakes beloved Soviet formats with modern twists as well as adopts Western formats, such a crime-enforcement reality shows and gritty dramas with Russian themes. Yet, for all the diversity in entertainment,

---

[6] Ellen Propper Mickiewicz, *Media and the Russian Public* (New York: Praeger, 1980); Thomas F. Remington, *The Truth of Authority: Ideology and Communication in the Soviet Union* (Pittsburgh: University of Pittsburgh Press, 1988).

[7] Fred S. Siebert, Theodore Peterson, and Wilbur Schramm, *Four Theories of the Press* (Chicago: University of Illinois Press, 1963, reprinted 1994).

there remain quite significant controls on mainstream news content.[8]

A key question in this is whether one perceives glasnost, the policy of greater media transparency introduced by Soviet leader Mikhail Gorbachev in the mid-1980s that led to widespread media diversity by 1991, as a change in nature of the Soviet media or merely an amplification of the media as lapdogs for powerful political factions. Glasnost was widely hailed as a significant shift in the role of the media from mere voices of propaganda to fitting far more closely to the Western role of the journalist to inform and enlighten the public. What is interesting is that there was indeed a switch in the nature of the media, as Soviet media outlets quickly adapted to this new policy of "transparency" (the best translation of the word *glasnost*). At first relatively limited — one of the first sensational stories was a *Pravda* newspaper report revealing how better goods were reserved for elite Communist Party stores — the reporting quickly spread to reveal and discuss forbidden topics, such as the shocking misuse of psychiatric hospitals to control dissidents and unreported Soviet army massacres during World War II. There is no question that the late 1980s and early 1990s fostered one of the most unfettered periods in journalism, not just in Russia but indeed anywhere.

However, the idea that glasnost represented a fundamental, permanent shift in the media's role in Russia from state lapdog to champion of the public interest would be a mistake. Media outlets were encouraged to push the boundaries of media frames and agenda — indeed re-invent them with great rapidity — due to two fundamental factors. First, media outlets were able to reflect the political divisions that developed among different elements of Soviet society during the CPSU's ill-fated perestroika campaign: between

---

8   Sarah Oates, *Television, Elections and Democracy in Russia* (London: Routledge, 2006); Sarah Oates and Tetyana Lokot, "Twilight of the Gods?: How the Internet Challenged Russian Television News Frames in the Winter Protests of 2011-12" (paper presented at the International Association for Media and Communication Research Annual Conference, Dublin, Ireland, 2013); Oates, *Revolution Stalled*.

hard-liners and reformers, between Soviet supporters and nationalists, between various individual politicians themselves such as Gorbachev and future Russian president Boris Yeltsin. Thus, the Russian (and somewhat universal) expression "he who pays for the music calls the tune" was appropriate, as divergent media outlets had political patrons who could give them authority and support. At the same time, this fragmentation of the political elites—never seen to this level before or after this period since the October Revolution—created an environment not only free from state control, but unfettered by dominant norms or frames. Unlike the "War on Terror" frame after 9/11 in the United States[9] or the Russian nationalist frame under Putin today,[10] the Soviet media in the late glasnost period were free not only of the constraints of the Soviet system, but of the normative frames of any system at all. While once the Soviet media had reflected the central ideology of the CPSU, by 1991 it reflected a very fragmented social and political landscape. A majority view that emerged in Russia was that of Russian nationalism and support for Yeltsin in lieu of Gorbachev.

Thus, glasnost was not a policy that supported "freedom" of the press, but diversity of the press emerged due to lack of controls. While the Soviet journalists were not trained as watchdog journalists, the splintering of central control, the rise of a range of political viewpoints, as well as the coverage of this new diversity across the media spectrum created many different voices. As a result, Soviet citizens were presented with perhaps one of the most diverse media environments in modern times during the late glasnost era. While media scholars might point to such an outpouring of different perspectives as a good thing, Soviet citizens themselves were less impressed.[11] Studies have shown that Soviet citizens viewed this media landscape as a cacophony of voices that encouraged a dangerous division of power. Indeed, in one survey they judged the media during the glasnost period as the worst era for the media in either

---

9   Robert M. Entman, "Cascading Activation: Contesting the White House's Frame after 9/11," *Political Communication* 20 (2003): 415-32.
10   Oates and Lokot, "Twilight of the Gods."
11   Oates, *Television, Elections and Democracy.*

Soviet or Russian times: In a survey of 2,000 Russians in 2001, respondents showed little enthusiasm for the glasnost style of news: they preferred either the media under Putin (43 percent) or even in Soviet times (17 percent) rather than during the Yeltsin era or during glasnost.[12] In a series of 24 focus groups in Russia in 2000, Russians expressed dismay at the chaotic nature of information and society during the glasnost period and in the first years of the young Russian state.[13] Thus, while the media went through profound changes during glasnost, Russians did not necessarily appreciate these changes. The Russian audience expressed support for order and authority over a diversity of opinions on the pages of newspapers or via their television screens. The open question is whether there is still the preference for order over information in the Internet age in Russia.

Ultimately, neither journalistic philosophy nor audience reaction was the key factor in the (unintended) ability of glasnost to transform Soviet society in ways counter to Gorbachev's intentions. What glasnost did was ruin the façade of an effective state. All states are flawed, but citizens usually accept some measure of incompetence or corruption if the broader image of the state is that of control and competence. Western analysts assumed that Russians were enraged by the way in which media transparency (or media cacophony) under glasnost revealed a non-democratic state. Public opinion surveys from this period and soon after, however, showed that there was little permanent support for democracy as defined by Western experience.[14] Thus, the Soviet audience was more profoundly disturbed by the lack of competence and authority in their state, which was amply demonstrated during glasnost. This reached a head in August 1991, when a CPSU reactionary coup failed within days and the full inability of the Party to continue to lead the country was revealed, not least by the shaking hands of the leaders in a wooden press conference on state television. Nor did

---

12 Ibid., 155.
13 Oates, *Television, Elections and Democracy*.
14 Stephen White, *Understanding Russian Politics* (Cambridge: Cambridge University Press, 2011).

the newly acquired habits and skills of Soviet journalists help the coup makers hold on to power for the CPSU, as the prime state television channel defied armed guards to send cameras onto the streets and record not only the broad civic unrest, but even more significantly, the failure of the military to support the coup. In this moment, the actions of the Soviet media under glasnost and any free media anywhere converged. The Soviet media in August 1991 had huge latitude because there literally was no longer a central government to control them, not because the idea of control was gone from the minds of the journalists or the citizens. At the time, however, many mistakenly saw this as the dawning of a Western-style journalistic freedom in Russia. They were wrong; the dearth of control came from the non-existence of a functional state, not from a shift in journalistic norms or audience expectations. Meanwhile, citizens suffered in this new era of "freedom" in the young Russian state, when jobs, pensions, savings, and security disappeared virtually overnight for tens of millions of Russians

3. *Glasnost* Then and Russia Now

How does the glasnost period compare with the current media landscape in Russia? Even prior to the advent of the Internet, the Russian media sector was notably more diverse than the Soviet media. In particular, a vibrant commercial sector has developed, including the national *NTV* television network and many other outlets (online and offline). However, this did not mean it developed into a system that included media and journalism as a watchdog of the state or as a champion of the public. In particular, it is significant what is not reported on the mainstream media (especially television). Issues such as widespread corruption, the collapse of social services, the problems of rural life, endemic unemployment in some areas, and particularly ongoing violence in Chechnya are not reported in any meaningful way in the Russian mainstream media.

Can the Internet, then, bring further and useful glasnost or transparency to Russia? Raising such a question is not even asking if the Internet can bring freedom of the media, given that the lesson of the glasnost era is that transparency alone can bring about profound change. There are some significant parallels between the glasnost period and the new digital age for Russia, not least in the noteworthy increase in diverse reporting and opinions. After the foundation of the Russian state, media freedom as measured by Western standards steadily declined in Russia. Indeed, Russia has slipped far down the list of free countries compiled by Freedom House, now ranked 176th out of 197 countries, between Sudan and Azerbaijan.[15] Although there is a relatively lively commercial broadcast sphere in Russia, Putin signaled a lack of tolerance for political challenge by commercial media through a forced financial takeover of the main commercial broadcaster (*NTV*) in 2001.[16] The performance of the Russian media at elections has highlighted many flaws in the system, particularly in the bias and slanted reporting of the central state-run television on *Pervyy kanal* (*Channel 1*). Despite electoral laws that guarantee equal coverage to candidates and parties, there is a marked bias toward pro-Putin candidates and the United Russia party.[17] Political opponents, from the communists to liberals, are mostly ignored and occasionally vilified in the main state-run media. Commercial television does produce news that is slightly more challenging to the dominant state narrative, but it does not call into serious question any aspect of the state (particularly widespread corruption or the long-running conflict in Chechnya).

While information sources have diversified and become technically more professional, the idea of the media as "objective" or "balanced" has never been widely accepted. All segments of Rus-

---

15 See the report by Freedom House, a U.S.-based non-governmental organization, at http://www.freedomhouse.org/report-types/freedom-press
16 Oates, *Television, Elections and Democracy*.
17 See reports from the European Institute for the Media on media performance in Russian elections from 1993 to 2000, archived at http://www.media-politics.com/eimreports.htm as well as reports on Russian elections from the Organization for Security and Co-operation in Europe/Office for Democratic Institutions and Human Rights (OSCE/ODIHR) at http://www.osce.org/odihr-elections/. Also see Stephen White, Richard Rose, and Ian McAllister, *How Russia Votes* (Washington, DC: CQ Press, 1996).

sian society, from politicians to the public to the journalists themselves, perceive the mass media as political actors themselves rather than watchdogs that can provide a check on political power.[18] Thus, while there is no overt system of top-down state censorship in Russia today, the media are not free to contribute to the democratic process. This limit results from an intertwined set of societal factors. These elements include a lack of professional acceptance of the concept of journalistic balance or objectivity; the use of the media as political pawns by leaders; and the public's acceptance of the media as a voice of authority rather than the purveyor of information.

4. The Internet in the Post-Soviet Information Ecosystem: Stability or Change?

Until late 2011, there was little evidence that the democratizing potential of the Internet was bringing any fundamental change to citizens in Russia, even as growth in Internet use exploded in the country. Between 2000 and 2010, the percentage of people online in Russia grew 1,826 percent.[19] Figures from World Telecommunications/ICT Indicators Database show that 43 percent of the Russian population was online by March 31, 2011, with almost 60 million users out of a population of just under 140 million. The percent of the population online has since expanded to about 47 percent, according to World Internet Stats.[20] Although Russia now has the most people online of any European nation, it came late to the digital revolution. Moving from a relatively low uptake for its level of economic development,[21] Russia's Internet use grew more quickly

---

18   Pasti, "Two Generations"; Voltmer, "Constructing Political Reality."
19   "World Telecommunications/ICT Indicators Database," United Nations, http://data.un.org/Data.aspx?d=ITU&f=ind1Code%3aI99H#ITU.
20   "Europe," Internet World Stats, http://www.internetworldstats.com/stats4.htm#europe.
21   Julian Cooper, "The Internet in Russia – Development, Trends and Research Possibilities" (paper presented at the CEELBAS Post-Soviet Media Research Methodology Workshop, University of Birmingham, Birmingham, UK, 28 March 2008).

than any other significant European nation over the same time period.[22] Russia's experience parallels the online population in Egypt, where use accelerated sharply in the period just before the Arab Spring. The two countries' experience suggests that considering not only the percent of a population online, but the pace of the growth of the outline audience, is important to understanding the relationship between the Internet and political protests. In both the case of Egypt and Russia, significant public protests occurred as the adoption of the Internet hastened.

At the same time that both the online audience and online content continued to grow at a rapid rate, the Russian state failed to extend its traditional system of mass media control to the online sphere. Such slow reactions are not unusual, in that there is significant variation in state control of the Internet across all types of regimes. However, it is important to note that Russia pursued a relatively laissez-faire approach to monitoring the online sphere up to the end of 2011.[23] The hands-off approach was in direct contrast to the way in which Russia uses a range of controls, from media law that asymmetrically gives power to the state and the inculcation of journalistic self-censorship, to controlling the traditional mass media. That being said, Russia has developed a range of laws over the past decade that technically allow for mass surveillance and control of the Internet, most notably its SORM legislation.[24] The interesting question is why the Russian authorities, for the most part, allowed the Internet to exist outside of the regime of repressive law and self-censorship. Allowing such freedom to flourish could be due to a lack of understanding of the Internet as a mass medium or the conviction that there was little dissent to fear within the society (or some combination of both these factors). The Internet might have been viewed as a useful "safety value" or showpiece for freedom of speech, much in the same way that the opposition newspaper *Novaya gazeta* (*The New Newspaper*) continues to publish reports highly critical of the Putin regime. Any views of the Internet as a benign

---

22 "World Telecommunications/ICT Indicators Database," United Nations.
23 Oates, *Revolution Stalled*.
24 Ibid.

or relatively powerless institution on the part of the government were significantly challenged by mass protests triggered by anger over electoral manipulation in late 2011 and early 2012.

5. The 2011–2012 Russian Protests: The Winter of Discontent

Until the end of 2011, there were relatively few street protests in Russia and virtually no meaningful coverage of these demonstrations in the mainstream media. While an examination of the traditional media would show minimal citizen opposition to the regime (aside from some token coverage of the Communist Party of the Russian Federation), there was evidence that people were aggregating interests online and even taking action locally or on targeted issues, such as health care or treatment for children with genetic disabilities.[25] Such activism was apparent not only in the ways that Russians responded to widespread forest fires in 2010 by setting up a crowd-sourced map of areas needing help or through online protests about the development of forest lands near Moscow, but also via smaller-scale protests to gain access to social benefits taking place in various parts of Russia.[26] Some social action spread on the Internet, such as the "blue buckets" campaign that saw motorists affixing blue buckets to the roofs of their cars across Russia to mock the overuse of blue police lights on official cars. Such innovation showcased the Russian flair for graphic humor and mockery as social protest. Alexei Navalny and other social-activist bloggers had gained significant followings online by the end of 2011, particularly with Navalny's anti-corruption campaigns that had broad resonance in a population frustrated by the high levels of fraud in Russia. However, it would have been difficult to identify any widespread, populist Russian political movement or street demonstrations linked to the Internet prior to late 2011.

The first major evidence of change in the scale and scope of protests in Russia occurred when relatively small protests about the

---

25 Ibid.
26 Ibid.

December 2011 parliamentary elections quickly escalated in Moscow and further afield. The protests were triggered by election rigging for the 450-seat Duma (the lower house of the Russian parliament and the only federal legislative chamber that is directly elected). Election fraud is nothing new in Russia and arguably was not worse in 2011 than in previous elections. Problems have included suspected falsification of returns (particularly in Chechnya), unfair treatment at the ballot box, vote buying, as well as highly biased coverage of candidates and parties by national media, especially on state-run television. Elections have been heavily manipulated by the Kremlin, not only via the state-dominated media, but also through an electoral law increasingly aimed at consolidating state-backed parties at the expense of grass-roots opposition.[27]

The Kremlin-backed United Russia won 53 percent of the vote in December 2011, which was not far off the predicted result, but anomalies in the vote as well as reports of electoral irregularities were widespread. The first protests appeared in Moscow just after the December 4 election day. The largest number of arrests (estimated at hundreds) occurred during the early protests and included the detention of Navalny along with other opposition figures. A larger protest was quickly organized for December 10 in Moscow under the banner of "For Fair Elections," managing to gain permission for the event and a sanctioned area on which to protest. The crowd was estimated at about 50,000 by the *BBC*. Other protests were planned for around the country, aided significantly by communication online. The protest numbers peaked on December 24, with the largest demonstration held on Sakharov Avenue in Moscow and attracting an estimated crowd of 80,000. There were additional rallies across the country. Although the movement called for new Duma elections, the removal of the chair of the Central Electoral Commission, as well as an investigation into falsification in the Duma results, none of these demands were met by the end of

---

27   Regina Smyth, "Beyond United Russia: The Kremlin's Efforts to Engineer Ruling Majorities," *PONARS Eurasia Policy Memo* No. 302, September 2013, http://www.ponarseurasia.org/memo/beyond-united-russia-kremlin's-efforts-engineer-ruling-majorities.

the 2011–2012 protests. Another set of protest meetings were organized for February 4, again at Bolotnaya Square in Moscow and around the country. Pro-Putin demonstrations started to appear as well, with the largest in Moscow also on February 4, with a reported 130,000 participants.[28]

The nature and scale of the protests caught many observers and analysts completely off guard. Russians were certainly aware of electoral manipulation, but arguably the Internet made them conscious of the scope of the problem for the first time in 2011. Although the first protests followed the usual script of state repression and arrests, the subsequent demonstrations were marked by few arrests and the participation of a broad range of the population as opposed to a narrow circle of committed dissidents. The size of the anti-regime protests is evidence that the online sphere can be a game-changer in terms of the ability to spark street protests in non-free states. Similar elections and high levels of corruption had been occurring for years, with no organized street demonstrations or virtually any protest at all. However, it is not the mere existence of the online sphere or even the electoral fraud. Rather, it is possible to identify a set of factors all linked to the online sphere that combined to produce an extraordinary level of dissent for Russian citizens. These factors are the particularly flagrant electoral manipulation made visible via the Internet; online alternative news sources; room for public aggregation of anger via social-networking sites; and the ability to logistically organize online. At the same time, the ability to witness via the online sphere removed one of the most powerful elements of a repressive regime to isolate and intimidate individual citizens through arrest. Private discontent had evolved into public

---

28 The estimates of the crowds varied widely between official numbers released by the police and the protestors themselves. Estimates from the British media are used as they are from a relatively objective viewpoint. See "'First we take Sakharov Avenue': The capital sees its biggest demonstration yet against the Kremlin," *The Economist*, 31 December 2011, http://www.economist.com/node/21542205, and "Moscow: Thousands join pro- and anti-Putin protests," *BBC Online*, 4 February 2012, http://www.bbc.co.uk/news/world-europe-16885446.

outrage, facilitated by the communicative affordances of the online sphere.

As during the glasnost period, state-run media could not maintain a unified narrative dictated by the Kremlin.[29] The First Channel's flagship news show *Vremya* (*Time*) attempted to frame the protestors as either dedicated troublemakers or foolish thrill-seekers, but it was impossible to maintain that narrative with almost half of the population having access to direct witnessing and relatively unbiased reports from the events themselves via the Internet. There was a noticeable shift in the frame of the events by state-run television to concede that the protests were much broader in both size and scope,[30] although *Vremya* avoided reporting that the main rallying cry for the protestors was "Russia without Putin." This shift was forced from the "bottom up" by the wealth of information online, ranging from full reports from reliable online news outlets to reports on social media from the protestors themselves. While the protests faded at the end of winter with little beyond a minor change in the electoral law to make it easier for political parties to register, arguably the change in the public sphere is permanent. Meanwhile, repressive laws aimed at controlling online dissent in Russia have accelerated since the 2011–2012 protests.[31]

The most telling example of how the Kremlin is failing to control the narrative relates to the fate of Navalny, who was arrested on charges of embezzlement and convicted of misappropriating about US$500,000 worth of lumber from a state-owned company in a trial that most viewed as politically motivated.[32] Although he was sentenced to five years in prison, he was released almost immediately on bail and continued to campaign for the Moscow mayoral election in September 2013. Navalny had risen to prominence

---

29   Oates and Lokot, "Twilight of the Gods?"
30   Ibid.
31   Regina Smyth, " 'Welcome to North Korea': Predicting the Effect of Russia's New Protest Law," *Policy Blog for PONARS Eurasia*, 4 July 2012, http://www.ponarseurasia.org/article/"welcome-north-korea"-predicting-effect-russia's-new-protest-law.
32   Miriam Elder, "Russia: Alexei Navalny found guilty of embezzlement," *The Guardian*, 18 July 2013.

online with his website that encouraged the reporting of corruption via the submission of evidence (much like the Wikileaks model). Once a member of the liberal Yabloko party, but long an independent activist, Navalny is the most prominent Internet innovator in Russia. His rise to prominence has led to harassment and attention from officials, notably his arrest at one of the earliest protests after the 2011 elections. Navalny went on to win a respectable 27 percent of the votes for an outsider/liberal candidate in the mayoral race.[33] Eventually, his prison sentence was suspended, although he was banned from the online sphere in February 2014.[34]

What is notable about Navalny's case is that it does not fit the post-Soviet power paradigm, which is the most compelling evidence yet that there is actually a lack of a central power plan in Russia. No one was able to pretend that the charges against Navalny were fair or reasonable. The court proceedings and decision were clearly politically motivated, as Navalny himself said when his sentence was suspended: "Everything that happened last summer and everything that happens today depends on Putin."[35] It appeared that the state was operating its usual machinery against those they deemed powerful enough to be a threat, a strategy that starts with charges and can lead to indefinite detention. This model was consolidated, in particular, by the case of Mikhail Khodorkovsky, the former head of the state energy concern Yukos, who was convicted of fraud charges in 2005 and released in December 2013. The state's ability to put away a billionaire oligarch consolidated the Putin regime's power, authority, and regime of intimidation. Following this playbook, Navalny needed to be imprisoned, preferably indefinitely, in the same manner as Khodorkovsky. However, the surprise release of Khodorkovsky in December 2013 raises intriguing

---

33 Will Englund, "Kremlin critic Alexei Navalny has strong showing in Moscow mayoral race, despite loss," *The Washington Post*, 9 September 2013, http://www.washingtonpost.com/world/kremlin-critic-alexei-navalny-has-strong-showing-in-moscow-mayoral-race-despite-loss/2013/09/09/dc9504e4-1924-11e3-a628-7e6dde8f889d_story.html.
34 Andrew E. Kramer, "Navalny Is Spared Prison Term in Russia," *The New York Times*, 16 October 2013, http://www.nytimes.com/2013/10/17/world/europe/russian-opposition-leader-is-spared-jail.html?_r=1&.
35 Ibid.

questions: was this a decision by the Kremlin to look "merciful" or a calculated move to respond to the need to appear more democratic in the Internet age? If the latter, it would suggest that the 2011–2012 protests have changed government strategy.

There have been many theories as to why Navalny was not left in prison, although few observers put forth the idea that Russian officials felt the case was unfair or were following any legal precedents (as politics rather than law dictates action for political challengers such as Navalny). It would appear that the case of Navalny simply did not fit the playbook. By imprisoning him and turning him into a martyr, the state risked giving him more power, visibility, and greater legitimacy. His visibility in the international media increased markedly via reports of his arrest in the first December 2011 elections protest. By letting him remain free, especially as he ran for public office and continues as a powerful opposition leader both online and off, he also remains a threat. The Kremlin, it would appear, simply has no particular strategy for dealing with an online social entrepreneur. As a result, there is no way to predict what will happen to Navalny, which opens a new and interesting era in Russian politics. And this era would be impossible without the *glasnost* that is brought about by the Internet. As during the glasnost period, there is little evidence that journalistic norms have changed, but there is a huge diversity of views available to the ever-growing Russian online audience. As in the glasnost era, this suggests that there is a cacophony of media frames, meaning that the state cannot control the narrative. And if a non-free state cannot control the narrative, it is at equal risk of coup or revolution. By admitting in February 2014 that Navalny is too dangerous to have online, the Russian state may have actually amplified his power and influence yet again.

A wild card factor in this shift is the Russian media audience, as a factor that has evolved significantly from late Soviet times is the media choice of the Russian audience. A Russian government report in 2011 predicted that by 2015, virtually all Russians under the age of 40 would be online.[36] At the same time, older Russians are far less likely to be online for economic and social reasons. Older Russians still report state-run television as their most important media source, while younger Russians select website portals in the same surveys.[37] Thus, the turn away from television and to the smaller screens of the Internet (computer, tablet, phone and whatever the future holds) is accelerated in Russia, which has a particularly rapid rise of the younger generation due to significantly lower life expectancy for Russians than most Western counterparts. Russia is changing fast, augmented by the shift in the delivery and sharing of information made available by the online sphere. It would take a smart and responsive repressive regime to adapt and capitalize on that shift in the public sphere, and the Navalny case, in particular, suggests that the regime is falling behind.

Research by Gallup for the U.S. Broadcasting Board of Governors has identified rapid shifts toward the digital sphere among the Russian audience.[38] In a series of surveys of nationwide samples of 2,000 Russians aged 15 and older, reports of Internet access have grown from 45 percent of the population in 2010 to 63 percent in 2012 to 71 percent in 2013. This shift means that Internet use surged 58 percent over just two years. The Gallup surveys have found that television still has massive penetration in Russia, with usage at 98 percent in 2013, but the trend is away from the big screen and toward smaller screens: From 2010 to 2012, reported daily television viewing fell from 89 percent of the Russian adult population to 85 percent while Internet use rose from just 29 percent for daily use to 46 percent. While television still saturates the Russian population, it is now augmented — or challenged — by information that Russians encounter in the online sphere.

---

36 "Internet v Rossii: sostoyanie, tendentsii i perspektivy razvitiya," Russian Federal Agency on the Press and Mass Communication, http://www.fapmc.ru/magnoliaPublic/rospechat/activities/reports/2011/item6.html.
37 Ibid.
38 For full results, see "BBG Research series: Contemporary media use in Russia," Broadcasting Board of Governors, http://www.bbg.gov/blog/2014/01/08/bbg-research-series-contemporary-media-use-in-russia/.

Gallup conducted more in-depth research on media use in November 2013 with a nationwide survey of 5,012 people. Although social networking was the most popular activity online in Russia in late 2013, with half of the respondents reporting they had used it during the past week, almost as many (46 percent) reported using the Internet to find information on a topic. Thirty-seven percent of the respondents had used the Internet to find news in the past week—indeed, four out of 10 Russians claimed to access news online two times or more each day. About a third of the respondents reported that they used social networking sites to share news regularly. When the results are shown by socio-economic characteristics, younger, more educated, wealthier, and urban respondents are likely to use the Internet more. The differences are particularly marked among the generations; indeed, those 15–24 years old were more likely to have been online (82 percent) in the previous day rather than watching television (73 percent). This compares with the middle age group (aged 35–44) who were more likely to have watched television (87 percent) compared with being online (55 percent). The Gallup surveys over several years have found that this rise in the use of the online sphere parallels a drop in allegiance to the Russian status quo. Approval of Putin has fallen from 83 percent in 2008 to 54 percent in 2013. At the same time, conviction that the Russian leadership is headed in the right direction has decreased from 63 percent to 45 percent. While this fall in approval is correlated with the rise in Internet access, it is important not to make direct causal links, although it raises interesting questions. Tellingly, considering an "active opposition" to be "very important" has risen from 35 percent in 2008 to 43 percent in 2013.

6. *Glasnost* 2.0 and the Acceleration of Dissent

Online communication offers new and formidable tools to spread information in ways that subvert the power of authoritarian regimes to censor and repress. At the same time, however, domestic factors ranging from political culture to media history shape these affordances in different ways. Underlying this already complex situation is the concern that the authoritarian regimes themselves can hijack the informative capability of the Internet for their own ends. Thus, analysts should be looking for ways to fit the affordances of the Internet into the media culture and media history of a particular country. In other words, the Internet is a game-changer, but the games it changes vary significantly. In the comparison of the Egyptian uprising of 2011 and the Russian street protests of 2011–2012, there are factors that point to how the Internet challenges the Russian state. At the same time, however, the history of late Soviet media and the experience of *glasnost* encourage us not to confuse media diversity—or even media cacophony—with freedom of the press. Changes in the media landscape were a significant factor in the collapse of the Soviet Union, but an over-determination of the role of the media in regime collapse blinds us to other factors. The most useful way to consider the Arab Spring effect on Russia is to consider how the new sources of information distribution and communication will specifically affect Russian political institutions.

One of the classic myths about Soviet history is that glasnost was a type of freedom of the press. Ultimately, however, the fact that the Soviet media system did not become a Western media system under glasnost did not matter to the leaders at the time. What the "cacophony" model created was the lack of confidence in the central power structure. From Lenin onwards, the Soviet system relied heavily on the media in building the image of a powerful state. The actual capabilities of the Soviet state were challenged, particularly at the beginning of the Soviet system, by a range of internal and external factors. The image of a strong central state and a shared vision, however, did not waver significantly in the Soviet media until the glasnost period. Once the illusion was shattered, chaos ensued. Under Putin, the Russian state has again managed to project an image of power and shared vision, with a particular emphasis on nationalism and regaining a significant role in the world order. The Internet threatens the ability of the Putin regime to maintain the useful illusion of cogency and power that non-democratic states critically need for legitimacy.

At the next major trigger event in Russia—ranging from anger over spending cuts, reports of high-level corruption, protests over social conditions such as failing healthcare—there will be a public memory of the right and the ability to take to the streets. As in the glasnost period, a lack of a strong central narrative makes this sort of mobilization even more likely and the Internet will be there to facilitate that protest. If Russian officials do not want more protests of this nature, they have two choices: accommodate greater engagement of the Russian public in governance or control the Internet. They may not choose to do the former, but it looks unlikely that they can pull off the latter as well. And now that the latest digitally driven revolution has taken place just over the border in Ukraine, change seems more likely.

Worryingly, a third option emerged for Russia in February 2014. This wild card is the use of nationalism to trump calls for individual freedoms, particularly a Russian-led invasion of another country to "liberate" fellow Russians. The threat of the Internet to "repression-as-usual" would encourage the Russian government to pursue military incursions or other nationalist acts to overwhelm this new media ecology and re-establish control of the narrative.

The Persistence of Media Control under Consolidated Authoritarianism: Containing Kazakhstan's Digital Media

Luca Anceschi, The University of Glasgow

On 5 February, 2014, Nurali Aytelenov, Rinat Kibrayev, and Dmitriy Shelokov—three bloggers operating in Kazakhstan—received 10-day sentences for hooliganism charges after being arrested for publicly protesting their exclusion from a meeting between selected bloggers and Akhmetzhan S. Yesimov—the *akim* of the Almaty *oblast'*.[1] A fourth blogger, Dina Baidildayeva, was briefly detained on 8 February, after she had staged a one-woman demonstration in central Almaty to express solidarity with her imprisoned colleagues. On both occasions,[2] police interrogators reportedly demanded lengthy explanations—in some cases provided by the detainees themselves—of the nature and scope of Internet blogging. Almaty authorities (or at least the police personnel tasked to conduct interrogations in these two cases) had apparently never heard of—let alone read—an online blog.

This account of the repressive wave of February 2014 in many ways represents a microcosm of the politics of digital media in post-Soviet Kazakhstan. Despite their niche status within the Kazakhstani socio-political landscape, new media—and blogging in particular—have not escaped the repressive attention of the regime headed by Nursultan A. Nazarbayev. The enforcement of government control over the media landscape and, more generally, the

---

[1] "Arest blogerov v Almaty prokommentirovali v sude," *TengriNews*, http://tengrinews.kz/events/arest-blogerov-v-almatyi-prokommentiroval i-v-sude-250053/; Joanna Lillis, "Kazakhstan arrests four bloggers in a week," *EurasiaNet.org*, http://www.eurasianet.org/node/68027.

[2] Anonymous. Interviewed by Luca Anceschi, Almaty, 31 March 2014. The author has respected the wishes of those interviewees who asked to remain anonymous.

limitation of freedom of expression are standard power technologies in authoritarian Kazakhstan.[3] Containing digital media, in this sense, does not represent an instance of discontinuity in the evolution of Kazakhstani authoritarianism.

In early 2014, repressive measures were enforced with the deliberate intention of blocking relatively prominent Internet activists from gaining access to Kazakhstan's limited public sphere.[4] In so doing, Nazarbayev and his associates demonstrated that they had rapidly assimilated the many lessons of Egypt and Tunisia, where digital media were instrumental in "spreading protest messages, [while] connecting frustrated citizens with one another."[5] It was the translation of on-line activity into political activism, and not the publication of controversial or subversive posts, that led the regime to detain the Almaty bloggers.

The visibly exaggerated response to the minor protests of 2014 might suggest that the élite in Astana had ultimately concluded that new media had come to represent a potentially destabilizing force within the Kazakhstani domestic landscape. The government's preoccupation with containing digital media, however, featured heavily in pre-2014 political developments and, in December 2011, characterized decisively the regime's posture throughout one of the most dramatic political crises that erupted in post-Soviet Kazakhstan. In the aftermath of the brutal repression of a workers' strike in Zhanaozen (Mangystau *oblast'*, Western Kazakhstan), the Naz-

---

3 In 2015, Reporters without Borders ranked Kazakhstan in 160th place in its Global Press Freedom index. For more on media freedom in Kazakhstan, see: Barbara Junisbai, "Oligarchs and ownership: The role of financial-industrial groups in financing Kazakhstan's 'independent' media," in Eric Freeman and Richard Shafer, eds., *After the Czars and Commissars – Journalism in Authoritarian Post-Soviet Central Asia* (East Lansing, Mich.: Michigan State University Press, 2012).

4 Peter Dahlgren, "The Internet, Public Spheres, and Political Communication: Dispersion and Deliberation," *Political Communication* 22:2 (2005): 147–62; Peter Van Aelst and Stefaan Walgrave, "New media, new movements? The role of the internet in shaping the 'anti-globalization' movement," *Information, Communication & Society* 5:4 (2002): 465–93.

5 Philip N. Howard and Muzammil M. Hussain, "The role of digital media," *Journal of Democracy* 22:3 (July 2011): 41.

arbayev regime imposed a strict block on phone and Internet services over a radius of 65 km around the city center in order to avoid the diffusion of independent accounts of the government-sanctioned violence through social media.[6] Through the establishment of a suffocating legislative framework and the consolidation of adversarial relations between government and independent digital media, post-Zhanaozen Kazakhstan evolved into an inhospitable milieu for new media.[7] It was against this authoritarian backdrop that the multiple arrests of February 2014 took place.

The logic of regime control, therefore, offers an appropriate lens to analyze the numerous regulatory linkages connecting government policies and digital media in Kazakhstan. The Nazarbayev regime endeavored to control new media by applying the same combination of persuasive tactics and intensively restrictive methods[8] by which it had constrained broadcast and print media since the achievement of independence. Unlike more traditional outlets, however, digital media came to prominence at a time when local authoritarianism had already reached a position of monopolistic control over domestic political dynamics. This chapter argues that there is a strong link between the progressive de-politicization of Kazakhstan's cyberspace and the consolidation of non-political Internet consumption patterns across the Kazakhstani users' community. In other words, the regime's desire to stay in power decisively shaped the outlook of Kazakhstani cyberspace, while influencing directly the consumption habits of those segments of the local population that access the Internet regularly.

---

6   Wefightcensorhip.org—a subsidiary project of Reporters without Borders—has prepared an exhaustive page of resources on Zhanaozen, including a list of censored news outlets that offered alternative coverage of the events in Western Kazakhstan, https://www.wefightcensorship.org/censored/kazakhstan-zhanaozen-city-cut-rest-world-year-agohtml.html-forbidden-content.

7   Since 2012, Reporters without Borders has included Kazakhstan within the list of countries that practice systematic censure of the Internet.

8   On the alternation of repression and more persuasive methods in the advancement of Kazakhstani authoritarianism, see: Edward Schatz and Elena Maltseva, "Kazakhstan's Authoritarian 'Persuasion'," *Post-Soviet Affairs* 28:1 (2012): 45–65; "Kazakhstan: Waiting for Change," *Asia Report* No. 250, International Crisis Group, 30 September 2013, 11–15.

To unveil the multiple impacts of this dual policy of containment, our analysis will go beyond Kazakhstan's cyberspace, which will be predominantly discussed through an investigation of the population's Internet consumption habits. The second segment of the chapter, in turn, will shift its attention onto the containment of Kazakhstan's new media landscape, with the ultimate goal of describing both the restrictive legislative frameworks and the coercive processes through which virtually every pocket of the Kazakhstani cyberspace ended up under the suffocating control of the Nazarbayev regime.

1. Internet Consumption Habits in Kazakhstan

The proliferation of access options has complicated the identification of reliable data on Kazakhstan's total Internet users. At the end of 2014, official statistics reported that 2.1 million Kazakhstani citizens had subscribed to a fixed Internet connection.[9] Approximately 41.6 percent of this category of users was reportedly located in Almaty and Astana: the concentration of fixed accesses in selected urban settings is therefore a defining trait of Kazakhstan's Internet consumption patterns. Regional distribution of fixed connections is an area where the Kazakhstani government has failed to improve its performance, as at the end of 2004, Kazakhstan's two main cities accounted for 44 percent of fixed subscriptions.

However, urban concentration notwithstanding, access patterns have noticeably changed since the emergence of GSM technology and the progressive diffusion of 3G and 4G connectivity, launched in 2010 and 2013 respectively. The ratio of fixed connections over total accesses decreased by 40 percent between 2007 and 2012, when, according to Kazakhtelekom data, fixed subscriptions represented only 34 percent of total accesses.[10] The majority of Kazakhstani users access the Internet through mobile connections,

---

9   "Chislo abonentov fiksirovannogo Interneta," Stat.gov.kz, http://www.stat.gov.kz/faces/wcnav_externalId/homeNumbersCommunication?_afrLoop=533188689158354#%40%3F_afrLoop%3D533188689158354%26_adf.ctrl-state%3D19yionbrr_158.

10 Data extracted from Kazakhtelekom's official site, http://www.telecom.kz/page/single/strategija-kompanii?lang=ru.

which have more than tripled in number since 2006,[11] reaching a remarkable 59 percent penetration rate in 2012.[12]

The government is boasting about a relatively unrealistic overall Internet penetration rate of over 70 percent,[13] claiming that, in October 2014, 12 million Kazakhstani citizens had stable access to the Internet.[14] Inflating data on total accesses is integral to a central regime narrative, namely one which sought to portray, both domestically and internationally, Kazakhstan as a rapidly developing country. A closer look at wider policy frameworks — including *Nurly Zhol*, which Astana is currently presenting as Kazakhstan's key document defining economic development — does, on the other hand, indicate that the achievement of universal Internet access normally is not included among the regime's long-term development targets.[15] Moving away from the government's fabricated data, and combining all the available statistics on different connection typologies, it might be therefore reasonable to estimate a nominal 53–54 percent total penetration rate for late 2014, when approximately 40 percent[16] of the Kazakhstani population is thought to be using the Internet on a regular basis.

Katy Pearce observed that trying to develop a true picture of what is happening based on penetration rate statistics is ultimately

---

11   Frederick Emrich, Yevgeniya Plakhina, and Dariya Tsyrenzhapova, *Mapping Digital Media: Kazakhstan* (Almaty: Open Society Foundation, 2013), 7.
12   "Kazakhstan," in *Freedom of the Net 2013 — A Global Assessment of Internet and Digital Media* (Washington, DC: Freedom House, 2013), 439.
13   "V Kazakhstane proniknovenie internet dostiglo bolee 70% - A. Zhumagaliev," www.zakon.kz, 15 July 2010, http://www.zakon.kz/463 9322-v-kazakhstane-proniknovenie-interneta.html.
14   Indira Kaumetova, "A. Isekeshev: V Kazakhstane chislo internet-pol'zovateley dostiglo 12 mln chelovek," strategy2050.kz, 7 October 2014, http://strategy2050.kz/ru/news/13777.
15   For the full draft of the presidential speech underpinning the *Nurly Zhol* programme, see: "Poslanie Glavy gosudarstva N. Nazarbayeva narodu Kazakstana. 11 noyabrya 2014 g.," strategy2050.kz, http://strategy2050.kz/ru/page/message_text2014/.
16   This figure has been also confirmed in numerous interviews conducted with bloggers and communication experts in Kazakhstan in March and April 2014.

"futile."[17] Her argument can be appropriately extended to Kazakhstan, where state-run operator Kazakhtelekom controlled approximately 80 percent of fixed Internet connections at the end of 2013.[18] Kazakhstan's mobile Internet market, although visibly more fragmented, is far from being thoroughly competitive. At the end of 2012, KCell's market share of 47 percent was almost as large as the combined shares of its three main competitors, namely Beeline (32 percent), Tele2 (12 percent), and Altai (5 percent).[19] Kcell had been operating under Kazakhtelekom's control until 2012, when it was acquired by Swedish company Teliasonera[20] through a series of not entirely uncontroversial[21] transactions.

The political implications of a non-competitive Internet market are evident:[22] the state owns 51 percent of Kazakhtelekom, which controls, in turn, 70 percent of Kazakhstan's Internet accesses. Regime hegemony over network infrastructure places the issue of physical control at the epicenter of every strategy of Internet censorship put into practice in Kazakhstan.[23] A similar infrastructural context, when imposed in non-democratic political landscapes, usually leads to the consolidation of a networked form of

---

17　Katy Pearce, "Why Technology-Penetration Rates Are Worthless," *RFE/RL*, 21 December 2012.

18　Data extracted from Kazakhtelekom's official site, http://www.telecom.kz/page/single/strategija-kompanii?lang=ru.

19　Data retrieved by the author from the annual reports of the four companies in question.

20　Isabel Gorst, "KCell IPO priced at up to $650m," *Financial Times*, http://blogs.ft.com/beyond-brics/2012/11/29/kcell-ipo-priced-at-up-to-650m/.

21　Joanna Lillis, "In Kazakhstan, What Did Embattled TeliaSonera Learn From Uzbekistan?," *eurasianet.org*, 4 April 2014, http://www.eurasianet.org/node/68233.

22　John L. Couper, Adil Nurmakov, and Tyrone Adams, "Political uses of social media in Kazakhstan," in Cui Litang and Michael H. Prosser, eds., *Social Media in Asia* (Doerzbach: Dignity Press, 2014).

23　Eric Harwit and Duncan Clark, "Shaping the Internet in China. Evolution of Political Control over Network Infrastructure and Content," *Asian Survey* 41:3 (May/June 2001): 381.

authoritarianism, in which dissuading[24] politicized Internet consumption patterns goes hand in hand with the creation of a false sense of freedom associated with widely available Internet access.[25] A dual core of de-politicization (of established consumption habits) and non-politicization (of the emerging usership) underpins the Kazakhstani version of networked authoritarianism. Higher penetration rates—like those that Kazakhstan is reportedly achieving—hold the key to the crystallization of similar authoritarian dynamics, which are sustained, most crucially, by the systematic application of more or less invisible censorship strategies.

In Kazakhstan, the providers[26] allowed to connect to the international Internet are thus compelled to use infrastructure and technology controlled by the state-run company, reinforcing Kazakhtelekom's unfettered dominance over data transfer and, ultimately, enhancing the regime's filtering potential.[27] This context, in turn, facilitates the introduction of specific policies designed to restrict the content of websites and blogs and, more notably, has supported the regime through the adoption of targeted strategies of censorship. In Kazakhstan, a relatively restricted number of websites is permanently blocked, while, in other instances, the regime intervened with temporary *ad hoc* outages to block the population's access to normally available websites.

The relatively mild intensity of the regime's censorship drive—which will be analyzed in greater detail in the chapter's second segment—sets Kazakhstan apart from the inflexible praxis of Internet control that has crystallized throughout post-Soviet Central Asia in the last two decades. However inflated official data might ultimately be, the statistical reality of Internet penetration in Kazakhstan points to wide access—a contextual framework that departs from the norm established in Turkmenistan, where Internet

---

24 Katy E. Pearce and Sarah Kendzior, "Networked Authoritarianism and Social Media in Azerbaijan," *Journal of Communication* 62:2 (April 2012): 288.
25 Rebecca MacKinnon, "China's 'Networked Authoritarianism'," *Journal of Democracy* 22:2 (April 2011): 33.
26 In late 2014, the government listed 11 companies as Internet providers authorized to operate within Kazakhstan.
27 "Kazakhstan," 440.

access options have been severely limited by the government, both prior to the leadership change of 2006–2007 and following it.[28] Kazakhstan's choice to allow its population relatively open access to the international Internet[29] differs, in turn, from the strategy implemented in neighboring Uzbekistan, where the regime headed by Islam A. Karimov endeavored to create a set of "homegrown" social networks—strikingly similar to Facebook and Twitter—with the view to insulate local users from exogenous (and hence destabilizing) influences.[30] Finally, Kazakhstan's censorship practice does not appear to be as extensive and erratic as that put into place in Tajikistan, where local authorities have regularly blocked social media outlets and popular websites, without offering any explanation as to the rationale for such blatant mass censorship acts.[31]

On the one hand, this regional contextualization highlights the relative freedom enjoyed by Kazakhstan's Internet users. On the other, Central Asia's low standards prevent the formulation of positive assessments for the Kazakhstani digital media policy. As suggested by a closer look at domestic social media consumption patterns and, most importantly, the progressive de-politicization of Kazakhstan's blogosphere, the Nazarbayev regime managed with some success to monitor and regulate the Kazakhstani cyberspace, and social media in particular.

Social media are an emerging influence within the Kazakhstani socio-political landscape but, quantitatively, have to be seen as peripheral features within the Internet consumption habits emerging in Kazakhstan. Vkontakte and Odnoklassniki remain the

---

28 Luca Anceschi, "Reinforcing authoritarianism through media control: The case of post-Soviet Turkmenistan" in Freeman and Shafer, eds., *After the Czars and Commissars*, 63–64.
29 On the (allegedly negative) economic impacts of the internationalization of the Kazakhstani cyberspace, see: B. Kisikov, "Ne kazakhstanskiy Kaznet," *vlast.kz*, http://vlast.kz/?art=407.
30 Murat Sadykov, "After Cloning Facebook, Uzbekistan Launches Twitter Imitation," *eurasianet.org*, 13 February 2014, http://www.eurasianet.org/node/68043.
31 Casey Michel, "Tajikistan Cracks Down on Internet… Again," *The Diplomat*, 8 October 2014; Chris Rickleton, "Tajikistan: Can Dushanbe Keep the Lid on the Internet?," *eurasianet.org*, 11 August 2014, http://www.eurasianet.org/node/69481.

most popular social networks to operate in the Kazakhstani cyberspace, with a combined total of more than 4.5 million registered users.[32] "Western" social networks are numerically more marginal but seem to feature a more active community of users. Only 14 percent of Kazakhstan's Internet users have a Facebook account,[33] while an even smaller percentage of users (7.37 percent) micro-blogs through Twitter.[34] This limited number of users, moreover, has to date engaged in mostly non-political discussions,[35] as the content of Kazakhstan's social media pages remains essentially lowbrow. There is perhaps no better way to capture the essence of this latter proposition than by examining Kazakhstan's most-followed Twitter accounts.

Sport personalities, celebrities, and pop-stars are currently topping Kazakhstan's Twitter rankings,[36] while major companies — including Air Astana, KCell, and Beeline — usually manage accounts with substantive numbers of followers (more than 50,000), suggesting that Twitter, within Kazakhstan, is seen as a PR tool rather than a medium for more meaningful exchanges.[37] Government personalities, including President Nazarbayev, are generally alien to micro-blogging. However, a Klout-index analysis of the Kazakhstani Twitter-sphere reveals that the presidential party *Nur Otan*, the Ministry of Foreign Affairs, and the Press Service of the Presidential Administration — which, in spite of its information remit, joined Twitter only in June 2012 — are amongst the ten top performers. At the top of the list was Prime Minister Karim Masimov,[38] who is generally regarded as a smooth social media operator: his Twitter

---

32   Emrich, Plakhina, and Tsyrenzhapova, *Mapping Digital Media: Kazakhstan*, 48.
33   Anonymous. Interviewed by Luca Anceschi, Almaty, 5 April 2014.
34   Emrich, Plakhina, and Tsyrenzhapova, *Mapping Digital Media: Kazakhstan*, 48.
35   Couper, Nurmakov, and Adams, "Political uses of social media in Kazakhstan."
36   Available at http://kaznet.me/rating/.
37   Anonymous. Interviewed by Luca Anceschi. Almaty, 2 April 2014.
38   Local media also monitored quite closely the social media activity of Kazakhstani politicians, as in: Sabina Serikova, "Rating of the most popular blogs of Kazakhstan politicians," *TengriNews,* 29 November 2011, http://en.tengrinews.kz/internet/Rating-of-the-most-popular-blogs-of-Kazakhstan-politicians-5886/.

activity, rather interestingly, has been often openly discussed on national media.[39] Nevertheless, Masimov's two accounts were largely inactive during 2013 and 2014, revealing the PM's progressive detachment from micro-blogging and, more widely, the fundamentally non-political nature of Kazakhstan's Twitter-sphere.

The engagement potential of social networking, at least initially, was not recognized by the Kazakhstani élite.[40] In more recent times, however, Facebook seems to have emerged as a viable avenue to express both aligned and, more interestingly, dissenting opinions. The non-free elections of 2011 and 2012 featured a significant social network dimension, with several candidates setting up Facebook pages for their campaigns and updating them on a regular basis.[41] Mid-way through the campaign for the snap presidential election held on 26 April 2015, only one of the two[42] candidates registered to run against Nazarbayev had an active Facebook page on which he published campaign updates and posted information on his political platform.

In contrast, the opposition forces currently allowed to operate at the margins of the political arena within Kazakhstan have a visible Facebook presence. Most prominent is the page devoted to the unstructured and numerically small anti-Eurasianist movement that emerged throughout Kazakhstan in the lead-up to the signing of the treaty that established the Eurasian Economic Union (EEU). Prominent Eurasian-sceptics — including Marat Tazhin, Rasul Zhumaly, and Serikzhan Mambetalin — engaged in articulate Facebook campaigns to disseminate their criticism of the regime's foreign policy.[43] Following the violent repression that crushed the anti-devaluation protests of February 2014, Eurasia-sceptics opted to maintain a low profile in their activities, relying on word-of-mouth

---

39   See, for instance, "Medvedev is now following Massimov on Twitter," *TengriNews,* 13 May 2011, http://en.tengrinews.kz/kazakhstan_news/Medvedev-is-now-following-Massimov-on-Twitter--1722/.
40   Couper, Nurmakov, and Adams, "Political uses of social media in Kazakhstan."
41   "Kazakhstan."
42   Data as of 21 March 2015.
43   Luca Anceschi and Paolo Sorbello, "Kazakhstan and the EEU: The rise of Eurasian scepticism," *Open Democracy Russia,* 15 May 2014.

and, to a lesser extent, social networking to inform the Kazakhstani population about the inaugural anti-EEU forum, held in Almaty on 12 April 2014.[44]

Kazakhstan's tiny blogosphere ultimately has adopted a de-politicized outlook. At the end of 2014, there was no established blogging tradition in Kazakhstan: whereas the absence of political blogs has to be seen as the net effect of the authoritarian context that encapsulates the wider Kazakhstani cyberspace, the lack of more mundane forms of blogging—including gastronomy or travel—points to the crystallization of disengaged Internet consumption patterns among Kazakhstani users.[45] A relatively small number of Western expats living in Kazakhstan blog about their local experiences; local users, on the other hand, "do not write blogs [...] and do not read blogs."[46] At the end of 2014, approximately 80,000 local bloggers kept journals at Yvision.kz, which, due to the closure or the intermittent availability of other major platforms, has become Kazakhstan's most popular blogging website.[47] The potential of such a numerically small blogosphere, however, has not failed to attract the attention of the Kazakhstani government, which, following a well-established regional praxis, proceeded to manipulate new media with propagandistic aims in mind. For example, several new blogs related essentially pro-government accounts of the court trials for the Zhanaozen events throughout 2012 and 2013.[48]

The exception to this norm of de-politicization is represented by *Blogbasta.kz*, a niche website that publishes blog entries on politics, arts, and urban development.[49] By targeting Kazakhstan's "creative urban youth,"[50] the blog's underpinning ambition is to challenge the "profound apathy"[51] that is engulfing the Kazakhstani

---

44   The author was in Almaty during the lead-up to this meeting, researching the politics of anti-Eurasianism in Kazakhstan.
45   Anonymous. Interviewed by Luca Anceschi, Almaty, 7 April 2014.
46   Anonymous. Interviewed by Luca Anceschi. Almaty, 29 March 2014.
47   "Kazakhstan," 2014, 446.
48   Kaznis Toguzbaev, "Usililis' postzhanaozenskie batalii blogerov," *Radio Azattyk*, 20 August 2012, http://rus.azattyq.org/content/twitter-bloggers-battle-about-zhanaozen-trial/24680408.html.
49   Anonymous. Interviewed by Luca Anceschi, Almaty, 7 April 2014.
50   "Kazakhstan."
51   Anonymous. Interviewed by Luca Anceschi, Almaty, 7 April 2014.

polity and that allegedly is the by-product of the government's restrictive media policies. To date, however, *Blogbasta* remains a peripheral outlet in Kazakhstani cyberspace: peak access on the blog's website has been quantified at no more than 1,000 hits per day.[52] While *Blogbasta*'s entries—which are increasingly featuring an international authorship—are published mostly in Russian, a timidly growing segment of the Kazakhstani blogosphere has begun to operate in Kazakh. *Urimtal*, more specifically, constitutes the most visible web-publication in this restricted context. The team at *Urimtal*—which is blogging through the international platform Wordpress—has devoted substantial energies to training Kazakh-language bloggers, holding a series of workshops across Kazakhstan's expansive territory. [53] The blog's diverse content is, however, not political and certainly does not aspire to challenge the Kazakhstani establishment. Overall, *Urimtal*'s readership continues to be limited: peak access, in April 2014, had been estimated at only 300 hits per day.[54]

Given the marginal influence that social media and blogs have been allowed to wield upon the local population, continuing to contain Kazakhstan's restricted new media landscape should not represent a challenging undertaking for Nazarbayev and his associates. The Kazakhstani regime, in the words of one of the digital media operators interviewed while researching this chapter, "should not be afraid of the bloggers, but [it] is."[55] Kazakhstan's digital media, ultimately, "remains constrained and state interference remains prominent."[56] This statement identifies the paradoxical outlook of Kazakhstan's new media policy. Containing Kazakhstan's essentially de-politicized cyberspace suggests, on one hand, that the regime—rhetoric notwithstanding—continued to regard its own stability as a critical driver for its digital media policy. On the other, the persistent repression of local new media reveals the profound disconnect that has come to characterize the interplay between the

---

52 Anonymous. Interviewed by Luca Anceschi, Almaty, 7 April 2014.
53 Anonymous. Interviewed by Luca Anceschi, Almaty, 9 April 2014.
54 Anonymous. Interviewed by Luca Anceschi, Almaty, 9 April 2014.
55 Anonymous. Interviewed by Luca Anceschi, Almaty, 31 March 2014.
56 Emrich, Plakhina, and Tsyrenzhapova, *Mapping Digital Media: Kazakhstan*, 8.

élite's authoritarian outlook and the population's political behavior. Repression, in this sense, emerges as the connecting link between progressive Internet de-politicization and the consolidation of non-political consumption habits across Kazakhstan. There is no better way to capture the essence of this interrelated dynamic than by illustrating the strategy of systematic control through which the Kazakhstani government attempted to "regulate" the social media landscape illustrated above. It is precisely to the analysis of these repressive processes that our attention now turns.

2. Containing Kazakhstan's Digital Media

Kazakhstan's digital media policy has had, since its very onset, a profoundly repressive disposition. Its initial formulation related directly — albeit not openly — to the resolution of intra-élite conflicts that emerged within Kazakhstan's first family. International observers[57] as well as local media operators[58] agreed in linking the containment of the "subversive" activities of the late Rakhat Aliyev[59] to the imposition of an access ban on the Russian blogging platform LiveJournal (*Zhivoy Zhurnal* or *ZhZh*) and, eventually, the enactment of draconian legislative measures to regulate the emergence of a new media landscape in Kazakhstan. Containing Ali-

---

57 Martha Brill Olcott, *Kazakhstan: Unfulfilled promise?* (Washington, DC: Carnegie Endowment for International Peace, 2010), 260–61; Carl Schreck, "Kazakhstan puts pressure on bloggers," *The National*, 25 August 2009; "Kazakhstan," 442; "V Kazakhstane vse sayty stali SMI," *Polit.ru*, 11 July 2009, http://polit.ru/news/2009/07/11/00/.

58 This connection emerged clearly during several of the interviews conducted throughout 2014 in preparation for this article, particularly those held in Almaty by the author on 29 March, 31 March, 5 April, 7 April, and 10 April.

59 For intra-elite conflict in Kazakhstan, and the Nazarbayev-Aliyev rivalry in particular, see: Sébastien Peyrouse, "The Kazakh neopatrimonial regime: balancing uncertainties among the 'family', oligarchs and technocrats," *Demokratizatsiya* 20:4 (Fall 2012): 354–56; Schatz and Maltseva, "Kazakhstan's Authoritarian 'Persuasion'," 57–59; Erica Marat, "Nazarbayev prevails over political competitors, family members," *The Central Asia-Caucasus Institute Analyst*, 9:11 (30 May 2007).

yev's blog was the key political imperative that led to Internet censorship in Kazakhstan: pre-2008 policies, albeit equally repressive, operated through more discrete strategies.[60]

The insulation of Kazakhstani cyberspace from the supposedly destabilizing information contained in Aliyev's blog entries was the key objective pursued by the earliest iteration of the regime's new media policy, which was implemented through a combination of pre-emptive censorship and restrictive law-making. Interestingly, this repressive mix has continued to characterize the interplay between regime and digital media until the time of writing.

An in-depth look at the access ban imposed on LiveJournal unveils a clear connection between Aliyev's anti-regime campaign and the establishment of a durable practice of Internet censorship in Kazakhstan. The platform was initially blocked in October 2008 and the ban was strictly enforced until 13 November 2010.[61] Throughout this period, the government provided no official explanation for the access ban, while *Kazakhtelekom* denied any involvement in censoring *ZhZh*.[62] The ban was significant because, at the time it was imposed, LiveJournal was hosting "32 percent of all active Russian-language blogs in Kazakhstan, or nearly 230,000 users."[63] Two events catalyzed the suspension of this restrictive measure. First, the LiveJournal team—in a decision that was to be eventually reversed[64]—announced the cancellation of Rakhat Aliyev's

---

60   Eric McGlinchey and Erica Johnson, "Aiding the Internet in Central Asia," *Democratization* 14:2 (2007): 283–85.
61   On the regime's treatment of LiveJournal, see Adil Nurmakov's numerous reports for *Global Voices Online*, including: "Kazakhstan: LiveJournal Still Blocked," posted on 5 January 2009 and "Kazakhstan: LiveJournal unblocked after two years of filtering," published on 17 November 2010.
62   "V "Kazakhtelekome" utverzhdayut, chto ne imeyut otnosheniya k blokirovke blog-portala LiveJournal," Zakon.kz, 15 October 2014, http://www.zakon.kz/123296-v-kazakhtelekome-utverzhdajut-chto-ne.html.
63   "Kazakhstan."
64   In late 2014, when Rakhat Aliyev was facing a sentence for murder in an Austrian jail, the blog operating under his LiveJournal account was fully accessible at http://rakhataliev.livejournal.com. Pre-2011 blog-entries, however, had been cancelled by the platform's administrators.

account.[65] Second, the organization of the OSCE summit in Astana (1–2 December 2010) led the regime to relax temporarily its suffocating control of the Kazakhstani blogosphere. In this sense, the suspension of the Livejournal access ban represented a cosmetic measure. The platform's operations in Kazakhstan, as a consequence, were destined to be short-lived: in late 2011—in a move that local bloggers connected with the Aliyev case—the Saryarkinskiy District Court in Astana decreed its definitive closure.[66]

The simultaneous introduction of a new legislative framework meant to deter the proliferation of anti-regime views across the wider Kazakhstani cyberspace. In the first half of 2009, the Kazakhstani Parliament discussed a bill that intended to subject all forms of Internet content to Kazakhstan's restrictive media code. The outlook of such legislative reform was repressive by design, as it applied Kazakhstan's draconian anti-defamation measures—which had severely curtailed the freedom of traditional media operators—to bloggers in particular and, more widely, every Internet user operating from within Kazakhstan. Throughout 2009, local[67] and international[68] outrage accompanied the enactment of this legislation. The then OSCE Representative on Freedom of the Media Miklos Haraszti asked Nazarbayev to veto the law[69] since the restriction of

---

65 "LiveJournal blocked the blog of the former son-in-law of Kazakh President," *Ferghana.ru*, 10 November 2010, http://enews.ferganaews.com/news.php?id=1910.

66 Sergey Park, "Kazakhstan: Bloggers Denounce Repeated Blockage of LiveJournal," *GlobalVoices*, 3 September 2011, http://globalvoicesonline.org/2011/09/03/kazakhstan-bloggers-denounce-repeated-blockage-of-livejournal/.

67 A concise list of Kazakhstan's protests against the introduction of the 2009 legislation is included in: "2010 Media Sustainability Index—The Development of Sustainable Independent Media in Europe and Eurasia," IREX, Washington, DC, 2010, 217.

68 "Kazakhstan: Rescind New Media Restrictions," Human Rights Watch, Press Release, 14 July 2009.

69 "OSCE media freedom representative urges Kazakh President to veto new Internet law," OSCE, Press Release, 25 June 2009.

Internet freedom violated Kazakhstan's 2007 Madrid commitment.[70] The Kazakhstani president ignored Haraszti's request and proceeded to sign the bill into law on July 10, 2009.[71]

The strategies of Internet containment devised by the government in 2008–2009 aligned Kazakhstan to the wider authoritarian practice then consolidating throughout Eurasia. More specifically, the censorship strategy introduced by blocking LiveJournal imported to Kazakhstan the model of digital media containment that had crystallized in China, where pre-emptive censorship and large-scale access bans represented standard regime practices.[72] At the same time, the 2009 legislative reforms pushed Kazakhstan beyond repressive norms then prevalent in neighboring Russia, where digital media have been predominantly contained through extensive law-making efforts, but actual bans on content were not widely enforced until 2012, after the prominent protests of 2011.[73]

The measures of 2008–2009, furthermore, exerted both immediate and, crucially, long-lasting influences on the politics of new media in Kazakhstan. Containing LiveJournal—a popular blogging platform that was started in the United States and later purchased by Russian owners—was primarily intended to address short-term matters of regime preservation related to the Nazarbayev-Aliyev rivalry. The new media legislation enacted in 2009 meant to set, in the medium term, the tone for future debates to be held across the Kazakhstani blogosphere. The most durable imprint that these measures left upon Kazakhstan's new media panorama, nevertheless, is connected to the consolidation of unencumbered regime authority over the Kazakhstani cyberspace, and the amalgamation of

---

70 "Kazakhstan and the so-called 'Madrid Commitments'," RC.GAL/6/10, 1 October 2010.
71 For the full text of the law, see: "Zakon Respubliki Kazakhstan ot 10 iyulya 2009 goda No. 179–IV 'O vnesenii izmeneniy i dopolneniy v nekotorye zakonodatel'nye akty Respubliki Kazkhstan po voprosam intellektual'noy sobstvennosti'," *Kazakhstanskaya pravda*, 28 July 2009, 2.
72 Rebecca MacKinnon, "Flatter world and thicker walls? Blogs, censorship and civic discourse in China," *Public Choice* 134:1–2 (January 2008): 31–46.
73 Sarah Oates, *Revolution Stalled: The Political Limits of the Internet in the Post-Soviet Sphere* (New York and Oxford: Oxford University Press, 2013), 94–97.

the Internet to the authoritarian norm of media control established by Nazarbayev and his associates in the mid- and late-1990s.

As the government's new media policy became integral to the regime's power technologies, control over the Kazakhstani cyberspace had to remain strict. Throughout 2010, when Kazakhstan held the OSCE Chairmanship, the regime restrained from adopting excessively repressive strategies vis-à-vis the regulation of local digital media, failing, however, to liberalize Kazakhstan's cyberspace in any significant way. Astana's attention, most specifically, focused at the time on filtering the website of the opposition newspaper *Respublika*. In this context, the country's largest Internet provider contributed in decisive fashion to the successful application of the repressive measures dictated by Nazarbayev and his associates: the Committee to Protect Journalists, reporting to the OSCE, noted that *Respublika* "readers served by Kazakhtelecom [...] could not load the [newspaper's] site, while readers served by other providers were able to access it."[74] The restriction of *Respublika* and 125 other websites found to host illegal information in 2010 was not regulated through court cases based on the 2009 legislation, but was enforced unilaterally by the Kazakhstani regime.[75]

The combination of restrictive law-making and repressive methods resurfaced yet again in late 2011 to shape decisively the Kazakhstani new media landscape and, ultimately, determine its transition to today's status of nearly total de-politicization. In November 2011, as previously mentioned, the Saryarkinskii Court imposed a permanent access ban on LiveJournal and twelve other websites, dealing a nearly fatal blow to the freedom of the Kazakhstani blogosphere. It is in the aftermath of the Zhanaozen crisis, however, that the containment of social media emerged as a crucial element in Kazakhstan's technologies of power, confirming that Nazarbayev and his associates had come to regard digital media as a severely destabilizing influence at times of regime vulnerability.

---

[74] "Disdaining press freedom, Kazakhstan undermines OSCE," RC.NGO/59/10, 4 October 2010.

[75] Tamara Kaleeva, "Situatsiya so svobodoy slova v Kazakhstane v 2010 godu (analiticheskiy doklad)," Adil soz, http://www.adilsoz.kz/politcor/show/id/20.

This proposition is better appreciated by observing the quasi-total isolation imposed on Zhanaozen and its surroundings immediately after the brutal repression of workers' demonstrations in the city's main square: Twitter, YouTube, and other key websites—including *Novosti Kazakhstana, RIA Novosti's* local partner—were inaccessible throughout 16–17 December 2011.[76] Yet again, Kazakhtelekom publicly denied that it extended any technological support to the isolation of the city, while the Kazakhstani Ministry of Communication and Information explained the interruption of Internet services through electricity shortages and damaged connection lines.[77] As the disruption was imposed on a large scale, it brought significant economic losses for the population of the Mangystau *oblast'*.[78] While it is difficult to quantify the financial loss incurred by the population during the Zhanaozen outage, the economic impact of network disruptions in Kazakhstan certainly represents a further facet of the regime's instrumental use of communication infrastructure across the Kazakhstani territory.

After the intransigence of December 2011, the Kazakhstani government returned to approach the management of the Zhanaozen crisis through traditionally milder authoritarian tones. In the final week of 2011, the government—through the office of Twitter-savvy PM Masimov[79]—invited a delegation of selected bloggers to visit the Mangystau *oblast'*, in order to grant new media operators the first hand access that was denied in late December. This group of bloggers ended up producing an account of the events that closely matched[80] the official version disseminated by the government immediately after the Zhanaozen riots. This group—soon to

---

76 Kaleeva, "Situatsiya so svobodoy slova."
77 "MSI raz"yasnilo situatsiyu so svyaz'yu v Zhanaozene," *TengriNews*, 17 December 2011, http://tengrinews.kz/kazakhstan_news/msi-razyyasnilo-situatsiyu-so-svyazyu-v-janaozene-204082/.
78 See, on this point: Anita R. Gohdes, "Pulling the plug: Network disruptions and violence in civil conflict," *Journal of Peace Research* (2015) (Online First).
79 Makpal Mukankyzy, "Sobytiya v Zhanaozene raskololi internet-auditoriyu," *Radio Azattyk*, 9 January 2012.
80 "Kazakhstan's Zhanaozen Information Confrontation," Cybernautika, http://cybernautika.com/2012/01/02/kazakhstans-zhanaozen-information-confrontation/.

be known as the *Krovavye Blogery* (bloody bloggers) — was rapidly discredited by Kazakhstan's independent blogging community, which, to re-establish some equilibrium, proceeded to organize its own fact-finding mission to the Mangystau *oblast'*. This second delegation, perhaps not unsurprisingly, produced a critical account of the government's responsibilities in the Zhazaozen events, calling for the resignation of the region's *akim*.[81]

The information war fought over the Zhanaozen crisis captures two critically important issues that, while holding the key to this chapter's core argument, encapsulate the essence of Kazakhstan's post-2011 media policy. To begin with, the information war confirmed that social media manipulation in late 2011 was contributing directly to the strategies through which the Nazarbayev regime sought the consolidation of its domestic power. It also revealed the regime's deliberate intention to split Kazakhstan's blogging community. Both issues re-emerged at regular intervals to characterize Kazakhstan's digital media policy in the post-Zhanaozen years — a policy that has been in turn underpinned by an apparently paradoxical correlation. On the one hand, the access options available to local Internet users became more stable while staying relatively inexpensive:[82] such circumstances, ultimately, led to a substantive rise in the Internet penetration rate. On the other, the regime continued in its persistent strategy of containment, endeavoring to restrict even further the opportunities for politicized Internet use. Kazakhstan's cyberspace, in other words, had become wider, but remained strictly controlled. This latter proposition aligns the argument advanced in this paper with the recent findings of Rød and Weidmann, who concluded that Internet expansion might indeed play some positive roles vis-à-vis the solidification of authoritarian stability.[83]

---

81 For a first-hand account of this second mission to Zhanaozen, see Dmitriy Shelokov's blog at http://yvision.kz/post/217205.
82 "Kazakhstan," 439.
83 Espen Geelmuyden Rød and Nils B. Weidmann, "Empowering activists or autocrats? The Internet in authoritarian regimes," *Journal of Peace Research* (2015) (Online First).

An unrelenting strategy of repression continued to underpin the regime's approach to social media. The most visible manifestation of this crackdown was certainly the multiple arrests of bloggers in February 2014. The protests that led to the 2014 arrests erupted in relation to the regime's attempt to split the blogging community.[84] A. S. Yesimov's dinner with selected Almaty bloggers represented a deliberate attempt to co-opt a segment of the blogging community active in Kazakhstan's cultural capital.[85] The split in the Kazakhstani blogosphere became more evident in the lead-up to the 2015 snap presidential election. In mid-February 2015, as the Kazakhstani political landscape was abuzz with rumors about the imminent decision to call a presidential vote, the Alliance of Bloggers in Kazakhstan (ABK) suggested skipping the election and requested instead the organization of a referendum that would confirm Nazarbayev until 2022.[86] The more independent segment of the Kazakhstani blogosphere expressed vocal criticism of ABK's political stand and questioned its legitimacy with vehemence.[87] Both the establishment and public advocacy of the ABK, ultimately, confirmed that digital media are currently playing an integral role in the power technologies of the Kazakhstani regime.

Post-Zhanaozen containment of new media did not exclude the implementation of legislative reforms. While international pressure targeted the 2009 media law and called for the de-penalization

---

84   Anonymous. Interviewed by Luca Anceschi. Almaty, 31 March 2014.
85   Alexander Sodiqov, "Some Kazakh bloggers dine with Mayor, some get jail terms," *GlobalVoices*, 8 February 2014, http://advocacy.globalvoicesonline.org/2014/02/08/some-kazakh-bloggers-dine-with-mayor-some-get-jail-terms/.
86   Asemgul' Kasenova, "Al'yans blogerov predlagaet prodlit' polnomochiya Nazarbayeva do 2022 goda," *TengriNews*, 18 February 2015, http://tengrinews.kz/kazakhstan_news/alyans-blogerov-predlagaet-prodlit-polnomochiya-Nazarbayeva-270308/.
87   Criticism of ABK, more precisely, pre-dated the 2015 campaign. To question the credentials of the pro-government blogging association, the collective blog community *Ostrosotsial'nye razmyshleniya* published a complete list of ABK members, alluding to their scarce familiarity with blogging and social media in general. Ernar Prediktor, "Participants in the Alliance of Bloggers of Kazakhstan," Your vision, 9 October 2014, http://yvision.kz/post/433209.

of defamation in Kazakhstan,[88] the regime proceeded to increase the government's discretionary powers in relation to new media control. In April 2014, an amendment to Article 41.1 of Kazakhstan's media legislation conferred on the Attorney General extrajudicial blocking power vis-à-vis websites that host information deemed to be causing damage to Kazakhstani society at large.[89] The amendment allowed the regime to block websites or wider networks—including WhatsApp and Skype—without waiting for a court decision. The rationale for this legislative amendment is entrenched in the turbulent days that followed the tenge devaluation of February 2014, when, after a viral WhatsApp message falsely announced the imminent collapse of the national banking system, residents of Almaty and Astana crowded into local bank branches to withdraw their savings.[90]

The Kazakhstani regime did not have to wait long for the application of this controversial amendment. On 29 May 2014, during the signing of the controversial EEU treaty, the website of *Radio Free Europe/Radio Liberty's Kazakhstani service*—locally known as *Radio Azattyk*—was partially blocked: the government specifically targeted *Azattyk*'s EEU-related content, which remained inaccessible inside Kazakhstan until the signature ceremony had concluded.[91]

Equating the dissemination of false information to a violation of national security brings Kazakhstan's censorship practices closer

---

88   "Defamation to remain criminal charge in Kazakhstan and 27 European countries: no freedom of speech for Kazakhstan only?," *TengriNews*, 14 January 2014, http://en.tengrinews.kz/laws_initiatives/Defamation-to-remain-criminal-charge-in-Kazakhstan-and-27-European-countries-no-25286/.

89   Asemgul' Kasenova. "Sotsseti v Kazakhstane smogut blokirovat' bez resheniya suda," *TengriNews*, 9 April 2014, http://m.tengrinews.kz/ru/kazakhstan_news/253345.

90   Anonymous. Interviewed by Luca Anceschi. Almaty, 9 April 2014. On this, also see: Charles Recknagel, "Kazakh bank run apparently latest to be fueled by social media," *RFE/RL*, 18 February 2014.

91   Partial blocking was not the only means through which the Kazakhstani government attempted to silence *Radio Azattyk* while the EEU treaty was signed in Astana. Journalist Orken Bisenov was arrested on 27 May, while covering a meeting of EEU-sceptics in the nation's capital. On this see: Adilsoz, "Narusheniya svobody slova v Kazakhstane, may 2014 goda," Adil soz, http://www.adilsoz.kz/monitoring/show/id/68.

to those established in Uzbekistan, where the concept of information security is normally manipulated to restrict freedom of expression.[92] Security considerations were certainly central to the regime's decision to block online material featuring Islamic State propaganda,[93] but were also more loosely applied to justify the numerous bans imposed upon different websites throughout 2013 and 2014.[94] Imposing systematic censorship under the rubric of national security[95] allows the regime to limit even further the freedom of Kazakhstan's new media: in a move that is reminiscent of China's large-scale blocking strategy, prominent élite members have called for the imposition of targeted access bans to several Facebook and Twitter pages that are reportedly hosting "messages of general and religious terrorism."[96] The forced de-politicization of Kazakhstan's social media landscape is another step in the persistently repressive new media policy implemented in Kazakhstan from 2008 onwards.

3. Conclusion

The stability of contemporary Eurasian authoritarianism is often attributed to the leaderships' ability to contain digital media. The rise of Internet penetration rates throughout much of the region forced the Eurasian élites to rethink their approaches to the containment of cyberspace. In this sense, a new set of repressive strategies came to be implemented across the region, with the ultimate view to mould the Internet consumption habits of Eurasian users. Locating

---

92   Zhanna Kozhamberdiyeva, "Freedom of expression on the Internet: A case study of Uzbekistan," *Review of Central and East European Law* 33:1 (2008): 116–22.
93   Joanna Lillis, "Kazakhstan: Children Star in Islamic State Propaganda Video," *EurasiaNet*, 24 Novembr 2014, http://www.eurasianet.org/node/71071.
94   Kaleeva, "*Situatsiya so svobodoy slova.*"
95   See, on this: Philip N. Howard, Sheetal D. Agarwal, and Muzammil M. Hussain, "When do states disconnect their digital networks? Regime responses to the political uses of Social Media," *The Communication Review* 14:3 (2011): 226–29.
96   Renat Tashkinbayev, "Kazakhstan authorities unable to block Facebook and Twitter," *TengriNews*, 4 October 2013, http://en.tengrinews.kz/internet/Kazakhstan-authorities-unable-to-block-Facebook-and-Twitter-23079/.

Kazakhstan's place vis-à-vis the regional praxis of new media repression constituted the core objective of this chapter, which concluded that Kazakhstan's digital media policy is fully consistent with the authoritarian norm crystallizing throughout the post-Soviet space and wider Eurasia.

In Kazakhstan, the rapid diffusion of 3G and 4G connectivity led to the emergence of a new category of users, able to access the Internet more often, more quickly, and at relatively low cost. Promoting non-political consumption habits among this specific — and rapidly expanding — category of users represents a critically important end for the Nazarbayev regime, particularly throughout the 2010–2014 quadrennium, when the number of total mobile accesses rose rather sharply. The regime, in early 2015, might be said to have achieved this objective in full, as the great majority of local users came to see the Internet as an essentially lowbrow medium, and approached social media — and Twitter in particular — as PR instruments rather than avenues for intellectual engagement or more meaningful exchanges. The rise of new media in Kazakhstan occurred under conditions of consolidated authoritarianism: this milieu profoundly influenced the outlook of the great majority of new Internet users, while the cyberspace segments that did not automatically align to the regime's outlook clashed in turn with the élite's repressive ambitions. A combination of occasional censorship and systematically restrictive law-making supported the Kazakhstani leadership in its attempts to influence the popular perception of the political undertone of social media, promoting the de-politicization of consumption habits amongst the most recalcitrant segment(s) of Kazakhstan's cyberspace. This mix, ultimately, replicated closely the methods of media control adopted in neighboring Uzbekistan, Tajikistan, and the more distant China.

The adjustment of Kazakhstan's more established power technologies to the emergence of social media was not, however, limited to the promotion of de-politicized and non-political consumption patterns. Indeed, the regime manifested a growing understanding of the propagandistic potential held by digital media. The incorporation of social media manipulation within the élite's strategies of power preservation became particularly visible at times of crisis, including the 2011 Zhanaozen riots and, more recently, the devaluation protests of early 2014. In these contexts, the Kazakhstani élite made a deliberate attempt to split the local blogging community, to ultimately transform the country's small blogosphere into another vehicle for the official propaganda.

It is by focusing on the small size of Kazakhstan's blogosphere that we, however, might draw some more specific conclusions about the nexus between regime stability and digital media in Kazakhstan. The persistent control of Internet blogging—which remains an overall marginal and essentially non-political medium—captures the government's methodically authoritarian outlook. It also highlights the profound disconnect between the élite and the wider population: this divide, in the ultimate analysis, represents a further indicator of the slow, yet inexorable decline currently experienced by the Nazarbayev regime.

Friends, Foes, and Facebook: Blocking the Internet in Tajikistan

Abdulfattoh Shafiev and Marintha Miles,
The George Washington University

Tajikistan offers a unique case study for examining the role of the Internet in national politics. Within the context of its Central Asian neighbors, the country allows more space for on-line autonomy than Turkmenistan or Uzbekistan, but put in place an offensive strategy of blocking access to sites and trolling long before Kazakhstan did. Moreover, because Tajikistan's population of roughly 8 million people relies heavily on remittances from 1.17 million migrant workers in Russia,[1] the Internet plays an influential role for public discussion in connecting the diaspora with their family and friends who stay at home. At the same time, Tajikistan's civil society seeks to protect and expand the democratic ideals and principles that the Internet offers them. Against this background, regular localized armed conflicts in the Rasht Valley and Badakhshan province, political threats to the ruling regime from the opposition preceding the November 2013 presidential and 2015 parliamentary elections, and unsolved economic and social problems influenced the government's decisions to block access to certain web sites. During these waves of attack, which began in 2012, organizations and activists demand access to blocked sites and take action, mostly via social media, to open dialogue with the authorities.

While the growing fight over the Internet in Tajikistan figures in reports by independent media and advocacy groups, there has been little scholarly research that lays out the chronology of this struggle and assesses its scope. In this chapter, we investigate the Tajik authorities' change of strategy toward the Internet: while the

---

1   "Novye pravila v"ezda dlya grazhdan Tadzhikistana ne snizyat potok migrantov v RF, uvereny eksperty," *Newsru.com*, 24 June 2014, http://www.newsru.com/russia/24jun2014/taj.html.

government previously controlled Internet access, periodically blocking YouTube, Facebook and some top local news outlets in 2010–2011, the bans imposed in 2012 signaled a new wave of censorship and marked a new and determined war against unrestricted Internet access. After a brief overview of Internet penetration in Tajikistan, we address the growing focus on the Internet by both the authorities and the opposition. Next we establish a chronology for Tajikistan's censorship policy. Finally, we move on to discuss the remaining spaces of dialogue existing between the authorities, independent media, the opposition, and external actors, such as the international community and Internet providers.

1. Internet Penetration and Accessibility

Research indicates that countries with higher Internet penetration are more likely to seek democratic governance and institutions, and that participants active in social networking groups are more politically active than their peers.[2] However what constitutes a sufficient threshold of access to make a tangible difference in political activism is not easily perceptible. To complicate matters, it is difficult to determine actual levels of Internet penetration in many countries. The 2010 Tajikistan Electronic Readiness Assessment (TERA) report notes: "The number of online users at a given time is considered one of the best parameters of the population's access to Internet. In developing countries, it is not easy to figure out the exact number of online users. Tajikistan is not an exemption to this challenge."[3]

Because of differences in methodologies used in data collection, there are large discrepancies in the reported levels of Internet penetration in Tajikistan. These differences are clear in the World Bank (WB)

---

2   Erik C. Nisbet, Elizabeth Stoycheff, and Katy E. Pearce, "Internet Use and Democratic Demands: A Multinational, Multilevel Model of Internet Use and Citizen Attitudes about Democracy," *Journal of Communication* 62:2 (April 2012): 249–65; Florence Passy and Marco Giugni, "Social Networks and Individual Perceptions: Explaining Differential Participation," *Sociological Forum* 16:1 (2001).

3   "Tajikistan Electronic Readiness Assessment," Public Fund "Internet" Tajikistan, 2010, 49.

reports, Internet World Statistics, and the 2012 Tajikistan Electronic Readiness Assessments (TERA), prepared by a non-governmental organization in Tajikistan. The World Bank claims that Internet penetration is just 16 percent. In contrast, the 2012 TERA calculates Internet penetration (access to a home computer with Internet access) at 47 percent, with users numbering 3.7 million. However, regarding the combined coverage of the four main telecom providers, both Tajikistan's government and the World Bank estimate that 90 percent of Tajikistan's territory has mobile phone coverage. TERA notes that this coverage affords accessibility to 99 percent of the population. Theoretically this infrastructure would also make the Internet accessible to 99 percent of the population via mobile phone. According to the official data, there are about 11.1 million mobile phone subscriptions, exceeding the Tajik population by over two million. Of these, 6.5 mobile phones subscriptions are active.[4]

Mobile phones are particularly important because they offer easy and on-the-go access to social media. Poor Internet penetration via fixed connections and lack of infrastructure make mobile connections an especially attractive option. Mobile access is important in helping the large migrant population and their families stay connected. As noted in these reports, Tajikistan is, in theory, well wired for Internet access. However, its cost remains prohibitive for most people, even as prices are dropping. Figure 1 illustrates the monthly amount in dollars spent on data access in 2010 and 2012. Not only has data cost declined, people are willing to spend more to access it.

---

4   Payrav Chorshanbiev, "Chislennost' abonentov mobil'noy svyazi v vos'mi-millionnom Tadzhikistane prevyshaet 11,1 mln," *Asia Plus*, 18 August 2014, http://news.tj/ru/news/chislennost-abonentov-mobilnoi-svyazi-v-vosmi-millionnom-tadzhikistane-prevyshaet-111-mln.

Figure 1. Dollars Spent Monthly on Internet Access, 2012 and 2010

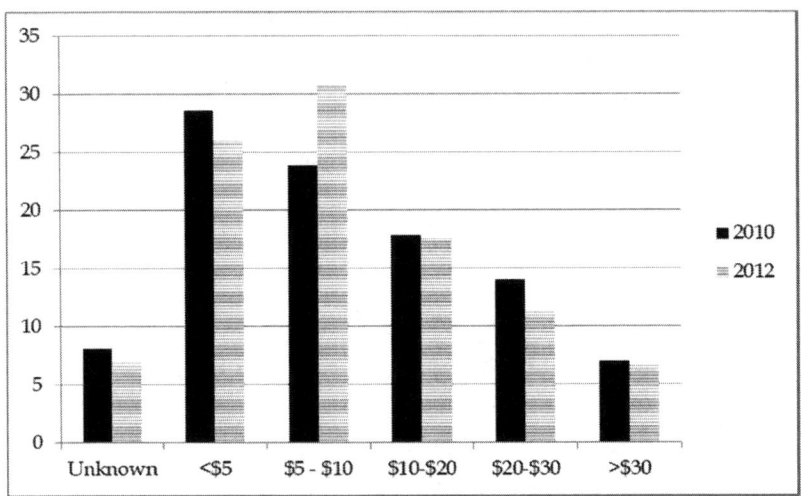

Source: Author's own calculation

The 2012 TERA report shows that an increasing number of people use the Internet, especially mobile connectivity, primarily to access social networking sites. The most popular social media platforms used in Tajikistan and by the diaspora are Odnoklassniki, VKontakte, Moy Mir, and Facebook. As of mid-2014, the total number of users on Odnoklassniki who identify their location as in Tajikistan is 2,449,365; the total number on VKontakte 211,239. The total number of Facebook users within Tajikistan is approximately 90,000; 72 percent men and 28 percent women (see Figure 2).[5] However determining the number of social media users in Facebook poses some problems. This figure reported here indicates how many users there are within the country, but it does not include the number of Tajik diaspora users. Yet, even if it is hard to measure its exact size, the diaspora cannot be left out of discussions surrounding civil society and civil liberties within Tajikistan because its members are among the most active agitators for the development of both.

---

5   Mehrangez Tursunzoda, "Facebook dostupen na tadzhikskom yazyke," *Asia Plus*, 22 August 2014, http://news.tj/ru/news/facebook-dostupen-na-tadzhikskom-yazyke.

Figure 2. Number of Tajik Social Media Users

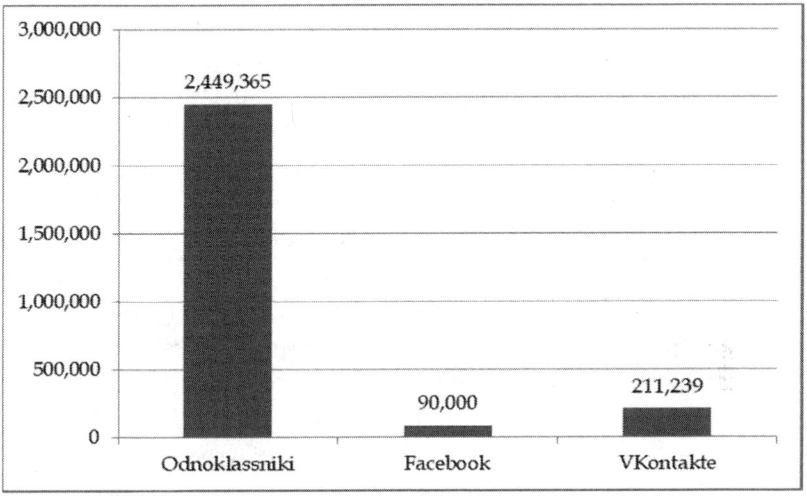

Odnoklassniki	2,449,365
Facebook	90,000
VKontakte	211,239

Source: Author's own calculation

One reason behind the popularity of the Russian social networks in Tajikistan is that they were the first to enter the market in the Central Asia. By the time American social media introduced their Russian language versions, Odnoklassniki, Moy Mir, and VKontakte were already in wide use. Russian social networks, especially Odnoklassniki, also introduced versions in local languages, including Tajiki. However, as we will discuss below, during 2014 some oppositional groups and accounts of activists were dissolved in Odnoklassniki, which forced these netizens and groups to go to Facebook and YouTube with their comparatively smaller targeted audience.

2. The Regime's Crackdown on the Opposition

Tajikistan's political system is unique in Central Asia. It is the only country in the region which faced five years of civil war (1992–1997), and whose peace agreements formalized the official recognition of an Islamic party, the Islamic Revival Party of Tajikistan (IRPT), one of the members of the Unified Tajik Opposition (UTO) that fought against the Dushanbe central authorities during the civil war. However, with the progressive strengthening of President Emomali Rahmon's regime, the spirit of the peace agreement weakened: the central authorities gradually reduced the autonomy given to regional elites and especially to former warlords, which contributed to the revival of localized armed conflicts in the Rasht Valley in 2009–2010 and in the autonomous region of Badakhshan in 2012. Moreover, Rahmon's regime also reduced the role of the IRPT to a simple façade, harassing its leaders, and wiping out its role in the parliament. The legislative elections of March 2015 put a symbolic end to the peace agreements period, with the IPRT losing its last two seats in the parliament. The Tajik political system thus moved closer in form to that of Uzbekistan, where there is an increasingly despotic and nepotistic regime with no recognized opposition. However, because of its important diaspora in Russia, and a small but energetic civil society, it remains more diversified than its neighbor, and this plurality is visible in the struggles over Internet.

While Tajikistan formally boasts many features of democracy, such as multiple political parties, elections, and laws that protect civil liberties, the authorities persecute and arrest journalists and political opposition leaders and curtail the free flow of information. The Tajik authorities justify their authoritarianism as the only way to prevent massive violence and reactivate the civil war that raged during the 1990s. During those years the regime did not grant a lot of attention to the Internet world, but since 2012, it has begun to repress Tajikistan's opposition through more pro-active on-line measures.

Until the fall of 2012 Tajikistan's legal code included a defamation law, which the authorities frequently used to curtail free speech. In March 2013, Rahmon signed new legislation guaranteeing free press and canceling the previous legislation. In his speech to mark the event, Rahmon championed the media: "Every democratic society needs mass media, information about the activities of government agencies, and all the branches of its power. It is one of the fundamental foundations of a free democratic society."[6] Yet in the same speech Rahmon reiterated the government's authority to censor the press:

> Along with this I remind you that the media should not abuse their professional authority. They must not allow the emergence of material instigating and inciting hate, inattention to national values and interests, insults and slander in relation to distinguished persons, and the promotion of immoral behavior.[7]

Thus, the new law meant little change in practice.

Tajikistan requires licensing for news agencies and journalists without providing corresponding transparency as to what constitutes the government's right to withhold licensing. For instance, in December 2012 the Ministry of Foreign Affairs refused to renew the journalism accreditation of popular and longtime U.S. Congress-financed *Radio Ozodi* journalist, Abdulqayoum Qayoumzod, without giving any reason and despite local and international campaigns to support his reinstatement. Qayoumzod is known for actively interviewing political opposition leaders and not mincing words in his reporting style. His censoring added pressure to journalists and independent media outlets, resulting in an increase of self-censorship, at the same time increasing the role of social media and bloggers in news delivery and analyses to wider audiences. Bloggers and social media activists became increasingly vocal about the lack of access to government and civil information, against human rights abuses, and a general lack of access to digital information.

In 2013–2014 several attempts to organize political protests used the Internet as their main platform for rallying participants. The authorities' reaction switched from inattention to the implementation of tight security measures. In April 2013, Gruppa24, a political opposition group founded in late 2012 in Moscow by Tajik business tycoon Umarali Quvvatov and heavily propagated on Odnoklassniki, planned a protest in Dushanbe. While online the pro-

---

6   "2012 god—god krizisa dlya tadzhikskikh SMI?," *Asia Plus*, 7 March 2013, http://news.tj/en/node/.
7   Ibid.

test garnered more than 400 supporters, the actual event never materialized. A few timid protesters showed up at the appointed time and place but, wary of the police presence, waited for someone else to be brave enough to make the first move toward a visible protest. Later that year, in December 2013, a bid in social media forums to gather protesters at the High Court building of Tajikistan to protest against the detention of new political party leader Zaid Saidov was equally unsuccessful, perhaps because Tajik police were noticeably prepared for the event with special anti-protest Jeeps.

A third wave of calls for protest, propagated widely via social media in Tajikistan, produced visible demonstrations by the Tajik diaspora in Moscow, Yekaterinburg, and other Russian cities against the Rahmon government in 2014. These rallies caused a sharp rise in tensions in Tajikistan and the government scrambled to curtail attention to social media and the spread of dissent and discontent amongst the diaspora. Government fears of a rumored protest to take place in Dushanbe on October 10 resulted in the appearance of armed vehicles in Dushanbe, the blocking of dozens of websites country-wide, the complete shuttering of Internet access in the northern part of the country, disabling texting service throughout the country on the scheduled protest day, and accelerated court hearings to list Gruppa24 as an illegal, extremist group. In subsequent days, several high-ranking officials were sent to Russia to meet with the Tajik diaspora, hoping to ease tensions.[8]

3. Building a "Networked Authoritarianism" in Tajikistan

Although until 2012 online discussion did not translate into action in the real world, popular voices undeniably grew louder in Tajikistan's social media. The growing perception of social media as a threat to the authorities pushed them to take measures to control the online doings of opposition activists. In the course of just three years, from 2012 to 2014, Tajikistan's authorities evolved from

---

[8] "Ubaidulloev v Moskve. Ot osuzhdeniya sanktsiy do vstrechi s migrantami," *Radio Ozodi*, 23 October 2014, http://rus.ozodi.org/content/article/2665 2074.html.

maintaining a purely passive approach to imposing an assertive "networked authoritarianism" that sought to repress the new freedoms the Internet provided.

The First Site Blocking Strategies of 2012

The first efforts to block web sites, in March 2012, resulted from an article published by the Russian online magazine *Polyarnaya Zvezda* (zvezda.ru), suggesting that the weakness and volatility of Rahmon's regime would result in his downfall during the 2013 presidential elections.[9] The site published scanned copies of the full minutes from a secret government meeting, where the authorities ordered increased pressure on the Islamic Revival Party of Tajikistan (IRPT). Despite state denials that the leaks were authentic, pressure on the IRPT by security forces, government officials, and state-run media increased. The minutes, known as "*Protokol* 32–20," enflamed political discontent in civil society and social media. Consequently, *Polyarnaya Zvezda*, Facebook, and other sites were blocked. Facebook was the first to go, indicating government recognition of Facebook as a meeting place for Tajik activists and a forum for civil discourse and political thought. The sites were unblocked after several days. Ironically, media attention garnered because of the blocking served to increase the number of Tajik Facebook users by an additional 5,000.[10] Netizens rushed to participate in Facebook discussions they had not been previously aware of, creating a "Face-boom."

The second wave of blocking efforts in 2012 occurred at the end of June, when government troops conducted a military operation in the Badakhshan autonomous province that left 23 soldiers, 21 militants, and 18 civilians dead, according to official sources and

---

[9] Sergey Strokan, "Tadzhikistan nakanune revolutsii," *Polyarnaya zvezda*, 1 March 2012, http://zvezda.ru/geo/2012/03/01/rachmon.htm.

[10] Mehrangez Tursunzoda, "V srednem kazhdyy den' v Facebook registriruyutsya do 500 pol'zovateley iz Tadzhikistana," *Asia Plus*, 13 March 2012, http://news.tj/ru/news/v-srednem-kazhdyi-den-v-facebook-registriruyutsya-do-500-polzovatelei-iz-tadzhikistana.

possibly more according to independent reports.[11] Phone service was suddenly cut to the region, sparking wide protests at embassies worldwide and in the streets of Moscow by the Tajik diaspora, who could no longer contact their families or send remittances home. The Head of the State Communications Service, Bek Zuhurov, denied the government's hand in cutting phone access in Badakhshan, claiming: "During the events in Khorugh a bullet reached the communications wires, you know that the wires there are in the air, not the ground." When pressed by journalists as to how then high ranking officials continued to have uninterrupted service in the area, Zuhurov responded "They have expensive mobiles to use and also they love their wives."[12] Zuhurov also boasted that a new group of volunteers was monitoring websites and social media, informing relevant state authorities when national interests and the state image were in danger or the country was being humiliated.[13] These volunteers would play a significant role in future blockings, as we will discuss later.

The state crackdown on the Internet was covered widely by independent media, as well as by representatives of illegal armed groups who used YouTube and Facebook to speak out against government actions. Media coverage and activities on social networking sites led the Tajik authorities to close the offending sites.[14] The *BBC*, *Radio Liberty*'s Tajik service, the independent news website *Asia Plus*, many Russian news websites, as well as YouTube, Facebook, and all Google services including Google Translate were subsequently blocked. The websites were unblocked days later after military action had ended. However, the unblocking was selective.

---

11 "Khorugh. Pas az yak sol...," *Radio Ozodi*, 24 July 2013, http://www.ozodi.org/content/khorog-security-clashes/25054904.html.

12 Payrav Chorshanbiev, "B. Zukhurov: Odna pulya popala v provoda, poetomu s Khorogom net svyazi," *Asia* Plus, 26 July 2012, http://news.tj/ru/news/b-zukhurov-odna-pulya-popala-v-provoda-poetomu-s-khorogom-net-svyazi.

13 "Tadzhikistan sozdaet 'gruppu nablyudateley za Internetom," *BBC*, http://www.bbc.co.uk/russian/international/2012/07/120712_tajikistan_Internet_censorship.shtml.

14 "Tajikistan Blocks YouTube, Steps Up Info Restrictions After Clashes," *Eurasianet.org*, 26 July 2012, http://www.eurasianet.org/node/65709.

Some Internet providers opened access to all websites while others continued to block selected websites. For example, *Tojnews*, a local news agency, and many Russian news websites were unblocked only at the end of summer 2012. *TeliaSonera*'s Tcell continued to block *BBC* websites in Russian, Tajik, and Farsi until the end of summer 2013. When asked why *BBC* remained blocked while other websites were unblocked, Tcell stated on its Facebook page, "Tcell did not get any order to unblock the named website...." At least two other major providers did not block *BBC*, and officials at the *BBC*'s Dushanbe Media Bureau remained silent regarding its continued blocking by Tcell. In August, a letter from Reporters without Borders to State Communications Service head Zuhurov protested the blocking and asked for transparency.[15] There was no response from the government.

The third wave of blocking, in November 2012, was intrinsically tied to the second. A press conference by Zuhurov became the foundation for a widespread satire campaign against him throughout social media, and sites that posted insulting comments were immediately blocked. Zuhurov justified the move by saying "hundreds of citizens" had called him to ask that Facebook be shut down because it was a "hotbed of slander."[16] During this time numerous new political groups were created on Facebook and Odnoklassniki, and political opposition leaders actively engaged in social media as a platform to criticize the Tajik government.

Three days after access to Facebook was shuttered, Radio Ozodi's Tajik Service interviewed Zuhurov about the blocking. Zuhurov naively asked the correspondent, "Who owns Facebook?" and wondered, "Does he pay taxes?" Zuhurov added that he would receive a visit from him [Mark Zuckerberg] to discuss the future of

---

15   Olivier Basille and Nuriddin Karshiboyev, "Joint Letter to Tajik Director of Communication Services, Beg Zuhurov," *Reporters without Borders*, 7 August 2012, http://en.rsf.org/tadjikistan-joint-letter-to-tajik-director-of-07-08-2012,43179.html.

16   Lukas I. Alpert and Olga Razumovskaya, "Tajikistan Unfriends Facebook," *The Wall Street Journal*, 27 November 2012, http://blogs.wsj.com/emergingeurope/2012/11/27/tajikistan-unfriends-facebook/.

Facebook accessibility in Tajikistan, "during my office hours on Saturdays."[17] The interview only increased the backlash against Zuhurov and inspired additional political satire and numerous memes. Figures 3 and 4, memes aimed at Zuhurov, were widely circulated in social media. This increase in ridicule strengthened the government resolve to control political discourse. Thus, *Radio Ozodi* was blocked. However, pressure from the local and international community, especially the U.S. Department of State, persuaded authorities to unblock access to *Ozodi* within two days.[18]

Figure 3. **Meme Critical of Zuhurov**

Thought bubble: "Where is McDonalds?"

---

17 "Beg Zukhurov: "Dobrovol'tsy ne pozvolyayut okryt' dostup k Facebook," *Radio Ozodi*, 29 November 2012, http://rus.ozodi.org/content/interview-beg-zuhurov-facebook/24785172.html.
18 "Somonai "Ozodi" dubora dastras shud," *Radio Ozodi*, 3 December 2012, http://www.ozodi.org/content/ozodi-site-blocked-removed-in--tajikistan/24787445.html.

Figure 4.   Meme Critical of Zuhurov

Caption: "I own this website"

The last wave of blocking in 2012 began on 24 December. All Internet service providers (ISPs) in Tajikistan received an official letter from the State Communications Service to block access to a list of 131 websites. The list included music and media downloading sites, media outlets and news sites, and social networking sites.[19] Russian online giants Mail.ru, *Moi Mir*, blogs at Mail.ru, Odnoklassniki, and Vkontakte were all ordered blocked. Facebook and YouTube were also again blocked, as well as all language services of *Radio Ozodi* and *Asia Plus*. Perhaps not coincidentally, the blocking order came the same day that political dissident and founder of the opposition group Gruppa24 in Moscow Quvvatov was arrested in Dubai at the request of the Tajik government.[20] Support for his new movement had grown in the days before his arrest, and social media was the popular avenue where his supporters gathered.

---

19   "Spisok 131 saytov, podlezhashchikh zakrytiyu," *Radio Ozodi*, 25 December 2012, http://rus.ozodi.org/media/photogallery/24808058.html.

20   "Lider tadzhikskoy oppozitsionnoy 'Gruppy-24' Umarali Kuvatov zaderzhan v Dubae," *Fergana News*, 24 December 2012, http://www.fergana news.com/news.php?id=19963.

The Russian social networking site, VKontakte, stated that it was "surprised to be included on this list."[21] While Tajik ISPs usually complied with orders to block the Internet, the new longer list, combined with outrage at Zuhurov for blocking Facebook and other sites earlier in the month, caused an immediate and strong backlash. Representatives of Tajikistan's ISPs gathered on 24 December and invited international organizations, embassy representatives from Western governments, and media, in an appeal for help to petition the government for restored access to blocked sites, specifically social media. Providers also worried about losing an important sector of their clientele. The pressure worked. Negotiations between the State Communications Service and Tajik Internet and mobile providers were successful and the blocking order and blacklist were cancelled.[22]

What can one conclude from these site blocking patterns? First, blocking systematically followed an event, such as military action, which the government did not want publicized; or when articles, audio or video leaks, or discussions that made the government uncomfortable appeared online. Second, the authorities claimed technical difficulties were to blame each time the blockings occurred, subsequently denying any state orders for censorship. Yet in 2012 a written order from the government to block sites, as well as less official phone text messages from the State Communications Service to ISPs were published by media outlets. Third, Tajikistan continues to live under the shadow of its civil war. Government officials frequently appeal to the collective memory and fears of civil war, warning that views on the Internet could cause a resurgence in violence. More recently, unrest in the Arab world has been used by the officials and supporters of Internet blocking to justify

---

21   Abdullo Ashurov, "'Vkontakte' dasturi Khadamoti aloqaro 'hayratovar' khond," *Radio Ozodi*, 22 December 2012, http://www.ozodi.org/content/vkontakte-says-surprised-by-tajik-authorities-decision-to-block-the-network/24805755.html.

22   "Khadamoti aloqa: 131 somonaro bubanded..., e"...boz kuned!," *Millat.tj*, 31 December 2012, http://millat.tj/component/content/3455.html?task=view.

their actions. Zuhurov followed this blocking pattern by first claiming there were technical problems, then claiming slander, and finally justified the actions, citing the potential for war.

Site Blocking in 2013: Unclear Reasoning

In 2013 there appeared to be a shift as to why blocking took place and who ordered it. In January Facebook and several other websites were blocked for several days. While previous periods of blocking were linked to current events, this time the blocking did not appear to be explicitly linked to specific events in the country. Zuhurov, while again claiming that lack of access to websites was caused by "technical error," said that he and his volunteers were discontent with comments posted on Facebook and in discussion areas after news articles. He said:

> There's no claim [of ownership] to the websites, but comments are posted by people under different nicknames. People write whatever comes to their minds… and I can't figure it out, is it just a comment? Or a provocation to cause us to limit access to the site?[23]

On March 29 YouTube was blocked for a short period. The official order from state authorities to ISPs stated the reason as "technical and maintenance work." Asomuddin Atoev, head of the Association of Tajik Internet providers, told Asia Plus that Internet providers had received a text message to block YouTube two weeks previously, but they ignored the order until they received an official letter on official letterhead.[24] Again it was not clear what precipitated the blocking in this instance.

On May 23, Dodojon Atovulloev, a prominent political dissident residing in Germany who faces outstanding arrest and extradition orders issued by Tajikistan for "attempted overthrow of the government," began broadcasting footage from Rahmon's son's

---

23   Turko Dikaev, "Beg Zukhurov: Ogranichenie s saytov budet snyato maksimum cherez 2-3 dnya," *Asia Plus*, 18 January 2013, http://news.tj/ru/n ews/beg-zukhurov-ogranichenie-s-saitov-budet-snyato-maksimum-cherez-2-3-dnya.

24   "V Tadzhikistane vnov' zablokirovali YouTube," *Asia Plus*, 1 April 2013, http://news.tj/ru/news/v-tadzhikistane-vnov-zablokirovali-youtube.

wedding.[25] Atovulloev insinuates Rahmon is drinking alcohol and he is seen dancing and singing. The video reached 230,000 hits in the days it was available.[26] The television station *K+* subsequently published several interviews with Tajik opposition leaders. The wedding video resulted in the blocking of YouTube and other video websites for about three months. Three weeks after the blocking of YouTube, news appeared that Rahmon's daughter married Zuhurov's son. [27]

While Zuhurov's role in blocking web-sites is seen as crucial and the subsequent arranged marriage between the Rahmon and Zuhurov families is evidence of the nepotism and patronage system with which Tajikistan's government functions,[28] it is not clear that there was a standard government policy on Internet blocking in 2013. Unlike blockings in 2012, official requests by government officials were elusive. Requests via texts were common and not received or carried out uniformly across ISPs. The possibility that the blockings were the result of individual lower level functionaries who felt it was their prerogative and duty to censor sites when something was amiss on the Internet cannot be dismissed. Governments and their employees are not monoliths. While it was the assumption of many that YouTube would remain blocked until after

---

25   "Tajik Journalist Allowed to Fly Back to Germany," *Reporters without Borders*, 21 August 2013, http://en.rsf.org/georgia-tajik-opposition-journalist-20-08-2013%2C45074.html.
26   "Tamoshoi rekordii tūyi Rustami Emomalī dar Yutub," *TojNews.org*, 13 April 2013, http://tojnews.org/tamoshoi-rekordii-tuyi-rustami-emomali-dar-youtube.
27   "Qudo shudani Emomalī Rahmon bo Bek Zuhurov," *TojNews.org*, 10 June 2013, http://tojnews.org/ovozaho-dar-borai-kudoi-navi-prsident.
28   Eric McGlinchey, "Patronage, Islam, and the Rise of Localism in Central Asia," *PONARS Eurasia Policy Memo* No. 2, 2008. Note: While McGlinchey projected a patronage system weakened by Islam in the case of Tajikistan, patronage networks still function in the political arena; Humayro Bakhtiyor, "Kheshutaborchigī (nepotizm) dar hukumati Tojikiston. Ovoza yo voqeiyat?," *Ozodagon.com*, 18 December 2013, http://www.ozodagon.com/13969-heshutabor-dar-ukumati-toikiston-afsona-e-voeiyat.html.

the presidential elections in November, the site was unblocked in August.[29]

2014 Blockings: Fear of Virtual Protests

In 2014, the Internet remained fairly free and open until June, when YouTube and all Google services, including Gmail, were blocked.[30] Civil unrest in Badakhshan forced a government response in May and the region was watched closely. Google's search engine was restored a few days later and other Google service over a matter of weeks. On 18 July, Odnoklassniki, was blocked, a date that correlates with the emergence of a video five days earlier, which shows an interview of a woman claiming Rahmon's wife's brother kidnapped and raped her 15-year-old daughter.[31] Although Odnoklassniki was blocked, the video was embedded into Facebook and VKontakte, both of which remained accessible.

The reason for continued blocking of YouTube from the month prior remains unclear. Some link the blocking to the appearance of propagandist videos by Tajik fighters in Syria. However, Odnoklassniki, where the videos were propagated, was not blocked until a month after the appearance of the jihadi videos. Odnoklassniki's owner, Mail.ru Group, issued a statement expressing concern over the blocking, saying no reason for blocking access was ever given.[32] Access to Odnoklassniki was restored on August 21 amid rumors spread via social media that all groups which actively agitated against the Tajik government had first been removed. The rumors appear to be at least somewhat accurate. For example, the

---

29   "Youtube dar Tojikiston dubora dastras shud," *Radio Ozodi*, 28 August 2013, http://www.ozodi.org/content/youtube-access-tajik-Internet-available-1/25086140.html.

30   "'Megafon' megūyad, islohi 'kambudi fannī' dar dasti on nest," *Radio Ozodi*, 17 June 2014, http://www.ozodi.org/content/Internet-providers-do-not-reveal-technical-reason/25424958.html.

31   "Group24," YouTube, 13 July 2014, http://www.youtube.com/watch?v=PrQHJQxvH6A.

32   "'Odnoklassniki' ba Dushanbe noma navisht," *Radio Ozodi*, 29 July 2014, http://www.ozodi.org/content/tajik-officials-didnt-respond-to-odnoklassniki-request/25474144.html.

Gruppa24 account vanished from Odnoklassniki, maybe deleted by the Mail.ru Group itself, or through self-censorship.

In September the Tajik media, including U.S.-funded *Radio Ozodi* and UK-funded *BBC*, remained silent about three protests organized by supporters of Gruppa24 in the Russian cities of Moscow, St. Petersburg, and Samara.[33] But videos of the events circulated on social media showing young men unabashedly demanding Rahmon to resign, marking the first time since Tajikistan's independence that a group of ordinary people openly gathered and demanded the president leave office. Even though the media outlets chose to self-censor, the videos circulated widely and quickly on social media. In this sense, it is likely that social media offered access to people who would not have otherwise known about the accusations and events. The examples of challenges in reaching traditional media by opposition groups to disseminate their events and views, and their choice, somewhat by default, to use social media for this aim show the vital role social media plays.

While YouTube remained blocked from June, Facebook, Odnoklassniki, VKontakte, many news websites, as well as dozens of anonymizers were added to the list of blocked websites on 3 October. Not coincidently, that date also marked the tightest security measures in the capital Dushanbe since the end of the civil war. Gruppa24, building on its experience organizing several relatively small protests in Russian cities, began a promotional campaign in social media for a rally in Dushanbe on 10 October. The resulting unprecedented preventive security measures included blocking social media and websites while cutting Internet access in the northern part of the country on 4–5 October, and disabling texting service throughout the country on October 10. All access, except to YouTube, was restored in the days following the absent protest on

---

33 "Iste"fo emomtapak Rakhmonov. Imruz dar Maskav, fardo dar Dushanbe," YouTube, 13 September 2014, https://www.youtube.com/watch?v=fbHf 1hHXi-w; "Bachakhoi Samara Iste"fo 02 Emomtapak Rakhmonov," YouTube, 20 September 2014, https://www.youtube.com/watch?v=0eVi4iyfeKQ.

10 October, deemed "the most silent day" in the history of Tajikistan.[34]

Yet access to social media remained open two weeks only. At the end of October, Facebook and VKontakte were again blocked for about a month with unknown reasons.[35] Usually, a list of anonymizers becomes available via social media each time a popular site such as YouTube is blocked. Articles about blocking are often followed by reader comments with recommendations on how to gain access to the censored pages. For example, when the news site *Asia Plus* was blocked in August 2012, one commenter wrote, "Dear brothers and sisters who look for ways to gain access to blocked websites. You can find more than 100 active proxy servers via this link...".[36] Figure 5 is a graph from the Tor project showing how the use of this anonymizing software grew during each blocking in 2014. However, the latest waves of blocking also targeted proxy servers and anonymizers.

Figure 5. Estimated Number of Directly-Connecting Tor Clients from Tajikistan

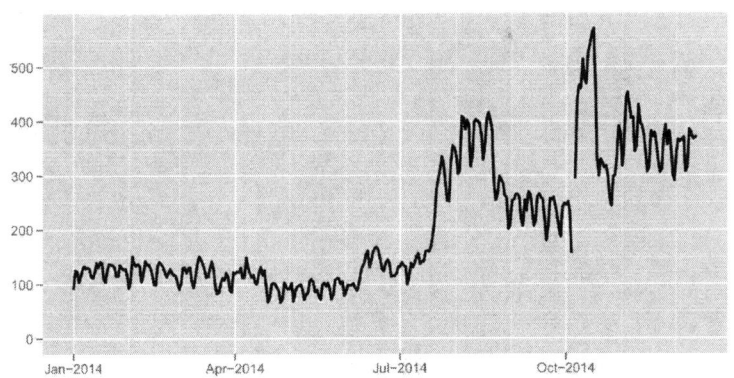

Source: The Tor Project – https://metrics.torproject.org/

---

34 "V Tadzhikistane vosstanovili dostup v sotsseti," *Rosbalt.ru*, 13 October 2014, http://www.rosbalt.ru/exussr/2014/10/13/1326231.html.
35 "Facebook i 'VKontakte' snova zablokirovali v Tadzhikistane," *Baltinfo.ru*, 31 October 2014, http://www.baltinfo.ru/2014/10/31/Facebook-i-VKontakte-snova-zablokirovali-v-Tadzhikistane-459035.
36 A comment posted under *Asia Plus* news by a user named Bakha, http://news.tj/ru/news/v-tadzhikistane-vnov-zablokirovan-sait-azii-plyus.

4. Tajnet as an Object of Struggle: Civil Society, "Volunteers," Media Outlets, and the ICT Industry

In the span of only a few years, the Tajik Internet became a space over which different groups fight for what they consider their cause. At least four actors can be identified: civil society activists, state officials and "volunteers" for trolling, independent and foreign media outlets, and ICT industries.

Civil Society Activists

Civil society activists have been fighting non-stop for a freer Internet. Journalists and other media workers are among the most engaged backers of Internet access. During blocking waves, organizations and people demanding access to the blocked sites took several actions, mostly via social media, posting memes, satire, and written complaints. The meme in Figure 6, circulated on Facebook, illustrates the perceived divide between state media and independent media. The caption shows state media reporting the opening of a kindergarten, while the same day independent media and social networks reported a protest in Dushanbe.

Odnoklassniki plays a unique role in connecting different social groups. Tajik migrant workers use Odnoklassniki not only to socialize and as a means to keep in contact with family members, but also as a gathering place to voice social and political dissent. The interactions between journalists and dissidents in Russia and elsewhere form the underpinnings of a strong, but unorganized political dissonance. These influences come from many different places, including Russian interests, internally organized opposition groups within Tajikistan, and grassroots digital political activism by individual actors.[37]

---

[37] Marintha Miles, *The Political Activities of the Tajik Diaspora in Russia: Implications for the Future of Tajikistan* (Forthcoming).

Figure 6. Meme Illustrating Divide between State Media and Social Networks

как подается информация в Таджикистане

05.04.2013

В Душанбе прошел митинг

Caption: Presentation of information in Tajikistan: 5 April 2013. Tajik TV: A kindergarten was opened in Dushanbe. Social media and independent web-sites: A protest was organized in Dushanbe.

Political dissidents like Dodojon Atovulloev, other vocal diaspora members in Russia, and journalists utilize social media to promote civil liberties and encourage public debate. Facebook and Odnoklassniki brought thousands of social network users together in protest against the arrest and jailing of Umarali Quvvatov in December 2012, and again on behalf of prominent businessmen Zayd Saidov in April 2013. The official Facebook and Odnoklassniki pages of Quvvatov and Saidov, Gruppa24 and Tojikistoni Nav, respectively, played a huge and vital role in attracting the attention of society to the legal proceedings and issues surrounding them, and increased the number of their supporters. The role of social media was particularly powerful in the case of Saidov.[38] Leaders of Tajik opposition groups claim that drawing attention to his case was the greatest accomplishment of civil society. Among those supporting this assessment are the head of the IRPT, Muhiddin Kabiri, who subsequently united with supporters of his group and others to run Oynihol Bobonazarova as the opposition candidate in the November 2013 presidential elections.[39]

Activists' efforts to organize virtual events and real flash mobs in 2012, garnered more than 200 participants, but ended unsuccessfully without any real discussion or outcome. The first event, "100 days for Tajnet (Tajikistan's Internet) freedom," was created on Facebook on 2 October by a journalist. The effort drew 145 guests and between 25–30 comments. Despite limited discussion, it was widely covered by the media, including *BBC Tajik*, *Ozodi*, *EurasiaNet*, and others. The founder pushed participants toward developing and adopting a charter for a free Tajnet, founding a National Civil Council on Tajnet monitoring, organizing round tables, and creating a platform for regular opinion sharing.

Another activist created the second event entitled "Group of Volunteers for Free Speech," on November 30, 2012.[40] The group, which had 70 guests, was named in mockery of Bek Zuhurov, who justified earlier blocking "at the requests of volunteers." The virtual

---

38   The official Facebook page of Tojikistoni Nav, Zayd Saidov's movement, is located at: https://www.facebook.com/newtajikistanparty?hc_location=stream, launched on May 2012.
39   Muhiddin Kabiri, IRPT head, interviewed in "Agar Zayd sazovori 26 soli zindon boshad, pas hama zindonii iakumraem," *Nahzat*, 2 January 2014, http://nahzat.tj/2/item/11054-zaid-saidov; Oynihol Bobonazarova, Tajik human rights activist and politician, then-unsuccessful presidential candidate, interviewed in "O. Bobonazarova: 'Novomu prezidentu budet ochen' slozhno," *Asia Plus*, 15 August 2013, http://news.tj/ru/newspaper/article/o-bobonazarova-novomu-prezidentu-budet-ochen-slozhno.
40   Public event "Gruppa dobrovol'tsev za svobodu slova," Facebook, https://www.facebook.com/events/119772151516619/.

event organizer noted, "I would like to see people who have responded to the invitation say they will gather in a group and work further for freedom of speech, and not only in social networks, a counterweight to [Zuhurov's] 'volunteers'." When the participants were asked what motivated them to join the event, one participant responded, "Freedom of speech for me is a value and necessary condition for personal development and for the development of the society in which I live. That's why I'm in this group." While enthusiasm appeared high, tangible results lagged.

The Authorities and Pro-State Volunteers

While Internet blocking did not curtail activism for an open Tajnet, the appearance of Bek Zuhurov's volunteers and active trolling of these individuals in social networking groups and attacks on individuals did. Blocking proved to be an inefficient way to fight against the spread of news stories and stop discussions in the virtual world. Netizens flocked to Facebook and Odnoklassniki, expressing anger over the realities of events and conditions in the country and the official state news line. Internet discussions about the detention of political opponents, pressures on the ruling party's main rival, the Islamic Revival Party of Tajikistan, and the events in Khorugh pushed Tajik authorities to adapt new ways to rule online. Authorities began to ride the Internet wave; beyond volunteers reporting slander, a large number of users with fake names and pictures now defend state positions. These volunteers, Zuhurov claimed, were "a group of patriots who will defend the country's image in social networks and control online society." In November 2012 Zuhurov told *Radio Ozodi*:

> *Ozodi*: Who are these volunteers? Some believe that you are talking about agents of the Special Forces, the KGB, not about social networking groups.
> Zuhurov: No, KGB and other government agencies are not linked to this. These people [volunteers] lost their relatives in the civil war, their parents, brothers and sisters. And they think that it is media's fault .... I tell them, go and talk to Ozodi or Asia Plus yourself and tell them about your discontent.

But they refuse, saying that you [Bek Zuhurov] are a representative of the Communications Service, and you should control everything.[41]

The appearance of volunteers coincided with increased attention from state special forces to active users of social networks. Users began gathering in closed digital spaces, making previously open public groups private, and choosing to associate online only with those whom they also knew outside of the Internet. Those who do not want to keep their political thoughts bound within closed social networking groups sometimes assume fake identities to open new accounts, sharing their views and opinions with less fear. Other social media users exited social networks altogether or deleted contacts and personal information. But these precautions offer users limited protections and are a bit naïve.

It is unlikely that Tajikistan's government does not have the capacity to monitor all aspects of citizens' online lives. In March 2013, Zuhurov announced that Tajikistan has the technology to censor digital communication and allows it to find "false information, cheating, abusive and bawdry postings, and sources of dissemination on the Internet." He further reminded citizens that, "falsehood and lies on the Internet are crimes to which the people who commit them should answer."[42] In August 2014, parliament passed a law which allows the government to shut down all mobile and Internet service during an emergency.[43]

To increase control over the Internet, the Tajik government entered into negotiation with several foreign firms providing technical support. If China is often denounced as the country selling Internet control software to the Central Asian states, it seems some Western firms are also participating in this lucrative business. In

---

41 Bek Zuhurov, head of the Tajikistan Communications Service, interviewed in "Beg Zukhurov: 'Dobrovol'tsy ne pozvolyayut otkryt' dostup k Facebook," *Radio Ozodi*, 29 November 2012, http://rus.ozodi.org/content/interview-beg-zuhurov-facebook/24785172.html.
42 "Ozodii bayon va Internet," *Khovar State News Agency*, 29 March 2013, http://khovar.tj/society/27086-ozodii-baen-va-Internet.html.
43 Tohir Safar, "Dar holati iztirorī aloqai mobilī va Internet qat" meshavand," *Radio Ozodi*, 4 August 2014, http://www.ozodi.org/content/no-mobile-connection-in-emergency-situation/25480111.html.

November 2014 Privacy International released a 96 page-report "detailing its findings from an extensive investigation into electronic surveillance technologies" in Central Asia. According to the report, Western companies sold sophisticated surveillance technology to Central Asian nations providing the Central Asian state security services "virtually unchecked power to monitor the communications of ordinary citizens."[44] Regarding Tajikistan, Privacy International notes that it obtained a document showing that "the German company Trovicor GmbH marketed a monitoring centre 'for all cellular networks' to the Ministry of the Interior of Tajikistan in 2009, together with what appears to be a mediation device provided by fellow German company, Utimaco."[45]

Media Outlets and the ICT Industry

On the other side of the coin, media outlets and the ICT industry took their own actions to negotiate open access to the Internet. While the president of the U.S. funded Radio Free Europe/Radio Liberty, Steven Korn, criticized the blocking of Ozodi's website, little was said publicly by most mass media outlets beyond short news briefs that sites were blocked.[46] Even the *BBC*'s Tajik service, blocked for more than a year by Swedish-owned Tcell, did not publicly complain about Internet blocking. Instead, media outlets preferred to negotiate unofficially with government officials for open Internet access, but only made these efforts on behalf of their own websites.

---

44   Craig Timberg, "U.S., Israeli companies supply spy gear to repressive regimes, report says," *The Washington Post*, 19 November 2014, http://www.washingtonpost.com/business/technology/us-israeli-companies-supply-spy-gear-to-repressive-regimes-report-says/2014/11/19/49da9b48-700b-11e4-893f-86bd390a3340_story.html.

45   Edin Omanovic, "Privacy International releases 'Private interests: Monitoring Central Asia'," *Privacy International*, 20 November 2014, https://www.privacyinternational.org/?q=node/59.

46   Payrav Chorshanbiev, "Mezhdunarodnoe soobshchestvo osuzhdaet blokirovku saytov v Tadzhikistane," *Asia Plus*, 1 December 2012, http://news.tj/ru/news/mezhdunarodnoe-soobshchestvo-osuzhdaet-blokirovku-saitov-v-tadzhikistane.

This negotiation process was difficult for media outlets and personalities who were not in a position to negotiate unofficially because of difficult political relationships with the authorities. Thus, these actors saw public demand for their rights as the only option. Among them were non-media outlets like the Islamic Revival Party of Tajikistan. The IRPT attempted to use official channels and sent letters to the State Communications Service, requesting the reasons that their website was blocked.[47] In its reply, the state agency denied any link between it and a lack of access to the party's website, and advised the party to clarify the issue with the companies that provide them with Internet service.[48]

Tajik media organizations and journalism unions, including the Union of Journalists of Tajikistan, the National Association of Independent Media of Tajikistan, Media Alliance of Tajikistan and Tajikistan Counsel on Media, condemned the blocking by the State Communications Service and demanded an, "immediate stop to the disregard of the law in the information sphere of the Republic." Tajik media organizations also expressed their concern about independent Internet and mobile providers, who obey "illegal demands of the Communications Service and join in violating the rights of juridical and individual persons."[49]

Increased criticism of non-state companies violating the rights of their clients, and the loss of considerable numbers of clients who mostly use the Internet for social networking, forced ISPs to change course. When the authorities prepared and disseminated the list of 131 websites to be blocked to Internet and mobile providers at the end of 2012, the companies held a meeting and invited international organizations and diplomatic missions to challenge the decision of

---

47 Avaz Yuldashev, "PIVT trebuyet ot B. Zukhurova ob"yasnit' prichiny blokirovki partiynogo sayta," *Asia Plus*, 8 May 2013, http://www.asiaplus.tj/ru/node/143644.

48 Mehrangez Tursunzoda, "Zukhurov dal ofitsial'nyy otvet po povodu nedostupnosti partiynogo sayta PIVT," *Asia Plus*, 14 May 2013, http://news.tj/ru/node/144431.

49 Nargis Khamrabaeva, "Media-organizatsii trebuyut ot Sluzhby svyazi prekratit' bezzakonie," *Asia Plus*, 3 August 2012, http://news.tj/ru/news/media-organizatsii-trebuyut-ot-sluzhby-svyazi-prekratit-bezzakonie.

the Communications Service to block social networks, namely Odnoklassniki, YouTube, and Facebook. The companies urged their invitees to write official letters to parliament and government agencies requesting a nullification of the Communications Service's demands.[50]

5. Conclusion

The case of Tajikistan highlights the many factors that affect the Internet as an increasingly important public space. The decision to block independent media and social media is taken at the government level, but it cannot be assumed that an official chain of command automatically implements the decision. Some senior officials may autonomously make individual decisions that have an impact on the Internet. In other cases, government spies disguised as "volunteers" may intervene, causing activists to change their on-line behavior. To this list should be added the state structures' lack of fully mastered technical capabilities, and some inconsistencies in the way that websites are targeted. Moreover, the Tajik government is under pressure from the international community, the latter being able to force government decisions to re-open websites. More importantly, large migrant outflows and a well-established Tajik diaspora abroad are critical players in Tajikistan's online activism. Journalists at home and abroad worked in a concerted effort and with political opposition groups to campaign for an open Internet, with some success.

Tajikistan's online protest organizers provide evidence that street demonstrations do not always materialize offline. However the relative safety of the digital commons does not always cancel the threat of violence in the public square. Internet access and social media should thus not been seen as a panacea against authoritarianism. For Internet access and social media to move democracy forward there must be enough political space to speak freely, or the state must lack the ability or will to effectively censor the Internet or utilize it to its advantage. How Tajikistan chooses to employ

---

50   "Khadamoti aloqa," Millat.tj.

these technologies in the future and the abilities of in-country citizens and diaspora to circumvent technologies will largely determine the political climate of the country's future. Tajikistan provides an important case study of both the power and limits of social media in consolidating opposition movements in authoritarian states. In this context, Abdulghaffor Abduljabborov of the Ministry of Culture, under which media outlets and journalists must be registered, noted, "The Internet is like a river. Despite the fact that some people might try, no one can block its way."[51]

---

51   "Soli intikhobot soli sonsuri Internet?," *Radio Ozodi*, 12 March 2013, http://www.ozodi.mobi/a/24925762.html.

Youth Media Consumption and Perceptions of Electoral Integrity in Kazakhstan and Kyrgyzstan

Olena Nikolayenko, Fordham University

Central Asian societies have recently experienced spectacular growth in Internet use.[1] The share of Internet users soared from 1 percent in 2001 to 50.6 percent in 2011 in Kazakhstan.[2] The proportion of Internet users also grew, albeit at a slower pace, in Kyrgyzstan, increasing from 3 percent in 2001 to 20 percent in 2011. A related phenomenon was a surge in secure Internet servers, defined as servers using encryption technology in Netcraft. The number of secure Internet servers climbed from 8 (2001) to 105 (2011) in Kazakhstan and from 1 (2001) to 14 (2011) in Kyrgyzstan.[3] By the same token, there occurred a dramatic growth in online content. According to the Internet Domain Survey semi-annually conducted by the Internet Systems Consortium, the number of Internet hosts with the country domain name *kz* skyrocketed from 4,404 in January 2001 to 61,205 in July 2011.[4] Likewise, the number of Internet hosts with the country domain name *kg* exponentially increased from 1,873 in January 2001 to 111,930 in July 2011. Yet, it is unclear whether this rapid spread of digital technology poses a formidable threat to po-

---

[1] An earlier version of this article was presented at the workshop "Youth in Kazakhstan: Societal Changes, Challenges, and Opportunities" (Central Asia Program, George Washington University, 21 April 2014). I thank workshop participants and *Demokratizatsiya*'s anonymous reviewers for their helpful comments. I am also thankful to the World Values Survey research team for generously providing public access to survey data.

[2] "Cyberwellness Profile: republic of Kazakhstan," The World Telecommunication/ICT Indicators Database, http://www.itu.int/en/ITU-D/Cybersecurity/Documents/Country_Profiles/Kazakhstan.pdf.

[3] "World Development Indicators Database," World Bank, http://data.worldbank.org/data-catalog/world-development-indicators.

[4] "Distribution by Top-Level Domain Name by Host Count," Internet Systems Consortium's Internet Domain Survey, https://www.isc.org/services/survey.

litical stability in the non-democratic regimes that have been installed in the former Soviet republics since the collapse of communism.

Scholars disagree over the political implications of rapidly increasing Internet use in non-democracies. Internet optimists argue that the Internet has the potential to instantly connect a large number of citizens, swiftly disseminate information, and eventually facilitate mass mobilization against the incumbent government.[5] Larry Diamond, for example, uses the term "liberation technology" to denote "any form of information and communication technology (ICT) that can expand political, social, and economic freedom."[6] Emphasizing the power of social media, some journalists and analysts described post-election protests held in Moldova in spring 2009 as the Twitter Revolution,[7] while a popular uprising that brought down the long-serving president of Egypt Hosni Mubarak was nicknamed the Facebook Revolution.[8] Other observers of world politics, however, question the crucial role of web-based communication in sustaining mass protests. In particular, Internet pessimists contend that the Internet might undercut citizens' drive

---

[5] See, for example, Cass Sunstein, *Infotopia: How Many Minds Produce Knowledge* (New York: Oxford University Press, 2008); Clay Shirky, "The Political Power of Social Media," *Foreign Affairs* 90:1 (2011): 28–41.

[6] Larry Diamond, "Liberation Technology," *Journal of Democracy* 21:3 (2010): 70.

[7] Ellen Barry, "Protests in Moldova Explode, with the Help of Twitter," *New York Times*, 7 April 2009, http://www.nytimes.com/2009/04/08/world/europe/08moldova.html?pagewanted=all&_r=0; Nathan Hodge, "Inside Moldova's Twitter Revolution," *Wired.Com*, 8 April 2009, http://www.wired.com/2009/04/inside-moldovas/; Alina Mungiu-Pippidi and Igor Munteanu, "Moldova's 'Twitter Revolution'," *Journal of Democracy* 20:3 (2009): 137–42. For an alternative perspective, see Henry E. Hale, "Did the Internet Break the Political Machine? Moldova's 'Twitter Revolution that Wasn't'," *Demokratizatsiya: The Journal of Post-Soviet Democratization* 21:4 (2013): 481–505.

[8] Nahed Eltantawy and Julie Wiest, "Social Media in the Egyptian Revolution: Reconsidering Resource Mobilization Theory," *International Journal of Communication* 5 (2011): 1207–24; Catharine Smith, "Egypt's Facebook Revolution: Wael Ghonim Thanks the Social Network," *The Huffington Post*, 11 February 2011, http://www.huffingtonpost.com/2011/02/11/egypt-facebook-revolution-wael-ghonim_n_822078.html; Jose Antonio Vargas, "Spring Awakening: How an Egyptian Revolution Began on Facebook," *New York Times*, 17 February 2012, http://www.nytimes.com/2012/02/19/books/review/how-an-egyptian-revolution-began-on- facebook.html?pagewanted=all.

for democratic change because it can create an illusion of vibrant civil society in the absence of viable offline social networks.[9] Furthermore, autocrats might devise a wide arsenal of repressive methods to harness the power of digital technology. Recent empirical research, for example, shows how the Russian government seeks to subvert the use of the Internet for regime-threatening political action.[10] The dramatic spread of digital technology in Central Asia provides an excellent opportunity for further analysis of the political consequences of Internet growth in non-democracies.

This chapter examines the linkage between young people's media consumption and confidence in the electoral process in Kazakhstan and Kyrgyzstan. Specifically, the analysis compares the effects of television and the Internet on young people's perceptions of electoral integrity. The study hypothesizes that consumption of TV news boosts citizens' confidence in having free and fair elections in the country, whereas exposure to web-based news negatively affects the level of public confidence in the electoral process. The underlying assumption is that the Internet is subject to less state censorship than television and thus supplies more opportunities for learning about politics from different perspectives, which facilitates a more critical assessment of the quality of national elections.

The chapter focuses on public confidence in the electoral process because these political attitudes have a significant impact on political behavior. The concept of electoral integrity here refers to "international conventions and global norms, applying universally to all countries worldwide throughout the electoral cycle, including during the pre-electoral period, the campaign, on polling day, and

---

9 For a critical assessment of the role of the Internet, see Evgeny Morozov, *The Net Delusion: The Dark Side of Internet Freedom* (New York: Public Affairs, 2011).

10 Sarah Oates, *Revolution Stalled: The Political Limits of the Internet in the Post-Soviet Sphere* (New York: Oxford University Press, 2013); Andrei Soldatov and Irina Borogan, "Russia's Surveillance State," *World Policy Journal* 30:3 (2013): 23–30; Florian Toepfl, "Managing Public Outrage: Power, Scandal, and New Media in Contemporary Russia," *New Media and Society* 13:8 (2011): 1301–19.

its aftermath."[11] Recent empirical work clearly demonstrates that public confidence in the electoral process affects the likelihood of voting.[12] Birch, for example, finds a positive relationship between perceptions of electoral fairness and the propensity to vote.[13] Furthermore, public outrage over electoral fraud might trigger backlash against the incumbent. For example, vote rigging fomented post-election protests, culminating in the resignation of the incumbent governments in Georgia (2003), Ukraine (2004), and Kyrgyzstan (2005).[14] In light of previous research on behavioral consequences of mass perceptions of electoral integrity, it is important to uncover sources of public confidence in the electoral process.

This study uses the cases of Kazakhstan and Kyrgyzstan to investigate media effects on mass perceptions of electoral integrity in two countries with different levels of press freedom. Kazakhstan and Kyrgyzstan are similar in many ways.[15] These Central Asian states share common cultural heritage. The titular nations trace their origins to Turkic-speaking tribes pursuing a nomadic lifestyle. Most of their land was colonized by the Russian empire in the nineteenth century and subsequently incorporated into the Soviet Union. The former Soviet republics gained national independence and embarked upon transition from communism in 1991. Despite these historical legacies, the political trajectories of the two post-Soviet

---

11   Pippa Norris, "The New Research Agenda Studying Electoral Integrity," *Electoral Studies* 32:4 (2013): 564.
12   Miguel Carreras and Yasemin Irepoglu, "Trust in Elections, Vote Buying, and Turnout in Latin America," *Electoral Studies* 32:4 (2013): 609–19; Olena Nikolayenko, "Do Contentious Elections Depress Turnout?," in Pippa Norris, Richard W. Frank, and Ferran Martinez i Coma, eds., *Contentious Elections: From Ballots to Barricades* (New York: Routledge, 2015), 25–44; Pippa Norris, *Why Electoral Integrity Matters* (New York: Cambridge University Press, 2014); Alberto Simpser, "Does Electoral Manipulation Discourage Voter Turnout? Evidence from Mexico," *Journal of Politics* 74:3 (2012): 782–95.
13   Sarah Birch, "Perceptions of Electoral Fairness and Voter Turnout," *Comparative Political Studies* 43:12 (2010): 1601–22.
14   On the mobilizing effects of electoral fraud, see Joshua Tucker, "Enough! Electoral Fraud, Collective Action Problems, and the 2nd Wave of Post-Communist Democratic Revolutions," *Perspectives on Politics* 5:3 (2007): 537–53.
15   For an overview, see Sally Cummings, *Understanding Central Asia: Politics and Contested Transformations* (London: Routledge, 2012).

states diverged. Kyrgyzstan of the early 1990s was often hailed as "Central Asia's island of democracy," surrounded by more authoritarian neighbors.[16] Compared to most rulers in the former Soviet republics, the first president of Kyrgyzstan, Askar Akayev, had less political experience in the ranks of the Communist Party and introduced more economic liberalization reforms in the early 1990s. Akayev's popularity, however, plummeted due to the bleak performance of the national economy, high incidence of poverty, and rising corruption within the ruling elite. Scattered mass protests against deteriorating living standards broke out in 2000 and 2001.[17] Growing public discontent with the incumbent government, along with increasing elite divisions, engendered larger mass protests, known as the Tulip Revolution, in March 2005 and resulted in Akayev's removal from office.[18] Another series of protest events held in April 2010 led to the resignation of Kyrgyzstan's second president Kurmanbek Bakiyev. As a result of the 2011 election, Almazbek Atambayev was elected as president with 63.2 percent of the popular vote.[19] In contrast, there has been little turnover of power in Kazakhstan, where authoritarian practices are more firmly entrenched. President Nursultan Nazarbayev has held the post from 1991 to the present day. According to the official results of the 2011 presidential election, Nazarbayev received 95.5 percent of the popular vote.[20] In addition, the political party Nur Otan (Radiant Fatherland), which is closely associated with the incumbent president, secured the majority of seats in the national parliament.

---

16   John Anderson, *Kyrgyzstan: Central Asia's Island of Democracy?* (Amsterdam: Harwood Academic Publishers, 1999).

17   "Kyrgyzstan at Ten: Trouble in the 'Island of Democracy'," *Asia Report* No. 22, International Crisis Group, 2001, 15–16, http://www.crisisgroup.org/en/regions/asia/central-asia/kyrgyzstan/022-kyrgyzstan-at-ten-trouble-in-the-island-of-democracy.aspx.

18   For an analysis of Akayev's downfall, see Scott Radnitz, "What Really Happened in Kyrgyzstan?," *Journal of Democracy* 17:2 (2006): 132–46.

19   "The Kyrgyz Republic Presidential Elections 30 October 2011: OSCE/ODIHR Election Observation Mission Final Report," Office for Democratic Institutions and Human Rights (ODIHR), Warsaw, Poland, 2012, 24.

20   "Republic of Kazakhstan Early Presidential Election 3 April 2011: OSCE/ODIHR Election Observation Mission Final Report," Office for Democratic Institutions and Human Rights (ODIHR), Warsaw, Poland, 2011, 29.

Given the cross-country differences in the degree of authoritarianism, media outlets in Kyrgyzstan enjoy a higher level of press freedom than their counterparts in Kazakhstan. According to the U.S.-based non-governmental organization Freedom House, the 2011 score for press freedom in Kazakhstan was 81, compared to 69 for Kyrgyzstan, on a scale from 0 to 100, with a higher score signifying a lower level of press freedom.[21] Similarly, Freedom House's score for Internet freedom is higher in Kazakhstan (58 vs. 35 in 2011), indicating that there is more state control over the Internet in the country.[22]

The present study focuses on Central Asian youth. Opinion polls consistently show that young people are the most active Internet users. The data from the sixth wave of the World Values Survey, for example, indicate that 38.7 percent of 18–29 year old respondents in Kazakhstan obtain political news daily on the net, compared to only 5.3 percent of those over 55.[23] Similarly, 32.7 percent of 18–29 year old respondents reported daily consumption of online political news in Kyrgyzstan in 2011, compared to 7.1 percent of those over 55. Recent ethnographic work traces how Internet use affects the cultural identity of urban youth in Central Asia.[24] In addition, Internet use is likely to influence the development of youth's political identity. For example, the blog *Akaevu.net* provided an im-

---

21 For more information, visit "Freedom of the Press Report, 2012," Freedom House, http://www.freedomhouse.org/report/freedom-press/freedom-press-2012#.U58sISho718.
22 For details, see "Freedom on the Net, 2012," Freedom House, http://www.freedomhouse.org/report/freedom-net/freedom-net-2012#.U58sqSho718.
23 The reported statistics are based upon the author's calculations. For detailed information about the World Values Survey and access to the data files for Wave 6, 2010–2014, see http://www.worldvaluessurvey.org/wvs.jsp.
24 Douglas Blum, *National Identity and Globalization: Youth, State, and Society in Post-Soviet Eurasia* (New York: Cambridge University Press, 2011); Hans Ibold, "Disjuncture 2.0: Youth, Internet Use and Cultural Identity in Bishkek," *Central Asian Survey* 29:4 (2010): 521–35; Stefan Kirmse, *Youth and Globalization in Central Asia: Everyday Life between Religion, Media, and International Donors* (Frankfurt-on-Main, Germany: Campus Verlag, 2013).

portant platform for dissemination of information about anti-government protests in Kyrgyzstan in spring 2005.[25] The patterns of youth's media habits and political behavior merit further academic attention because the young generation growing up in the post-Soviet period has the potential to act as an agent of social change and bring about dramatic political transformations in the region.

The remainder of the chapter proceeds as follows. Section 2 discusses the media environment in Kazakhstan and Kyrgyzstan. Section 3 describes the survey methodology. The next section presents findings from public opinion polls conducted in 2011. That year, both countries held presidential elections amidst concerns about the integrity of electoral procedures. The concluding section lays out implications of these findings for prospects for democracy in Central Asia.

1. Media Environment in Kazakhstan and Kyrgyzstan

There are numerous media outlets in Kazakhstan. According to the 2013 data released by the Kazakhstan Ministry of Communication and Information, there were 1,357 newspapers, 48 radio stations, and 51 TV companies in the country, which had a population of 17.5 million people in 2013.[26] Only one-fourth of newspapers and one-fifth of TV companies were state-owned that year.[27] An abundance of private media, however, does not translate into a high degree of pluralism in the public sphere because a sizeable share of private media outlets are controlled by individuals closely associated with

---

25   Svetlana Kulikova and David Perlmutter, "Blogging down the Dictator? The Kyrgyz Revolution and Samizdat Websites," *The International Communication Gazette* 69:1 (2007): 29–50.

26   Ministry of Information and Communication of Kazakhstan, "Statistics on the Mass Media in Kazakhstan as of 15 March 2013," http://mki.gov.kz/ru s/komitety/komitet_informacii_arxivov/upravlenie_pechatnyh_smi/statis tika_otrasli/.

27   Ibid.

the incumbent president.[28] The president's daughter, Dariga Nazarbayeva, founded the news agency Khabar and captured a large segment of the media market.

Numerous reports indicate that press freedom is systematically violated in Kazakhstan.[29] According to the International Foundation for the Protection of Freedom of Speech *Adil soz*, there were 13 physical attacks on media professionals and 19 libel suits against journalists in 2011, while the government denied access to public information in 325 cases and denied public access to certain web sites in more than 200 cases.[30] Political pressures on the mass media escalated during the national elections. For example, the web site of the weekly *Respublika*, known for its critical coverage of domestic politics, was blocked during the 2011 presidential election.[31] Another major assault on the freedom of expression occurred during a strike of oil workers in the city of Zhanaozen.[32] Several web sites, including Twitter, were blocked during the government's crackdown on outspoken labor union members in December 2011.[33] A team of researchers affiliated with the OpenNet Initiative (ONI) estimated that Kazakh authorities widely used selective online filter-

---

28   Bruce Pannier, "Kazakhstan: Media Ownership Leaves Little Room for Independence," *Radio Free Europe/Radio Liberty*, 25 May 2007, http://www.rferl.org/content/article/1076718.html.

29   For example, see "Attacks on the Press," Committee to Protect Journalists, http://www.cpj.org/attacks/; "Press Freedom Index 2011/2012," *Reporters without Borders*, http://en.rsf.org/press-freedom-index-2011-2012,1043.html.

30   "Statistics on Press Freedom Violations in Kazakhstan in 2011," Adil soz, http://www.adilsoz.kz/programms/statistika/ctatistika-narushenij-prav-smi-i-zhurnalistov-v-kazaxstane-v-2011-godu/.

31   Joanna Lillis, "Kazakhstan: The News Weekly that Won't Be Silenced," *Eurasianet.org*, 29 March 2011, http://www.eurasianet.org/node/63176.

32   "Kazakh Authorities Censor News on Deadly Clashes," Committee to Protect Journalists, 20 December 2011, http://cpj.org/2011/12/kazakh-authorities-censor-news-on-deadly-clashes.php.

33   "Striking Oil, Striking Workers: Violations of Labor Rights in Kazakhstan's Oil Sector," Human Rights Watch, 101, https://www.hrw.org/report/2012/09/10/striking-oil-striking-workers/violations-labor-rights-kazakhstans-oil-sector.

ing, defined as "narrowly targeted filtering that blocks a small number of specific sites across a few categories or filtering that targets a single category or issue."[34]

Moreover, amendments to the Law on Media that went into effect on July 11, 2009 ratcheted up the level of Internet censorship in Kazakhstan.[35] In accordance with the law, all forms of online content, including blogs, personal web pages, and chat rooms, are legally defined as mass media. This legal definition makes the Internet resources liable to the same regulations as traditional media outlets. Under the amendments, the government is authorized to suspend or block any web resource that propagates ethnic strife, terrorism, war, or violent overthrow of the constitutional order. Acting upon these legal provisions, state authorities blocked public access to the blog-hosting platform LiveJournal in 2011 in an alleged attempt to prevent the propaganda of terrorism and religious extremism.[36] The government's ban ostensibly came after Rakhat Aliyev, Nazarbayev's former son-in-law and author of the provocative book *Godfather-in-Law*, posted compromising material about the Kazakh elite on his LiveJournal blog.

Despite the government's infringements on the freedom of expression, the volume of online content has grown at a staggering pace in Kazakhstan. In particular, efforts are underway to expand the scope of Kazakh-language content and divert domestic users from the consumption of Russian-language resources. A group of like-minded individuals, for example, spearheaded the production of the Kazakh-language content for the web-based encyclopedia Wikipedia. As a result of this initiative, the number of the Kazakh-language Wikipedia articles skyrocketed from merely 1 in January 2005 to 212,000 in January 2015.[37] For comparison, the number of

---

34 On the ONI methodology and findings, see https://opennet.net/country-profiles.
35 For a full text of the law, visit http://adilet.zan.kz/rus/docs/Z090000178_.
36 "Mounting Concern about Kazakhstan's Use of Cyber-Censorship," Reporters without Borders, 26 August 2011, http://en.rsf.org/kazakhstan-mounting-concern-about-kazakhstan-26-08-2011,40858.html.
37 "Wikipedia: Kazakh," Wikimedia Statistics, http://stats.wikimedia.org/EN/TablesWikipediaKK.htm.

Kyrgyz-language Wikipedia articles increased from 2 in January 2005 to 29,000 in January 2015.[38]

Compared to Kazakhstan, Kyrgyzstan has a less saturated media market. There were 159 newspapers, 26 radio stations, and 25 TV channels in the country with a population of 5.5 million people in 2013.[39] Since Akayev's ouster, the government of Kyrgyzstan continued to curtail press freedom. Most analysts concur that the media situation worsened with the start of Bakiyev's presidency.[40] Bakiyev seized control over the local broadcasting media and banned transmission of the international radio stations *Radio Free Europe* and *BBC Radio* in the winter of 2008. As in the early 2000s, the mass media were threatened with legal suits and hefty fines for investigative journalism. Furthermore, there were at least 83 threats and attacks on media professionals between 2007 and 2011.[41] For example, the office of the newspaper *Kyrgyz Rukhu* was burned down by unidentified assailants after the paper criticized presidential administration head Kurmanbek Temirbaev in February 2007.[42] The murders of investigative journalists Alisher Saipov (2007), Almaz Tashiev (2009), and Gennady Pavlyuk (2009) were also seen as attacks on press freedom.[43]

---

38   "Wikipedia: Kirghiz," Wikimedia Statistics, http://stats.wikimedia.org/EN/TablesWikipediaKY.htm.

39   "Freedom of the Press 2014," Freedom House, http://freedomhouse.org/report/freedom-press/2014/kyrgyzstan#.U7mWDbFI6So.

40   Erica Marat, "Bakiyev Anticipates a Harsh Winter and an Energy Crisis, Further Restricts Free Speech," *Eurasia Daily Monitor*, 12 December 2008, http://www.jamestown.org/programs/edm/archives/edm2008/?tx_publicationsttnews_pi2[issue]=237; Muzaffar Suleymanov, "Kyrgyzstan's Familiar Path: Press Repression, Ousted Leaders," *Committee to Protect Journalists Blog*, 8 April 2010, https://cpj.org/blog/2010/04/kyrgyzstan-media-crackdown-bakiyev-ousted.php.

41   B. D. Usenova, ed., *Is Journalist Work Safe in Kyrgyzstan?* (Bishkek: Institute of Media Policy of the Kyrgyz Republic, 2012), 7, http://www.media.kg/category/publications.

42   "Political Extremism, Terrorism and Media in Central Asia," Research Report, Public Association Journalists, Kyrgyzstan and International Media Support, Denmark, 2008, 31, http://www.mediasupport.org/wp-content/uploads/2012/11/ims-political-extremism-central-asia-2008.pdf.

43   Farangis Najibullah, "Violent Death of Kyrgyz Journalist Follows a Disturbing Pattern," *Radio Free Europe/Radio Liberty*, 22 December 2009, http://w

A steep decline in the number of registered media outlets took place in recent years. The number of newspapers per 1,000 people dropped from 193 in 2008 and 179 in 2011 to 143 in 2012.[44] In particular, Uzbek-language media took a big hit in the aftermath of ethnic violence in the south of the country in June 2010. According to a Bishkek-based NGO spokesperson interviewed by Eric Freedman in May 2012, "Uzbek-language media were completely wiped out of the media landscape, with only one 1,000-circulation newspaper left in the South, but it is state-funded and on the brink of survival."[45] Some ethnic Uzbek journalists fled the region, while others fell victim to physical attacks. Owners of two local TV channels providing Uzbek-language programming—Khalil Khudaiberdiyev of *Osh TV* and Dzhavlon Mirzakhodzhayev of *Mezon TV*—fled the country under threat of imprisonment.[46] In another widely publicized case, members of the Asaba Party broke into the office of the news agency *24kg* in the city of Osh and threatened the agency's ethnically diverse staff using ethnic slurs.[47] Another alarming development in 2011 was the parliament's move to nationalize the privately-owned *Pyatyy kanal* (*Channel 5*) and transform it into a state parliamentary TV channel.[48] Despite the precarious media environment, the level of press freedom is usually estimated to be higher in Kyrgyzstan than in Kazakhstan.

---

ww.rferl.org/content/Violent_Death_Of_Kyrgyz_Journalist_Follows_A_Disturbing_Pattern/1910726.html.

44 "Annual Statistics Report of the Kyrgyz Republic, 2008–2012," National Statistics Committee of the Kyrgyz Republic, Bishkek, 59.

45 Eric Freedman, "Press Rights and Constraints in Kyrgyzstan: The First Year of President Atambaev," *Central Asia and the Caucasus: Journal of Social and Political Studies* 14:1 (2013).

46 Muzaffar Suleymanov, "Kyrgyzstan No 'Island of Democracy' as It Censors the Press," *Committee to Protect Journalists Blog*, http://www.cpj.org/blog/2011/06/an-island-of-democracy-where-freedom-of-speech-is.php.

47 Tolgonai Osmongazieva, "Kyrgyzstan: Playing Nationalist Card?," *24kg News Agency*, 1 August 2011, http://info.24.kg/community/2011/08/01/19482.html; "Disturbing Spate of Physical Attacks on Journalists," *Reporters Without Borders*, 20 May 2011, http://en.rsf.org/kirghizistan-disturbing-spate-of-physical-20-05-2011,40326.html.

48 "Kyrgyz Parliament Gets Own TV Channels despite President's Veto," *Radio Free Europe/Radio Liberty*, 23 September 2011, http://www.rferl.org/content/kyrgyz_parliament_gets_own_tv_channel_despite_presidents_veto/24338296.html.

Another prominent feature of Kyrgyzstan's media landscape is the growth of online media. Several popular Russian-language newspapers, including the weekly *MSN* (http://www.msn.kg), launched their online versions in the mid-2000s.[49] In addition, there was a boom in Kyrgyz-language news content. The largest Kyrgyz-language news portal *Barakelde*, for example, saw a significant increase in Internet traffic during the 2011 election.[50] The political implications of this online content growth have yet to be analyzed.

2. Methodology

This study uses data from the sixth wave of the World Values Survey conducted in Kazakhstan and Kyrgyzstan in 2011. A total of 1,500 respondents per country participated in the survey based upon a national representative sample. Respondents aged 18–29 comprised approximately one-third of the sample (N=475 in Kazakhstan and N=495 in Kyrgyzstan). These age boundaries closely correspond to the legal definition of youth in each country. According to state laws on youth policy, youth is legally defined as 14–29 year old persons in Kazakhstan and 14–28 year old persons in Kyrgyzstan.[51]

The survey gauges the frequency of news consumption from different sources, including newspapers, TV channels, radio stations, the Internet, and discussions with friends and colleagues. The question wording is, "People learn what is going on in this country and the world from various sources. For each of the following sources, please indicate whether you use it to obtain information daily, weekly, monthly, less than monthly, or never."

---

49 Claire Wilkinson, "Kyrgyzstan: E-Revolution," *EurasiaNet*, 20 July 2012, http://www.eurasianet.org/departments/insight/articles/pp072105.shtml; "Political Extremism, Terrorism and Media," 30.
50 *Media Sustainability Index 2012* (Washington, DC: IREX, 2012), 304.
51 "The Law on State Youth Policy in the Republic of Kazakhstan," YouthPolicy.org, http://www.youthpolicy.org/national/Kazakhstan_2004_National_Youth_Policy.pdf; "The Law on Principles of State Youth Policy in the Kyrgyz Republic," YouthPolicy.org, http://www.youthpolicy.org/national/Kyrgyzstan_2009_Youth_Policy_Law.pdf.

An advantage of using the WVS data is that the survey includes multiple measures of public confidence in the electoral process. These measures tap into citizens' evaluations of the country's compliance with such international electoral standards for democratic elections as the right to freedom of expression and freedom of association; a fair, honest and transparent vote count; and the independence and impartiality of electoral management bodies (EMBs).[52] Respondents were asked to report how often the following electoral (mal)practices occur during the country's national elections:

- Votes are counted fairly.
- Opposition candidates are prevented from running.
- TV news favors the governing party.
- Journalists provide fair coverage of elections.
- Election officials are fair.
- Voters are bribed.
- Rich people buy elections.
- Voters are threatened with violence at the polls.
- Voters are offered a genuine choice in the elections.

Using these survey items, this study computes nine variables: (1) fair vote count, (2) low likelihood (LL) of obstacles to the opposition's campaigning, (3) LL of media bias in favor of the ruling party, (4) fair media coverage, (5) EMB competence, (6) LL of voter bribery, (7) LL of vote buying by the rich, (8) LL of violence at the polls, and (9) genuine choice. The five variables referring to electoral malpractices are recoded so that a higher value corresponds to a higher level of electoral integrity. It must also be noted that the "don't know/difficult to answer" response option is recoded into the middle category so each variable ranges from 1, the lowest level of perceived electoral integrity to 5, the highest. Based upon the principal

---

52 For a full list of international election standards, see International Institute for Democracy and Electoral Assistance, *International Electoral Standards: Guidelines for Reviewing the Legal Framework of Elections* (Stockholm, Sweden: IDEA, 2002).

component analysis,[53] this study distinguishes two dimensions of perceived electoral integrity and constructs two indices. The first index, labeled index of youth's confidence in politicians' compliance with electoral procedures, is made up of five variables: LL of vote bribery, LL of vote buying by the rich, LL of violence at the polls, LL of media bias in favor of the ruling party, and LL of obstacles to the opposition's campaigning (Cronbach's alpha=.679). The second index, labeled index of youth's confidence in electoral institutions, includes the remaining four variables: EMB competence, fair vote count, fair media coverage, and genuine choice (Cronbach's alpha=.643).

Additional attitudinal variables included in the multivariate statistical analysis are interest in politics, party identification, interpersonal trust, and satisfaction with the family financial situation. Interest in politics is coded as a dichotomous variable, with 1 for those interested in politics and 0 for those disinterested in politics. Citizens with high levels of interest in politics are likely to evaluate the quality of elections more critically due to greater awareness of political developments in the country. Furthermore, those who identify with the ruling party are likely to place a larger amount of confidence in the electoral process than supporters of opposition political parties or non-partisans. Party identification is coded as a dichotomous variable, with 1 signifying electoral support for the political party closely associated with the incumbent president (Nur Otan Party in Kazakhstan and Social Democratic Party in Kyrgyzstan). Perceptions of electoral integrity might be further affected by the individual's propensity to trust others. The level of interpersonal trust is measured with the help of the following survey item, "Generally speaking, would you say that most people can be trusted or that you need to be very careful in dealing with people?" Moreover, citizens' satisfaction with the family financial situation,

---

53 Principal component analysis is a statistical technique used to reduce the number of variables in a data set into a smaller number of components or dimensions. For an overview, see Ian Jolliffe, *Principal Component Analysis*, 2nd ed. (New York: Springer-Verlag New York, 2006).

measured on a ten-point scale, is likely to influence their evaluation of electoral procedures in the country.

Such socio-demographic variables as education, employment status, gender, ethnicity, and urban residence are also included in the multivariate analysis. Better-educated individuals are likely to report less confidence in having free and fair elections in the country due to a greater amount of political knowledge. Loss of employment might also lower youth's trust in government. University education is a dichotomous variable, with 1 for university students and those with a university degree. Employment status is another dichotomous variable, with 1 signifying part-time or full-time employment. In addition, given dominant gender norms,[54] it is hypothesized that men are more likely to place confidence in the electoral process than women. Ethnicity is also included as a control variable in multivariate analysis. Members of the titular nation might be more inclined to report confidence in the electoral process than ethnic minorities. In particular, interethnic violence in southern Kyrgyzstan is likely to have alienated the majority of ethnic Uzbeks from the incumbent government.[55] Finally, urbanites are likely to differ from rural residents in their perceptions of electoral integrity. The degree of urbanization ranges from 1, settlement of less than 2,000 people, to 7, a city with more than 500,000 people.

3. Findings

Sources of Political News

Table 1 reports the percentage of young people who learn daily about politics from various sources. Television is the main source of political news for nearly 80 percent of youth in Kazakhstan and Kyrgyzstan. The second most popular source of political news is an

---

[54] Lori Handrahan, "Gender and Ethnicity in the 'Transitional Democracy' of Kyrgyzstan," *Central Asian Survey* 20:4 (2001): 467–96.

[55] On ethnic tensions in Kyrgyzstan, see Vicken Cheterian, "Kyrgyzstan: Central Asia's Island of Instability," *Survival* 52:5 (2010): 21–27; International Crisis Group, "Kyrgyzstan: Widening Ethnic Tensions in the South," *Asia Report* No. 222, http://www.crisisgroup.org/en/regions/asia/central-asia/kyrgyzstan/222-kyrgyzstan-widening-ethnic-divisions-in-the-south.aspx.

informal social network. Almost two-thirds of young people report having a daily discussion of politics with their friends and colleagues. In contrast, newspapers are the least frequently used source of political news among youth. Approximately one-tenth of Kazakh youth and one-fifth of Kyrgyz youth report daily newspaper readership. The findings also show that 38.7 percent of Kazakh youth and 32.7 percent of Kyrgyz youth are daily exposed to political news on the net. To date, a higher percentage of Kyrgyz youth (52.7 percent) obtain political news via the radio than the Internet. Nonetheless, a sizable proportion of youth in both countries regularly consumes political news online.

Table 1.   Sources of Political News, Percent

Source	Country	
	Kazakhstan	Kyrgyzstan
TV	80.6	78.1
Radio	28.6	52.7
Newspapers	11.2	20.0
Internet	38.7	32.7
Friends and colleagues	71.4	62.8

Note: The column entries are percentages of 18–29 year old respondents who report daily consumption of political news from the above-mentioned sources.
Source: World Values Survey, 2011

Additional statistical analysis investigates how different sources of political news are related to each other. As shown in Table 2, online news consumption in both countries is positively correlated with newspaper readership and political discussions with friends and colleagues. These findings suggest that citizens with a high level of interest in politics tend to consume news from multiple sources. Another noteworthy finding is that the correlation between Internet news consumption and TV news consumption is negative and statistically significant in Kazakhstan, but it is positive and statistically insignificant in Kyrgyzstan. These results suggest that some youth in Kazakhstan choose not to consume news on state-controlled TV channels and turn to the Internet in their search for alternative information.

Table 2. Correlation Matrix for News Consumption

News Source	TV	Radio	Newspapers	Friends and Colleagues
Kazakhstan				
Internet	-.140**	.251**	.158**	.256**
TV		.025	.169**	.180**
Radio			.213**	.082
Newspapers				-.017
Kyrgyzstan				
Internet	.059	.033	.149**	.233**
TV		.294**	.161**	.230**
Radio			.199**	.128**
Newspapers				.083

Note: The column entries are Pearson's correlation coefficients, **$p<.01$.
Source: World Values Survey, 2011

Youth's Confidence in the Electoral Process

Figure 1 displays the level of youth's confidence in having free and fair elections in the country. Youth's opinions in both countries converge regarding their assessment of media performance. Notwithstanding cross-country differences in Freedom House scores, approximately two-thirds of young people in Kazakhstan and Kyrgyzstan feel that TV news is frequently biased in favor of the ruling party during national elections. Remarkably, however, Kazakhstani youth tend to place more confidence in various dimensions of the electoral process than Kyrgyz youth. For example, 41.1 percent of Kazakhstani youth, compared to 29.5 percent of Kyrgyz youth, agree with the statement that election officials in their home country are fair. A higher percentage of Kazakhstani youth also report that candidates affiliated with opposition political parties are rarely prevented from running for office (48.6 percent vs. 40 percent). In light of violent post-election protests in Kyrgyzstan, it is not surprising that Kyrgyz youth exhibit lower levels of confidence in having violence-free elections than their peers in Kazakhstan (53.1 percent vs. 61.6 percent). In addition, Kyrgyz youth are less likely to believe that vote buying is absent during an election campaign. Specifically, only 30.1 percent of Kyrgyz youth, compared to 48.8 percent of Kazakh youth, report that voters are rarely bribed in their home country. Overall, the results suggest that young people differ in the extent to which they perceive the country's elections as free and fair.

Figure 1. Youth's Perceptions of Electoral Integrity, Percent

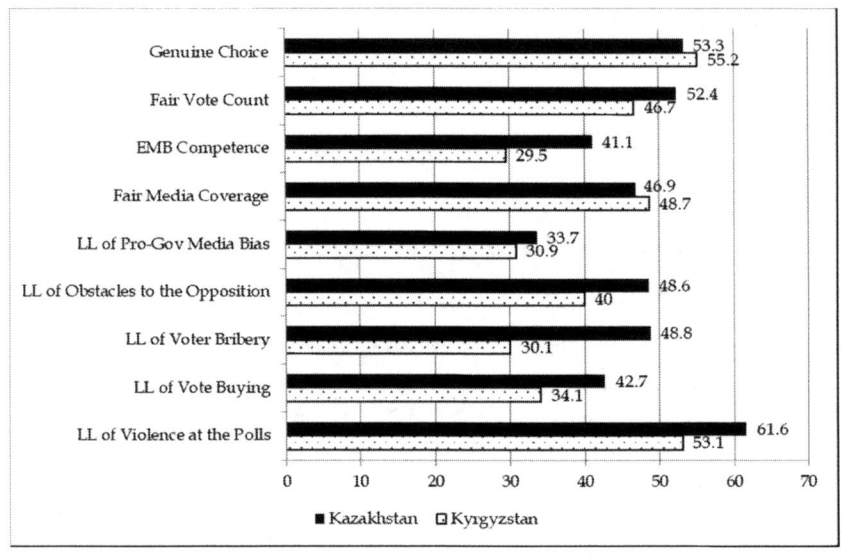

Source: Author's own calculations

Correlates of Youth's Confidence in the Electoral Process

Table 3 presents the results of ordinary least squares (OLS) regression analysis, with the index of youth's confidence in politicians' compliance with electoral procedures as the dependent variable. Model 1 includes data for both countries, with the dummy variable "country" and the interaction term "news source: Internet*country." The analysis finds that youth's confidence in politicians' compliance with electoral procedures is weakly related to their consumption of political news on the Internet and radio. In contrast, the analysis registers a statistically significant negative correlation between trust in politicians and TV news consumption, while newspaper readership is positively associated with trust in politicians. The divergent effects of TV channels and newspapers might arise from differences in media ownership structure and state censorship. As seen in Model 1, the regression coefficient for the dummy variable "country" is statistically significant, indicating that there are cross-country differences in the level of youth's confidence in politicians' compliance with electoral procedures. The next model estimates the effects of media consumption on trust in politicians separately for each country. The regression coefficient for "news source: TV" is negative and statistically significant in Model 2b (Kyrgyzstan), while the regression coefficient for "news source: newspaper" is positive and statistically significant at .10 level in Model 2a (Kazakhstan). The impact of online news consumption on trust in politicians appears to be negligible in both countries.

Table 3. Results of OLS Regression Analysis for the Index of Youth's Confidence in Politicians' Compliance with Electoral Procedures

Variables	Model 1 B (St. Error)	Model 1 Beta	Model 2a (Kazakhstan) B (St. Error)	Model 2a (Kazakhstan) Beta	Model 2b (Kyrgyzstan) B (St. Error)	Model 2b (Kyrgyzstan) Beta
News Source: Internet	.031 (.116)	.013	.087 (.111)	.041	-.014 (.127)	-.006
News Source: Internet*Country	.027 (.153)	.013				
News Source: TV	-.300+ (.170)	-.057	.010 (.249)	.002	-.587* (.242)	-.120
News Source: Radio	.053 (.094)	.019	.155 (.117)	.064	.006 (.159)	.002
News Source: Newspapers	.191+ (.108)	.059	.250+ (.146)	.086	.100 (.163)	.030
Interest in Politics	-.406 (.265)	-.049	-.008 (.355)	-.001	-.553 (.408)	-.066
Identification with the Ruling Party	.883*** (.277)	.105	1.040** (.400)	.121	.717+ (.392)	.087
Interpersonal Trust	-.348 (.266)	-.041	-.224 (.361)	-.029	-.506 (.401)	-.059
Satisfaction with the Family Financial Situation	-.002 (.055)	-.001	.128+ (.075)	.080	-.113 (.081)	-.065
University Education	-.665** (.276)	-.081	-.972** (.364)	-.130	-.247 (.434)	-.030
Employment Status (employed=1)	-.442 (.273)	-.053	-.625+ (.377)	-.080	-.183 (.396)	-.022
Gender (male=1)	-.192 (.265)	-.023	-.258 (.360)	-.035	-.196 (.393)	-.024
Ethnicity (titular nation=1)			-.136 (.356)	-.018	-.816+ (.453)	-.090
Urban	.111* (.051)	.073	.019 (.071)	.013	.206** (.074)	.141
Country (Kazakhstan=1)	2.199*** (.576)	.267				
Intercept	10.877*** (.984)		10.726*** (1.439)		13.684*** (1.344)	
R-Square	13.0		5.04		3.3	

Source: Author's own calculation

Note: Cell entries are regression coefficients (b) with standard errors in parenthesis and standardized regression coefficients (beta). Significance levels: ***p<.001; **p<.01; *p<.05; +p<.10.

Table 4 reports the results of OLS regression analysis, with the index of youth's confidence in electoral institutions as the dependent variable. The empirical strategy adopted here is the same as in the previous analysis. Model 1 includes the dummy variable "country" and the interaction term "news source: Internet*country," while Models 2a and 2b estimate the effects of media consumption on confidence in electoral institutions separately for each country.

Table 4. Results of OLS Regression Analysis for the Index of Youth's Confidence in Electoral Institutions

Variables	Model 1 B (St. Error)	Beta	Model 2a (Kazakhstan) B (St. Error)	Beta	Model 2b (Kyrgyzstan) B (St. Error)	Beta
News Source: Internet	.099 (.100)	.049	-.211* (.102)	-.105	.131 (.103)	.066
News Source: Internet*Country	-.316* (.132)	-.187				
News Source: TV	.311* (.147)	.070	.420+ (.230)	.085	.168 (.196)	.043
News Source: Radio	-.096 (.082)	-.041	-.251* (.108)	-.111	.168 (.128)	.065
News Source: Newspapers	.095 (.093)	.035	-.030 (.134)	-.011	.228+ (.132)	.085
Interest in Politics	.026 (.229)	.004	-.053 (.326)	-.007	.119 (.330)	.018
Identification with the Ruling Party	.978*** (.239)	.140	1.291*** (.369)	.160	.773* (.318)	.116
Interpersonal Trust	.449* (.229)	.063	.115 (.332)	.016	.733* (.325)	.106
Satisfaction with the Family Financial Situation	.032 (.047)	.022	.073 (.069)	.048	-.010 (.066)	-.007
University Education	-.278 (.238)	-.041	.067 (.335)	.010	-.441 (.352)	-.067
Employment Status (employed=1)	-.463* (.235)	-.067	-.839* (.347)	-.115	-.052 (.321)	-.008
Gender (male=1)	.077 (.229)	.011	-.054 (.332)	-.008	.154 (.318)	.023
Ethnicity (titular nation=1)			-.009 (.328)	-.001	-.082 (.367)	-.011
Urban	-.066 (.044)	-.053	.005 (.066)	.004	-.113+ (.060)	-.096
Country (Kazakhstan=1)	1.653*** (.497)	.241				
Intercept	7.163*** (.849)		8.672*** (1.325)		6.493*** (1.089)	
R-Square	6.7		8.9		5.4	

Source: Author's own calculation
Note: Cell entries are regression coefficients (b) with standard errors in parenthesis and standardized regression coefficients (beta). Significance levels: ***p<.001; **p<.01; *p<.05; +p<.10.

As shown in Table 4, news consumption produces divergent effects on youth's confidence in electoral institutions in Kazakhstan and Kyrgyzstan. The regression coefficient for the interaction term "news source: Internet*country" is statically significant, indicating that the impact of web-based news consumption on confidence in electoral institutions varies across the two countries. As reported in the table, Internet news consumption is negatively correlated with confidence in electoral institutions in Kazakhstan (Model 2a), but it has negligible effects on confidence in electoral institutions in Kyrgyzstan (Model 2b). Furthermore, the results suggest that TV news consumption boosts public confidence in electoral institutions in Kazakhstan, but it exerts weak effects on confidence in electoral institutions in Kyrgyzstan. The regression coefficient for "news source: radio" is negative and statistically significant in Model 2a, indicating that radio station listeners are less likely to report confidence in electoral institutions in Kazakhstan. Newspaper readership, on the contrary, is positively associated with confidence in electoral institutions in Kyrgyzstan.

As seen in Table 3 and Table 4, party identification is a strong determinant of youth's confidence in the integrity of the electoral process. Consistent with previous research on winners and losers in elections,[56] young people who identify with the ruling party are more likely to report confidence in the electoral process.

Another noteworthy finding is that ethnicity affects the level of youth's confidence in politicians' compliance with electoral procedures in Kyrgyzstan. The regression coefficient for "ethnicity" is negative and statistically significant at the .10 level, indicating that ethnic minorities are less likely to place trust in politicians than the titular nation. In particular, Uzbek youth in Kyrgyzstan might be less inclined to trust the incumbent government in the aftermath of violence against the minority group. The regression coefficient for "ethnicity" is statistically insignificant in the case of Kazakhstan, suggesting that ethnic origin has weaker effects on youth's trust in politicians in the country. Furthermore, the impact of ethnicity on confidence in electoral institutions is insignificant in both countries,

---

56   Christopher J. Anderson et al., eds., *Losers' Consent: Elections and Democratic Legitimacy* (New York: Oxford University Press, 2005); Emily Beaulieu, "From Voter ID to Party ID: How Political Parties Affect Perceptions of Election Fraud in the U.S.," *Electoral Studies* 35:1 (2014): 24–32.

suggesting similar levels of dissatisfaction with the performance of electoral institutions across ethnic lines.

The results also suggest that socioeconomic status has stronger effects on youth's confidence in the electoral process in Kazakhstan. As seen in Table 3 and Table 4, employment status has a significant impact on youth's confidence in the electoral process in the country. Unemployed youth are less prone to report confidence in the electoral process. In addition, youth dissatisfied with the family financial situation are significantly less likely to believe that politicians comply with electoral procedures in Kazakhstan. The level of trust in politicians also tends to be lower among college-educated youth in Kazakhstan. The regression coefficients for employment status, education, and satisfaction with the family financial situation are statistically insignificant in the case of Kyrgyzstan. Instead, urban residence affects the level of youth's confidence in the electoral process in Kyrgyzstan. Interestingly, Kyrgyz youth in large cities are more likely to report confidence in politicians' compliance with electoral procedures, but they are less likely to place confidence in electoral institutions.

4. Conclusion

This study provides partial support for the argument that consumption of online news erodes public confidence in the electoral process in a repressive political regime. Internet news consumption is negatively associated with youth's confidence in electoral institutions in Kazakhstan, but it is weakly related to youth's confidence in the electoral process in Kyrgyzstan. The results suggest that the impact of exposure to web-based news might be stronger in a country with a lower level of press freedom. An implication of these findings is that increasing access to the Internet might eventually undermine the political legitimacy of the ruling elite in a non-democratic regime. But the impact of online news consumption on youth's political attitudes currently remains rather modest.

A limitation of this study is that it uses cross-sectional data to examine the relationship between media consumption and confidence in the electoral process. The use of panel data is necessary to arrive at stronger conclusions regarding media effects on political trust. Furthermore, an oversample of ethnic minority youth can help us better understand the effects of digital technology on the political outlook of young people from disadvantaged backgrounds.

Another limitation of this research is that it analyzes the frequency of news consumption across different types of mass media. Further research needs to be done to determine how news content influences citizens' confidence in the electoral process. As Ronald Deibert et al. point out, the most recent forms of state control over the Internet focus "less on *denying* access than successfully *competing* with potential threats through effective counter-information campaigns that overwhelm, discredit, or demoralize opponents."[57] As a result, web-based publications in repressive political regimes are becoming replete with news content that essentially supports state-sanctioned interpretations of current events in mainstream media, rather than challenging state propaganda. Compared to television, however, there remains a greater amount of political pluralism on the net. Do Internet users actively seek out uncensored news or devour a web-based portion of state propaganda? Under which conditions does consumption of online news lead to a substantial change in citizens' political outlook? Answering these questions will shed additional light on the transformative power of online media in repressive political regimes.

Obviously, economic obstacles hinder greater use of Internet resources in low-income countries. Unlimited access to the Internet is out of reach for a large segment of the local population in Central Asia, especially in poverty-stricken Kyrgyzstan. Citizens of Kazakhstan, where the 2011 gross domestic product (GDP) per capita based on purchasing power parity (ppp) was US$20,772,[58] paid

---

57 Ronald Deibert et al., eds., *Access Controlled: The Shaping of Power, Rights, and Rule in Cyberspace* (Cambridge, Mass.: Massachusetts Institute of Technology Press, 2010), 27.
58 "World Development Indicators Database," World Bank, http://data.worldbank.org/data-catalog/world-development-indicators.

US$17.20 for a monthly broadband subscription.[59] In contrast, the monthly broadband subscription tariff was 2.7 times higher (US$48.10) and GDP per capita, ppp, was seven times lower (US$2,920) in Kyrgyzstan in 2011, making Internet access prohibitively expensive for most citizens. As the living standards improve in these Central Asian states, online media is bound to reach a wider audience and exercise greater influence in the public sphere.

---

59   Barney Warf, "The Central Asian Digital Divide," in Massimo Ragnedda and Glenn Muschert, eds., *The Digital Divide: The Internet and Social Inequality in International Perspective* (London: Routledge, 2013), 275.

Social Media and Online Public Debate in Central Asia: A Journalist's Perspective

Navbahor Imamova, Voice of America

The emergence of the Internet and the growing participation of people, especially youth, in social media constitute positive change for Central Asia.[1] Uzbekistan, Kazakhstan, Kyrgyzstan, Tajikistan and Turkmenistan are more connected to the world than ever before. Despite several of the governments' wide-ranging attempts to restrict the Internet, the flow of information through social media is unstoppable. While some political observers debate whether these governments would block access to social media altogether to curtail politically sensitive discussions, this author contends that by doing so, they would be making a serious and ultimately unsuccessful gamble for three specific reasons.

First, to varying degrees, all of the Central Asian governments have already accepted that the world has gone online. They understand that in order to be seen as a modern society, attempts must be made, however superficial, to adapt to the Internet landscape; even in Central Asia the idea of "e-government" has become the word of the day. Kazakhstan now offers electronic government services, an ambitious project that was launched in 2005.[2] In cooperation with South Korea and the United Nations Development Program (UNDP), Uzbekistan started its electronic government in 2014.[3] Perhaps not fully cognizant of its ramifications, authorities at the highest levels have made the political decision that state institutions should begin to provide online services and also promote state policies and interests over the Internet.

---

1   This article does not reflect the views of the *Voice of America*.
2   "Index," Electronic government of the Republic of Kazakhstan, http://egov.kz/wps/portal/index.
3   "Home Page," The Single Interactive State Services Portal (Uzbekistan), https://my.gov.uz/en.

Second, people under 49, who tend to be active online, are the overwhelming majority in each of the countries of Central Asia.[4] As such, any attempt to constrain access to the broader world or to slow down the free exchange of ideas presents these governments with an impossible choice: become modern or maintain repressive control.

Third, in social media, as in any other mass medium, what drives the audience is the quality of the content and the way it is communicated. As any social media user, whether very experienced or just beginning, will readily share that what keeps her engaged in social media is a sense of forward motion, the anticipation of what will come next, and a desire to shape it. A journalist's perspective on the power and promise of social media in Central Asia is that it creates unprecedented opportunities for critical thinking and discussion of the region's challenging realities for a wider audience than had hitherto been possible.

Drawing on the author's long experience using social media as a broadcast tool as well as a way to moderate and facilitate discussions on news, politics, and various social topics, this chapter explores the significance of social media for Central Asia not only by examining the phenomenon from a macro-level perspective, but also by explaining the logics that drives social media users. The analysis looks at the strategies and concerns of Central Asians as they increasingly engage on Facebook, Twitter, Odnoklassniki, and other social networks. Personal experience as a social media user, both as a journalist and a native of the region also inform what follows.

1. Access to the Internet

Social media cannot exist without widespread access to the Internet. Central Asia is far behind many regions in terms of Internet penetration and especially the speed of the worldwide web. But this relative lack of infrastructure has not prevented the governments

---

[4] "International Programs," United States Census Bureau, http://www.census.gov/population/international/.

of the region from boasting improvements to the network. In Uzbekistan, for example, authorities claim that in just the first month of 2014, the Internet became 15 percent faster.[5] According to Netindex.com, which reports on real-time global broadband and mobile performance data, speeds of accessing the Internet in Uzbekistan have increased from an average 0.46 Mbps in 2004 to 2.71 Mbps in 2014.[6] However, Uzbekistan still lags far behind Kazakhstan at 16.7 Mbps, Kyrgyzstan at 12.9 Mbps, and Tajikistan at 15.2 Mbps. There is no data on Turkmenistan. To give a comparison, Russia's rate stands at 23.9 Mbps whereas China is at 23.3 Mbps.[7]

Research by the author has shown that the average cost of monthly Internet access, such as 1-Mbps Internet service, is about US$60 (140,000 Uzbek sums). Users in Uzbekistan have said that fast Internet access in 2014, for example, cost them over US$200/month, which is above the average monthly salary in the country. Despite this high cost, Internetworldstats.com estimated that by the end of 2014 over 11 million people out of Uzbekistan's population of 31 million, or over 38 percent, would be accessing the Internet. Similarly, 55 percent of Kazakhstan's nearly 18 million population, 39 percent of Kyrgyzstan's 5.6 million population, 16 percent of Tajikistan's 8 million population, and 9.6 percent of Turkmenistan's 5.1 million population would be online.[8]

With more people going online in the region, more local web sites are popping up. UzInfoCom[9] reports that there are 18,000 websites registered in the .uz domain. Kazakhstan's Network Information Center registry[10] showed 103,590 sites registered to the .kz

---

5   Maksim Yeniseyev, "Uzbek internet service becomes faster, cheaper," *Central Asia Online*, 11 August 2014, http://centralasiaonline.com/en_GB/articles/caii/features/business/2014/08/11/feature-01.
6   "Household Download Index Uzbekistan," Netindex, http://www.netindex.com/download/2,100/Uzbekistan/.
7   Ibid.
8   "Asia Internet Use, Population Data and Facebook Statistics," InternetWorldStats, http://www.internetworldstats.com/stats3.htm.
9   "Development of national network segment," Uzinfocom, http://www.uzinfocom.uz/en/page/show?alias=uznet.
10 "Detailed .KZ and .ҚАЗ Domain Names Registration Statistics," Nic.kz, http://www.nic.kz/stats.

domain. No official, credible data exists on Kyrgyzstan's .kg, Tajikistan's .tj, and Turkmenistan's .tm domains.

Among social networks used in Central Asia, Russia-based Odnoklassniki and VKontakte are the leading ones. However, US-based Facebook and Twitter also have found millions of new users in recent years. This author's research uncovered that Central Asians look at Facebook and Twitter as platforms for free expression, specifically for sharing and discussing political opinion. Odnoklassniki and VKontakte, as well as Moy Mir, are preferred for keeping in touch. Viber, Whats App and Google Hangouts have joined the list of popular messaging and calling programs along with Skype. The usage data varies. With the largest population in the region and a large number of migrant workers in Russia, Uzbekistan is estimated to lead among the Central Asian states in the use of Odnoklassniki, while VKontakte is the most popular such site in Kyrgyzstan. Facebook has the largest number of users in Kazakhstan. California-based Alexa.com, which analyzes global web traffic, shows that Kazakhstan ranks third among all Odnoklassniki users with 5.3 percent of visitors.[11] Usage data available from the U.S. State Department shows that Facebook has the following numbers of users in Central Asia: Kyrgyzstan—75,380; Kazakhstan—452,200; Uzbekistan—128,780; Tajikistan—34,600 and Turkmenistan—5,860.[12] These numbers are similar to data provided by the web-analysis site SocialBakers.[13] It is important to note that online data is mostly based on where a person says he or she is from and some, especially in Central Asia, may not want to reveal his or her real locations. Additionally, IP addresses can be misleading because in countries like Uzbekistan, Tajikistan, and Turkmenistan many people use proxy addresses to access banned sites. The above data is provided to help the reader understand how complicated, yet dynamic, the growth of social networking in the region is.

---

11 "Audience Geography: Where are this site's visitors located?," Alexa.com, http://www.alexa.com/siteinfo/odnoklassniki.ru.
12 Joe Witters, "Transcript of Social Media in Central Asia," Prezi, 9 April 2014, http://prezi.com/95vbjintigtw/social-media-in-central-asia/.
13 "Analytics," SocialBakers, http://analytics.socialbakers.com/home/.

2. Internet as a Tool for Empowerment

As the Internet began to permeate various aspects of life, many in Central Asia have started to realize what a powerful tool it is. From teenagers to seniors, Central Asians know about social media and are learning how to sign on to Facebook, join Odnoklassniki, message on WhatsApp, or watch YouTube. This author's travels to Kyrgyzstan and Kazakhstan in the summer of 2014 revealed that even in some remote villages, people are eager to share moments of their lives with the rest of the world online. While Internet speeds vary, mobile phones are the backbone of day-to-day social media activity.

Most phones come equipped with social media applications and, therefore, almost every customer is a potential user. Once a person finds out what he or she can do with a phone, they start posting what they see and experience. This does not necessarily mean that what they are putting up on social media is seen or shared by many other users. But once connected, the potential to reach large numbers of people is there.

According to official sources, there are over 20 million mobile phones in use in Uzbekistan, which means that about two-thirds of the population has its own phone. In Kazakhstan, cell phone penetration is over 175 percent; 110 percent in Kyrgyzstan; 90 percent in Tajikistan, and 50–60 percent in Turkmenistan. Almost every social medium is primarily accessed through mobile phones, as analyzed by data providers such as Internetworldstats.com and BuddeCom.[14]

As an example, during a one and half-hour drive from Jalal-Abad to the Arslanbob Valley in southern Kyrgyzstan, four passengers and a driver used at least five social networks. Odil, the driver, was taking constant phone calls through Viber from Europe, where his business partners were discussing car sales and clients in Kyrgyzstan. He was also using Telegram Messenger, Android, and an iOS-based Russian App. One of the passengers, the author, was WhatsApp-ing with people in Uzbekistan, Turkey, and Australia.

---

14 "Country Research: Telecoms, Mobile, Broadband and Forecasts," BuddeComm, http://www.budde.com.au/Research/Uzbekistan-Telecoms-Mobile-Broadband-and-Forecasts.html.

Another passenger, a local health specialist, was on Twitter, Facebook, and WordPress. Another, an international aid worker, was tweeting, and the fifth person, a housewife, was chatting on her cell.

Put simply, what social media has given people, whether they are from a city or a village, are the necessary tools to communicate with the wider world and think in new ways. A school teacher this author interviewed in the Suzaq district of Jalal-Abad, Kyrgyzstan, said that information technology has challenged people, rural or urban, to re-think and improve their communication skills. More effective communication, he observed, helps lead to more critical thinking. Such developments are especially important in Central Asia, where people on the whole have had little experience of freedom, and lack the space to intellectually or otherwise challenge prevailing socio-political norms.[15]

A local journalist in Fergana, Uzbekistan, said that social media is also helping to improve how people write. "If you write well, people understand your points and tend to follow you."[16] More importantly, however, is the way that social media enables people to interact with one another and exchange views, including on politically or culturally sensitive and even "forbidden" subjects, such as the criticism of the National Security Service, open discussion of homosexuality or atheism.

Mobile communication is a critical necessity. Perhaps the most important factor driving the use of cell phones, social networks and applications such as Viber, WhatsApp and Facebook, is the fact that in countries like Uzbekistan and Tajikistan almost every other family has someone working abroad. These platforms provide free calls and texting and are easy to use.[17]

What Central Asians discuss on social media today is what they had been able to only whisper about in private earlier. Social media has become a genuine public square for the region. Central Asians, who have long been denied the right to openly express their

---

15   Abdugapirov. Interviewed by Navbahor Imamova, Arslanbab, 6 August 2014.
16   Aslonov. Interviewed by Navbahor Imamova, on Facebook, 19 April 2014.
17   Begimov. Interviewed by Navbahor Imamova, on Viber and WhatsApp, 10 July 2014.

political and social views, now inspire and empower each other through new media and acquire their own voices.

Years of being active on social media has taught this author the following: For many Central Asians social media is a pastime — sharing or enjoying music and video, discussing food, clothes and style, exchanging various commentary — while for others it is a platform they are using to create a public square where people gain information, receive diverse analysis of social and political problems, and use that new knowledge to transform their societies. They are using social media to discuss the most challenging, persistent, yet central questions for the region, including how to resolve ethnic tensions, create jobs, fight domestic violence, end corruption, implement reforms, and become active citizens.

The majority of Central Asians are under the age of 35, making it an opportunity-hungry part of the world. Independent journalists of the region, where most of the media remain under the tight grip of the governments, use social media as platforms to showcase their work. Alongside these journalists, there are also restricted international media outlets, such as *Voice of America* (*VOA*), *Radio Liberty* (*RL*), *British Broadcasting Corporation* (*BBC*) and aggregators such as the *Ferghana.ru* news agency. Editors who run the pages of these organizations say that what motivates them is the audience's desire to know more than they are able to get inside their own societies.[18]

While the data shown above is ever-changing, one can say that those Central Asians who are already active on social media are having a disproportionate impact on their societies, which in many cases has been quite positive. Several million Central Asian migrant workers use social media to keep in touch with home and connect with their peers.

In a region that lacks political and economic integration, professional communities and networks have been created online. One of the most popular groups in Uzbek is called "Professional and

---

18 Social media conversations. Interviewed online by Navbahor Imamova, April 2014

amateur translators" (*Professional va havaskor tarjimonlar*), where experienced as well as emerging linguists and writers discuss the nuances of the Uzbek, Russian and English languages.[19]

Central Asian Civic Forum [Grazhdanskiy forum Tsentral'noy Azii] is run by activists and NGO workers promoting interethnic unity and harmony.[20] Colleagues are finding and sharing with each other, and exploring opportunities for partnership through each other. The Internet is helping empower many across an overall repressive region.

Why has social media become so popular? Because it addresses two of the most basic human instincts: to be an individual and to be a part of society. One study describes the significance of social media in the following terms: "Social media employ mobile and web-based technologies to create highly interactive platforms via which individuals and communities share, co-create, discuss, and modify user-generated content.[21]

The primary reason behind social media's appeal is that it is quintessentially personal. As Timothy B. Lee asks in his 2012 essay, "Do social media platforms promote or limit individual liberty?"[22] Social media is not going to change society all by itself, but it can be a powerful tool for increasing public awareness and support.

While one can reach thousands through social media, sharing almost always begins with one individual connected to the world through his or her computer, mobile phone or tablet. This is a profound change for an environment like Central Asia, where society has always been structured around a collective, not the individual; where you are taught that your personal opinion does not matter;

---

19 "Professional va khavaskor tarzhimonlar," Facebook, https://www.facebook.com/groups/438868872860349/.
20 "Grazhdanskiy forum Tsentral'noy Azii," https://www.facebook.com/groups/1450996138494730/.
21 Jan H. Kietzmann et al., "Social Media? Get Serious! Understanding the Functional Building Blocks of Social Media," *Business Horizons* 54 (2011): 241–51.
22 Timothy B. Lee, "Do Social Media Platforms Promote or Limit Individual Liberty?," Big Questions Online, https://www.bigquestionsonline.com/content/do-social-media-platforms-promote-or-limit-individual-liberty.

where it is about your family, your community, and local sources of authority.

Users of social media in Central Asia cannot escape a certain fear factor. Being online and openly expressing one's view entails risks. But at the same time, the exposure to the critical views of others seems to help social media users learn and gain courage.[23] This is not, however, always the case. One example is the Twittersphere. Uzbek users on Twitter with considerable popularity studiously avoid political topics. Peculiar things can happen when Uzbek tweeters inside Uzbekistan, who tend to adhere to strict censorship and avoidance of political topics, interact with ethnic Uzbek tweeters across the border in Kyrgyzstan. For example, Uzbekistan-based tweeters become concerned when their views or posts are "favorited" by critical outsiders. Likewise, popular Uzbek-language tweeters from Kyrgyzstan avoid discussing politics or other sensitive topics with people in Uzbekistan so as to maintain appeal with that potential audience. An Uzbek blogger in Kyrgyzstan told the author: "Because I want to have a following in Uzbekistan, I try to be careful about what I say."

When a politically sensitive subject is posted, careful Facebookers and tweeters usually give their feedback through private and direct messages rather than writing comments publicly. This author has observed an evolution in Central Asian social media usage by constantly interacting with people publicly and privately. Many who started out carefully limiting their statements gradually became vocal communicators and moderators of public heated discussions.

Twitter is not very popular in Uzbekistan. Until recently, the most powerful Uzbek persona on Twitter was Gulnara Karimova, daughter of Uzbekistan's President Islam Karimov. As her legal problems grew, spectacular revelations about the first family and her own feuds with the National Security Service attracted thousands of Uzbeks to Twitter along with many others. Between Octo-

---

23 Mamatova. Interviewed online by Navbahor Imamova, Tashkent-Istanbul, 2014.

ber 2013 and February 2014, @GulnaraKarimova was being followed by 40,000–50,000 people, and the account was making news almost on a daily basis. While Karimova was suspected of having thousands of fake followers and orchestrating hype on Twitter, her tweets perhaps were the most scandalous of any statements coming out of Uzbekistan. Never before had anyone with a profile like hers accused the ruling elite in Uzbekistan of so much corruption and other abuses. @GulnaraKarimova was going after her own mother, sister, and eventually even after her father, and all the people in their closest circle.

Before her troubles began, Karimova had not been quite as active on social media. While she maintained an official presence on various platforms, these pages were used to mainly promote her celebrity status, fashion and lifestyle, PR projects and public activity. When she started sending out "political" tweets, many in the media wondered why she had chosen Twitter as her main vehicle. This author's study revealed that Karimova's choice was based on the fact that she wanted to tell her story to the outside world, mainly to the West. She decided it was the most appropriate place to fight her enemies, who are concentrated around her powerful father, with a tool that is widely used by Western politicians, analysts, journalists and celebrities.

It is hard to imagine in today's Uzbekistan anyone tweeting in a way similar to Karimova — using one's name and face, making regular claims about how the political elites abuse power. Interestingly, there was no response from the authorities. While her tweets made many news stories and spurred debates within Uzbek circles and elsewhere, @GulnaraKarimova disappeared as an account by the end of February 2014. Karimova allegedly remains under house arrest and it is hard to determine whether she is presently online or not. But she did leave a legacy, according to Uzbek tweeters, and some of them are still cheering for her.

While Karimova herself is the subject of hotly contested opinions, there is no doubt that she created a space for the discussion of certain topics, like the abuses of the country's feared National Security Service (SNB), which had not existed previously. Karimova refused to answer many difficult questions, especially those from critical media, but as a tweeter she was forced to confront thousands of comments that challenged her credibility, her legitimacy and her words. In the eyes of many Uzbeks and other Central Asians, this powerful and wealthy figure, untouchable in real life, became accessible on Twitter. What also became clear is that the more you interact, the more you gain followers and attention. @GulnaraKarimova capitalized on that. Even people who hated her wanted to follow her.

3. Social Media is a Separate Platform

There is no doubt that social media is a unique platform. It is not something that journalists or activists use just to post or promote content. It is also a medium where people come not only for news, but to hear what others are saying about it. Users prefer to spend significant time in social media and to immerse themselves in conversations. Put simply, people want to communicate with the rest of society and connect with the world and social media provide them with the platform. They want to read, watch or listen. And they want to comment.

More importantly, the line between consuming information and generating it has been blurred on social media. People can instantly react to what is shared. Everyone is able to have his or her "say"; they do not depend on some media organization or a journalist to be able to project their views. They may not be reaching millions at one time, but what they say has an ability to travel wider and faster than ever before. Their problem may not be resolved through social media, but they have a megaphone now and can instantly find many who support or advise them on any matter that they raise.

However, in a tightly controlled political environment, social media also becomes a much-needed platform for political participation. What is remarkable about social networks is that people are there by choice and yet, in many cases, they become part of a discussion that they would not otherwise have access to. For example, would dozens of people go to discuss a health care issue in Namangan, Uzbekistan, where some ordinary folks share their horrible experience at a local hospital? Would they get up and express their view? Probably not, but on Odnoklassniki or Facebook, they will. This author's report about forced sterilization in Uzbekistan caused a firestorm on Facebook. She ended up deleting many comments because people became verbally abusive and women who shared their stories felt threatened. But the fact that it was discussed meant a great deal.[24]

This author has observed over the past several years that many Central Asians have come to social media to express themselves and debate with one another. Earlier social media seemed to be exclusively about simply being there, connecting, and entertainment. But it is no longer simply about sharing pictures. It has become much more about telling stories through images. It has increasingly become about explaining one's life, work, and exploring the problems around them.

Three or four years ago, when this author would post an article about unemployment in Uzbekistan, she did not see any public comments at all. People would privately message her about the story. Now these types of stories have become more popular on social media and get discussed widely. When President Karimov announced in early 2013 that more than one millions jobs were created in Uzbekistan in 2012, the story was debated on Facebook for days, most of the comments either denouncing the policy or accusing the Uzbek leader of lying to the nation or pointing out the fact that new jobs did not mean better paying jobs. This author's timeline received dozens of open and private comments.[25] Central Asians are more willing to talk about food prices, living standards and domestic matters than they were a couple of years ago. Consumer [26] and

---

24 Several debates on Facebook led by Navbahor Imamova. December 2013 and January 2014.
25 Facebook debate and private conversations led by Navbahor Imamova.
26 "'Potrebitel'.Uz' community page," Facebook, https://www.facebook.com/groups/Potrebitel.Uz.

Public Monitoring UZ24[27] are popular platforms where Uzbekistanis discuss their rights as consumers. These developments do not necessarily mean people have become braver politically. They are just becoming more comfortable interacting on social media.

Central Asians are also learning how to communicate more effectively with each other and, in some cases, developing more tolerance than they would have had, had they not become engaged in social media. One can observe anger, frustration and hatred on any network on any given day, but users on the whole have come to accept that if you are using any social media, you have to be ready to have your views challenged. Users learn quickly that once they become part of a conversation and express their opinion, they are left with a binary choice: Stay in or get out. On social media, atheist Uzbeks argue with conservative Muslims. Opposition members joust with pro-government Uzbeks. Secular Tajiks debate the future of their country with Islamists. Turkmen migrant workers abroad are speaking with their relatives and friends inside one of the world's most closed regimes. There are a great many issues hotly debated over social media that many of the same users would not dream of discussing on the ground.

While fear is still prevalent, people feel a certain level of risk when they express themselves through words and images. Many Central Asians choose to be anonymous or use nicknames. Nonetheless, they are online. Even those who appear to be not fully straightforward about their identity or not entirely honest, often present online relevant issues.[28] Take, for example, the extremely sensitive issue of domestic violence. Would a woman in Central Asia write a letter or a column in a local newspaper about experiencing domestic violence? Most likely she would not, but there is a greater chance she will discuss it on social media.

The speed of social media is another draw. Because information travels faster, and an immediate digital record is created, it

---

27   Facebook, "'Obshchestvennyy kontrol' UZ24' community page," https://www.facebook.com/control.uz24.
28   Nick-named Facebook users talking about religion and state. March and April 2014.

can also easily be translated into other languages. A migrant worker in Russia far from home is able to record his frustrations into a video, post it on YouTube, and immediately share his personal story with thousands of others. Users who see his video may share that post on Facebook or Twitter, embed it in their blogs, and before long create a firestorm.

4. Social Media and the Search for Identity

One of the most popular topics among Central Asians is a question of identity. Who are we? Who have we been? Who should we be? Any social media discussions that relate to history, anthropology, or culture produce a flood of comments. Often discussions on these topics become emotional and incredibly expressive because questions of identity are intensely personal. Everyone who comments has his or her own idea of what constitutes a "real" Uzbek.

One example of this type of discussion occurred when the Kremlin presented a prestigious award, the Order for Service to the Fatherland, in 2013 to billionaire businessman and ethnic Uzbek Alisher Usmanov. As he stood next to President Vladimir Putin during the ceremony, Usmanov, who has long lived in Russia, spoke of his enormous pride to be a Russian citizen as well as an Uzbek.[29] This author posted a video of his comments on her Facebook page and commented that if Usmanov was so proud to be Uzbek then perhaps he should demonstrate it by supporting the millions of Uzbek migrant workers who live and work in abusive conditions throughout Russia and receive no support from their own government. Hundreds of people commented on the Facebook post, even while no one would agree to comment on the record for any official news story. People did not want to be officially quoted or speak on the air, but they were comfortable voicing their opinions on a Facebook wall.

Social media also allows Central Asians traveling abroad to learn what is happening on the inside of their countries while also

---

29 Alisher Usmanov, "Ya gorzhus', chto ya Uzbek," http://youtu.be/8k77wyvqnFw.

having an impact from the outside—something that makes the governments in Central Asia nervous. Over the past three years Tajikistan has repeatedly blocked access to Facebook, Gmail, and YouTube, usually in the wake of sensitive political developments, such as the unrest in Gorno-Badakhshan in July 2012. However, people continue going online, finding ways to be there, wanting to know more and to participate.

Foreign news organizations such as *VOA*, *BBC* and *RFE/RL* are blocked in Uzbekistan. Proxy addresses are constantly generated and regular users know ways to bypass the blockage in most cases. As Daniil Kislov, managing editor of *Ferghana.ru*, has stated, "blocking [the Internet] is stupid and a waste of money and time."[30] In this author's view, blocking access to the Internet is a potentially counterproductive game that governments play, because ultimately they know it has little effect. Before the appearance of social media, it was easy for the state and state-controlled media to control information. But now social media means that increasing numbers of people have their own sources of information and are able to share it with one another bypassing official channels.

In Uzbekistan, state-controlled television has been conducting a campaign against the use of social media. The message is that social networks are increasingly threatening Uzbekistan by promoting corrosive pop culture, which President Karimov himself has said is dangerous for youth, especially young women.[31] Perhaps not appreciating the irony, the state and state journalists have promoted these anti-social media shows using social media, which in itself has provoked debate. In 2013 Uzbek state-controlled media released a propaganda film entitled Odnoklassniki. The film depicts how a group of young, promising students become "brainwashed" by using social media. One character is turned into an "extremist," while another foolishly migrates to Russia in the hopes of striking it rich. The film promotes the idea that social networks and

---

30 Daniil Kislov, "Blocking information is stupid," *VOA*, http://www.amerikaovozi.com/content/press-freedom-central-asia-kislov/1552370.html.
31 "Uzbekistan: Tashkent Trying to Keep Culture from Going Pop," *EurasiaNet*, http://www.eurasianet.org/node/66369.

the Internet in general corrupt young minds. Interestingly, however, this "propaganda" film still recognizes some bitter facts of life in the country: lack of quality education, a lack of critical thinking, and unemployment. The young people sitting on Odnoklassniki want to know' more about the world, religion, and opportunities.

Despite the fact that some governments are not comfortable with the emergence and popularity of social media, they know they can use it to promote their own positions and policies. While Central Asian politicians are not as visible as their Russian counterparts online, some Kyrgyz and Kazakh lawmakers, diplomats, and other important figures are quite active on social media. In general, the region's political and business elites are coming to accept social media, even if grudgingly, as a way to respond to criticism.

5. What Draws the Most Followers on Social Media?

Just like anywhere in the world, it is people with some level of authority, social standing, cultural recognition, or professional credibility who draw the most attention and followers on social media. Beyond these categories, those who draw and maintain large followings are the most active users—those who engage in frequent exchanges. One can have a fan page and many "likes" on Facebook, but users will quickly lose interest absent an exchange.

To have an impact on social media one needs to be curating material, moderating discussions or debates, and asking questions. Despite being ridiculed by many, the "*Qo'rqmaymiz*" (We are not afraid) movement has attracted more than 10,000 followers within a few months. The group focuses on repression in Uzbekistan and many share their own painful experiences with the regime.[32] *Nur.kz*, one of the popular Kazakh sites, claims to have attracted over three million social media users since 2009.[33] Often the most popular are individuals or pages that post things others will not.

---

32 "'Kurkmaimiz' public group page," Facebook, https://www.facebook.com/groups/qorqmaymiz/.
33 "'Nur.kz' public group page," Facebook, https://www.facebook.com/PortalNURKZ/.

Sources with huge followings are often those who are willing to teach others to conduct a civil discourse online and express themselves. For example, a person can not just verbally abuse somebody and get away with it. He or she will lose followers and eventually people stop commenting or sharing their opinion. One has to have a certain discipline to be a part of a conversation if you want to be taken seriously. A colleague in journalism in Kyrgyzstan remarked about the number of Kyrgyz politicians who had taken to Twitter and quickly developed massive followings.[34] However, more than one of these figures has experienced a social media "fall from grace," by using their account to discuss issues far too mundane, or even worse, getting into personal attacks with individual followers. Following such incidents, the Kyrgyz journalist observed, many followers decided it was time to "unfollow" these accounts.

Radio Liberty's Central Asian language services are perhaps the most popular pages on Facebook. The Turkmen Service has over 67,000 followers.[35] But "liking" does not mean being a part of debates. Ozodlik, Radio Liberty's Uzbek Service, leads in generating discussions on sensitive topics.[36] It has more than 25,000 Facebook followers and nearly a quarter of a million members on Odnoklassniki. Over the years, this author has seen certain users evolve from angry nutcases to thoughtful participants, as they became more practiced in online etiquette and discourse.

Most of the popular topics on social media in Central Asia, as anywhere else, include sports, show business, culture, and religion. Among the fan pages and official pages of celebrities, the most popular one is that of Yulduz Usmanova, Uzbek prima donna, who has close to 53,000 followers.[37] There are other pages dedicated to her and they show thousands of followers too.[38] The region's legendary

---

34 Journalist who wishes to remain anonymous. Interview with Navbahor Imamova, August 2014.
35 "Azatlyk Radiosy," Facebook, https://www.facebook.com/azatlykradiosy.
36 "Ozodlik radiosi," Facebook, https://www.facebook.com/ozodlikradiosi.
37 "'Yulduz Usmanova' official page," Facebook, https://www.facebook.com/yildizusmanova.
38 "'Yulduz Usmanova' community page," Facebook, https://www.facebook.com/pages/Yulduz-Usmonova/49505051919.

literary figures such as Kyrgyz writer Chingiz Aytmatov,[39] Uzbek poet Muhammad Yusuf[40] and pages focusing on world literature such as ziyouz.com[41] generate vibrant social media interaction. Farhod Sulton, publisher of Vatandosh newspaper, based in New York, does not have thousands of followers on Facebook, but his posts ranging from politics to religion, family to morality attract dozens of Uzbeks—liberal, conservative, pro-Western, anti-Western, secular, Islamist and fundamentalist.[42] Pages on Islam appeal to thousands of users too. Islom.uz[43] and its sister pages such as Oilam.uz (My family)[44] and Shaykh Muhammad Sodiq Muhammad Yusuf,[45] former mufti of Uzbekistan, have a large following and their posts are widely shared.

Why are social media firestorms caused by topics that touch on politics, identity, and even daily realities? Someone's post may concern a mundane fact of life. All of a sudden someone else from his or her network may leave a critical comment regarding the person's character or behavior which will draw in numerous people into the conversation, transforming the conversation into something else entirely. For example, a young woman boasts about her exciting life in New York City and a friend suggests that she wear something more decent. That sparks a debate on morality, freedom, gender rules, religion, economy, family, education and even crime. It often becomes necessary to have a moderator who can lead the discussion and help people to focus as they express their opinions.

---

39 "'Chingiz Aytmatov' fan page," Facebook, https://www.facebook.com/pages/Chinghiz-Aitmatov/105607642807192?rf=109582482400641.
40 "Muhammad Yusuf poetry page," Facebook, https://www.facebook.com/MuhammadYusufSherlari.
41 "Ziyo istagan qalblar uchun!," Facebook, https://www.facebook.com/ziyouzcom.
42 "'Farhod Sulton' personal page," Facebook,https://www.facebook.com/sfarhod.
43 "Islom.uz community page," Facebook, https://www.facebook.com/www.islom.uz.
44 "Oilam.uz community page," Facebook, https://www.facebook.com/OilamUz.
45 "Muhammad Sodiq Muhammad Yusuf fan page," Facebook, https://www.facebook.com/ShaikhMSMY.

Many migrant Central Asian activists and experts use social media to make an impact from outside the region and learn from the inside. This is the case with Tashabbus, a web-based non-governmental organization (NGO), registered in the United States, whose mission is to educate the Uzbek public about the laws, legislation, human rights and legal obligations that affect them. The group is run by young, Western-educated Uzbek lawyers who use social media to promote awareness. The founders say that Facebook has played a crucial role in allowing them to disseminate legal information and engage with the public. Thousands have shared their materials. Many thousands more have discussed and learned something from the website.

Tashabbus' president, Dilorom Abdulloeva, has observed an interesting phenomenon. She notices that people seem to feel more confident expressing their views on Facebook rather than on the site itself:

> One might think that leaving an honest comment with a nickname is easier and safer on the web page than showing one's face and real name on Facebook. But many tend to share their opinions on social media because it stirs a rapid discussion and they want to have a real-time conversation. On the web page what you say is just a comment. But on social media, it becomes an organic debate. On social media, you can easily see where the person speaking comes from; what she or he does. Even if they don't reveal much, you can get some sense of who the individual is by looking at their Facebook page."[46]

Steve Swerdlow, Central Asia researcher at Human Rights Watch, describes some of the ways the human rights community uses social media to monitor abuses and raise awareness in and outside the region:

> When authorities detained a group of artists during a peaceful protest in Tashkent in the spring of 2014, we used Twitter to monitor and collect information about their detention in real-time, and also to raise alarm among journalists and diplomats who might not otherwise be following the situation. To some extent, the timely publication on social media of accurate information about human rights abuses sometimes acts as a deterrent. In this

---

46   Dilorom Abdulloeva. Interviewed by Navbahor Imamova, Washington, DC, 2014.

case, some of the artists were released quickly, in less than 24 hours, likely due to the widespread attention on social media.[47]

Swerdlow adds that while social media is a tool human rights activists use to collect data on abuses and inform the public, it also teaches him and other lawyers about the emergence of a newer generation and a dimension of independent civil society in even the most closed of the Central Asian countries, Turkmenistan and Uzbekistan:

> The posting online in August 2014 of Ashgabat residents resisting authorities' attempts to expropriate their air conditioning units in the middle of summer revealed the existence of rare public demonstrations in a country known for crushing all forms of dissent. Likewise, the emergence and growing popularity among Uzbeks in and outside the country of the hashtag #Qorqmaymiz, which translates to 'We are not afraid,' demonstrates that there are many ordinary citizens who are ready and willing to speak out for their rights who need our support.

In a region where international media presence is restricted, social media has become an alternative way to collect and deliver information. *VOA, RL, BBC* and many other Western outlets offering content in regional languages have long used social networks to reach and widen their audiences, and, most importantly, interact with them. While they realize the penetration is still limited they see that their impact through social media is growing. On any given day, their posts are shared or commented by at least a few dozen people and ultimately reach thousands.

As the numbers of users grow, the media treatment of social networks has become more sophisticated as well. Journalists are now accustomed to the fact that their reporting is no longer just one-way communication. Once you report, you get immediate feedback. As a journalist one must be ready for the reality that people will tell you that they either love or hate your content, whether it is a TV show, an article or a column. Your job is no longer just to cover a story, but to discuss the matter on social media. Some choose not to, but many are learning to curate and moderate the

---

47   Steve Swerdlow, telephone interview with Navbahor Imamova, Washington, DC, 2014.

conversations. For them, it is a way to earn more credibility. You may not like what you get from the public, disagree or get upset with the responses, but by engaging with the social media user you are taking advantage of your chance to have an impact. In Central Asia, where users often lack the opportunity to be online easily or for a long time, audiences do not want to browse much. They want the content to be brought right to them by posting material directly on Facebook or Odnoklassniki.

Just like anywhere else online, there is abuse and discrimination on social media. As watchdogs, journalists and activists have an obligation to educate people. Hopefully a social media leader is someone who brings the conversation to a higher level by being both respectful and reasonable. For example, in one case in 2013, male Uzbek users posted online an insulting cartoon depicting the brain of an Uzbek woman. Dozens of users "liked" it on a Facebook group page and left demeaning and sexist comments on the site. Even more upsetting, some Uzbek women also "liked" the cartoon. It was necessary for someone with stature to enter the discussion and put the problem in context and explain what was wrong with the cartoon. Once this had happened, one constructive comment was able to quickly change the tone. Soon dozens of other remarks were made supporting that view. Social media interactions occur through the use of powerful words and images. The sharper they are, the stronger the impact.

Even the repressive governments that doubted the role and effect of social media are slowly changing their minds. The regimes in Central Asia, famous for blockages and restrictions, are now promoting themselves on social media. When the Uzbek government finally appeared on Facebook and Twitter in 2013, the pages were received with cheer and criticism. Many Uzbeks were furious that the communication was in Russian. This fact itself stirred up a heated conversation about the state of the national language and the influence of Russian. Moreover, when the Uzbek Foreign Ministry launched a Facebook fan page, it was also denounced for having a Russian title. Uzbek state media are incapable of covering such issues so social media users are left to discuss it on their own. When it came to this issue, they were eager to let the government know that they were unhappy.

6. Conclusion

Skeptics may conclude that this social media activity is ultimately insignificant in the face of widespread human rights abuses, corruption, and surveillance. They may feel that social media discussion does not automatically translate into progress nor equate with genuine political or social protest. But the counter argument is that social media, through more or less visible ways, is changing the dynamic of life in the region. Critical comments online can and do lead to awareness. Awareness leads to an increase in critical thinking, which can trigger a will and an increased confidence that enables change. Change does not always mean regime change or revolution. Social media is about changes in attitudes and in thinking. It is about people being exposed to diverse ideas and developments, and participating in the analysis of world events. In an age when the world is getting smaller and the inhabitants in it more connected, Central Asians want to be more integrated into the international system, which makes social media an absolutely critical platform in which they can engage.

The question is not whether the average Central Asian joins social media; it is about when they join social media. The power and promise of social media for Central Asia is that it gives an unprecedented opportunity for critical thinking and the discussion of the region's challenging realities with a broader audience than had hitherto been possible. The words of one former politician, an opposition member, who is also an Uzbek poet, sum up the social media "revolution" quite well:

> Social media is what I looked for all my life—a free platform, where I can state my view, hear what people have to say, and then make up my own mind. It's also where I showcase my poems. Publications, TV or radio can't do it. On social media, I know that my work is clearly reaching people. They praise it or denounce it. I'm not on Facebook or Odnoklassniki to find friends or gain popularity. I'm here to interact with people, whoever can be there, to talk with me. We just talk. Yes, the Internet is slow, and the security services may trace me, perhaps punish me, but I have a tool in my hand that can amplify my opinion.[48]

---

48 Uzbek poet who wishes to remain anonymous. Online interview with Navbahor Imamova, August 2014.

SOVIET AND POST-SOVIET POLITICS AND SOCIETY

Edited by Dr. Andreas Umland

ISSN 1614-3515

1 Андреас Умланд (ред.)
Воплощение Европейской
конвенции по правам человека в
России
Философские, юридические и
эмпирические исследования
ISBN 3-89821-387-0

2 Christian Wipperfürth
Russland – ein vertrauenswürdiger
Partner?
Grundlagen, Hintergründe und Praxis
gegenwärtiger russischer Außenpolitik
Mit einem Vorwort von Heinz Timmermann
ISBN 3-89821-401-X

3 Manja Hussner
Die Übernahme internationalen Rechts
in die russische und deutsche
Rechtsordnung
Eine vergleichende Analyse zur
Völkerrechtsfreundlichkeit der Verfassungen
der Russländischen Föderation und der
Bundesrepublik Deutschland
Mit einem Vorwort von Rainer Arnold
ISBN 3-89821-438-9

4 Matthew Tejada
Bulgaria's Democratic Consolidation
and the Kozloduy Nuclear Power Plant
(KNPP)
The Unattainability of Closure
With a foreword by Richard J. Crampton
ISBN 3-89821-439-7

5 Марк Григорьевич Меерович
Квадратные метры, определяющие
сознание
Государственная жилищная политика в
СССР. 1921 – 1941 гг
ISBN 3-89821-474-5

6 Andrei P. Tsygankov, Pavel
A. Tsygankov (Eds.)
New Directions in Russian
International Studies
ISBN 3-89821-422-2

7 Марк Григорьевич Меерович
Как власть народ к труду приучала
Жилище в СССР – средство управления
людьми. 1917 – 1941 гг.
С предисловием Елены Осокиной
ISBN 3-89821-495-8

8 David J. Galbreath
Nation-Building and Minority Politics
in Post-Socialist States
Interests, Influence and Identities in Estonia
and Latvia
With a foreword by David J. Smith
ISBN 3-89821-467-2

9 Алексей Юрьевич Безугольный
Народы Кавказа в Вооруженных
силах СССР в годы Великой
Отечественной войны 1941-1945 гг.
С предисловием Николая Бугая
ISBN 3-89821-475-3

10 Вячеслав Лихачев и Владимир
Прибыловский (ред.)
Русское Национальное Единство,
1990-2000. В 2-х томах
ISBN 3-89821-523-7

11 Николай Бугай (ред.)
Народы стран Балтии в условиях
сталинизма (1940-е – 1950-е годы)
Документированная история
ISBN 3-89821-525-3

12 Ingmar Bredies (Hrsg.)
Zur Anatomie der Orange Revolution
in der Ukraine
Wechsel des Elitenregimes oder Triumph des
Parlamentarismus?
ISBN 3-89821-524-5

13 Anastasia V. Mitrofanova
The Politicization of Russian
Orthodoxy
Actors and Ideas
With a foreword by William C. Gay
ISBN 3-89821-481-8

14 *Nathan D. Larson*
Alexander Solzhenitsyn and the Russo-Jewish Question
ISBN 3-89821-483-4

15 *Guido Houben*
Kulturpolitik und Ethnizität
Staatliche Kunstförderung im Russland der neunziger Jahre
Mit einem Vorwort von Gert Weisskirchen
ISBN 3-89821-542-3

16 *Leonid Luks*
Der russische „Sonderweg"?
Aufsätze zur neuesten Geschichte Russlands im europäischen Kontext
ISBN 3-89821-496-6

17 *Евгений Мороз*
История «Мёртвой воды» – от страшной сказки к большой политике
Политическое неоязычество в постсоветской России
ISBN 3-89821-551-2

18 *Александр Верховский и Галина Кожевникова (ред.)*
Этническая и религиозная интолерантность в российских СМИ
Результаты мониторинга 2001-2004 гг.
ISBN 3-89821-569-5

19 *Christian Ganzer*
Sowjetisches Erbe und ukrainische Nation
Das Museum der Geschichte des Zaporoger Kosakentums auf der Insel Chortycja
Mit einem Vorwort von Frank Golczewski
ISBN 3-89821-504-0

20 *Эльза-Баир Гучинова*
Помнить нельзя забыть
Антропология депортационной травмы калмыков
С предисловием Кэролайн Хамфри
ISBN 3-89821-506-7

21 *Юлия Лидерман*
Мотивы «проверки» и «испытания» в постсоветской культуре
Советское прошлое в российском кинематографе 1990-х годов
С предисловием Евгения Марголита
ISBN 3-89821-511-3

22 *Tanya Lokshina, Ray Thomas, Mary Mayer (Eds.)*
The Imposition of a Fake Political Settlement in the Northern Caucasus
The 2003 Chechen Presidential Election
ISBN 3-89821-436-2

23 *Timothy McCajor Hall, Rosie Read (Eds.)*
Changes in the Heart of Europe
Recent Ethnographies of Czechs, Slovaks, Roma, and Sorbs
With an afterword by Zdeněk Salzmann
ISBN 3-89821-606-3

24 *Christian Autengruber*
Die politischen Parteien in Bulgarien und Rumänien
Eine vergleichende Analyse seit Beginn der 90er Jahre
Mit einem Vorwort von Dorothée de Nève
ISBN 3-89821-476-1

25 *Annette Freyberg-Inan with Radu Cristescu*
The Ghosts in Our Classrooms, or: John Dewey Meets Ceauşescu
The Promise and the Failures of Civic Education in Romania
ISBN 3-89821-416-8

26 *John B. Dunlop*
The 2002 Dubrovka and 2004 Beslan Hostage Crises
A Critique of Russian Counter-Terrorism
With a foreword by Donald N. Jensen
ISBN 3-89821-608-X

27 *Peter Koller*
Das touristische Potenzial von Kam''janec'–Podil's'kyj
Eine fremdenverkehrsgeographische Untersuchung der Zukunftsperspektiven und Maßnahmenplanung zur Destinationsentwicklung des „ukrainischen Rothenburg"
Mit einem Vorwort von Kristiane Klemm
ISBN 3-89821-640-3

28 *Françoise Daucé, Elisabeth Sieca-Kozlowski (Eds.)*
Dedovshchina in the Post-Soviet Military
Hazing of Russian Army Conscripts in a Comparative Perspective
With a foreword by Dale Herspring
ISBN 3-89821-616-0

29 Florian Strasser
Zivilgesellschaftliche Einflüsse auf die Orange Revolution
Die gewaltlose Massenbewegung und die ukrainische Wahlkrise 2004
Mit einem Vorwort von Egbert Jahn
ISBN 3-89821-648-9

30 Rebecca S. Katz
The Georgian Regime Crisis of 2003-2004
A Case Study in Post-Soviet Media Representation of Politics, Crime and Corruption
ISBN 3-89821-413-3

31 Vladimir Kantor
Willkür oder Freiheit
Beiträge zur russischen Geschichtsphilosophie
Ediert von Dagmar Herrmann sowie mit einem Vorwort versehen von Leonid Luks
ISBN 3-89821-589-X

32 Laura A. Victoir
The Russian Land Estate Today
A Case Study of Cultural Politics in Post-Soviet Russia
With a foreword by Priscilla Roosevelt
ISBN 3-89821-426-5

33 Ivan Katchanovski
Cleft Countries
Regional Political Divisions and Cultures in Post-Soviet Ukraine and Moldova
With a foreword by Francis Fukuyama
ISBN 3-89821-558-X

34 Florian Mühlfried
Postsowjetische Feiern
Das Georgische Bankett im Wandel
Mit einem Vorwort von Kevin Tuite
ISBN 3-89821-601-2

35 Roger Griffin, Werner Loh, Andreas Umland (Eds.)
Fascism Past and Present, West and East
An International Debate on Concepts and Cases in the Comparative Study of the Extreme Right
With an afterword by Walter Laqueur
ISBN 3-89821-674-8

36 Sebastian Schlegel
Der „Weiße Archipel"
Sowjetische Atomstädte 1945-1991
Mit einem Geleitwort von Thomas Bohn
ISBN 3-89821-679-9

37 Vyacheslav Likhachev
Political Anti-Semitism in Post-Soviet Russia
Actors and Ideas in 1991-2003
Edited and translated from Russian by Eugene Veklerov
ISBN 3-89821-529-6

38 Josette Baer (Ed.)
Preparing Liberty in Central Europe
Political Texts from the Spring of Nations 1848 to the Spring of Prague 1968
With a foreword by Zdeněk V. David
ISBN 3-89821-546-6

39 Михаил Лукьянов
Российский консерватизм и реформа, 1907-1914
С предисловием Марка Д. Стейнберга
ISBN 3-89821-503-2

40 Nicola Melloni
Market Without Economy
The 1998 Russian Financial Crisis
With a foreword by Eiji Furukawa
ISBN 3-89821-407-9

41 Dmitrij Chmelnizki
Die Architektur Stalins
Bd. 1: Studien zu Ideologie und Stil
Bd. 2: Bilddokumentation
Mit einem Vorwort von Bruno Flierl
ISBN 3-89821-515-6

42 Katja Yafimava
Post-Soviet Russian-Belarusian Relationships
The Role of Gas Transit Pipelines
With a foreword by Jonathan P. Stern
ISBN 3-89821-655-1

43 Boris Chavkin
Verflechtungen der deutschen und russischen Zeitgeschichte
Aufsätze und Archivfunde zu den Beziehungen Deutschlands und der Sowjetunion von 1917 bis 1991
Ediert von Markus Edlinger sowie mit einem Vorwort versehen von Leonid Luks
ISBN 3-89821-756-6

44 *Anastasija Grynenko in Zusammenarbeit mit Claudia Dathe*
    Die Terminologie des Gerichtswesens der Ukraine und Deutschlands im Vergleich
    Eine übersetzungswissenschaftliche Analyse juristischer Fachbegriffe im Deutschen, Ukrainischen und Russischen
    Mit einem Vorwort von Ulrich Hartmann
    ISBN 3-89821-691-8

45 *Anton Burkov*
    The Impact of the European Convention on Human Rights on Russian Law
    Legislation and Application in 1996-2006
    With a foreword by Françoise Hampson
    ISBN 978-3-89821-639-5

46 *Stina Torjesen, Indra Overland (Eds.)*
    International Election Observers in Post-Soviet Azerbaijan
    Geopolitical Pawns or Agents of Change?
    ISBN 978-3-89821-743-9

47 *Taras Kuzio*
    Ukraine – Crimea – Russia
    Triangle of Conflict
    ISBN 978-3-89821-761-3

48 *Claudia Šabić*
    "Ich erinnere mich nicht, aber L'viv!"
    Zur Funktion kultureller Faktoren für die Institutionalisierung und Entwicklung einer ukrainischen Region
    Mit einem Vorwort von Melanie Tatur
    ISBN 978-3-89821-752-1

49 *Marlies Bilz*
    Tatarstan in der Transformation
    Nationaler Diskurs und Politische Praxis 1988-1994
    Mit einem Vorwort von Frank Golczewski
    ISBN 978-3-89821-722-4

50 *Марлен Ларюэль (ред.)*
    Современные интерпретации русского национализма
    ISBN 978-3-89821-795-8

51 *Sonja Schüler*
    Die ethnische Dimension der Armut
    Roma im postsozialistischen Rumänien
    Mit einem Vorwort von Anton Sterbling
    ISBN 978-3-89821-776-7

52 *Галина Кожевникова*
    Радикальный национализм в России и противодействие ему
    Сборник докладов Центра «Сова» за 2004-2007 гг.
    С предисловием Александра Верховского
    ISBN 978-3-89821-721-7

53 *Галина Кожевникова и Владимир Прибыловский*
    Российская власть в биографиях I
    Высшие должностные лица РФ в 2004 г.
    ISBN 978-3-89821-796-5

54 *Галина Кожевникова и Владимир Прибыловский*
    Российская власть в биографиях II
    Члены Правительства РФ в 2004 г.
    ISBN 978-3-89821-797-2

55 *Галина Кожевникова и Владимир Прибыловский*
    Российская власть в биографиях III
    Руководители федеральных служб и агентств РФ в 2004 г.
    ISBN 978-3-89821-798-9

56 *Ileana Petroniu*
    Privatisierung in Transformationsökonomien
    Determinanten der Restrukturierungs-Bereitschaft am Beispiel Polens, Rumäniens und der Ukraine
    Mit einem Vorwort von Rainer W. Schäfer
    ISBN 978-3-89821-790-3

57 *Christian Wipperfürth*
    Russland und seine GUS-Nachbarn
    Hintergründe, aktuelle Entwicklungen und Konflikte in einer ressourcenreichen Region
    ISBN 978-3-89821-801-6

58 *Togzhan Kassenova*
    From Antagonism to Partnership
    The Uneasy Path of the U.S.-Russian Cooperative Threat Reduction
    With a foreword by Christoph Bluth
    ISBN 978-3-89821-707-1

59 *Alexander Höllwerth*
    Das sakrale eurasische Imperium des Aleksandr Dugin
    Eine Diskursanalyse zum postsowjetischen russischen Rechtsextremismus
    Mit einem Vorwort von Dirk Uffelmann
    ISBN 978-3-89821-813-9

60 Олег Рябов
«Россия-Матушка»
Национализм, гендер и война в России XX века
С предисловием Елены Гощило
ISBN 978-3-89821-487-2

61 Ivan Maistrenko
Borot'bism
A Chapter in the History of the Ukrainian Revolution
With a new introduction by Chris Ford
Translated by George S. N. Luckyj with the assistance of Ivan L. Rudnytsky
ISBN 978-3-89821-697-5

62 Maryna Romanets
Anamorphosic Texts and Reconfigured Visions
Improvised Traditions in Contemporary Ukrainian and Irish Literature
ISBN 978-3-89821-576-3

63 Paul D'Anieri and Taras Kuzio (Eds.)
Aspects of the Orange Revolution I
Democratization and Elections in Post-Communist Ukraine
ISBN 978-3-89821-698-2

64 Bohdan Harasymiw in collaboration with Oleh S. Ilnytzkyj (Eds.)
Aspects of the Orange Revolution II
Information and Manipulation Strategies in the 2004 Ukrainian Presidential Elections
ISBN 978-3-89821-699-9

65 Ingmar Bredies, Andreas Umland and Valentin Yakushik (Eds.)
Aspects of the Orange Revolution III
The Context and Dynamics of the 2004 Ukrainian Presidential Elections
ISBN 978-3-89821-803-0

66 Ingmar Bredies, Andreas Umland and Valentin Yakushik (Eds.)
Aspects of the Orange Revolution IV
Foreign Assistance and Civic Action in the 2004 Ukrainian Presidential Elections
ISBN 978-3-89821-808-5

67 Ingmar Bredies, Andreas Umland and Valentin Yakushik (Eds.)
Aspects of the Orange Revolution V
Institutional Observation Reports on the 2004 Ukrainian Presidential Elections
ISBN 978-3-89821-809-2

68 Taras Kuzio (Ed.)
Aspects of the Orange Revolution VI
Post-Communist Democratic Revolutions in Comparative Perspective
ISBN 978-3-89821-820-7

69 Tim Bohse
Autoritarismus statt Selbstverwaltung
Die Transformation der kommunalen Politik in der Stadt Kaliningrad 1990-2005
Mit einem Geleitwort von Stefan Troebst
ISBN 978-3-89821-782-8

70 David Rupp
Die Rußländische Föderation und die russischsprachige Minderheit in Lettland
Eine Fallstudie zur Anwaltspolitik Moskaus gegenüber den russophonen Minderheiten im „Nahen Ausland" von 1991 bis 2002
Mit einem Vorwort von Helmut Wagner
ISBN 978-3-89821-778-1

71 Taras Kuzio
Theoretical and Comparative Perspectives on Nationalism
New Directions in Cross-Cultural and Post-Communist Studies
With a foreword by Paul Robert Magocsi
ISBN 978-3-89821-815-3

72 Christine Teichmann
Die Hochschultransformation im heutigen Osteuropa
Kontinuität und Wandel bei der Entwicklung des postkommunistischen Universitätswesens
Mit einem Vorwort von Oskar Anweiler
ISBN 978-3-89821-842-9

73 Julia Kusznir
Der politische Einfluss von Wirtschaftseliten in russischen Regionen
Eine Analyse am Beispiel der Erdöl- und Erdgasindustrie, 1992-2005
Mit einem Vorwort von Wolfgang Eichwede
ISBN 978-3-89821-821-4

74 Alena Vysotskaya
Russland, Belarus und die EU-Osterweiterung
Zur Minderheitenfrage und zum Problem der Freizügigkeit des Personenverkehrs
Mit einem Vorwort von Katlijn Malfliet
ISBN 978-3-89821-822-1

75 Heiko Pleines (Hrsg.)
    Corporate Governance in post-
    sozialistischen Volkswirtschaften
    ISBN 978-3-89821-766-8

76 Stefan Ihrig
    Wer sind die Moldawier?
    Rumänismus versus Moldowanismus in
    Historiographie und Schulbüchern der
    Republik Moldova, 1991-2006
    Mit einem Vorwort von Holm Sundhaussen
    ISBN 978-3-89821-466-7

77 Galina Kozhevnikova in collaboration
    with Alexander Verkhovsky and
    Eugene Veklerov
    Ultra-Nationalism and Hate Crimes in
    Contemporary Russia
    The 2004-2006 Annual Reports of Moscow's
    SOVA Center
    With a foreword by Stephen D. Shenfield
    ISBN 978-3-89821-868-9

78 Florian Küchler
    The Role of the European Union in
    Moldova's Transnistria Conflict
    With a foreword by Christopher Hill
    ISBN 978-3-89821-850-4

79 Bernd Rechel
    The Long Way Back to Europe
    Minority Protection in Bulgaria
    With a foreword by Richard Crampton
    ISBN 978-3-89821-863-4

80 Peter W. Rodgers
    Nation, Region and History in Post-
    Communist Transitions
    Identity Politics in Ukraine, 1991-2006
    With a foreword by Vera Tolz
    ISBN 978-3-89821-903-7

81 Stephanie Solywoda
    The Life and Work of
    Semen L. Frank
    A Study of Russian Religious Philosophy
    With a foreword by Philip Walters
    ISBN 978-3-89821-457-5

82 Vera Sokolova
    Cultural Politics of Ethnicity
    Discourses on Roma in Communist
    Czechoslovakia
    ISBN 978-3-89821-864-1

83 Natalya Shevchik Ketenci
    Kazakhstani Enterprises in Transition
    The Role of Historical Regional Development
    in Kazakhstan's Post-Soviet Economic
    Transformation
    ISBN 978-3-89821-831-3

84 Martin Malek, Anna Schor-
    Tschudnowskaja (Hrsg.)
    Europa im Tschetschenienkrieg
    Zwischen politischer Ohnmacht und
    Gleichgültigkeit
    Mit einem Vorwort von Lipchan Basajewa
    ISBN 978-3-89821-676-0

85 Stefan Meister
    Das postsowjetische Universitätswesen
    zwischen nationalem und
    internationalem Wandel
    Die Entwicklung der regionalen Hochschule
    in Russland als Gradmesser der
    Systemtransformation
    Mit einem Vorwort von Joan DeBardeleben
    ISBN 978-3-89821-891-7

86 Konstantin Sheiko in collaboration
    with Stephen Brown
    Nationalist Imaginings of the
    Russian Past
    Anatolii Fomenko and the Rise of Alternative
    History in Post-Communist Russia
    With a foreword by Donald Ostrowski
    ISBN 978-3-89821-915-0

87 Sabine Jenni
    Wie stark ist das „Einige Russland"?
    Zur Parteibindung der Eliten und zum
    Wahlerfolg der Machtpartei
    im Dezember 2007
    Mit einem Vorwort von Klaus Armingeon
    ISBN 978-3-89821-961-7

88 Thomas Borén
    Meeting-Places of Transformation
    Urban Identity, Spatial Representations and
    Local Politics in Post-Soviet St Petersburg
    ISBN 978-3-89821-739-2

89 Aygul Ashirova
    Stalinismus und Stalin-Kult in
    Zentralasien
    Turkmenistan 1924-1953
    Mit einem Vorwort von Leonid Luks
    ISBN 978-3-89821-987-7

90 *Leonid Luks*
Freiheit oder imperiale Größe?
Essays zu einem russischen Dilemma
ISBN 978-3-8382-0011-8

91 *Christopher Gilley*
The 'Change of Signposts' in the Ukrainian Emigration
A Contribution to the History of Sovietophilism in the 1920s
With a foreword by Frank Golczewski
ISBN 978-3-89821-965-5

92 *Philipp Casula, Jeronim Perovic (Eds.)*
Identities and Politics During the Putin Presidency
The Discursive Foundations of Russia's Stability
With a foreword by Heiko Haumann
ISBN 978-3-8382-0015-6

93 *Marcel Viëtor*
Europa und die Frage nach seinen Grenzen im Osten
Zur Konstruktion ‚europäischer Identität' in Geschichte und Gegenwart
Mit einem Vorwort von Albrecht Lehmann
ISBN 978-3-8382-0045-3

94 *Ben Hellman, Andrei Rogachevskii*
Filming the Unfilmable
Casper Wrede's 'One Day in the Life of Ivan Denisovich'
Second, Revised and Expanded Edition
ISBN 978-3-8382-0594-6

95 *Eva Fuchslocher*
Vaterland, Sprache, Glaube
Orthodoxie und Nationenbildung am Beispiel Georgiens
Mit einem Vorwort von Christina von Braun
ISBN 978-3-89821-884-9

96 *Vladimir Kantor*
Das Westlertum und der Weg Russlands
Zur Entwicklung der russischen Literatur und Philosophie
Ediert von Dagmar Herrmann
Mit einem Beitrag von Nikolaus Lobkowicz
ISBN 978-3-8382-0102-3

97 *Kamran Musayev*
Die postsowjetische Transformation im Baltikum und Südkaukasus
Eine vergleichende Untersuchung der politischen Entwicklung Lettlands und Aserbaidschans 1985-2009
Mit einem Vorwort von Leonid Luks
Ediert von Sandro Henschel
ISBN 978-3-8382-0103-0

98 *Tatiana Zhurzhenko*
Borderlands into Bordered Lands
Geopolitics of Identity in Post-Soviet Ukraine
With a foreword by Dieter Segert
ISBN 978-3-8382-0042-2

99 *Кирилл Галушко, Лидия Смола (ред.)*
Пределы падения – варианты украинского будущего
Аналитико-прогностические исследования
ISBN 978-3-8382-0148-1

100 *Michael Minkenberg (ed.)*
Historical Legacies and the Radical Right in Post-Cold War Central and Eastern Europe
With an afterword by Sabrina P. Ramet
ISBN 978-3-8382-0124-5

101 *David-Emil Wickström*
Rocking St. Petersburg
Transcultural Flows and Identity Politics in Post-Soviet Popular Music
With a foreword by Yngvar B. Steinholt
Second, Revised and Expanded Edition
ISBN 978-3-8382-0600-4

102 *Eva Zabka*
Eine neue „Zeit der Wirren"?
Der spät- und postsowjetische Systemwandel 1985-2000 im Spiegel russischer gesellschaftspolitischer Diskurse
Mit einem Vorwort von Margareta Mommsen
ISBN 978-3-8382-0161-0

103 *Ulrike Ziemer*
Ethnic Belonging, Gender and Cultural Practices
Youth Identitites in Contemporary Russia
With a foreword by Anoop Nayak
ISBN 978-3-8382-0152-8

104 Ksenia Chepikova
     ‚Einiges Russland' - eine zweite
     KPdSU?
     Aspekte der Identitätskonstruktion einer
     postsowjetischen „Partei der Macht"
     Mit einem Vorwort von Torsten Oppelland
     ISBN 978-3-8382-0311-9

105 Леонид Люкс
     Западничество или евразийство?
     Демократия или идеократия?
     Сборник статей об исторических дилеммах
     России
     С предисловием Владимира Кантора
     ISBN 978-3-8382-0211-2

106 Anna Dost
     Das russische Verfassungsrecht auf dem
     Weg zum Föderalismus und zurück
     Zum Konflikt von Rechtsnormen und
     -wirklichkeit in der Russländischen
     Föderation von 1991 bis 2009
     Mit einem Vorwort von Alexander Blankenagel
     ISBN 978-3-8382-0292-1

107 Philipp Herzog
     Sozialistische Völkerfreundschaft,
     nationaler Widerstand oder harmloser
     Zeitvertreib?
     Zur politischen Funktion der Volkskunst
     im sowjetischen Estland
     Mit einem Vorwort von Andreas Kappeler
     ISBN 978-3-8382-0216-7

108 Marlène Laruelle (ed.)
     Russian Nationalism, Foreign Policy,
     and Identity Debates in Putin's Russia
     New Ideological Patterns after the Orange
     Revolution
     ISBN 978-3-8382-0325-6

109 Michail Logvinov
     Russlands Kampf gegen den
     internationalen Terrorismus
     Eine kritische Bestandsaufnahme des
     Bekämpfungsansatzes
     Mit einem Geleitwort von
     Hans-Henning Schröder
     und einem Vorwort von Eckhard Jesse
     ISBN 978-3-8382-0329-4

110 John B. Dunlop
     The Moscow Bombings
     of September 1999
     Examinations of Russian Terrorist Attacks
     at the Onset of Vladimir Putin's Rule
     Second, Revised and Expanded Edition
     ISBN 978-3-8382-0608-0

111 Андрей А. Ковалёв
     Свидетельство из-за кулис
     российской политики I
     Можно ли делать добро из зла?
     (Воспоминания и размышления о
     последних советских и первых
     послесоветских годах)
     With a foreword by Peter Reddaway
     ISBN 978-3-8382-0302-7

112 Андрей А. Ковалёв
     Свидетельство из-за кулис
     российской политики II
     Угроза для себя и окружающих
     (Наблюдения и предостережения
     относительно происходящего после 2000 г.)
     ISBN 978-3-8382-0303-4

113 Bernd Kappenberg
     Zeichen setzen für Europa
     Der Gebrauch europäischer lateinischer
     Sonderzeichen in der deutschen Öffentlichkeit
     Mit einem Vorwort von Peter Schlobinski
     ISBN 978-3-89821-749-1

114 Ivo Mijnssen
     The Quest for an Ideal Youth in
     Putin's Russia I
     Back to Our Future! History, Modernity, and
     Patriotism according to Nashi, 2005-2013
     With a foreword by Jeronim Perović
     Second, Revised and Expanded Edition
     ISBN 978-3-8382-0578-6

115 Jussi Lassila
     The Quest for an Ideal Youth in
     Putin's Russia II
     The Search for Distinctive Conformism in the
     Political Communication of Nashi, 2005-2009
     With a foreword by Kirill Postoutenko
     Second, Revised and Expanded Edition
     ISBN 978-3-8382-0585-4

116 Valerio Trabandt
     Neue Nachbarn, gute Nachbarschaft?
     Die EU als internationaler Akteur am Beispiel
     ihrer Demokratieförderung in Belarus und der
     Ukraine 2004-2009
     Mit einem Vorwort von Jutta Joachim
     ISBN 978-3-8382-0437-6

117 Fabian Pfeiffer
Estlands Außen- und Sicherheitspolitik I
Der estnische Atlantizismus nach der
wiedererlangten Unabhängigkeit 1991-2004
Mit einem Vorwort von Helmut Hubel
ISBN 978-3-8382-0127-6

118 Jana Podßuweit
Estlands Außen- und Sicherheitspolitik II
Handlungsoptionen eines Kleinstaates im
Rahmen seiner EU-Mitgliedschaft (2004-2008)
Mit einem Vorwort von Helmut Hubel
ISBN 978-3-8382-0440-6

119 Karin Pointner
Estlands Außen- und Sicherheitspolitik III
Eine gedächtnispolitische Analyse estnischer
Entwicklungskooperation 2006-2010
Mit einem Vorwort von Karin Liebhart
ISBN 978-3-8382-0435-2

120 Ruslana Vovk
Die Offenheit der ukrainischen
Verfassung für das Völkerrecht und
die europäische Integration
Mit einem Vorwort von Alexander
Blankenagel
ISBN 978-3-8382-0481-9

121 Mykhaylo Banakh
Die Relevanz der Zivilgesellschaft
bei den postkommunistischen
Transformationsprozessen in mittel-
und osteuropäischen Ländern
Das Beispiel der spät- und postsowjetischen
Ukraine 1986-2009
Mit einem Vorwort von Gerhard Simon
ISBN 978-3-8382-0499-4

122 Michael Moser
Language Policy and the Discourse on
Languages in Ukraine under President
Viktor Yanukovych (25 February
2010–28 October 2012)
ISBN 978-3-8382-0497-0 (Paperback edition)
ISBN 978-3-8382-0507-6 (Hardcover edition)

123 Nicole Krome
Russischer Netzwerkkapitalismus
Restrukturierungsprozesse in der
Russischen Föderation am Beispiel des
Luftfahrtunternehmens "Aviastar"
Mit einem Vorwort von Petra Stykow
ISBN 978-3-8382-0534-2

124 David R. Marples
'Our Glorious Past'
Lukashenka's Belarus and
the Great Patriotic War
ISBN 978-3-8382-0674-5 (Paperback edition)
ISBN 978-3-8382-0675-2 (Hardcover edition)

125 Ulf Walther
Russlands "neuer Adel"
Die Macht des Geheimdienstes von
Gorbatschow bis Putin
Mit einem Vorwort von Hans-Georg Wieck
ISBN 978-3-8382-0584-7

126 Simon Geissbühler (Hrsg.)
Kiew – Revolution 3.0
Der Euromaidan 2013/14 und die
Zukunftsperspektiven der Ukraine
ISBN 978-3-8382-0581-6 (Paperback edition)
ISBN 978-3-8382-0681-3 (Hardcover edition)

127 Andrey Makarychev
Russia and the EU
in a Multipolar World
Discourses, Identities, Norms
ISBN 978-3-8382-0529-8

128 Roland Scharff
Kasachstan als postsowjetischer
Wohlfahrtsstaat
Die Transformation des sozialen
Schutzsystems
Mit einem Vorwort von Joachim Ahrens
ISBN 978-3-8382-0622-6

129 Katja Grupp
Bild Lücke Deutschland
Kaliningrader Studierende sprechen über
Deutschland
Mit einem Vorwort von Martin Schulz
ISBN 978-3-8382-0552-6

130 Konstantin Sheiko, Stephen Brown
History as Therapy
Alternative History and Nationalist
Imaginings in Russia, 1991-2014
ISBN 978-3-8382-0565-6

131 Elisa Kriza
Alexander Solzhenitsyn: Cold War
Icon, Gulag Author, Russian
Nationalist?
A Study of the Western Reception of his
Literary Writings, Historical Interpretations,
and Political Ideas
With a foreword by Andrei Rogatchevski
ISBN 978-3-8382-0689-9 (Paperback edition)
ISBN 978-3-8382-0690-5 (Hardcover edition)

132 Serghei Golunov
Elephant in the Room
Corruption and Cheating in Russian Universities
ISBN 978-3-8382-0670-7

133 Manja Hussner, Rainer Arnold (Hrsg.)
Verfassungsgerichtsbarkeit in Zentralasien I
Sammlung von Verfassungstexten
ISBN 978-3-8382-0595-3

134 Nikolay Mitrokhin
Die "Russische Partei"
Die Bewegung der russischen Nationalisten in der UdSSR 1953-1985
Aus dem Russischen übertragen von einem Übersetzerteam unter der Leitung von Larisa Schippel
ISBN 978-3-8382-0024-8

135 Manja Hussner, Rainer Arnold (Hgg.)
Verfassungsgerichtsbarkeit in Zentralasien II
Sammlung von Verfassungstexten
ISBN 978-3-8382-0597-7

136 Manfred Zeller
Das sowjetische Fieber
Fußballfans im poststalinistischen Vielvölkerreich
Mit einem Vorwort von Nikolaus Katzer
ISBN 978-3-8382-0787-2

137 Kristin Schreiter
Stellung und Entwicklungspotential zivilgesellschaftlicher Gruppen in Russland
Menschenrechtsorganisationen im Vergleich
ISBN 978-3-8382-0673-8

138 David R. Marples, Frederick V. Mills (Eds.)
Ukraine's Euromaidan
Analyses of a Civil Revolution
ISBN 978-3-8382-0700-1 (Paperback edition)
ISBN 978-3-8382-0740-7 (Hardcover edition)

139 Bernd Kappenberg
Setting Signs for Europe
Why Diacritics Matter for European Integration
With a foreword by Peter Schlobinski
ISBN 978-3-8382-0703-2

140 René Lenz
Internationalisierung, Kooperation und Transfer
Externe bildungspolitische Akteure in der Russischen Föderation
Mit einem Vorwort von Frank Ettrich
ISBN 978-3-8382-0751-3

141 Juri Plusnin, Yana Zausaeva, Natalia Zhidkevich, Artemy Pozanenko
Wandering Workers
Mores, Behavior, Way of Life, and Political Status of Domestic Russian labor migrants
Translated by Julia Kazantseva
ISBN 978-3-8382-0713-1

142 David J. Smith (eds.)
Latvia – A Work in Progress?
100 Years of State- and Nation-Building
ISBN 978-3-8382-0718-6

143 Инна Чувычкина (ред.)
Экспортные нефте- и газопроводы на постсоветском пространстве
Анализ трубопроводной политики в свете теории международных отношений
ISBN 978-3-8382-0822-0

144 Johann Zajaczkowski
Russland – eine pragmatische Großmacht?
Eine rollentheoretische Untersuchung russischer Außenpolitik am Beispiel der Zusammenarbeit mit den USA nach 9/11 und des Georgienkrieges von 2008
Mit einem Vorwort von Siegfried Schieder
ISBN 978-3-8382-0837-4

145 Boris Popivanov
Changing Images of the Left in Bulgaria
The Challenge of Post-Communism in the Early 21st Century
ISBN 978-3-8382-0717-9

146 Lenka Krátká
A History of the Czechoslovak Ocean Shipping Company 1948-1989
How a Small, Landlocked Country Ran Maritime Business During the Cold War
ISBN 978-3-8382-0716-2

147 Alexander Sergunin
Explaining Russian Foreign Policy Behavior
Theory and Practice
ISBN 978-3-8382-0782-7

148 Darya Malyutina
    Migrant Friendships in
    a Super-Diverse City
    Russian-Speakers and their Social
    Relationships in London in the 21st Century
    With a foreword by Claire Dwyer
    ISBN 978-3-8382-0702-5

149 Alexander Sergunin and
    Valery Konyshev
    Russia in the Arctic
    Hard or Soft Power?
    ISBN 978-3-8382-0783-4

150 John J. Maresca
    Helsinki Revisited
    A Key U.S. Negotiator's Memoirs on the
    Development of the CSCE into the OSCE
    With a foreword by Hafiz Pashayev
    ISBN 978-3-8382-0872-5

151 Jardar Østbø
    The New Third Rome
    Readings of a Russian Nationalist Myth
    With a foreword by Pål Kolstø
    ISBN 978-3-8382-0900-5

152 Simon Kordonsky
    Socio-Economic Foundations of the
    Russian Post-Soviet Regime
    The Resource-Based Economy and Estate-
    Based Social Structure of Contemporary
    Russia
    With a foreword by Svetlana Barsukova
    ISBN 978-3-8382-0875-6

153 Duncan Leitch
    Assisting Reform in Post-Communist
    Ukraine 2000–2012
    The Illusions of Donors and the Disillusion of
    Beneficiaries
    With a foreword by Kataryna Wolczuk
    ISBN 978-3-8382-0874-9

154 Abel Polese
    Limits of a Post-Soviet State
    How Informality Replaces, Renegotiates, and
    Reshapes Governance in Contemporary
    Ukraine
    With a foreword by Colin C. Williams
    ISBN 978-3-8382-0885-5

155 Mikhail Suslov (ed.)
    Digital Orthodoxy in the
    Post-Soviet World
    The Russian Orthodox Church and Web 2.0
    With a foreword by Father Cyril Hovorun
    ISBN 978-3-8382-0881-7

156 Leonid Luks
    Zwei „Sonderwege"? Russisch-
    deutsche Parallelen und Kontraste
    (1917-2014)
    Vergleichende Essays
    ISBN 978-3-8382-0823-7

157 Vladimir V. Karacharovskiy, Ovsey I.
    Shkaratan, Gordey A. Yastrebov
    Towards a new Russian Work Culture
    Can Western Companies and Expatriates
    Change Russian Society?
    ISBN 978-3-8382-0962-3

158 Edmund Griffiths
    Aleksandr Prokhanov and Post-Soviet
    Esotericism
    ISBN 978-3-8382-0963-0

159 Timm Beichelt, Susann Worschech
    (eds.)
    Transnational Ukraine?
    Networks and Ties that Influence(d)
    Contemporary Ukraine
    ISBN 978-3-8382-0964-7

160 Mieste Hotopp-Riecke
    Die Tataren der Krim zwischen
    Assimilation und Selbstbehauptung
    Der Aufbau des krimtatarischen
    Bildungswesens nach Deportation und
    Heimkehr (1990-2005)
    Mit einem Vorwort von Swetlana
    Czerwonnaja
    ISBN 978-3-89821-940-2

161 Olga Bertelsen (ed.)
    Revolution and War in
    Contemporary Ukraine
    The Challenge of Change
    ISBN 978-3-8382-1056-8

162 Natalya Ryabinska
    Ukraine's Post-Communist
    Mass Media
    Between Capture and Commercialization
    With a foreword by Marta Dyczok
    ISBN 978-3-8382-1051-3

163 Alexandra Cotofana,
James M. Nyce (eds.)
Religion and Magic in Socialist and
Post-Socialist Contexts
Historic and Ethnographic Case Studies of
Orthodoxy, Heterodoxy, and Alternative
Spirituality
With a foreword by Patrick L. Michelson
ISBN 978-3-8382-1039-1

164 Nozima Akhrarkhodjaeva
The Instrumentalisation of Mass
Media in Electoral Authoritarian
Regimes
Evidence from Russia's Presidential Election
Campaigns of 2000 and 2008
ISBN 978-3-8382-1043-8

165 Yulia Krasheninnikova
Informal Healthcare in Contemporary
Russia
Sociographic Essays on the Post-Soviet
Infrastructure for Alternative Healing
Practices
ISBN 978-3-8382-1030-8

166 Peter Kaiser
Das Schachbrett der Macht
Die Handlungsspielräume eines sowjetischen
Funktionärs unter Stalin am Beispiel des
Generalsekretärs des Komsomol
Aleksandr Kosarev (1929-1938)
Mit einem Vorwort von Dietmar Neutatz
ISBN 978-3-8382-1052-0

167 Oksana Kim
The Effects and Implications of
Kazakhstan's Adoption of
International Financial Reporting
Standards
A Resource Dependence Perspective
With a foreword by Svetlana Vady
ISBN 978-3-8382-1037-7

168 Anna Sanina
Patriotic Education in
Contemporary Russia
Sociological Studies in the Making of the
Post-Soviet Citizen
ISBN 978-3-8382-1033-9

169 Rudolf Wolters
Spezialist in Sibirien
Faksimile der 1933 erschienenen
ersten Ausgabe
Mit einem Vorwort von Dmitrij Chmelnizki
ISBN 978-3-8382-0515-1

170 Michal Vít,
Magdalena M. Baran (eds.)
Transregional versus National
Perspectives on Contemporary Central
European History
Studies on the Building of Nation-States and
Their Cooperation in the 20th and 21st Century
With a foreword by Petr Vágner
ISBN 978-3-8382-1115-2

171 Philip Gamaghelyan
Conflict Resolution Beyond the
International Relations Paradigm
Evolving Designs as a Transformative
Practice in Nagorno-Karabakh and Syria
With a foreword by Susan Allen
ISBN 978-3-8382-1117-6

172 Maria Shagina
Joining a Prestigious Club
Cooperation with Europarties and Its Impact
on Party Development in Georgia, Moldova,
and Ukraine 2004–2015
With a foreword by Kataryna Wolczuk
ISBN 978-3-8382-1104-6

173 Alexandra Cotofana,
James M. Nyce (eds.)
Religion and Magic in Socialist and
Post-Socialist Contexts II
Baltic, Eastern European,
and Post-USSR Case Studies
ISBN 978-3-8382-1090-2

174 Barbara Kunz
Kind Words, Cruise Missiles, and
Everything in Between
The Use of Power Resources in U.S. Policies
towards Poland, Ukraine, and Belarus
1989–2008
With a foreword by William Hill
ISBN 978-3-8382-1085-8

175 Eduard Klein
Bildungskorruption in Russland und
der Ukraine
Eine komparative Analyse der Performanz
staatlicher Antikorruptionsmaßnahmen im
Hochschulsektor am Beispiel universitärer
Aufnahmeprüfungen
Mit einem Vorwort von Heiko Pleines
ISBN 978-3-8382-0995-1

177 Anton Oleinik
Building Ukraine from Within
A Sociological, Institutional, and Economic
Analysis of a Nation-State in the Making
ISBN 978-3-8382-1150-3

178   *Peter Rollberg,*
      Marlene Laruelle (eds.)
      Mass Media in the Post-Soviet World
      Market Forces, State Actors, and Political
      Manipulation in the Informational
      Environment after Communism
      ISBN 978-3-8382-1116-9

179   *Mikhail Minakov*
      Development and Dystopia
      Studies in Post-Soviet Ukraine and Eastern
      Europe
      ISBN 978-3-8382-1112-1

180   *Aijan Sharshenova*
      The European Union's Democracy
      Promotion in Central Asia
      A Study of Political Interests, Influence, and
      Development in Kazakhstan and Kyrgyzstan
      in 2007–2013
      With a foreword by Gordon Crawford
      ISBN 978-3-8382-1151-0

181   *Andrey Makarychev, Alexandra Yatsyk*
      Boris Nemtsov and Russian Politics
      Power and Resistance
      With a foreword by Zhanna Nemtsova
      ISBN 978-3-8382-1122-0

ibidem-Verlag / *ibidem* Press
Melchiorstr. 15
70439 Stuttgart
Germany

ibidem@ibidem.eu
ibidem.eu